Conflicting Humanities

ALSO AVAILABLE FROM BLOOMSBURY

The Subject of Rosi Braidotti, edited by Bolette Blaagaard and
Iris van der Tuin
Readings in the Anthropocene, Sabine Wilke
The Transformative Humanities, Mikhail Epstein
The Public Value of the Humanities, edited by Jonathan Bate

THEORY

Conflicting Humanities

EDITED BY
ROSI BRAIDOTTI AND
PAUL GILROY

Bloomsbury Academic
An imprint of Bloomsbury Publishing Plc

B L O O M S B U R Y
LONDON · OXFORD · NEW YORK · NEW DELHI · SYDNEY

Bloomsbury Academic

An imprint of Bloomsbury Publishing Plc

50 Bedford Square	1385 Broadway
London	New York
WC1B 3DP	NY 10018
UK	USA

www.bloomsbury.com

BLOOMSBURY and the Diana logo are trademarks of Bloomsbury Publishing Plc

First published 2016

British Library Cataloguing in Publication Data

A catalogue record for this book is available from the British Library.

ISBN:	HB:	9781474237543
	PB:	9781474237550
	ePDF:	9781474237536
	ePub:	9781474237567

Library of Congress Cataloging-in-Publication Data

A catalog record for this book is available from the Library of Congress.

Typeset by Fakenham Prepress Solutions, Fakenham, Norfolk NR21 8NN
Printed and bound in India

CONTENTS

LIST OF ILLUSTRATIONS

Cover image: Natasha Unkart

LIST OF CONTRIBUTORS

Ariella Azoulay is a professor at Brown University, curator and documentary filmmaker. Among her recent books: *From Palestine to Israel: A Photographic Record of Destruction and State Formation, 1947–1950* (Pluto Press, 2011); *Civil Imagination: The Political Ontology of Photography* (Verso, August 2012) and *The Civil Contract of Photography* (Zone Books, 2008). She is curator of *Potential History* (2012, Stuk/Artefact, Louven); *Untaken Photographs* (2010, Igor Zabel Award, The Moderna galerija, Ljubljana; Zochrot, Tel Aviv); *Architecture of Destruction* (Zochrot, Tel Aviv); *Everything Could Be Seen* (Um El Fahem Gallery of Art). Director of documentary films, among which are: *Civil Alliances, Palestine, 47–48* (2012), *I Also Dwell Among Your Own People: Conversations with Azmi Bishara* (2004) and *The Food Chain* (2004).

Étienne Balibar was born in Avallon (France) in 1942. He graduated at the École Normale Supérieure and the Sorbonne in Paris, later took his PhD at the University of Nijmegen (Netherlands) and has an Habilitation from Université de Paris I. He has been teaching at the Universities of Algiers, Sorbonne, Leiden, Nanterre, UC Irvine. He is Professor of Philosophy at Kingston University London, and Visiting Professor of French and Comparative Literature at Columbia University, New York. His books include: *Reading Capital* (with Louis Althusser) (New Left Books, 1970) (1965); *On the Dictatorship of the Proletariat* (François Maspero, 1976); *Race, Nation, Class. Ambiguous Identities* (with Immanuel Wallerstein) (Verso, 1991); *Masses, Classes, Ideas* (Routledge, 1994); *The Philosophy of Marx* (Verso, 1995); *Spinoza and Politics* (Verso, 1998); *Politics and the Other Scene* (Verso, 2002), and *We, the People of Europe? Reflections on Transnational Citizenship* (Princeton, 2004). Forthcoming are *The Proposition of Equaliberty*, *Violence and Civility*, and *Citizen Subject, Essays of Philosophical Anthropology*.

Akeel Bilgrami is the Johnsonian Professor of Philosophy and Global Thought at Columbia University. He earned his first degree from Bombay University in English Literature and then went as a Rhodes Scholar to read Philosophy, Politics, and Economics at Oxford University. He is the author of *Belief and Meaning* (Blackwell, 1992); *Self-Knowledge and Resentment* (Harvard University Press, 2006) and *Politics and the Moral Psychology of*

Identity (Harvard University Press, 2013). His two short books *Gandhi's Integrity* (Columbia University Press) and *What is a Muslim?* (Princeton University Press) are forthcoming. His current large project is on Practical Reason and its Relevance to Politics.

Rosi Braidotti (BA Hons, Australian National University, 1978; PhD, Université de Paris, Panthéon-Sorbonne, 1981; Honorary Degrees Helsinki, 2007 and Linkoping, 2013; Fellow of the Australian Academy of the Humanities *(FAHA)*, 2009; Member of the Academia Europaea *(MAE)*, 2014; Distinguished University Professor and founding Director of the Centre for the Humanities at Utrecht University. Her latest books are: *The Posthuman* (Polity Press, 2013); *Nomadic Subjects* (Columbia University Press, 2011a) and *Nomadic Theory. The Portable Rosi Braidotti* (Columbia University Press, 2011b). www.rosibraidotti.com

Judith Butler is Maxine Elliot Professor in the Departments of Rhetoric and Comparative Literature and the Co-director of the Program of Critical Theory at the University of California, Berkeley. She is active in gender and sexual politics and human rights, anti-war politics, and Jewish Voice for Peace. She is presently the recipient of the Andrew Mellon Award for Distinguished Academic Achievement in the Humanities. Her most recent publications include: *Antigone's Claim: Kinship Between Life and Death* (Columbia University Press, 2000); *Precarious Life: Powers of Violence and Mourning* (Verso, 2004); *Undoing Gender* (Routledge, 2004); *Who Sings the Nation-State?: Language, Politics, Belonging* (Seagull Books, 2008, with Gayatri Spivak); *Frames of War: When Is Life Grievable?* (Verso, 2009); and two co-authored volumes: *Is Critique Secular?* (Fordham University Press, 2009) and *The Power of Religion in Public Life* (Columbia University Press, 2011).

Paul Gilroy teaches American and English literature at King's College London. Before that he was the first holder of the Anthony Giddens Professorship in Social Theory at the London School of Economics and Political Science. He is well known for his critical explorations into the legacy of colonialism, the rich promises of culturally and ethnically diverse societies and the ideal of 'cosmopolitanism from below'. Gilroy taught at Yale University in the USA for some years and has been active in the artistic and cultural life of London, his home city, where he worked for the GLC between 1982 and 1986. Gilroy is a specialist in the field of musical culture. His most recent books include *Kuroi Taiseiyo to Chishikijin no Genzai* (The Black Atlantic and Intellectuals Today) (Shoraisha, 2009, co-author) and *Darker Than Blue* (Harvard University Press, 2010).

Stathis Gourgouris is Professor of Classics, English, and Comparative Literature and Society and Director of the Institute of Comparative

Literature and Society at Columbia University. He is the author of *Dream Nation* (Stanford University Press, 1996); *Does Literature Think?* (Stanford University Press, 2003) and *Lessons in Secular Criticism* (Fordham, 2013), as well as editor of *Freud and Fundamentalism* (Fordham, 2010). His forthcoming work includes *The Perils of the One*, the second volume of lessons in secular criticism with emphasis on political theology as monarchical thought, and *The Synaesthetics of the Polity*, a collection of essays on poetry, music and film.

Engin F. Isin is Chair in Citizenship and Professor of Politics in Politics and International Studies (POLIS) at the Faculty of Social Sciences, the Open University. He is the author of *Cities Without Citizens* (Black Rose Books, 1992); *Being Political* (University of Minnesota Press, 2002); *Citizens Without Frontiers* (Bloomsbury, 2012); and, with Evelyn Ruppert, *Being Digital Citizens* (Rowman & Littlefield, 2015). He has edited, with Greg Nielsen, *Acts of Citizenship* (Zed Books, 2008), and with Michael Saward, *Enacting European Citizenship* (Cambridge University Press, 2013). Edward Said's work has inspired his two edited collections, *Citizenship after Orientalism: An Unfinished Project* (Routledge, 2014) and *Citizenship after Orientalism: Transforming Political Theory* (Palgrave Macmillan, 2015).

Jamila M. H. Mascat is Post-doctoral Fellow at Nosophi – Université de Paris 1/Sorbonne. Her research interests focus on Hegel and contemporary Hegelianism – namely the reception of Hegel in twentieth-century French and German philosophy – as well as on the legacy of Enlightenment in post-colonial knowledge. Her book *Hegel a Jena. La critica dell'astrazione* was published in 2011 (Pensa Multimedia). In 2012 she co-edited *Femministe a parole. Grovigli da districare* (Ediesse), a critical dictionary at the inter-section between feminist, queer and post-colonial theories; in 2014 she co-edited and co-translated an anthology of Hegel's early writings (*Il bisogno di filosofia* (1801–1804), Mimesis). She also co-edited a special issue of the journal *Cultural Studies* on 'Relocating Subalternity' (forth-coming, 2016).

Aamir R. Mufti was born and raised in Karachi, Pakistan, and is currently Professor of Comparative Literature and Director of the Seminar in Global Critical Humanities at the University of California, Los Angeles. He pursued his doctoral studies in literature at Columbia under the supervision of Edward Said. Also trained in Anthropology at Columbia and the London School of Economics, he conducts research and teaching that reflect this disciplinary range. His work reconsiders the secularization thesis in a comparative perspective, with a special interest in Islam and modernity in India and the cultural politics of Jewish identity in Western Europe. He has published widely on a range of topics: colonial and post-colonial literatures of the Indo–British encounter, including nineteenth- and twentieth-century Urdu literature; nationalism and minority cultures; the partition of India; exile and displacement; refugees and statelessness; the notion of the 'post-secular'; language conflicts; global English and the vernaculars; and the history of anthropology. His books include *Enlightenment in the Colony: The Jewish Question and the Crisis of Postcolonial Culture* (Princeton University Press, 2007) and *Forget English! Orientalisms and World Literatures* (Harvard University Press, forthcoming). Among his current work are two book projects – one concerning exile and criticism and the other, the colonial reinvention of Islamic traditions. He serves on the editorial collective of the journal *boundary 2*.

Ankhi Mukherjee is Professor of English and World Literatures in the English Faculty at Oxford and a Fellow of Wadham College. She works on Victorian and Modern literature, post-colonial studies, critical theory and intellectual history. Mukherjee's first book is *Aesthetic Hysteria: The Great Neurosis in Victorian Melodrama and Contemporary Fiction* (Routledge, 2007). Her second monograph, *'What is a Classic?' Postcolonial Rewriting and Invention of the Canon* (Stanford University Press, 2014), was awarded the British Academy Rose Mary Crawshay Prize. She has published on a wide range of topics in PMLA, MLQ, *Contemporary Literature, Paragraph, Parallax* and others, and has co-edited the *Concise Companion to Psychoanalysis, Literature, and Culture* (Wiley-Blackwell, 2014). Mukherjee is currently working on her third monograph, *Unseen City: Travelling Psychoanalysis and the Urban Poor*, on psychoanalysis and its vexed relationship to race and poverty, and editing *After Lacan*, a collection of essays on the intellectual legacy of Jacques Lacan (Cambridge University Press, forthcoming).

Gayatri Chakravorty Spivak is University Professor and Founder of the Institute for Comparative Literature and Society at Columbia University. BA English (First Class Honours), Presidency College, Calcutta, 1959. PhD Comparative Literature, Cornell University, 1967. DLitt, University of Toronto, 1999; DLitt, University of London, 2003; DHum, Oberlin College, 2008. D.Honoris Causa, Universitat Roveri I Virgili, 2011; D.Honoris Causa, Rabindra Bharati, 2012; D.Honoris Causa, Universidad Nacional de San Martin, 2013; DLitt, University of St Andrews, 2014; D.Honoris Causa, Paris VIII, 2014; Presidency University, 2014; DHum, Yale University, 2015; DLitt, University of Ghana-Legon, 2015. The 2012 Kyoto Prize Laureate in the field of Arts and Philosophy. She was awarded Padma Bhushan by the President of India in 2013. Her most recent books include *An Aesthetic Education in the Age of Globalization* (Harvard University Press, 2012); *Readings* (Seagull Books, 2014) and *Du Bois and the General Strike* (forthcoming). Professor Spivak has been an activist in rural education and feminist and ecological social movements since 1986.

Marina Warner is a writer of fiction, cultural history and criticism. Her award-winning books include *Alone of All Her Sex: The Myth and the Cult of the Virgin Mary* (George Weidenfeld & Nicolson Ltd. and Alfred A. Knopf, Inc., 1976); *From the Beast to the Blonde* (Chatto & Windus, 1994) and *No Go the Bogeyman* (Chatto & Windus, 1998). In 1994 she gave the BBC Reith Lectures on the theme of *Six Myths of Our Time* (the year after Edward Said gave his Reith Lectures). Her recent books include *Fantastic Metamorphoses; Other Worlds* (Oxford University Press, 2002); *Stranger Magic: Charmed States and the Arabian Nights* (Chatto & Windus, 2012) and *Once Upon a Time: A Short History of Fairy Tale* (Oxford University Press, 2014). Marina Warner is Professor of English and Creative Writing at Birkbeck College London. She is a Chevalier de l'Ordre des Arts et des Lettres, a Fellow of the British Academy, was made an honorary DLitt by Oxford University (2008), awarded a DBE for services to higher education and literature in 2015, and the Holzberg Prize, also in 2015.

Robert J. C. Young is Julius Silver Professor of English and Comparative Literature at New York University. From 1989 to 2005 he was Professor of English and Critical Theory at Oxford University and a fellow of Wadham College. He earned his BA, MA and DPhil degrees in English from Exeter College, Oxford University. His books include *White Mythologies: Writing History and the West* (Routledge, 1990); *Colonial Desire: Hybridity in Culture, Theory and Race* (Routledge, 1995); *Torn Halves: Political Conflict in Literacy and Cultural Theory* (Manchester University Press, 1996); *Postcolonialism: An Historical Introduction* (Blackwell Publishers Ltd., 2001); *Postcolonialism: A Very Short Introduction* (Oxford University Press, 2003); *The Idea of English Ethnicity* (Blackwell Publishers Ltd., 2008) and *Empire, Colony, Postcolony* (Wiley-Blackwell, 2015). He is also editor of *Interventions: International Journal of Postcolonial Studies*, and was a founding editor of *The Oxford Literary Review*.

ACKNOWLEDGEMENTS

This book is the outcome of the commemoration of the 300th year anniversary of the Treaty of Utrecht in 2013. On that occasion the Centre for the Humanities at Utrecht University convened several major projects: the international visiting professorship scheme of the Treaty of Utrecht Chair, three commemorative conferences in 2013 and a Redrafting Kant's Perpetual Peace project. The Centre for the Humanities, under the directorship of Rosi Braidotti and with the support of multiple partners, had the honour to host almost all the contributors to this book, either as visiting professors in 2009–12, or as speakers in the Edward Said Memorial Conference which took place on 15–17 April 2013, inaugurating the commemoration of the 1713 Treaty of Utrecht. We thank them profoundly not only for their contributions to this volume, but also for embodying the yearning to remember and transform the legacy of the past into empowering futures through their work.

We are also grateful for Liza Thompson, our publisher, who due to her enthusiasm and hard work made sure that this volume saw the light of day. Our sincere thanks also go to Stephanie Paalvast and Goda Klumbyte for their critical and editorial assistance.

SERIES PREFACE

Theory is back.

Critical theorists of the universal, organic or situated kind used to be defined by their ethical-political commitment to account for power relations at work in the real world, as well as in scientific practice. But their prestige waned throughout the 1990s. The 'theory wars' in the USA targeted critical theory as an outdated ideological activity, dismissing the theorists as 'tenured radicals'. They got replaced by new 'content-providers', experts and consultants, in a context of increased privatization of academic research. By the turn of the millennium, with the Internet as the only true 'content-provider', former theorists were relocated to the market-oriented position of 'ideas brokers' and, in the best cases, 'ideas leaders'. By now, we are all entrepreneurs of the mind. The cognitive character of contemporary capitalism and its high technological mediation paradoxically produced a 'post-theory' mood and intensified attacks on radical thought and critical dissent. This negative mood also resulted in criticism of the social and scholarly value of the Humanities, in a neo-liberal corporate university ruled by quantified economics and the profit motive.

And yet, the vitality of critical thinking in the world today is palpable, as is a spirit of insurgency that sustains it. Theoretical practice may have stalled in the academic world, but it exploded with renewed energy in other quarters, in media, society, the arts and the corporate world.

New generations of critical 'studies' areas have grown alongside the classical radical epistemologies of the 1970s: gender, feminist, queer, race, postcolonial and subaltern studies, cultural studies, film, television and media studies. The second generation of critical 'studies' areas includes: animal studies and eco-criticism; cultural studies of science and society; religion studies; disability studies; fat studies; success studies; celebrity studies; globalization studies; and many more. New media has spawned new meta-fields: software studies, Internet studies, game studies, digital postcolonial studies and more. The end of the Cold War has generated: conflict studies and peace research; human rights studies, humanitarian management; human rights-oriented medicine; trauma, memory and recon-ciliation studies; security studies, death studies; suicide studies; and the list is still growing. These different generations of 'studies' by now constitute a theoretical force to be reckoned with.

Theory is back!

This series aims to present cartographic accounts of these emerging critical theories and to reflect the vitality and inspirational force of on-going theoretical debates.

Rosi Braidotti

Introduction

Rosi Braidotti and Paul Gilroy

The essays gathered in this volume were first presented as papers at the Edward Said Memorial Conference,[1] which inaugurated the official commemoration of the 1713 Treaty of Utrecht. The event aimed to assess the mixed legacy of this Treaty, which ended an era of religious wars, but also consolidated colonial power worldwide. The focus on Edward Said's life and work allowed the contributors to discuss geopolitical issues in close relation to the role of humanistic culture, literature and the arts in diplomacy and international peace-making. This approach resonated with Said's vision in combining scholarship in the humanities with the arts so as to support the quest for justice, self-determination and equality and notably to highlight the critical power of music to inspire resistance and to challenge the political imagination.

Taking the intellectual and political legacies of Edward Said as a point of departure, this collection pursues the difficult mission of exploring what might be involved in the reinvention of notions of the human in today's world and more especially in the critical practice of the humanities. That prospect has become urgent in the light of several contemporary developments. The first is the impact of more than a decade of renewed warfare on the understanding of human rights and human vulnerability in the context of economic globalization. We have become habituated to what we are told are inter-civilizational conflicts in many parts of the world where decolonization struggles were historically played out. However, in a sharp departure from previous patterns, the war on terror's global counterinsurgency campaign is partly conducted out of sight. Death is dealt remotely from the sky – by unmanned flying vehicles – while the rules of war are quietly rewritten to make post-colonial innovations and 'securitocratic' experiments appear both proportionate and legitimate.

The impact of wholesale technological change is the other factor inbuilt in this context. The human, social and environmental devastations induced by economic disparities and structural injustices in the access to the benefits of the global economy and its advanced technologies add another layer of violence to the contemporary world. The convergence between genetics and informatics has allowed the so-called 'Life' sciences, notably nanotechnologies, biotechnologies, information technologies and cognitive science, to alter received notions of what constitutes the basic unit of reference for the human. As a result of insights drawn from these new multidisciplinary fields of scientific enquiry, there is much talk today of replacing atomized visions of the self with new approaches to subjectivity: network theories, extended minds, social and environmental ecological self-organizing systems and other transversal redefinitions of distributed agency, predicated on process ontologies. Aspects of contemporary thought have acquired a posthumanist momentum in that the humanist image of Man as a self-regulating rational animal endowed with the universal powers of reason and language no longer benefits from scientific consensus. The authority of science and of scientific reason for instance is challenged when faced by the apparently intractable problem of climate change. And yet, such advanced under-standings of living matter – and of self-organizing non-human systems – are not matched by and are often overrun by the perpetuation of familiar forms of injustice: multiple new instances of death, killing and the threat of extinction of multiple species, including our own. These socio-political, scientific, military and juridical practices take both human and non-human agents as their objects. Overdetermined by the double imperative of bio-genetic productivity on the one hand and security on the other, which dominates other functions of government, a necro-political dimension emerges at the core of contemporary concerns about 'Life', in its human, non-human and inhuman inceptions, human rights and humanitarianism.

This volume addresses the effects of this new context and more. The history of European humanism, its definition of the human and of its inhumanity, is assessed in the light of Edward Said's legacy. Then it asks how a posthumanism – or de-centring of the human – nurtured by scien-tific developments can be related to the persistence of social and political practices that assume or seek to re-instate the primacy of the individual even and especially in the face of death and dispossession. Sometimes those assumptions are part of a challenge to the power of governments and of warmongering and other corporate interests, but elsewhere the very individuation through which they operate compounds the injustice that is being done.

The humanist core of 'Man' – namely the universal powers of reason, self-regulating moral inclinations and a set of preferred discursive and spiritual values – asserts an ideal of mental and bodily perfection. Together, they spell out a political ontology that combines belief in human uniqueness with enduring faith in a teleologically-ordained view of rational progress through scientific and cultural development manifested in European history.

This model not only set standards for individuals but also for whole supra-national cultures, including a certain idea of Europe. The imperial humanism that underpinned it developed into a civilizational model, which, in turn, has shaped the idea that the West coincided uniquely with the universalizing powers of self-reflexive reason. That self-aggrandizing vision has been consolidated amidst chronic economic and political crisis.

It still assumes Europe to be much more than a geopolitical location. As an expression of universal consciousness, Europe transcends its specificity and posits the conspicuous power of that transcendence as its most distinctive characteristic. It becomes a universal attribute of humanity that can invest its special character in any suitable object. The old rationale for colonialism endorsed this variety of assumption of hierarchy. It endures in contemporary projections of inter-civilizational strife and the firmly militarized varieties of economic development in which they culminate.

Edward Said's body of work can be placed in dialogue with insights drawn from a broad range of feminist, multicultural and post-colonial writing produced during the last thirty years. By carefully orchestrating these transversal discursive exchanges and convergences, this volume also aims to provide new insights into the limitations of European self-representation and the growing contestation of its humanist claims, as a consequence of the re-centring of the world away from the modernity of the Atlantic and other Europe-centred paradigms. Analysis of the lasting legacies of colonialism on the one hand and of the Israeli–Palestinian conflict on the other provide the historical frames of reference for critical assessments of Europe's chequered track record in terms of humanist, humane and humanitarian practices.

The life and work of Edward Said fulfil a number of distinct and interrelated functions for the contributors. Some of them (Young, Isin, Mufti, Azoulay, Gourgouris, Butler) address his *corpus* directly, offering innovative critical angles on his work. Others (Bilgrami, Balibar, Spivak, Mukherjee, Mascat, Gilroy, Braidotti) lean on Said's work to extrapolate key concepts and methodologies and apply them to a range of contemporary issues, stressing its lasting relevance for academic, cultural, artistic and political debates. The discussion is focused by concerns with the responsibilities borne by academics and intellectuals, as well as the fundamental issue of how or indeed whether the humanities might still foster resistance to power inside and outside the changing institutional climate of the university, in the context of the current bio-technological and information revolution. Contributors engage Said's approaches to the practice of democratic criticism, cultural translation and the importance of artistic and musical practice, as well as the disavowal of the colonial past and the relevance of feminist, anti-racist and post-colonial critiques. At the heart of the volume lies a deep, cosmopolitan concern with the idea of Europe, the cultural character of citizenship and the prospect of humanistic education shaped by non-violence and the pursuit of peace.

Edward Said remains an emblematic figure not only because of his critical acumen, but also because of his active involvement in artistic education and practice, notably through the co-creation of the East West Divan orchestra, together with Daniel Barenboim. Said thus foregrounds the privileged bond between the humanities and the arts. These issues emerge from and are reinforced by Edward Said's sharp analyses and original methods. As a critical but also an affirmative humanist, Said approached European humanism agonistically. He took care to distance himself from either hasty or general dismissals of humanism. Accordingly, the volume is structured around a series of interlinked questions that are inspired by but not confined to the parameters of his intervention.

For example, we ask which, if any, humanisms are still trustworthy and how might a new humanism come into being? What idea of the human would be involved in the revised theories and practices of such a humanism? What values and sense of responsibilities are opened up by a posthuman perspective? How do historical events such as settler colonialism in general and the Israeli-Palestinan conflict in particular – by now over a century old – illuminate these concerns? How do conflicting notions of humanity and of what counts as human relate to the numerous instances of exile, dispossession and eviction that have taken place during the last century? How do they affect our understanding of belonging to real and imagined homelands? How can the teaching and research practices of the humanities account for forgotten histories and absent geographies and for missing people? How do recent displacements of the centrality of the Human in the 'Life' sciences and digital media contribute to discourses about the posthuman which fail to account for significant power differentials among human and non-human agents and for the persistence of mechanisms of violent exclusion? To what extent do they open up new possibilities for the recomposition of Humanity on fundamentally new grounds: a posthumanist cosmo-politics?

Universities in general and the humanities in particular are at the centre of these debates. As economic and political crises gain hold of educational systems and institutions, the need to re-imagine humanistic education is being conditioned by economic imperatives and profit-oriented policies which respect neither the dignity of the classical humanistic tradition nor the innovations proposed by more radical interdisciplinary epistemologies.

The established traditions of academic freedom and the very idea of the university have been challenged not only by the imperatives of security that have eroded civil rights but also by the managerial transformation which has forced the humanities to seek not philosophical and political but economic justification for their continued place in the curriculum. What some perceive as the gradual divorce of capitalism from democracy results in the pervasive influence of governmental and institutional functions by the logic of profit, which is corrosive of the university ethos and seeks to overthrow the basic premises of unbounded curiosity and free scientific enquiry for its own sake. There is consequently an insidious form of institutional dispossession currently at work within the humanities as a field. It must be confronted by a resolution informed by Edward Said's 'secular' faith in democratic criticism as the key to the politics of intellectual work and an effective, accountable and discerning citizenship within and beyond the national state.

The classical university model that combines scientific excellence with civic probity and active citizenship has been reviewed recently in response to economic globalization. If historically the university has been expected to provide a modern education for a participant in 'civil society', now universities, students and faculty are increasingly urged to provide forms of training and research that will contribute to vocational outcomes and innovations to support economic growth, notably in the fields of science and technology. Higher education has often responded to these novel circumstances by embracing neoliberal approaches and seeking out opportunities for funding and research that they have fostered. The effects of these pressures are complex and penetrate well beyond the teaching curricula of universities to reshape the very idea of 'research' and its value to society.

By the terms of contemporary institutional governance, however, the humanities are often judged to be inessential if not peripheral to the more substantive business of education, with increasing emphasis on science and technology. The dominance of the profit factor over all other criteria has forced the humanities into the position of having to defend and justify their existence not only to the political class but also to the rest of the academic community. The energy for institutional change, which is sweeping across the EU at present, is conducted under the banners of austerity in the name of socially discriminatory reforms that derive directly from neoliberal economics and its hasty equations between performance indicators and the notion of 'excellence'. In the academic world as well as in society as a whole, a sense of systemic crisis is now pervasive, though it often remains unnamed.

The ongoing public debate about the function and value of the humanities is rich in implications that go far beyond the academic world and touch the very socio-political fibre of our times. Some universities have retreated towards more conservative and avowedly disinterested versions of humanistic study. In Europe this vision often goes under the cover of the methodological nationalism that historically has served disciplines such as history and literary studies. As Edward Said pointed out, how this nationalistic line of defence intersects with the broader challenges of globalization remains an open question, as does the problem of how cosmopolitan alternatives to it might be devised.

Moreover, the bio-genetically given and digitally mediated world of advanced capitalism is both neo- and post-colonial in terms of its political economy. It is fractured by forms of social, environmental and geopolitical conflict that appear to extend without apparent resolution into the future. At the same time, advanced capitalism can be described as a myopic system that functions only on short-term gains and cannot be sustained in terms of its human, natural and social ecologies. What the future stands for has itself been transformed by the loss of linear conceptions of progress and the attendant belief that the fate of rising generations will be better than the experiences that their fore-parents have enjoyed. The truth of the matter is that, in the overdeveloped countries, today's young will be poorer financially and informationally as well as far less secure than their parents, and much more likely to be un- and underemployed.

All of these developments have had grave implications for the social status of higher education and of the university, in particular for areas of the curriculum which lie outside of the disciplines that have been accorded immediate priority for funding. Many humanities disciplines have not been either able or willing to translate their historic strengths into the terms required by contemporary management's calculations of value. Their future looks more uncertain than ever.

A further contradiction that haunts the field of the humanities is the recent growth of the theory and practice of Humanitarianism, which also includes security issues and the 'Humanitarian' warfare already mentioned. If the humanities are to retain any distinctive voice in these complex circumstances, it is likely to be muted by the increasing split in a culture that claims to be oriented by human rights but enacts the profanation and destruction of human and non-human life on unprecedented scales. In this context, the rise in popularity enjoyed by moral philosophy and morality discourses in the contemporary university is problematic to say the least and calls for renewed critical scrutiny.

The distinguished international contributors to this volume do not share a single standpoint on these difficult issues, but they do converge on the propositions that the humanities must be defended as an exercise in democratic criticism and that education is better understood as a public good rather than a private or corporate enterprise. Furthermore, they agree that the influential work of Edward Said will be a valuable source of inspiration and guidance in navigating this new environment.

Edward Said was, they suggest, one model for a new kind of global, public intellectual operating across the whole field of contemporary political culture. Our difficult predicament requires that we are homeless, nomadic and exilic – in Said's terms, 'secular' – yet somehow able to maintain a worldly, 'cosmopolitical' perspective capable of speaking across the divisions between north and south and reaching the south lodged inside the north and the north secreted inside the south. Said's interventions insisted upon the social responsibilities of intellectuals in embattled situations characterized by increasing inequality and conflict made intelligible primarily in cultural terms.

Delivered implausibly – but not uncharacteristically – from deep inside the elite stratum of US universities, his untimely wisdom remains to guide artful, critical practitioners of the humanities whose reading of those traditions against the grain concedes nothing to the pressures of Manichaean and civilizationist thinking. Said's definition of the core task of the humanities as the pursuit of democratic criticism remains more urgent than ever, though it needs to be supplemented by gender, environmental, technological and antiracist perspectives as well as by detailed analysis of the necropolitical governmentality of our time in the midst of a 'Life' sciences and new media revolution.

This book brings together individuals working in a range of disciplinary settings to consider their practice in relation to Said's legacies. His work and his example must, they suggest, acquire a new importance in struggles to widen access to educational resources and to develop innovative forms of scholarship committed to the refusal if not the undoing of a world riven by new kinds of warcraft, injustice and exploitation.

Note

1   The conference was held in Utrecht on 15–17 April 2013. It was chaired by Mariam Said and directed by Rosi Braidotti. The scientific committee was composed of Étienne Balibar, Paul Gilroy, Peter van der Veer and Sandra Ponzanesi.

CHAPTER ONE

The Contested Posthumanities

Rosi Braidotti

To reintegrate himself with worldly actuality, the critic of texts ought to be investigating the system of discourse by which the 'world' is divided, administered, plundered, by which humanity is thrust into pigeon-holes, by which 'we' are 'human' and 'they' are not.

EDWARD SAID (2001: 26)

Introduction

In response to complex social, environmental and academic climate changes, this chapter adopts an affirmative position. I want to defend the productivity of a posthuman future for the humanities, accounting for the tensions of our times in a grounded manner without being reductive and critical while avoiding negativity. To achieve this, I will develop the following argument: starting from the legacy and the limitations of the debate on humanism between Said and Foucault, I will provide a cartography of the critical humanities in the contemporary university. Then I will proceed to map out some of the ways in which the posthumanities are currently being developed in response to and in dialogue with our globally linked and technologically mediated societies that are marked by increasing polarizations in terms of access to economic, technological and environmental resources.

What is human about the humanities?

Michel Foucault's distinction between universal, organic and specific intellectuals (Foucault and Deleuze 1977), modelled respectively on the Hegelian–Marxist scheme, on Gramsci's thought and on his own insights, reformulated the task of intellectuals as critical thinkers after Sartre's and Fanon's generation. As Edward Said (in Viswanathan 2001: 335) pointed out, the distinction between these categories is not fixed but porous, and the cyclical nature of these different positions allows them to cross over each other, adapting to changing historical circumstances. The common denominator for both the organic and the specific intellectual is the ethical-political commitment to provide adequate and reasoned cartographies of power in its immanent and situated historical formations, as well as in the production of discourse. As Said put it: 'part of intellectual work is understanding how authority is formed' (Said in Viswanathan 2001: 384), and especially for critical theorists working in the university, to represent the powerless and the dispossessed.

Loyal to this legacy, my generation of academics based our work on the politics of location (Rich 1987, 2001), the production of theoretical cartographies as diagrams of power and the creation of new concepts, combining philosophical critiques with feminist, post-colonial and anti-racist reconstructions of both knowledge and social relations (Braidotti 2014). The specific or situated intellectuals' practice rests on the rejection of universalism as both idea and representation, in favour of embedded and embodied relational forms of knowledge production. For my generation, this re-definition of the responsibilities of intellectuals went hand-in-hand with the rejection of European exceptionalism and its vehement and often belligerent universal pretensions (Said 1978, 2004). The critique of humanism formulated by poststructuralism – notably in Foucault's diagnosis of the death of 'Man' (1970) – targeted specifically the assumption about the 'Human' that is implied in the theory and practice of the academic humanities. That is to say the humanist idea of the 'Man of reason' (Lloyd 1984) as coinciding with masculinity, transcendental reason, rational consciousness and European civilization. Irigaray's critique of the Enlightenment-based project of emancipation, pointedly called 'Equal to whom?' (1994), expanded the same critique to social and discursive constructions of 'Woman', radicalizing feminist theory and practice. Anti-humanism emerges as the nodal point.

It is poignant to note, however, how fast the term 'intellectual' was phased out throughout the 1990s, becoming disconnected from its social vocation, till it came to be replaced by a new class of 'content-providers' (Anderson 1997). Also known as the regime of experts and consultants, in a context of increased privatization of research following the official end of the Cold War in 1989, this shift coincided with the 'theory wars' (Arthur and Shapiro 1995) and rising criticism of French philosophy. The impact of a new techno-scientific culture based on information technologies and bio-genetics was also a crucial factor in demystifying the role of intellectuals. Globalized information networks, the flows of data and capital and the speed and heterogeneity of digital access, induced multiple dislocations of the image and practice of academic 'knowing subjects'.

By the end of the 1990s it was obvious to all that the only 'content-provider' that really mattered was the Internet itself, which relocated the former intellectuals to the market-oriented position of 'ideas brokers' and, in the best case scenario, 'ideas leaders'. As Williams lucidly put it (2014: 166), 'now we are entrepreneurs of the mind and it wears us down'. By the end of the millennium the mutation of capitalism into a cognitive differential machine (Deleuze and Guattari 1977, 1987; Moulier-Boutang 2012) was in full swing, just as criticism of the humanities became dominant in a neoliberal university ruled by quantified economics and the profit motive. Critical theory was dismissed as an ideologically-biased activity and declared outdated (Fukuyama 1989), its intellectuals dismissed as 'tenured radicals' (Kimball 1990), while the humanities became down-graded as a glorified finishing school. Academic publishing went into a downward spiral, but seemed to be compensated by the rise of a new class of academic stars, who were both commercially successful and media-savvy, their visibility concealing the real impoverishment of the field (Collini 2013; Williams 2014). A mood of 'post-theoretical malaise' (Cohen, Colebrook and Miller 2012) resulted in critical theorists being contested in both the academy and society.

Deleuze and Guattari's anatomy of advanced capitalism as schizophrenia (1977, 1987) taught us that the global economy is a spinning machine that perverts global nature as well as global culture (Franklin, Lury and Stacey 2000) and subsumes all living materials – human and non-human – to a logic of commodification and consumption (Rose 2007; Cooper 2008). It functions as a deterritorializing flow of images without imagination (Braidotti 1994), organs without bodies (Braidotti 1989; Žižek 2004) and growth without progress. The manic-depressive proliferation of commodified differences and quantified selves makes for an unsustainable system – a 'future eater' (Flannery 1994) – that erodes its own foundations as it axiomatically shifts ground and sabotages the future (Patton 2000; Braidotti 2002; Protevi 2009, 2013; Toscano 2005). At the same time, as feminist and post-colonial theories (Grewal and Kaplan 1994) pointed out, global consumerism, while promoting an ideology of 'no borders', implements a highly controlled system of hyper-mobility of consumer goods, information bytes, data and capital (Braidotti 2002, 2006), whereas people do not circulate nearly as freely.

This political economy of controlled mobility produces dramatically different nomadic subject positions (Braidotti 1994, 2011a): registered and unregistered migrant workers, refugees, VIP frequent flyers, daily commuters, tourists, pilgrims and others. The violence of capitalist de-territorializations also induces evictions, homelessness and destitution, as well as the exodus of populations on an unprecedented planetary scale (Sassen 2012). As a result of such devastations, a global diaspora (Brah 1996) has replaced the exemplary condition of 'exile' (Said 2003) while structural injustices including increasing poverty and indebtedness (Deleuze and Guattari 1977; Lazzarato 2012) have condemned large portions of the world population to substandard life-conditions. A 'necro-political' governmentality (Mbembe 2003) is at work through technologically mediated wars and counterterrorism strategies. Security concerns have accordingly become paramount by now, also in the academic humanities and social sciences. I will return to this point.

In this context, the mood of the humanities is undefinable. It is as if, after the great explosion of theoretical creativity of the 1970s and 1980s, theoretical practice stalled in philosophy, but exploded with renewed energy in other quarters. On the right of the political spectrum the ruling philosophical idea became the 'end' of ideological time (Fukuyama 1989) after the official end of the Cold War, and the inevitability of civilizational crusades (Huntington 1996) after 9/11. The political left on the other hand expressed its sense of theoretical fatigue, both by manifest resentment against the previous intellectual generations (Badiou and Žižek 2009) and by self-declared impotence (Badiou 2013), while the centre faltered into self-doubt (Latour 2004). Peter Galison (2004), echoing Lyotard's idea of the decline of master narratives (1979), struck a more balanced note, welcoming the end of grand systems in favour of 'specific theory'. This pragmatic approach stands between universalistic pretensions on the one hand and narrow empiricism on the other, embracing 'just enough theory' to sustain socially relevant practice. In a critical analysis, Jeffrey Williams argues that today we are experiencing a double movement: on the one hand what was blasphemy in the 1980s has by now become banality. Foucault and Derrida, 'once discursive bomb-throwers and banes of traditionalists, are now standard authorities to be cited in due course' (Williams 2014: 25). On the other hand, we are also witnessing the shrinking of public support for the humanities. As a result of this conjuncture, our theoretical mood has become 'retrospective' (Williams 2014: 25), reflecting on its own history and conditions of possibility in an often autobiographical tone, much as I am doing in this essay.

But this crisis is far from universal. For instance, Matthew Fuller[1] argues that, 'in discussions of cyber-cultures, or new media, which then moved on to become software studies (Fuller 2008), the 1990s was a period of theoretical and practical exuberance that spread into the early years of the new millennium – marked in particular by a coming together of generations emerging from the Cold War'. It is significant that this upbeat account of both the side-effects of the end of Communism and the general health of the humanities is expressed from the discursive location of new media studies, whose object of enquiry is networks, codes and systems, that is to say non-anthropomorphic objects. This shift of perspective engenders renewed energy and optimism. I shall return to this point in the next section.

The idea of 'crisis' may not quite cover the institutional status of the contemporary humanities, given that this field operates through self-reflection and adaptation to changing historical circumstances. So much so that the 'crisis' may be taken as the humanities' *modus operandi*, as Gayatri Spivak astutely suggested in response to Foucault's analysis of the 'death of Man' (1988). Whether in a strong and self-assertive posture, or as 'weak thought' (Vattimo and Rovatti 2012), the theoretical humanities is the field that posits itself as a perennially open question, constitutionally Socratic, so to speak. Considering the concerted attacks moved against the humanities by Western governments of late, however, it is undeniable that its practitioners are investing disproportionate amounts of time defending themselves in the public sphere.

For instance, literature and the literary critic nowadays are perceived – by management, policy-makers and a large section of the media – as a luxury, not as a necessity, a trend that Marina Warner describes (2014: 42) as 'new brutalism in academia'. The pride Edward Said could take in the great tradition of literature, music and culture is no longer a point of consensus in a globalized and technologically mediated world. Moreover, a shared sensibility based on the knowledge of the canonical literary texts cannot be assumed or taken for granted, either in the West or in the rest of the world. Warner's trenchant comment (2015: 10) says it all: 'Faith in the value of a humanist education is beginning to look like an antique romance'. This general shift of sensibility is enough to make me almost nostalgic for the days of the modern–postmodern dispute, when Edward Said clashed with Harold Bloom on this very issue and defended an anti-elitist conception of culture, cultural access and production. Said replaced the heroic individualism of the 'lone genius' syndrome in cultural criticism and history – upheld by Bloom – with a more grounded analysis of the material conditions that favour cultural creativity as a collective activity and a form of democratic participation. Nowadays, the least we can say is that the humanities as a whole no longer occupies a hegemonic position within the hierarchy of knowledge production systems in the contemporary world and the critical intellectual, far from representing the idealized self-image of the developed world's subjects, is under severe scrutiny.

What is universal about the university?

The zig-zagging trajectory that traces the descending curve of the status and fortunes of the intellectuals is problematic not only in terms of this particular class of practitioners, but also for what it reveals about the institutional settings and the changing position of the university in general and the academic humanities in particular. The often acrimonious nature of the debate about the role of critical intellectuals is partly related to the modern–postmodern controversy of the 1980s and the theory wars of the 1990s, reaching a strident peak by the turn of the millennium (Lambert 2001). The institutional vulnerability of the humanities at this time is directly proportional to the extent to which the university itself comes under fire (Berubé and Nelson 1995). The 'post-theory' mood coincides with and of public financial support for higher education (Williams 2014) and 'a broader scaling down within the humanities and social sciences, of the kind of radicalism that anti-imperial and post-colonial work often enabled' (Nixon 2011: 259). Surveying this situation Coetzee (2013) suggests that the assault on the humanities which started in the 1980s has successfully rid this institution of all academics that were 'diagnosed as leftists or anarchist or anti-rational or anti-civilisational', so much so that 'to conceive of universities any more as seedbeds of agitation and dissent would be laughable'.

Government support and funding have been withdrawn from academic institutions across the Western world, despite their attempt at reinventing themselves as 'research' universities (Cole, Barber and Graubaud 1993), and this hit the humanities with particular violence. The 'last professors' who still believed in their intellectual mission (Donoghue 2008) and in academic freedom (Menand 1996) denounced 'the university in ruins' (Readings 1996) and took a stand against the corporate university and increasing tuition fees, refusing to be cast as merely managerial figures. Williams (2014: 6) argues that, in the last forty years, the public university in the USA was transformed 'from a flagship of the postwar welfare system to a privatized enterprise, oriented toward business and its own self-accumulation'. In continental Europe, the populist right-wing politicians who came to power in the aftermath of 9/11 and the wars that followed it are explicitly hostile to the fields of culture and the arts, both in society and as academic curricula. The field of the literary and cultural humanities, for instance, was dismissed as 'left-wing hobbies' by Geert Wilders in the Netherlands and became the target of large government cut-backs, having been down-classed to the level of a 'high-risk-no-gain' investment.

The question of the public value of the humanities (Small 2013) has come to the fore, as policy-makers apply narrowly economic criteria to assess the academic 'market'. The new labour structure within the university – especially in the USA – reflects the hierarchical values of neoliberal economics. A small (in the USA less than one third, according to Williams) percentage of tenured staff at the top is supported by a large section of intellectual 'precariat'[2]: part-time, temporary, untenured and underpaid teaching staff with hardly any entitlements or career prospects. With heavy teaching loads, increased pressure to generate income through grant submissions and few research opportunities, this mass of non-staff or temporary staff members experience working conditions of duress, stress and systemic exploitation (Gill 2010), which Marina Warner (2015: 9) describes as 'like working for a cross between IBM, with vertiginous hierarchies of command, and McDonald's'.

Progressive academics responded to this situation by pleading for a non-profit approach to the humanities and to higher education, following the classical liberal arts model (Nussbaum 2010), while more sceptical voices wondered if there was a future at all for the field (Collini 2012). One of the areas of growth within the humanities at institutional level today occurs at the intersection between national security matters, issues of surveillance and anti-terrorism. Ever since Lynne Cheney, speaking for the Bush administration in 2001, declared the academics the 'weak link' in the war on terror, much pressure was put on the university to fall in line with official government policy on defence and related matters. The relevance of the humanities for security studies has been growing ever since (Burgess 2014). In 1998 Said (in Viswanathan 2001: 331–2) commented on the affinity that the terms 'terrorist' and 'intellectual' seemed to have acquired in American consciousness since 9/11 and the subsequent reinforcement of nationalistic 'Western Judeo-Christian values' in the academic curriculum. Said saw it both as a sign of the reactionary times and as a failure on the part of left-wing intellectuals to make their voices heard. I tend to see this alliance between the humanities and security studies today as the contemporary variation on the methodological nationalism (Beck 2007) that has haunted the field since the nineteenth century and also made the humanities so crucial for the imperial project of European colonialism (Davies 1997). Today, nationalism protects 'Fortress Europe' from the new 'barbaric' invasions by diasporic peoples pushing at its gates. As Said lucidly put it, at such a conjuncture it is more crucial than ever for intellectuals to 'speak the truth to power' and side with 'the wretched of the earth' (Fanon 1963).

To sum up: the university as a material and discursive institution has come down from the universalist pedestal where it stood throughout the nineteenth century, following the models of Von Humboldt and Cardinal Newman (Collini 2010). But this mutation is not entirely negative, as I will argue in the next section.

From critical studies to posthuman discourses

Over the last thirty years the core of theoretical innovation in the humanities has emerged around a cluster of new, often radical and always interdisciplinary fields of enquiry that called themselves 'studies'. Gender, feminist, queer, race, post-colonial and subaltern studies, alongside cultural studies, film, television and media studies, are the prototypes of the radical epistemologies which have provided a range of new methods and innovative concepts. Institutionally, they have remained relatively under-funded in relation to the classical disciplines, yet alternative perspectives and sources of inspiration can be drawn from these highly creative, albeit marginalized 'studies' areas. This proliferation of infra-disciplinary discourses is both a threat and an opportunity in that it calls out for methodological innovations and theoretical creativity. Their relationship to the classical disciplines, in the same period of time, is a complex issue, which James Chandler (2004) called 'critical disciplinarily'. They have contributed to a rigorous revision of often implicit assumptions about humanism and Eurocentrism, and also to the implosion of anthropocentrism, causing both internal fractures and the dislocation of outer disciplinary boundaries in the humanities. The 'studies' areas, however, do not merely oppose humanism, but also create alternative visions of the self, the human, knowledge and society. Their insights have lasting consequences for the academic practice of the humanities.

These 'studies' are radical epistemologies that have exposed the persistence of the fatal flaw at the core of the humanities, namely their inbuilt Eurocentrism that unfolds into methodological nationalism, as I suggested above. The humanist vision of 'Man' includes both an ideal of bodily perfection and a set of mental, discursive and spiritual values. Since the Enlightenment, this ideal combines belief in human uniqueness with an intrinsically Eurocentric understanding of what counts as the basic unit of reference for the human (Foucault 1970). A firm belief in a teleologically ordained view of rational progress through scientific development is a consistent current in defining European cultures as well as individuals. Humanism historically developed into a civilizational model that shaped the idea of Europe as coinciding with the universalizing powers of self-reflexive reason (Said 1978). Europe as a fundamental attribute of the human mind posits transcendence as its specific trait and humanistic universalism as its particularity. This makes Eurocentrism into more than just a contingent matter of attitude: it is a structural element of our cultural practice, which is embedded in received ideas about scientific truth, and the task of theory, as well as institutional and pedagogical practices (Bart, Didur and Heffernan 2003). Humanistic 'Man' defined himself as much by what he excluded from as by what he included in his rational self-representation. Furthermore, by organizing differences on a hierarchical scale of decreasing worth, this humanist subject justified violent and belligerent exclusions of the sexualized, racialized and naturalized 'others' that occupied the slot of devalued difference and were socially marginalized at the best of times and reduced to the subhuman status of disposable bodies in the worst case scenarios (Braidotti 2002; 2006). Humanism's restricted notion of what counts as the human emerges therefore as one of the key points of criticism, with Foucault and Said as leading theoretical figures in this debate. This means that many aspects of their position on humanism are relevant for the current situation. Let us briefly go into them.

A high humanist in background, disposition and taste, Said developed however a trenchant critique of Eurocentric humanism. He showed the limitations of this ideal in the orientalist and discriminatory mode implemented by European powers over the last two centuries, and yet never relinquished his belief in humanistic values. Said's *Humanism and Democratic Criticism* is, in my reading, an exercise in affirmative critique of humanism. Said was both generationally and theoretically close to the work of Foucault, Derrida and Deleuze, his contemporaries. He had special affinity with Foucault's critique of the complicity between power and discourse (1977), that is to say the thick materiality of knowledge-production and theoretical representation. But Said (2003) grew progressively disenchanted with the post-structuralist project and his attachment to Foucault lessened over time, because of the deep Eurocentrism – in fact France-centrism – of Foucault's work. This parochial quality, which for some makes the post-structuralists into new orientalists (Almond 2007), was aggravated by the issue of politics. The problem with Foucault, according to Said, is that he lost the insurrectionary spirit and his scholarship evolved in the direction of quietism, or acquiescence with the status quo, believing that power could never be undone (Said 1998). Being a profound humanist, Said did not share in the deconstructive mode, rejected postmodern relativism and believed absolutely in values such as justice and non-coercive social systems. He abandoned Foucault as 'the scribe of domination' (in Viswanathan, 2001: 137) and turned to more robust theories of historical change, drawn from Fanon (1963, 1967) and Gramsci (1971). Said dismissed what he perceived as the opportunistic transnationalism of academic stars and emphasized instead two interrelated notions. The first is a political economy of ideas – based on Lukács and Fanon – that connects their circulation as 'traveling theory' (Said 1983: 226) to the analysis of what Rob Nixon (2011: 262) calls 'the socioenvironmental relations between internal colonialisms and offshore imperialisms in all their historical and geographical variability'. The second is the importance for critics to exit the text and be part of the world, the mundane, and the everyday politics of resistance. In spite of a brief encounter with Deleuze and Guattari's philosophy in *A Thousand Plateaus*, which he found 'mysteriously suggestive' (Said 1994: 402), Said's nomadism, as Iskander and Rustom lucidly put it (2010: 5), was 'theoretically unhoused, methodologically untidy and spatially fluid'.

I tend to concur with Radhakrishnan (2010: 437) that Said actually misread Foucault and Deleuze and that his project is much closer to the Foucauldian idea of a philosophy of the outside, materially embedded in micro-political practices, than he is willing to acknowledge. Said's declared hostility to poststructuralism marked an entire generation of post-colonial thinkers, but the debate has since acquired less polemical tones. Spivak's defence of Derrida (1988), Ann Stoler's path-breaking work on gender and race (1995), Paul Gilroy's *Black Atlantic* (1995) and Robert Young's insightful reappraisal of both Foucault and Deleuze (1990, 1995), as well as Homi Bhabha (1994), played a constructive role in this respect. The fast-growing field of Deleuzian post-colonial theory and studies of Edouard Glissant (1997; Patton and Bignell 2010; Burns and Kaiser 2012) is another significant factor in rebuilding missing links between these discursive communities, as are intersectional post-colonial studies (Ponzanesi 2014) and neo-materialist and queer race theory (Livingstone and Puar 2011).

The point of consensus is that humanist ideals of reason, secular tolerance, equality under the law and democratic rule, have not been, historically or logically, mutually exclusive with European imperialist practices of violent domination and systematic terror. Acknowledging the close proximity of Enlightenment-driven rationality and barbaric horror has been the core of the radical critique of humanism since the 1970s. The paradox, however, is that, as Said put it:

> It is possible to be critical of Humanism in the name of Humanism and that, schooled in its abuses by the experience of Eurocentrism and empire, one could fashion a different kind of Humanism that was cosmopolitan and text-and-language bound in ways that absorbed the great lessons of the past [...] and still remain attuned to the emergent voices and currents of the present, many of them exilic extraterritorial and unhoused. (2004: 11)

Complicit in genocides and crimes on the one hand, supportive of enormous hopes and aspirations to freedom on the other, humanism engenders productive contradictions that defeat linear criticism and can only remain open-ended.

But another layer of complexity emerges from the unresolved paradoxes of both humanist and antihumanist critique of humanism, namely the question of disciplinarity. Foucault was very much a philosopher, not particularly involved in the new interdisciplinary 'studies' areas that emerged also in response to his own work, as evidenced by his distant relationship to women's and gay studies in his own days. Foucault's objection – shared and made more explicit by Deleuze (Deleuze and Guattari 1987) – was that the change of scale introduced by these 'studies' areas may not be enough to introduce a qualitative shift in terms of conceptual and methodological tools. Similarly, Edward Said himself was not very keen on the field of 'post-colonial studies' that none the less celebrated him as a foundational figure. His objection was two-layered: on the one hand Said had a distinct preference for a classical humanistic education in traditional university departments and on the other he was sceptical of the term 'post'-colonial, preferring instead the critique of imperialism: he was 'more Gramsci than Derrida' (Nixon 2011: 283).

In Said's work as in Foucault's, one can detect a deep suspicion of identity politics, the appeal to authenticity and to ethnic or cultural purity. In different ways they both stress the migratory, non-unitary structure of subjectivity and warn us against proposing uncritically essentialized counteridentities. But the differences are striking. Whereas Foucault called for an antihumanist stance, Said strongly believed that humanism is still valid, but must shed its smug Eurocentrism and become an adventure in difference and in learning about and from alternative cultural traditions. This shift of perspectives requires prior consciousness-raising on the part of humanities scholars: 'Humanists must recognize with some alarm that the politics of identity and the nationalistically grounded system of education remain at the core of what most of us actually do, despite changed boundaries and objects of research' (Said 2004: 55). For Foucault, on the other hand, the project of European humanism is over. Contemporary European subjects of knowledge must meet the ethical obligation to be accountable for their nationalist and imperialist history of exclusions and the long shadow it casts on their present-day politics both in the academy and in society (Morin 1987; Passerini 1998; Balibar 2004; Bauman 2004; Braidotti 2011b, 2013). These different positions also engendered different thinking and writing styles. Both Foucault and Said were aware of the subtle powers of language, but handled it differently. Said, as Nixon put it (2004: x), 'thrived on intellectual complexity while aspiring to clarity', while Foucault – and Deleuze – more influenced by structuralism and Lacanian psychoanalysis, pursued the polysemic complexity of language with a view to expose it, producing an equally dense counter-language.

Since the 1970s however, as I argued in the first two sections of this essay, the institutional landscape has changed dramatically and the question of disciplinarity has acquired a more critical edge. Humanistic culture and its canonical texts no longer constitute a non-negotiable point of reference for a university education, let alone for society as whole. Far from marking the beginning of the end, however, the simultaneous rise of the 'studies' areas and of popular media cultures – both analogue and digital – has proved most invigorating. From this perspective, the real problem with the generation of both Said and Foucault lies elsewhere, namely in their lack of concern for both media culture and the environment, that is to say in the unacknowledged and implicit anthropocentrism of their mindset.

Thus, although the modern–postmodern and humanism–antihumanism debates loom ominously on the contemporary horizon, the real focus for me lies elsewhere, namely in a change of paradigm brought about by the emergence of posthuman discourses. The Said–Foucault quarrel is therefore relevant nowadays as a means to a broader aim, namely how the multilayered critique of humanism comes to bear on contemporary concerns about the dislocation of the human. I have argued (Braidotti 2013) that, far from being deconstructivist and relativistic, the posthuman turn is materialist and neo-foundationalist. It marks the convergence of antihumanism with post-anthropocentrism but moves beyond them both in a more complex direction, overcoming the limitations of both humanism and antihumanism (Braidotti 2013). Because the two-pronged process of negotiating new terms with the humanist tradition on the one hand, and de-centring *Anthropos* on the other, is fraught with tensions and contradictions, many aspects of the old debates on humanism are relevant for the current situation, but mostly as a cautionary tale.

The humanities in the Anthropocene

The academic humanities are built on structural anthropomorphism, which translates into a complicated relationship to the culture and institutional practice of science and technology – the never-ending debates about the 'two' cultures (Snow 1959) being almost emblematic of this difficulty. The lack of concepts and terminology to deal with the ecological environment and non-human others is a serious deficit in view of the mutation we are experiencing towards the posthuman predicament. Neither 'Man' as the universal measure of all things nor *Anthropos* as the emblem of an exceptional species can be said to occupy the centre of world-historical systems of knowledge production in the Anthropocene,[3] which coincides with an era of high technological mediation. The Anthropocene introduces the deconstruction of anthropocentrism in the sense of species supremacy – the rule of *Anthropos* – and shifts the parameters that are used to define it (Rabinow 2003). The compounded impacts of globalization and of technology-driven forms of mediation challenge also the separation of *bios*, as the prerogative of humans, from *zoe*, the life of animals and non-human entities. What comes to the fore instead is a nature–culture continuum in the very embodied structure of the extended self. This shift can be seen as a sort of 'anthropological exodus' from the dominant configurations of the human as the king of creation – a colossal hybridization of the species (Hardt and Negri 2000: 215).

This post-anthropocentric critique has far-reaching implications. Once the centrality of *Anthropos* is challenged, a number of new boundaries between 'Man' and the 'others' are exposed and challenged. Thus, if the multifaceted critiques and revisions of humanism empowered the sexualized and racialized human 'others' to emancipate themselves from the dialectics of oppositional hierarchical master–slave relations, the crisis of *Anthropos* relinquishes the planetary forces of the naturalized others. Animals, insects, plants, cells, bacteria, in fact the planet and the cosmos as a whole, are called into play in a planetary political arena. This places a different burden of responsibility on our species, which is the primary cause for the climate change and other environmental disasters.

The Anthropocene as a central symptom of the posthuman predicament, however, raises both methodological and conceptual problems. The issue of scale – both temporal and spatial – is a major one: how to develop planetary and very long-term perspectives in a geo-centred and not anthropocentric frame is quite a challenge for the disciplines in the humanities. Moreover, the necessity to contemplate the idea of extinction, that is to say, a future without 'us' – members of this particular species – opens up both theological and futuristic concerns which do not sit well with secular academic methods. Furthermore, these shifts in the basic parameters also affect the content of historical research, by 'destroying the artificial but time honoured distinction between natural and human histories' (Chakrabarty 2009: 206).

The post-anthropocentric, or geo-centred turn, however, also has serious implications for the more radical 'studies' areas that have perfected the critique of humanism but have not necessarily relinquished anthropocentrism. This tension arises first in the field of science and technology studies, signalling that the social constructivist, oppositional approach does not always help to deal with the challenges of a post-anthropocentric or geo-centred shift.

In 1985 Donna Haraway, the most prominent contemporary post-anthropocentric thinker, published her path-breaking 'Manifesto for Cyborgs', the first posthuman social-theory text of that generation. It guides us into the high-technology world of informatics and telecommunications and a post-anthropocentric universe marked by what Haraway (2003) would later define as non-human companion species. Haraway (2006) shows that contemporary technologies are enacting a qualitative shift in our understanding of how the human is constituted in its interaction with non-human others, which requires new politics, ethics and creative new cosmologies. She challenges specifically the long-standing association of females/non-Europeans with nature (Haraway 1990), stressing instead the need for feminist and anti-racist critiques that rest on a technologically mediated vision of a nature–culture continuum. She initiates a crossover dialogue between science and technology studies, race theory, socialist feminist politics and feminist neo-materialism by the figuration of the cyborg. A hybrid, or body-machine, the cyborg is a connection-making entity, a figure of inter-relationality, mobility, receptivity and global communication that deliberately blurs categorical distinctions (human/non-human; nature/culture; male/female; Oedipal/non-Oedipal; European/non-European). The cyborg as posthuman political subject exemplifies how Haraway combines competence in contemporary bio-sciences and information technologies with a firm programme of feminist social justice and critique of capitalist abuses.

Since this pioneering work, it has become clear that both the mainstream disciplines and the interdisciplinary 'studies' areas are affected by the fallout of post-anthropocentrism. The climate change issue and the spectre of human extinction, as Naomi Klein claims (2014), changes everything, including 'the analytic strategies that post-colonial and post-imperial historians have deployed in the last two decades in response to the postwar scenario of decolonization and globalization' (Chakrabarty 2009: 198).

Exposing the limitations of the Enlightenment-based humanist model of emancipation, as the 'studies' areas did, is a good starting point but, in the age of the Anthropocene, it just does not go far enough. We need to set a different agenda for the humanities, by challenging anthropocentric definitions of the Human and stressing the structural interdependence among species.

The anthropocentric core of the humanities, moreover, is challenged by another factor: the ubiquity and pervasiveness of technological mediation: the new 'human-non-human linkages, among them complex interfaces involving machinic assemblages of biological "wetware" and non-biological "hardware"' (Bono, Dean and Ziarek 2008: 3). The question of the future of the humanities and the issue of their renewal, therefore, is currently played out on the question of the complex re-configuration of knowledge led by new media and digital technological information: we have entered into global mediation.

The question is consequently what the humanities can become, in the posthuman era and after the decline of the primacy of 'Man' and of *Anthropos*. My argument is that, far from being a terminal crisis, these challenges open up new global, eco-sophical, posthumanist and post-anthropocentric dimensions for the humanities. They are expressed by a second generation of 'studies' areas. Thus animal studies and eco-criticism have grown into such rich and well-articulated fields that it is impossible to even attempt to summarize them.[4] Cultural studies of science and society; religion studies; disability studies; fat studies; success studies; celebrity studies; globalization studies are further significant examples of the exuberant state of the new humanities in the twenty-first century. New media has proliferated into a whole series of sub-sections and meta-fields: software studies, Internet studies, game studies and more. This vitality justifies the optimism expressed by Fuller about the future of the humanities, with media theory and media philosophy providing the new ontological grounds for knowledge production, while the curriculum of the traditional humanities disciplines – notably philosophy – resists any inter-disciplinary contamination.

These new 'studies' areas are the direct descendants of the first generation of the 1970s critical 'studies' areas and pursue the work of critique into new spaces. For instance, a growing field of posthuman research concerns the inhuman(e) aspects of our historical condition, namely the recurrence of devastations, mass migration, wars on terror, violent evictions and technologically mediated conflicts. These questions have been taken up by conflict studies and peace research; human rights studies; humanitarian management; human rights-oriented medicine; trauma, memory and reconciliation studies; security studies death studies; suicide studies – and the list is still growing. These are institutional structures that combine pastoral care with both a healing and a critical function in relation to the legacy of pain and hurt which they entail. They perpetuate and update the transformative impact of the humanities: humane posthumanities for inhumane times.

It follows therefore that, both institutionally and theoretically, the 'studies' areas, which historically have been the motor of both critique and creativity, innovative and challenging in equal measure, have an inspirational role to play also in relation to the posthuman context we inhabit. But in order to be productive, feminist, gender, queer, post-colonial and anti-racist, studies need to allow themselves to be affected by the posthuman turn. To return to the leading question of this essay, if the proper study of mankind used to be 'Man' and the proper study of humanity was the human, it seems to follow that the proper study for the posthuman condition is the complex human interaction with non-human agents. This new knowing subject is a complex assemblage of human and non-human, planetary and cosmic, given and manufactured, which requires major readjustments in our ways of thinking. The posthuman condition marks the end of what Shiva (1993) called 'monocultures of the mind'. The humanities need to embrace the multiple opportunities offered by the posthuman condition, while keeping up the analyses of power formations and the social forms of exclusion and dominations perpetuated by the current world-order of bio-piracy (Shiva 1997), necro-politics (Mbembe 2003) and worldwide dispossession (Sassen 2014).

Towards the posthumanities

So far I have ascertained a number of preliminary conclusions: the humanities in the posthuman era of the Anthropocene should not be restrained by the Human – let alone 'Man' – as its proper object of study. On the contrary, the field would benefit by being free from the empire of humanist anthropocentric 'Man', so as to be able to access in a post-anthropocentric manner issues of external and even planetary importance. These include relation to organic and inorganic non-human others, scientific and technological advances, ecological and social sustainability and the multiple challenges of globalization, including poverty and structural injustice.

Today the posthumanities are emerging as trans-disciplinary discursive fronts around the edges of the classical disciplines but also across the established 'studies' areas, as evidenced by environmental, evolutionary, cognitive, bio-genetic, medical and digital humanities. They rest on post-anthropocentric premises and technologically mediated emphasis on Life as a *zoe*-centred system of species egalitarianism (Braidotti 2006), which are very promising for new research in the field. They embrace creatively the challenge of our historicity without giving in to cognitive panic and without losing sight of the pursuit of social justice.

Let us take some examples: the first and probably the most successful one the digital humanities – pioneered by Katherine Hayles (1999), which deals with a rich agenda of thematic and methodological issues. In Europe and the UK the more traditional 'humanities Informatics' tends to be the preferred term of reference.[5] The agenda is focused on the continuing relevance of the science of texts and the role of the press – from Gutenberg to 3D printing – in shaping human knowledge and the imagination. The defining feature of the digital humanities is that they shift the focus from the mere effects of the development of technical applications for traditional humanities methods onto the study of the computational systems and protocols that go into the making of the information architecture, the codes and data types (Fuller 2005; Drucker, Burdick, Lunenfeld and Presner 2012). Also noteworthy is advanced reflection on new forms of technologically mediated sensibility, post-anthropocentric modes of perception (Hansen 2006) and the effects of new media not only on issues of community and ethics, but also in the fun and pleasure it induces (Goriunova 2014). The field is so advanced that it can boast its own advanced companion (Schreibman, Siemens and Unsworth 2004). As I suggested earlier, the field of new media theory and philosophy – which Fuller designates as 'digital media studies' – has emerged as the conceptual core of the digital humanities and it is the fastest-growing area of the posthumanities.

Another illuminating example of conceptual creativity is the environmental humanities, also known as 'green humanities' and, in the case of water-research, 'blue humanities',[6] inspired by the awareness of the Anthropocene and the issue of sustainability (Braidotti 2006). This interdisciplinary field of study spells the end of the idea of a denaturalized social order disconnected from its environmental and organic foundations, and calls for more complex schemes of understanding the multilayered form of interdependence between contemporary nature and culture. They combine theories of historical subjectivity with 'species thinking', proposing a post-anthropocentric configuration of knowledge which grants the earth the same role and agency as the human subjects that inhabit it. Environmental humanities also explore the social and cultural factors that underscore the public perception and representation of climate change issues. The humanities and more specifically cultural research are best suited to affect and restructure the social imaginary about the posthuman condition. These innovative agenda, which build on but are not confined to either humanism or anthropocentrism, set a new programme for the humanities today. They demonstrate the extent to which the field will prosper if it shows the ability and willingness to undergo a process of transformation in the direction of the posthuman.

What is posthuman about the digital and environmental humanities? It is a question of thematic, methodological and conceptual changes. Thematically, both discursive fields deal with non-human objects/subjects of study: the Digital with new media and computational culture in general (including its repercussions for social, economic and political life) and the Environmental with Gaia or the planet as a whole. Methodologically, the situation is slightly more complex but still quite discernible. On the analytical level, both areas work through a mixture of empirical data, including active cultural and technical practices, ethnographic observation and theoretical framing. They are openly relational in their approach but they differ on the degree of disengagement from *Anthropos* which they endorse. Both of them emphasize the intertwined destinies of humans and non-humans and call for an end to the epistemic violence that consists in metaphorizing the naturalized 'others' – animals, plants, the flora and fauna of the planet – with the anthropological aim of either exemplifying the humans' moral aspirations or of flattering our self-projections. These zoo-mythologies need critical revisions (Wolfe 2003, 2010), to be replaced by a more materialist, i.e. less metaphorical, mode of relation.

This does not mean, however, that all analytically post-anthropocentric discourses are automatically posthumanist. On the contrary, one of the paradoxes of the current situation in the humanities is a normative return to Humanism, coupled with a growing post-anthropocentric analytical framework. This is one of the reasons for the revival of the previous generation's debate on antihumanism. An explicit example of what I define as 'compensatory neo-humanism' (Braidotti 2013) is Peter Singer's animal rights theory (1975), where, much as Martha Nussbaum's liberal philosophy (2006), post-anthropocentric analytic premises are combined with a reassessment of a number of humanist values, notably moral rationality, empathy and solidarity. Post-anthropocentric neo-humanists converge on the need to uphold and expand on these values across all species and to practice an ethics of affirmation based on species-equality (Braidotti 2006). Eco-feminists also embrace this ontological form of solidarity and the critique of the destructive side of human individualism that entails selfishness and a misplaced sense of superiority. They (Donovan and Adams 1996, 2007) connect it to male privileges and the oppression of women and other 'others'.

For Shiva (1997), the political analysis of environmental issues is linked to Eurocentrism and Western supremacy, and speciesism is therefore held accountable as an undue privilege to the same degree as sexism and racism. Meat-eating is targeted as a legalized form of cannibalism by feminist vegetarian critical theory (Adams 1990).

One of the most vocal post-anthropocentric neo-humanists in the field of primatology and animal-studies is Frans de Waal (1996), who extends classical humanist values, like empathy and moral responsibility as a form of emotional communication, to the upper primates, notably the bonobos, striking also a note in support of the evolutionary role of the females of the species. De Waal (1996, 2009) argues that evolution has also provided the requisites for morality and empathy as both an innate and genetically transmitted moral tendency.

I think the analytically post-anthropocentric but normatively neo-humanist approach is problematic (Braidotti 2013). The reason why I am somewhat sceptical of this position is that it is uncritical about humanism itself and it leaves aside the critical evaluation of its limitations. At such a time of deep epistemological, ethical and political crises of values in human societies, extending the privileges of humanist values to other categories can hardly be considered as a selfless and generous, or a particularly productive move. Asserting a vital bond between the humans and other species is necessary, but to narrow down this bond to the effect of shared vulnerability is self-serving a historical time when the very category of the 'human' has become vulnerable. All the more so as this vulnerability is unevenly distributed among humans, with poorer classes across the globe and the South of the planet in general paying a disproportionate price for economic globalization and for climate change. The compensatory efforts on behalf of animals generate what I consider as a belated kind of solidarity between the human dwellers of this planet, currently traumatized by globalization, technology and the 'new' wars, and their animal others. It is at best an ambivalent phenomenon, in that it combines a negative sense of cross-species bonding with classical and rather high-minded humanist moral claims. In this cross-species embrace, anthropocentrism is actually being reinstated uncritically under the aegis of species egalitarianism and humanistic empathy. Is it not the case then that the humans have spread to non-humans their fundamental anxiety about their own future? I think that what we need instead is a change of paradigm, and some recent developments are pointing in that general direction.

The missing links

The present scholarly landscape in the humanities shows some glaring omissions and a new distribution of knowledge, mostly as a result of the high degrees of specialization required by the second generation of trans-disciplinary 'studies' areas. Firstly, the conceptual and methodological efforts made by the disciplines to address the post-anthropocentric challenge are such that they cave inwards under the strain of having to redefine their key concepts and methodology. This brings about a paradoxical return of disciplinarity in a highly defensive mode.

Secondly, and in order to remedy such tendencies, we need to make a cartographic account of the missing links in the emerging posthumanities: where do they leave feminist, queer, post-colonial, anti-racist, class-conscious analyses? Are we not witnessing a re-segregation of these discourses in the new posthuman landscape? Or, to translate this question into my main concern: what is the 'human' in the posthumanities? It is urgent to create border crossings between the new post-anthropocentric discourses and the multiple critiques of humanism emerging from the 'studies' areas, notably the feminist and post-colonial perspectives. Let us look at how feminist and post-colonial studies reacted to the posthuman turn.

By the late 1990s, posthuman feminism takes off,[7] building on the legacy of cultural studies (McNeil 2007), science and technology studies (Stengers 1997), media and film theory (Smelik and Lykke 2008) and the pioneering work of Donna Haraway. A convergence occurs between these discrete fields, producing a discursive boom in feminist theories of non- and posthuman subjectivity that relate specifically to non-anthropomorphic animal or technological others (Bryld and Lykke 2000; Parisi 2004; Braidotti 2006, 2013; Colebrook 2014; Alaimo 2010; Hird and Roberts 2011). Explicit references to the posthuman condition begin to circulate in feminist texts from the 1990s on (Braidotti 1994; Balsamo 1996; Hayles 1999; Halberstam and Livingston 1995). Exemplary of this development is the work of Barad (2003, 2007), who coins the terms 'posthumanist performativity' and 'agential realism' to signify this enlarged and, in my terms, post-anthropocentric vision of subjectivity.

New media and cultural studies, under the impact of the posthuman ethical turn (Braidotti 2006; MacCormack 2012), provided related genealogical sources. Franklin, Lury and Stacey (2000) contribute to a *de facto* displacement of the centrality of the human, through studies of molecular biology (Franklin 2007) and computational systems (Lury, Parisi and Terranova 2012). Eco-feminists (Plumwood 1993, 2003), who had already pioneered geo-centred perspectives, now embrace animal studies and radical veganism (MacCormack 2014). Parallel to these developments, feminist scholars' interest in Darwin, which had been scarce (Beer 1983), starts to grow proportionally by the end of the millennium (Rose and Rose 2000; Carroll 2004; Grosz 2011). 'Matter-realist' feminists (Fraser, Kember and Lury 2006) developed alongside neo-materialist feminism (Braidotti 1991; Dolphijn and Tuin 2012; Alaimo and Hekman 2008; Coole and Frost 2010; Kirby 2011). Deleuzian feminists also developed transversal nomadic subjectivity (Braidotti 1991, 1994) as well explicit discourses about the non-human in terms of the animal and the earth (Grosz 2004) and thus furthered the non-anthropocentric strand of feminist thought. There is no question that contemporary feminist theory is productively posthuman.

On the post-colonial front, things move very fast as well. Robert Nixon (2011) – a student of Said's – addresses head-on the missing links between post-colonial theories, the environmental humanities and indigenous epistemologies. As a contemporary USA-based critical thinker, Nixon can take as his starting point the institutional presence of the new trans-disciplinary posthuman areas such as the environmental and digital humanities. He can therefore proceed to develop a post-colonial critique of their omissions. He acknowledges a schism between these fields, which he traces back to the generation of Said, who tended to dismiss environmentalism as either irrelevant or complicit in imperialist practices. According to Nixon, 1970s USA environmentalism tended to be inward-looking and upheld a separation between human and natural ecology, which produced a retreat from analyses of global power relations and geopolitical differences. The ideology of preservation de-linked environmental degradation from the effects of poverty, warfare, social inequalities and economic exploitation in the global South.

Nixon argues moreover that the status of environmental activism among the poor in the global South has shifted in recent years towards the transnational environmental justice movement and the assessment of damage caused by warfare. Nixon's remedy to the parochialism of greening the humanities consists in bringing them into dialogue with post-colonial perspectives, notably the environmental justice movement, producing a transnational ethics of place. Academically, this results in the production of new areas of studies that crossover the complex post-anthropocentric axes of enquiry: post-colonial environmental humanities come therefore onto the agenda and transnational environmental literature emerges as a crossover between Native American studies and other indigenous studies areas and the environmental humanities.[8]

Starting from the assumption that in contemporary post-colonial studies 'green' politics is now replacing 'red' politics, Huggan and Tiffin (2015: 10) call for new alliances between these fields, so as to address the 'series of constitutive tensions and dilemmas' that characterize them. Identifying as the key issue today 'the clash between conservationist aims and the rights of local indigenous peoples' (Huggan and Tiffin 2015: 3), they also call for a revision of the Humanistic world view that, while celebrating Enlightenment-driven reason, with its implicit anthropocentrism and explicit Eurocentrism, 'provided both the ideological grounds and the practical basis for imperial expansion and colonial governance in many different regions of the world' (Huggan and Tiffin 2015: 3). Quoting Derrida they note that the very definition of humanity depends on both the construction and the exclusion of the non-human, the uncivilized, the savage, the animal. They conclude that 'a postcolonial environmental ethic necessitates an investigation of the category of the 'human' itself and the multiple ways in which this anthropocentric construction has been and is, complicit in racism, imperialism and colonialism, from the moment of conquest to the present day' (Huggan and Tiffin 2015: 7). This requires interdisciplinary networks to replace the discrete disciplines. The key issue is: 'no social justice without environmental justice; and without social justice – for *all* ecological beings – no justice at all' (Huggan and Tiffin 2015: 10).

Starting from the digital humanities, new developments are on the way to fill in other missing links. Ponzanesi and Leurs (2014) claim that post-colonial digital humanities is now a fully constituted field, digital media providing the most comprehensive platform to re-think transnational spaces and contexts. Relying on the work of pioneers like Lisa Nakamura (2002), contemporary activist-researchers Roopika Risam and Adeline Koh, editors of the website 'Post-colonial Digital Humanities'[9] describe their mission as being 'grounded in the literary, philosophical, and historical heritage of post-colonial studies and invested in the possibilities offered by digital humanities, we position post-colonial digital humanities as an emergent field of study invested in decolonizing the digital, foregrounding anti-colonial thought, and disrupting salutatory narratives of globalization and technological progress'.

The projects of setting up post-colonial digital humanities and de-colonizing new media are timely, considering that the fields are highly popular with corporate and institutional sponsors who see them as an indispensable economic tool and an essential element of the war on terror. These transversal projects pursue the critical analysis of power formation of the 'high' post-colonial studies era into the complex cultural analytics of the third millennium. Aware of the potential implications of their research for issues of security and anti-terrorism, Ponzanesi and Leurs (2014) are careful to ground their work empirically in the lived experiences of migrant communities across Europe and focus on digital diasporas that allow us to rethink connectivity and mobility as well as the lasting legacy of social inequalities and dissymmetries in access and power. Arguing that digital connectedness, in the dense materiality of its infrastructure as well as in multiple virtual applications, creates new opportunities for community-building and identity formations, they identify the 'digitally connected migrant' as the prototype of what I would call the contemporary posthuman subject.

Walter Mignolo and the decolonial movement propose a similar focus, but with a different approach. Taking distance from post-colonial studies in general and Said's work on the Orient in particular, as being over-academic and too literary, decoloniality focuses on the colonization of the Americas and notably Latin America from the sixteenth century. Mignolo defines coloniality as the matrix of European power and its quintessential logic: '*colonial* history is the non-acknowledged center in the making of *modern* Europe' (Mignolo 2011: 16). Mignolo (2011) calls for a very radical break from this tradition, suffering from none of the ambivalence and soul-searching complexity that distinguishes Said's work on the issue of multiple cultural belongings. The decolonial approach none the less shares with post-colonial studies the rejection of imperialism not only as a material system of structural inequality, but also as a system of thought: Eurocentrism. The mistaken idea that the history of human civilization culminates in Europe produces not only structural inequalities, but also the habit of racializing and naturalizing them: 'The first world has knowledge, the third world has culture' (Mignolo 2011: 2). The decolonial movement targets epistemic as well as material manifestations of Eurocentric power, namely coloniality and modernity. Modernity is postulated from the epistemic privilege of Europe's self-appointed role as the motor of world history and human development through its investment in scientific ration-ality on the one hand and colonial conquest on the other. Mignolo calls for 'epistemic disobedience' (2011: 122–3) as a way of 'de-linking' from this disastrous legacy, that is to say de-Westernizing the ideals of humanity: 'The *Anthropos* inhabiting non-European places discovered that s/he had been invented, as *Anthropos*, by a locus of enunciation self-defined as *humanitas*' (Mignolo 2011: 3). The decolonial move consists in freeing the human from the domination of European 'Man'.

Furthermore, this movement defines globalization as the contemporary form of Western imperialism, as such responsible for perpetuating the colonial legacy of exploitation and inequality, as evidenced by continuing racism, sexism, genocide and ecocide.[10] Concrete examples of resistance to globalization are movements for indigenous autonomy, like Zapatista self-government.[11] The key idea is that 'the regeneration of life shall prevail over primacy of production and reproduction of goods at the cost of life' (Mignolo 2011: 3).

Indigenous ways of knowing and non-Western epistemologies can provide inspirational material in this quest. As Clarke suggests, we need to be 'wary of the risks of aligning indigeneity with the primordiality of the earth, but [...] also mindful that integrating social history with geological, climatic or evolutionary history has its own potential to destabilize colonial narratives' (Clarke 2008: 739). New alliances between environmentalists, First Nation peoples, new media activists and anti-globalization forces constitute a significant example of these new political assemblages.[12] Mignolo concurs with Nixon about the importance of the transnational environmental justice movement and of taking indigenous epistemologies seriously not as a relic of the past but as a blueprint for the future.

The decolonial approach also proposes a crossover with the digital humanities, as evidenced by the Hasta Scholars Forum[13] that, explicitly inspired by Mignolo's work, focuses on 'Colonial Legacies, Post-colonial Realities and Decolonial Futures of Digital Media'. It starts from the assumption that Eurocentrism and the devastation of indigenous ways of knowing can be exacerbated by the adoption of digital technologies and argues for the need to 'challenge colonial legacies in new media and work towards decolonial futures using contemporary digital technologies, including creating artworks, indigenous archives, games and digital scholarship'. Issues raised include: neocolonialism; indigeneity and settler statuses; post-colonial approaches; white settler colonialism; tensions between decolonization, migration and diaspora; decolonial aesthetics; blackness and decolonization; queer and trans decolonization. The intersection of digital technologies with the humanities is especially targeted, as is research on alternative technologies that may work against colonization and 'post-colonial legacies that maintain social injustice'. These theoretically sophisticated transversal discursive developments constitute the emerging field of the posthumanities.

Contested reconstructions of knowledge

How are the posthumanities contested? They are so in a multilayered manner: firstly in relation to the original disciplines, which are also trying to reconfigure their profile in relation to the posthuman predicament, the Anthropocene included. A case in point is the fraught dialogue between 'eco-criticism' – which is mostly a literary phenomenon – and the broader interdisciplinary field of the environmental humanities, which has incorporated significant amounts of methodology from the social sciences.

Secondly, the posthumanities are contested in relation to the first generation of 'studies' areas, some of which are very anthropocentric and even militantly so – hence the traditional hostility of left-wing 'red' politics towards environmental 'green' politics. The political implications of the posthumanities' unwillingness to disengage from both humanism and anthropocentrism, and thus let go of the exclusively human political agent, are a highly contested matter. This takes me to the third dimension of the problem: the posthumanities are also contested in relation to mainstream humanist values like empathy and care. Different kinds of neo-humanism are emerging in this respect as well – including a revival of socialist humanism, which posit the human as the main point of resistance against the exploitation and dispossession of aggressive neoliberal politics. The human in question here, however, arises after the decline of the 'Man' of humanism and thus constitutes a new political subject. I shall return to this point.

Last but not least, not only is a variety of neo-humanist stances strengthening the attachment to a traditional sense of 'humanity', but it is also the case that new definitions of the 'human' are emerging, which tend to re-totalize the term. A neo-cosmopolitan redefinition of a new Humanity bonded in fear follows from this position. As I stated earlier, this generalized appeal to a new undifferentiated 'humanity' serves mainly the function of flattening out and disregarding all power differences.

These contestations and contradictions are constitutive of the contemporary posthumanities debate and we should not even attempt to resolve them. We need to think rhizomically, in terms of 'and … and' and not of 'either/or'. In order to support this shift of perspective, nomadic pedagogics of dis-identification from humanism and anthropocentrism values are needed, but I cannot pursue this further here.[14]

I want to go on now and suggest that Deleuze can provide the stimulus for a trans-disciplinary approach based on monistic philosophies of becoming. This vital materialism supports the convergence between the posthumanities and the radical epistemologies of the multiple 'studies' areas. We need to start from Spinoza and his materialist monistic ontology (Lloyd 1994, 1996), re-reading it with Deleuze and Guattari and others (Matheron 1969; Macherey 2011; Balibar 1998), that is to say with special emphasis on immanence. The focus of their approach is on theories and practices of subjectivity and subject formations, constituting a significant break from the dismissal of subjectivity, as proposed for instance by the object-oriented ontologists, following superficially on Latour's footsteps (Harman on Latour 2011; Braidotti and Vermeulen 2014). I would argue in favour of a non-unitary (nomadic), embodied and embedded (neo-materialist), affective and relational (vital) subject. The materiality of such a subject is of the dynamic, self-organizing kind (Maturana and Varela 1980; Deleuze and Guattari, 1987) which dissolves mind–body dualism in favour of a monistic integration of the two: embodiment of the brain and embrainment of the body (Marks 1998).

This extended self is moreover marked by the structural presence of practices and apparati of mediation that inscribe technology as 'second nature'. This eco-sophical 'milieu' is our living habitat, which Guattari (1995, 2000) reformulated in terms of the multiple ecologies of 'machinic autopoeisis'. Because the human and social sciences have historically been the main beneficiaries of the transcendental anthropology that posits anthropocentrism, rationality and transcendence as the basic units of reference for the human, they stand to gain the most by being recast today in the Spinozist mode of radical immanence and monistic materialism, enhanced by the high technological mediation and technology. A techno-ecological (Hörl 2013), posthuman turn is at work which means that the vital self-organizing powers that were once reserved for organic entities have now become an integral part of our technologically mediated universe. A nature–cultural continuum that also affects 'humanimals' (Hayward 2008, 2011) and their multiple activities, including the production of knowledge. There is no 'originary humanicity' (Kirby 2011: 233) but only 'originary technicity' (MacKenzie 2002).

We see traces of this approach in contemporary media studies (Fuller 2005; Hansen 2006; Parikka 2010), in neo-materialist philosophy of 'vibrant matter' (Bennett 2010) or 'inventive life' (Fraser, Kember and Lury 2006), that stress the self-organizing vitality and affective structure (Clough 2008) of all living systems, thereby dethroning anthropocentric exceptionalism. By choosing to bypass the binary between the material and the cultural, these process-ontologies focus on their interaction, the better to interrogate the boundaries between them. Posthumanists of many dispositions, building on the poststructuralist legacy but moving beyond it, are also calling for a transformation of the field in the direction of a new deal with the culture of science and technology (Haraway 1997; Hayles 1999; Parisi 2004; Clarke 2008); with comparative literature and cultural studies (Herbrechter 2013; Nayar 2013); new media studies (Fuller 2005; Parikka 2010); and in the framework of social theory (Lury, Parisi and Terranova 2012) and neo-Spinozist social theory (DeLanda 2006; Braidotti 2013).

In other words, however contested and contradictory, the changes and mutations in the direction of the posthumanities are already happening and the question is whether critical thinkers can rise to the occasion and be worthy of these transformations. The ethical and political stakes of these changes are high. They leave the task of posthuman critical thinkers exactly where Said would have wanted it: with the dispossessed and the disempowered, except that many of those are neither human nor anthropomorphic. This makes it imperative for critical thinkers to develop new genealogies, alternative theoretical and legal representations of the new relational systems we are trying to think our way through. We need adequate narratives to live up to this challenge and thus work towards an affirmative brand of posthuman thought. We need to work on counter-memories and new imaginaries and remain attuned to Foucault's focus on multiple archives of forgotten and erased memories. Echoing Haraway's call for new cosmological visions, DeLoughrey and Handley (2011) argue that, in this quest, the imagination plays a crucial role in reconstructing a memory, which Glissant (1997) described as a poetic and relational re-making of the world.

A reactive recomposition of humanity?

The selected overview of the fast-growing posthumanities I provided in the previous sections aimed at demonstrating a number of points. Firstly, that the humanities in the twenty-first century are alive and well, in spite of institutional cutbacks and a negative image in the media and policy-making circles. Secondly, that most of the growth in both thematic and methodological substantive issues emerges from trans-disciplinary 'studies' areas, which are very innovative and prolific but institutionally marginal in relation to the traditional disciplines. Thirdly, the posthumanities can be partly seen as the second generation of 'studies' areas, genealogically indebted to the first generation of the 1970s. But they go further and shed both ideological and tactical habits in order to develop more consistently transversal forms of enquiry. They differ from their predecessors in that they address directly and creatively the question of anthropocentrism, which had been left relatively under-examined.

In reaching the concluding section of this essay I want to return more explicitly to the question of the political implications of the posthuman turn. This is a multilayered dimension, which comes down to three basic issues. Firstly: how sustainable is the path of technological advances – which Paul Gilroy calls 'over-development'[15] – in a globally interlinked world? Secondly: what to do about the growing disparities in access to the riches of the global economy and its advanced technologies? And last but not least: what can be the contribution of the humanities to a better understanding of the issues involved?

These questions resonate across the field of the posthumanities. For instance, posthuman discourses of the digital and environmental humanities, crossed with post-colonial and feminist studies, raise more urgently than ever the question of scale: how can we re-think our interconnection in the era of the Anthropocene, while re-thinking our new ecologies of belonging? The connection to the natural environment and to the technosphere of new media recasts the issue of alterity in non-human terms that cannot be adequately dealt with in the discourses and language of poststructuralist difference, let alone universalist humanism.

There is a distinct tendency today to hastily recompose a new generic 'we' – a new endangered humanity after anthropocentrism. 'Humanity' is posited as a unitary category and as an object of intense debate, just as it emerges as a threatened or endangered category (Chakrabarty 2009). A panhuman bond of vulnerability engenders a negative or reactive sort of cosmopolitan interconnection (Beck 2006) that expresses intense anxiety about the future of our species and cannot fail to affect the construction of the human in the new (post-)humanities.

The literature on shared anxiety about the future of both our species and of our humanist legacy is by now an established genre, as shown by the statements of significant political and social thinkers like Habermas (2003), Fukuyama (2002), Sloterdijk (2009) and Borradori (2003). In different ways, they seem struck by moral and cognitive panic at the prospect of the human/non-human/posthuman turn, blaming our advanced technologies for the situation. The size of recent scholarship on the environmental crisis, extinction and the climate change also testifies to this state of emergency and to the emergence of the earth in the Anthropocene as a political agent. Both United Nations humanitarianism and corporate posthumanism assuage this anxiety by proposing a hasty reformulation of a panhuman 'we', who are supposed to be in *this* together.

There is no question that the generic figure of the human – 'we' – is in trouble and *this* is a serious matter. Donna Haraway puts is as follows: 'our authenticity is warranted by a database for the human genome. The molecular database is held in an informational database as legally branded intellectual property in a national laboratory with the mandate to make the text publicly available for the progress of science and the advancement of industry. This is Man the taxonomic type become Man the brand' (1997: 74). Massumi refers to this phenomenon as 'Ex-Man': 'a genetic matrix embedded in the materiality of the human' (1998: 60) and as such undergoing significant mutations: 'species integrity is lost in a bio-chemical mode expressing the mutability of human matter' (1998: 60). Karen Barad (2003) coins the term 'posthumanist performativity' to define new human–non-human interaction.

Such a sense of urgency, however, does not warrant generic reconstructions of 'Humanity' and a tacit new consensus about something we may call 'the human'. I would argue for the need to keep tracking the changing perceptions and multiple new formations of the 'human' in the globalized, technologically mediated and ethnically diverse world we inhabit. The differential politics of location affect the production of knowledge and self-representation. 'We' – the dwellers of *this* planet at this point in time – are confronted by a number of painful contradictions: an electronically linked pan-humanity which, however, is more fragmented than ever and split by convulsive internal fractures, economic disparities, xenophobic fears and violence. Humanity is re-created as a negative category, held together by shared vulnerability and the spectre of extinction, but also struck down by environmental devastation, by new and old epidemics, in endless 'new' wars that innovate on ways of killing, in the proliferation of migrations and exodus, detention camps and refugees' centres. The staggering inequalities engendered by the global economy make for violence and insurrection; the appeals for new forms of cosmopolitan relations or a global *ethos* (Kung 1998) are often answered by necro-political acts of violence, destruction and assassination, not only by the official enemies of the West – Muslim extremists – but also by home-grown killers, which in Europe are the likes of Anders Behring Breivik.[16]

In such a volatile context, it is important to keep the critical perspective wide open and not give in to foregone conclusions about the transition the 'human' and 'Humanity' is going through. Such 'closed' systems of thought would short-circuit the process of transformation. Nor can we assume that the shifting notions and social practices of human–non-human–posthuman relations are intrinsically progressive, or that they will automatically undo power relations based on class, gender, race, sexuality, age or disability (Braidotti 2002, 2013). There is in fact large and growing evidence that points to the exact contrary. What is needed instead is careful negotiations in order to constitute new subject positions as transversal alliances between human and non-human agents, which account for the ubiquity of technological mediation and the complexity of inter-species alliances (Livingston and Puar 2011). In a similar vein, arguing that ecologically oriented thinking has yet to come to terms with the deterritorializations induced by globalization, Ursula Heise (2008) concentrates on the missing links between post-colonial studies and media studies, and argues forcefully for the idea of a 'green' or eco-cosmopolitan citizenship. The posthumanities require productive and affirmative forms of de-familiarization or dis-identification from century-old habits of anthropocentric thought and humanist arrogance, which test the boundaries of what exactly is 'human' about them. De-familiarization involves shedding cherished habits of thought and representation, even at the risk of producing fear and nostalgia. It is a sobering process by which the knowing subject evolves from the vision of the self he or she had become accustomed to. Spivak calls it 'unlearning one's privileges', even and especially in the practice of critical theory. Instead of seeking for identity-bound recognition, the ethical emphasis falls on the expression of an affirmative mode of relations to multiple others. The frame of reference therefore becomes the world, in all its open-ended, interrelational, multi-sexed, and trans-species flows of becoming: a native form of cosmopolitanism (Braidotti 2006, 2013).

Acknowledging that engaging non-human agency creates these additional challenges, DeLoughrey and Handley (2011: 9) demand: 'a more nuanced discourse about the representation of alterity, a theorization of difference that post-colonialists, feminists, and environmental activists have long considered in terms of our normative representations of nature, human and otherwise'. In other words, we need a more 'cautious' hermeneutics, based on contingent and interdependent narratives to replace the previous, grandiose mythologies of universal human experience. More than ever, Said's concerns resonate in current geopolitical and academic concerns about the ways in which the 'human' is divided, administered, plundered and pigeonholed in violent oppositional ways.

Instead of taking a flight into an abstract idea of a 'new' pan-humanity, bonded in shared vulnerability or anxiety about survival and extinction, in a world risk society (Beck 1999), therefore, I want to plead for affirmative politics grounded on immanent interconnections, a transnational ethics of place. What we need are embedded and embodied, relational and affective cartographies of the new power relations that are emerging from the current geopolitical and post-anthropocentric world order. Class, race, gender and sexual orientations, age and able-bodiedness are more than ever significant markers of human 'normality'. They are key factors in framing the notion of and policing access to something we may call 'human' or 'humanity'. Yet, considering the global reach of the problems we are facing today, in the era of the 'Anthropocene', it is none the less the case that 'we' are indeed in *this* anthropocentric crisis together. Such awareness must not, however, obscure or flatten out the power differentials that sustain the collective subject ('we') and its endeavour (*this*). Labouring towards a neo-aboriginal, rather than a neo-Kantian brand of cosmopolitanism, 'we' need to acknowledge that there may well be multiple and potentially contradictory projects at stake in the complex recompositions of 'the human' in the posthumanities right now: many contested ways of becoming-world together.

Notes

1   Private communication with the author.

2   A portmanteau term obtained by merging precarious with proletariat. It designates the bottom social class in advanced capitalism with low levels of economic, cultural and social capital. Source: Wikipedia, consulted 1 June 2015.

3   Nobel Prize winning chemist, Paul Crutzen, in 2002 coined the term 'Anthropocene' to describe our current geological era. This term stresses both the technologically mediated power acquired by our species and its potentially lethal consequences for the geological sustainability of our planet as a whole.

4   A companion to animal studies has just been published (Gross and Vallely,

2012), whereas a complete eco-criticism reader has been available for a while (Glotfelty and Fromm, 1996). *The Journal of Ecocriticism* is quite established, while a recent issue of the prestigious *PMLA* papers (2012) was dedicated to the question of the animal. For an excellent historical analysis, see Bourke (2011). For a younger generation of scholars (Rossini and Tyler 2009) the animal is the posthuman question *par excellence*. Braidotti and Roets (2012); Davis (1997) and Goodley, Lawthorn and Runswick (2014).

5   With thanks to Matthew Fuller.

6   With thanks to Iris van der Tuin.

7   For a full analysis, see 'Posthuman feminist theory', Braidotti (2015).

8   With thanks to Sandra Ponzanesi.

9   Roopika Risam and Adleine Koh: http://dhpoco.org/about-us/. With thanks to Koen Leurs. Consulted 7 July 2015.

10   The term refers to any extensive damage or destruction of the natural landscape and disruption or loss of ecosystems of a given territory to such an extent that the survival of the inhabitants of that territory is endangered. Source: Wikipedia, consulted 7 July 2015.

11   Source: Wikipedia 'Decoloniality', consulted 6 July 2015.

12   See for instance the land/media/indigenous project based in British Columbia: Bleck, Dodds and Williams (2013).

13   Co-ordinated by Micha Cardenas, Noha F. Beydon and Alainya Kavaloski; see the website: http://www.hastac.org/forums/colonial-legacies-postcolonial-realities-and-decolonial-futures-digital-media. Consulted 7 July 2015. With thanks to Matthew Fuller.

14   For an illuminating example, see the project *'Posthumanism, the Affective Turn and Socially Just Critical Higher Education Pedagogies'*, directed by Vivienne Bozalek at the University of the Western Cape and funded by the National Research Foundation in South Africa.

15   Private communication with the author.

16   Anders Behring Breivik is the Norwegian mass murderer and the confessed perpetuator of the 2011 attacks in Oslo and on the island of Utoya, killing respectively eight and sixty-nine people, mostly Socialist youth.

References

Adams, C. J. (1990), *The Sexual Politics of Meat: A Feminist-Vegetarian Critical Theory*. New York and London: Continuum.

Alaimo, S. (2010), *Bodily Natures: Science, Environment and the Material Self*. Bloomington: Indiana University Press.

Alaimo, S. and S. Hekman (ed.) (2008), *Material Feminisms*. Bloomington: Indiana University Press.

Almond, I. (2007), *The New Orientalists. Postmodern representations of Islam from Foucault to Baudrillard*. London and New York: I. B.Tauris.

Anderson, L. (1997), 'Control Rooms and Other Stories: Confession of a Content Provider', *Parked* 49: 126–45.

Arthur, J. and A. Shapiro (1995), *Campus Wars. Multiculturalism and the Politics of Difference*. Boulder: Westwood Press.

Badiou, A. (2013), 'Our Contemporary Impotence', *Radical Philosophy* 181: 40–3.

Badiou, A. and Z. Slavoj (2009), *Philosphy in the Present*. Cambridge: Polity Press.

Balibar, É. (1998), *Spinoza and Politics*. London: Verso.

Balibar, É. (2004), *We, the People of Europe? Reflections on Transnational Citizenship*. Princeton: Princeton University Press.

Balsamo, A. (1996), *Technologies of the Gendered Body: Reading Cyborg Women*. Durham, NC: Duke University Press.

Barad, K. (2003), 'Posthumanist Performativity: Toward an Understanding of How Matter Comes to Matter', *Signs: Journal of Women in Culture and Society* 28 (3): 801–31.

Barad, K. (2007), *Meeting the Universe Halfway*. Durham, NC: Duke University Press.

Bart, S., J. Didur and T. Heffernan (eds) (2003), *Cultural Critique*, on Posthumanism, vol. 53.

Bauman, Z. (2004), *Europe: An Unfinished Adventure*. Cambridge: Polity Press.

Beck, U. (1999), *World Risk Society*. Cambridge: Polity Press.

Beck, U. (2006), *Cosmopolitan Vision*, trans. Ciaran Cronin. Cambridge: Polity Press.

Beck, U. (2007), 'The Cosmopolitan Condition. Why Methodological Nationalism Fails', *Theory, Culture & Society* 24 (7/8): 286–90.

Beer, G. (1983), *Darwin's Plots: Evolutionary Narrative in Darwin, George Eliot, and Nineteenth-Century Fiction*. London, Boston, Melbourne, and Henley: Routledge & Kégan Paul.

Bennett, J. (2010), *Vibrant Matter. A Political Ecology of Things*. Durham, NC: Duke University Press.

Berubé, M. and C. Nelson (eds) (1995), *Higher Education Under Fire. Politics, Economics and the Crisis of the Humanities*. New York and London: Routledge.

Bhabha, H. K. (1994), *The Location of Culture*. London and New York: Routledge.

Bignall, S. and P. Patton (eds) (2010), *Deleuze and the Postcolonial*. Edinburgh: Edinburgh University Press.

Bleck, N., K. Dodds and B. Chief Williams (2013), *Picturing Transformations*. Vancouver: Figure 1 Publishing.

Bono, James J., T. Dean and E. Plonowska (2008), *A Time for the Humanities. Futurity and the Limits of Autonomy*. New York: Fordham University Press.

Borradori, G. (2003), *Philosophy in a Time of Terror*. Chicago: University of Chicago Press.

Braidotti, R. (1989), 'Organs without Bodies'. In *Differences* 1: 147–61, Bloomington: Indiana University Press.

Braidotti, R. (1991), *Patterns of Dissonance: An Essay on Women in Contemporary French Philosophy*. Cambridge: Polity Press.

Braidotti, R. (1994), *Nomadic Subjects: Embodiment and Sexual Difference in*

Contemporary Feminist Theory [1st edn]. New York: Columbia University Press.

Braidotti, R. (2002), *Metamorphoses. Towards a Materialist Theory of Becoming*. Cambridge and Malden: Polity Press/Blackwell Publishers Ltd.

Braidotti, R. (2006), *Transpositions: On Nomadic Ethics*. Cambridge: Polity Press.

Braidotti, R. (2011a), *Nomadic Subjects: Embodiment and Sexual Difference in Contemporary Feminist Theory*. New York: Columbia University Press.

Braidotti, R. (2011b), *Nomadic Theory. The Portable Rosi Braidotti*. New York: Columbia University Press.

Braidotti, R. (2013), *The Posthuman*. Cambridge: Polity Press.

Braidotti, R. (2014), 'The Untimely'. In Bolette Blaagaard and Iris van der Tuin (eds), *The Subject of Rosi Braidotti*. London and New York: Bloomsbury.

Braidotti, R. (2015), 'Posthumanism'. In Lisa Disch and Mary Hawkesworth (eds), *Oxford Handbook of Feminist Theory*. Oxford: Oxford University Press.

Braidotti, R. and G. Roets (2012), 'Nomadology and Subjectivity: Deleuze, Guattari and Critical Disability Studies'. In Dan Goodley, Bill Hughes and Lennard Davis (eds), *Disability and Social Theory. New Developments and Directions*. New York: Palgrave Macmillan.

Braidotti, R. and T. Vermeulen (2014), 'Borrowed Energy. Interview by Timotheus Vermeulen'. In *Frieze*, No. 165, pp. 130–3. Also available at: http://www.frieze.com/issue/article/borrowed-energy/

Brah, A. (1996), *Cartographies of Diaspora-Contesting Identities*. New York and London: Routledge.

Bryld, M. and N. Lykke (2000), *Cosmodolphins. Feminist Cultural Studies of Technologies, Animals and the Sacred*. London: Zed Books.

Burgess, P. (2014), *The Future of Security Research in the Social Sciences and the Humanities*. European Science Foundation.

Burns, L. and B. Kaiser (eds) (2012), *Postcolonial Literature and Deleuze. Colonial Pasts, Differential Futures*. London: Palgrave.

Carroll, J. (2004), *Literary Darwinism. Evolution, Human Nature and Literature*. London and New York: Routledge.

Chakrabarty, D. (2009), 'The Climate of History: Four Theses', *Critical Enquiry* 35: 197–222.

Chandler, J. (2004), 'Critical Disciplinarity', *Critical Inquiry* 30 (2): 355–60.

Cheney, L. (2001), 'Defending Civilization: How our Universities are Failing America and What can be Done about it'. Washington: American Council of Trustees and Alumni, http://totse.mattfast1.com/en/politics/political_spew/162419.html (accessed 13 November 2015).

Clarke, B. (2008), *Posthuman Metamorphosis: Narrative and Systems*. New York: Fordham University Press.

Clough, P. (2008), 'The Affective Turn: Political Economy, Biomedia and Bodies', *Theory, Culture & Society*, 25 (1): 1–22.

Coetzee, J. M. (2013), 'Take a Stand on Academic Freedom', *University World News*. No. 298. http://www.universityworldnews.com/article.php?story=20131126223127382

Cohen, T., C. Colebrook and H. Miller (2012), *Theory and the Disappearing Future. On de Man, on Benjamin*. New York and London: Routledge.

Cole, J., Barber, E. and Graubard, S. (eds) (1993), *The Research University in a Time of Discontent*. London and Baltimore: Johns Hopkins University Press.

Colebrook, C. (2014), *Death of the Posthuman*. Ann Arbor: Open Humanities Press/University of Michigan Press.

Collini, S. (2010), 'Brown's Gamble', *London Review of Books* 32 (21): 23–5.

Collini, S. (2012), *What Are Universities For?* London: Penguin Books.

Collini, S. (2013), 'Sold Out', *London Review of Books* 35 (2): 3–12.

Coole, D. and S. Frost (2010), *New Materialisms: Ontology, Agency, and Politics*. Durham, NC: Duke University Press.

Cooper, M. (2008), *Life as Surplus. Biotechnology & Capitalism in the Neoliberal Era*. Seattle: University of Washington Press.

Davies, T. (1997), *Humanism*. London: Routledge.

Davis, Lennard J. (ed.) (1997), *The Disability Studies Reader*. New York and London: Routledge.

DeLanda, M. (2006), *A New Philosophy of Society: Assemblage Theory and Social Complexity*. New York and London: Continuum.

Deleuze, G. and F. Guattari (1977), *Anti-Oedipus. Capitalism and Schizophrenia*. New York: Viking Press/Richard Seaver.

Deleuze, G. and F. Guattari (1987), *A Thousand Plateaus: Capitalism and Schizophrenia*. Minneapolis: University of Minnesota Press.

DeLoughrey, E. and G. B. Handley (2011), *Postcolonial Ecologies. Literatures of the Environment*. Oxford: Oxford University Press.

Derrida, J. (1992), *The Other Heading: Reflections on Today's Europe*. Bloomington: Indiana University Press.

Dolphijn, R. and I. van der Tuin (2012), *New Materialism: Interviews & Cartographies*. Ann Arbor: Open Humanities Press.

Dongen, E. van (2002), 'Humanimals, Huchines and Glokin: Bodies and Medical Technology', *Medische Antropologie* 14 (1): 134–48.

Donoghue, F. (2008), *The Last Professors. The Corporate University and the Fate of the Humanities*. New York: Fordham University Press.

Donovan, J. and C. J. Adams (eds) (1996), *Beyond Animal Rights. A Feminist Caring Ethic for the Treatment of Animals*. New York: Continuum.

Donovan, J. and C. J. Adams (eds) (2007), *The Feminist Care Tradition in Animal Ethics*. New York: Columbia University Press.

Drucker, J., A. Burdick, P. Lunenfeld and T. Presner, (2012), *Digital Humanities*. Cambridge, MA: MIT Press.

Fanon, F. (1963), *The Wretched of the Earth*. New York: Grove Press.

Fanon, F. (1967), *Black Skin, White Masks*. New York: Grove Press.

Flannery, T. (1994), *The Future Eaters*. New York: Grove Press.

Foucault, M. (1970), *The Order of Things: An Archaeology of Human Sciences*. New York: Pantheon Books.

Foucault, M. (1977), *Discipline and Punish*. New York: Pantheon Books.

Foucault, M. and G. Deleuze, (1977), 'Intellectuals and Power: A Conversation between Foucault and Deleuze'. In Donald Bouchard (ed.), *Language, Counter-Memory and Practice*. Ithaca: Cornell University Press.

Franklin, S. (2007), *Dolly Mixtures*. Durham, NC: Duke University Press.

Franklin, S., C. Lury and J. Stacey (2000), *Global Nature, Global Culture*. London: Sage.

Fraser, M., S. Kember and C. Lury (eds) (2006), *Inventive Life. Approaches to the New Vitalism*. London: Sage.

Fukuyama, F. (1989), 'The End of History?', *National Interest* 16: 3–18.

Fukuyama, F. (2002), *Our Posthuman Future. Consequences of the BioTechnological Revolution*. London: Profile Books.

Fuller, M. (2005), *Media Ecologies: Materialist Energies in Art and Technoculture*. Cambridge, MA and London: MIT Press.

Fuller, M. (2008), *Software Studies. A Lexicon*. Cambridge, MA: MIT Press.

Galison, P. (2004), 'Specific Theory', *Critical Inquiry* 30 (2): 379–83.

Gill, R. (2010), 'Breaking the Silence: The Hidden Injuries of the Neoliberal Universities'. In Rosalind Gill and Roisin Ryan Flood (eds), *Secrecy and Silence in the Research Process: Feminist Reflections*. London and New York: Routledge.

Gilroy, P. (1995), *The Black Atlantic. Modernity and Double Consciousness*. Cambridge, MA: Harvard University Press.

Glissant, E. (1997), *Poetics of Relation*. Ann Arbor: University of Michigan Press.

Glotfelty, C. and H. Fromm (eds) (1996), *The Ecocriticism Reader*. Athens and London: University of Georgia Press.

Goodley, D., R. Lawthorn and K. Runswick (2014), 'Posthuman Disability Studies', *Subjectivity* 7 (4): 341–61.

Goriunova, O. (2014), *Fun and Software. Exploring Pleasure, Paradox and Pain in Computing*. London: Bloomsbury.

Gramsci, A. (1971), *Selections from the Prison Notebooks*. New York: International Publishers.

Grewal, I. and C. Kaplan (eds) (1994), *Scattered Hegemonies: Postmodernity and Transnational Feminist Practices*. Minneapolis: University of Minnesota Press.

Gross, A. and A. Vallely (2012), *Animals and the Human Imagination: A Companion to Animal Studies*, New York: Columbia University Press.

Grosz, E. (2004), *The Nick of Time*. Durham, NC: Duke University Press.

Grosz, E. (2011), *Becoming Undone*. Durham, NC: Duke University Press.

Guattari, F. (1995), *Chaosmosis. An Ethico-aesthetic Paradigm*. Sydney: Power Publications.

Guattari, F. (2000), *The Three Ecologies*. London: The Athlone Press.

Habermas, J. (2003), *The Future of Human Nature*. Cambridge: Polity Press.

Halberstam, J. and I. Livingston (eds) (1995), *Posthuman Bodies*. Bloomington: Indiana University Press.

Hansen, M. (2006), *Bodies in Code: Interfaces with Digital Media*. New York: Routledge.

Haraway, D. (1985), 'A Manifesto for Cyborgs: Science, Technology, and Socialist Feminism in the 1980s', *Socialist Review* 5 (2): 65–107.

Haraway, D. (1990), *Simians, Cyborgs and Women*. London: Free Association Press.

Haraway, D. (1997), *Modest_Witness@Second_Millennium. FemaleMan©_Meets_Oncomouse™*, London and New York: Routledge.

Haraway, D. (2003), *The Companion Species Manifesto. Dogs, People and Significant Otherness*. Chicago: Prickly Paradigm Press.

Haraway, D. (2006), 'When we have Never been Human, What is to be Done?', *Theory, Culture & Society* 23 (7–8): 135–58.

Hardt, M. and A. Negri (2000), *Empire*. Cambridge, MA: Harvard University Press.

Harman, G., B. Latour and P. Erdélyi (2011), *The Prince and the Wolf: Latour and Harman at the LSE*. Alresford: Zero Books.

Hayles, K. (1999), *How We Became Posthuman. Virtual Bodies in Cybernetics, Literature and Informatics*. Chicago: University of Chicago Press.

Hayward, E. (2008), 'More Lessons from a Starfish: Prefixial Flesh and Transspeciated Selves', *Women's Studies Quarterly* 36 (3–4): 64–85.

Hayward, E. (2011), 'Sensational Jellyfish: Aquarium Affects and the Matter of Immersion', *Differences* 25 (5): 161–96.

Heise, U. (2008), *Sense of Place and Sense of Planet*. Oxford: Oxford University Press.

Herbrechter, S. (2013), *Posthumanism: A Critical Analysis*. London and New York: Bloomsbury Publishing.

Hird, M. and C. Roberts (eds) (2011), 'Feminism Theorises the Nonhuman', *Feminist Theory* 12:2.

Hörl, E. (2013), 'A Thousand Ecologies: The Process of Cyberneticization and General Ecology'. In *The Whole Earth: California and the Disappearance of the Outside*. Diedrich Diederichsen and Anselm Franke (eds), Berlin: Sternberg Press.

Huggan, G. and H. Tiffin (2008), 'Green Postcolonialism', *Interventions. International Journal of Postcolonial Studies*, 9 (1): 1–11.

Huggan, G. and H. Tiffin (2015), *Postcolonial Ecocriticism. Literature, Animals, Environment*. London and New York: Routledge.

Huntington, S. (1996), *The Clash of Civilizations and the Remaking of World Order*. New York: Simon & Schuster.

Hussein, A. (2004), *Edward Said: Criticism and Society*. New York: Verso.

Husserl, E. (1970), *The Crisis of European Sciences and Transcendental Phenomenology*. Evanston: Northwestern University Press.

Kirby, V. (2011), *Quantum Anthropologies: Life at Large*. Durham, NC and London: Duke University Press.

Irigaray, L. (1994), 'Equal to Whom?', trans. Robert L. Mazzola. In Naomi Schor and Elizabeth Weed (eds), *The Essential Difference*. Bloomington: Indiana University Press.

Iskandar, A. and H. Rustom (eds) (2010), *Edward Said. A Legacy of Emancipation and Representation*. Berkeley: University of California Press.

Kimball, R. (1990), *Tenured Radicals*. Chicago: Ivan R. Dee.

Kirby, V. (2011), *Quantum Anthropologies: Life at Large*. Durham, NC: Duke University Press.

Klein, N. (2014), *This Changes Everything. Capitalism vs. the Climate*. New York: Simon & Schuster.

Kung, H. (1998), *A Global Ethic for Global Politics and Economics*. Oxford: Oxford University Press.

Lambert, G. (2001), *Report to the Academy. Re the New Conflict of the Faculties*. Aurora, CO: The Davies Group Publishers.

Latour, B. (2004), 'Why has Critique Run Out of Steam? From Matters of Fact to Matters of Concern', *Critical Inquiry* 30 (2): 225–48.

Lazzarato, M. (2012), *The Making of the Indebted Man: An Essay on the Neoliberal Conditi (Semiotext(e) / Intervention Series)*, trans. Joshua David Jordan. Los Angeles: Semiotext(e).

Livingston, J. and J. K. Puar (2011), 'Interspecies', *Social Text* 29/1: 3–13.

Lloyd, G. (1984), *The Man of Reason: Male and Female in Western Philosophy*. London: Methuen.

Lloyd, G. (1994), *Part of Nature: Self-knowledge in Spinoza's Ethic*. Ithaca and London: Cornell University Press.

Lloyd, G. (1996), *Spinoza and the Ethics*. London and New York: Routledge.

Lyotard, J.-F. (1984), *The Postmodern Condition*, Manchester: Manchester University Press.

Lury, C., Luciana Parisi and Tiziana Terranova (2012), 'Introduction: The Becoming Topological of Culture', *Theory, Culture and Society* 29 (4–5): 3–35.

MacCormack, P. (2012), *Posthuman Ethics*. London: Ashgate.

MacCormack, P. (2014), *The Animal Catalyst. Towards Ahuman Theory*. London and New York: Bloomsbury.

Macherey, P. (2011), *Hegel or Spinoza*. Minneapolis: University of Minnesota Press.

MacKenzie, A. (2002), *Transductions: Bodies and Machines at Speed*. New York: Continuum.

McNeil, M. (2007), *Feminist Cultural Studies of Science and Technology*. London: Routledge.

Marks, J. (1998), *Gilles Deleuze. Vitalism and Multiplicity*. London: Pluto Press.

Massumi, B. (1998), 'Requiem for our prospective dead! (Toward a participatory critique of capitalist power)'. In Eleanor Kaufman and Kevin Jon Heller (eds), *Deleuze and Guattari. New Mappings in Politics, Philosophy and Culture*. Minneapolis: University of Minnesota Press.

Matheron, A. (1969), *Individu et communauté chez Spinoza*, Paris: Les Editions de Minuit.

Maturana, H. R. and F. J. Varela (1980), *Autopoiesis and Cognition: The Realization of the Living*, Dordrecht: Kluwer Academic Publishing Group.

Mbembe, A. (2003), 'Necropolitics', *Public Culture*, 15 (1): 11–40.

Menand, L. (ed.) (1996), *The Future of Academic Freedom*. Chicago: University of Chicago Press.

Mignolo, W. (2009), 'Epistemic Disobedience, Independent Thought and De-colonial Freedom', *Theory, Culture & Society* 267 (7–8): 1–23.

Mignolo, W. (2011), *The Darker Side of Western Modernity: Global Futures, Decolonial Options*, Durham, NC: Duke University Press.

Morin, E. (1987), *Penser l'Europe*. Paris: Gallimard.

Moulier Boutang, Y. (2012), *Cognitive Capitalism*. Cambridge: Polity Press.

Nakamura, L. (2002), *Cybertypes. Race, Ethnicity and Identity on the Internet*. London and New York: Routledge.

Nayar, Pramod K. (2013), *Posthumanism*. Cambridge: Polity Press.

Nixon, R. (2004), 'Edward Said', *Politics and Culture* 1 (1).

Nixon, R. (2011), *Slow Violence and the Environmentalism of the Poor*. Cambridge, MA: Harvard University Press.

Nussbaum, M. (2006), *Frontiers of Justice. Disability, Nationality, Species Membership*. Cambridge, MA: Harvard University Press.

Nussbaum, M. (2010), *Not for Profit. Why Democracy Needs the Humanities*. Princeton: Princeton University Press.

Parikka, J. (2010), *Insect Media. An archaeology of Animals and Technology*. Minneapolis: University of Minnesota Press.

Parisi, L. (2004), *Abstract Sex. Philosophy, Bio-Technology, and the Mutation of Desire*. London: Continuum Press.

Passerini, L. (ed.) (1998), *Identità Culturale Europea. Idee, Sentimenti, Relazioni*. Florence: La Nuova Italia Editrice.

Patton, P. (2000), *Deleuze and the Political*. London and New York: Routledge.

Plumwood, V. (1993), *Feminism and the Mastery of Nature*. London and New York: Routledge.

Plumwood, V. (2003), *Environmental Culture*. London: Routledge.

Ponzanesi, S. (ed.) (2014), *Gender, Globalization and Violence. Postcolonial Conflict Zones*. New York: Routledge.

Ponzanesi, S. and K. Leurs (2014), 'Introduction to the Special Issue: On Digital Crossings in Europe', *Crossings, Journal of Migration and Culture* 4(1): 3–22.

Protevi, J. (2009), *Political Affect*. Minneapolis: University of Minnesota Press.

Rabinow, P. (2003), *Anthropos Today*. Princeton: Princeton University Press.

Radhakrishnan, R. (2010), 'Edward Said and the Possibilities of Humanism'. In A. Iskander and H. Rustom (eds), *Edward Said. A Legacy of Emancipation and Representation*. Berkeley: University of California Press.

Readings, B. (1996), *The University in Ruins*. Cambridge, MA: Harvard University Press.

Rich, A. (1987), *Blood, Bread and Poetry*. London: Virago Press.

Rich, A. (2001), *Arts of the Possible: Essays and Conversations*. New York: W. W. Norton & Company.

Risam, R. and A. Kph (eds) (2015), *Postcolonial Digital Humanities*. Website. http://dhpoco.org/about-us/ (accessed June 10).

Rose, H. and S. Rose. (2000), *Alas, Poor Darwin: Arguments against Evolutionary Psychology*. New York: Harmony Books.

Rose, N. (2007), *The Politics of Life Itself: Biomedicine, Power and Subjectivity in the Twentieth-first Century*. Princeton: Princeton University Press.

Rossini, M. and T. Tyler (eds) (2009), *Animal Encounters*. Leiden: Brill.

Said, E. W. (1978), *Orientalism*. Harmondsworth: Penguin Books.

Said, E. W. (1983), *The World, the Text and the Critic*. Cambridge, MA: Harvard University Press.

Said, E. W. (1994), *Culture and Imperialism*. London: Vintage.

Said, E. W. (1996), 'Identity, Authority and Freedom: the Potentate and the Traveler'. In L. Menand (ed.), *The Future of Academic Freedom*. Chicago: University of Chicago Press.

Said, E. W. (1998), 'Interview: Edward Said, in Conversation with Neeladri Bhattacharya, Suvir Kaul and A. Loomba, New Delhi', *Interventions: International Journal of Postcolonial Studies* 1 (1): 81–96.

Said, E. W. (2003), *Reflections on Exile and Other Essays*. Cambridge, MA: Harvard University Press.

Said, E. W. (2004), *Humanism and Democratic Criticism*. New York: Columbia University Press.

Sassen, S. (2012), *Cities in a World Economy*. Los Angeles: Sage Publications.

Sassen, S. (2014), *Expulsions – Brutality and Complexity in the Global Economy*. Cambridge, MA: Harvard University Press.

Schreibman, S., R. Siemens and J. Unsworth (2004), *A Companion to Digital Humanities*. Oxford: Blackwell.

Shiva, V. (1993), *The Monocultures of the Mind: Perspectives in Biodiversity*. London: Zed Books.

Shiva, V. (1997), *Biopiracy. The Plunder of Nature and Knowledge*. Boston: South End Press.

Singer, P. (1975), *Animal Liberation: A New Ethics for Our Treatment of Animals*. New York: Random House.

Sloterdijk, P. (2009), *Rules for the Human Zoo*: A Response to the 'Letter on Humanism'. *Environment and Planning D: Society and Space*, 27: 12–28.

Small, H. (2013), *The Value of the Humanities*. Oxford: Oxford University Press.

Smelik, A. and N. Lykke (eds) (2008), *Bits of Life. Feminism at the Intersection of Media, Bioscience and Technology*. Seattle: University of Washington Press.

Snow, C. P. (1959), *The Two Cultures*. Cambridge: Cambridge University Press.

Spivak, G. C. (1988), 'Can the Subaltern Speak?'. In Cary Nelson and Lawrence Grossberg (eds), *Marxism and the Interpretation of Culture*. Chicago: University of Illinois Press.

Spivak, G. C. (1999), *A Critique of Postcolonial Reason. Toward a History of the Vanishing Present*. Cambridge, MA: Harvard University Press.

Stengers, I. (1997), *Power and Invention. Situating Science*. Minneapolis: University of Minnesota Press.

Stoler, A. L. (1995), *Race and the Education of Desire: Foucault's* History of Sexuality *and the Colonial Order of Things*. Durham, NC and London: Duke University Press.

Toscano, A. (2005), *Axiomatic. The Deleuze Dictionary* (ed. Adrian Parr), 17–8. Edinburgh: Edinburgh University Press.

Viswanathan, G. (ed.) (2001), *Power, Politics and Culture. Interviews with Edward Said*. London and New York: Bloomsbury.

Vattimo, G. and P. A. Rovatti (eds) (2012), *Weak Thought*. Albany: State University of New York Press.

Waal, F. de (1996), *Good Natured*. Cambridge, MA: Harvard University Press.

Waal, F. de (2009), *The Age of Empathy*. New York: Three Rivers Press.

Warner, M. (2014), 'Why I Quit', *London Review of Books* 36 (17): 42–3.

Warner, M. (2015), 'Learning My Lesson', *London Review of Books*, 37 (6): 8–14.

Williams, J. (2014), *How To Be an Intellectual. Essays on Criticism, Culture & the University*. New York: Fordham University Press.

Wolfe, C. (ed.) (2003), *Zoontologies. The Question of the Animal*. Minneapolis: University of Minnesota Press.

Wolfe, C. (2010), *What is Posthumanism?* Minneapolis: University of Minnesota Press.

Young, R. (1990), *White Mythologies. Writing History and the West*. London and New York: Routledge.

Young, R. (1995), *Colonial Desire: Hybridity in Theory, Culture, and Race*. London and New York: Routledge.

Žižek, S. (2004), *Organs without Bodies*. New York: Routledge.

CHAPTER TWO

A Borderless World?

Gayatri Chakravorty Spivak

Introduction: On social justice

Radical teachers and thinkers must keep thinking and teaching a borderless world. Remembering Edward Said, and facing the wall separating the West Bank, it is on this theme that I will write. Border-thought calls for judgement and discrimination. Borders must be both removed and respected.

I will open with a general word on gender, the tacit globalizer before we could think a globe: in the simplest possible sense, the female body is seen as permeable. It is seen as permeable in perhaps the most basic gesture of violence. To respect the border of the seemingly permeable female body, which seems to be in the benign service of humanity itself for the continuation of the human race, to understand that one must attend to this border, respect it – we must nuance borderlessness, remember that citizenship is predicated on legitimate birth, breaking the border of the female body. The bordered female body opens the possibility of society.

In terms of respect for the bordered body, the short-term work is law, and its implementing. The long-term work is the work of a borderlessness that attends to borders. To be borderless is also a pleasure for the female and the male – to be borderless, to be permeable, can be a pleasure. So it is attending to borders rather than simply respecting them that is our first, gendered, lesson. This is a question of children's pedagogy, as will be suggested below. Even violence can be connected to desire. Here, at the border of gendering, we enter the space of the incalculable. With respect to the fraught cartography of the contemporary world, this surfaces as rape, displacement, asylum.

If, then, we situate border-thought into the broadest perspective, the gender-thought that is the condition and effect of all social formations, we begin to see that borders are amphibolic. In a symmetrical world, 'bordered' and 'borderless' would be substitutable. But all situations are marked by the asymmetry of interest and power. And to make individually altered word usage effective requires an impossible epistemological revolution, presupposing a 'borderless' world – a performative contradiction; and it would deny the world's wealth of languages, which would say 'borders', 'frontiers', 'borderless' in ways that we cannot know.

A world where 'bordered' and 'borderless' would be substitutable is a socially just world. We are commemorating not only the tenth anniversary of Edward Said's untimely death, but also the 300th anniversary of the Treaty of Utrecht. Daniel Barenboim was expected at the conference where this anthology took shape, so I began with some words of his. Given his resolute work against unjust borders by bringing together young Palestinian and Israeli musicians under the auspices of the West-Eastern Divan, I have preserved that opening.

I saw online that Daniel Barenboim had said 'the Divan ... [is] not going to bring peace, whether you play well or not so well. The Divan was conceived as a project against ignorance'. I want to quote myself here to show how much I agree with Mr Barenboim's words. Last November, I said this in front of rather a large crowd: 'I [also] do not believe there is a direct line from art and philosophy to social justice.' Barenboim's words – 'it is absolutely essential for people to get to know the other, to understand what the other thinks and feels ... [so that] the two sides can disagree and not resort to knives' – describe the most practical form of social justice – echoing Dr King's statement in 'Beyond Vietnam' in 1967: 'it helps us to see the enemy's point of view, to hear his questions, to know his assessment of ourselves. For from his view we may indeed see the basic weaknesses of our own condition, and if we are mature, we may learn and grow and profit from the wisdom of the brothers who are called the opposition' (King 1987: 139).

Here is my self-quotation:

> When artists and philosophers, then, call for social justice, they are acting as responsible citizens of the world, themselves perhaps changed by practicing art and philosophy, sometimes using the weight of their prestige as celebrated artists and philosophers in order to make an appeal. The real contribution of artists and philosophers is that they change minds. Art and philosophy, detached from their producers, become instruments for viewer, listener, player, teacher, to be changed from mere self-interest. You notice that word 'teacher', last on the list. I am neither artist nor philosopher, but I am indeed a teacher of the humanities. It is our task always to work for the future of humankind. The stream of art – within which is included literature and music, today the filmic and the hypertextual – must flow forever; the practice of philosophizing must be passed on from generation to generation, so that the human mind is prepared to use the technological setting-to-work of science for the betterment of the world.[1]

'Human' here marks the forever deferred promise of a posthumanism to come, a striving too easily claimed for the here and now.[2]

Palestine and Israel

One theme that I want to discuss here is 'Beyond Postcolonialism'. I remember two things when asked to think 'beyond'. One, that all attempts beyond also fall short of; even in 'Beyond Vietnam'. Necessarily within that frame, I take the beyond gesture to mean that, rather than take each case as an example of itself, a group of artists, intellectuals, and activists might try to think by listening to each other, how the specific example can enter a broader general sense for the philosophers of the future. I admire such efforts, but, like Barenboim in his own context, I do not have real-world confidence in the attendant claims. We must declare the claims in the mode of 'to come', as Phil Ochs, the Texas boy who killed himself, using the phrase 'futuristic' in the place of the more sexy 'to come', declared, also in 1967: 'I declare the war is over'. So Edward Said remarked, in 1978, when accused of partiality towards Palestinians by Donald Davie, 'I will be the first critic of the state of Palestine once it is established.' Death has obliged us to place that declaration in the future anterior. Edward W. Said *will have been* the first critic of the state of Palestine. The time is not there yet, when people will be able to disagree democratically. Israel is described times without number as 'the only democracy in the Middle East', although it plays the retaliation game energetically, basing it on a 'faith-based' – the word fills me with horror – narrative, quite opposed to the promise of democracy. Democracy is now equated with an operating civil structure, the functioning of a hierarchized bureaucracy, and 'clean' elections. We have plenty of examples around the world, that unrelenting state violence on the model of revenge and retaliation can coexist with so-called democracy. Revenge is indeed a kind of wild justice that proves that no retribution is just to the outlines of the tribute. It has nothing, however, to do with a vision of social justice, which builds itself on its own indefinite continuation. It nests in all children's, and therefore all people's, capacity to *use* the right to intellectual and imaginative labour, not just in ease and speed of learning. All accountable efforts at social justice are no more (and no less) than the way in which we can access justice as such, if there is such a thing.

I mention Edward Said here again because I want to touch on two topics that tied me to him and still consume my life. Since it was a memorial occasion for him, I thought it would be appropriate to do so. Paul de Man introduced me to Edward Said in 1974. Over the years, I developed two kinds of public connection with Edward Said: 1) as a political ally to raise public awareness; and 2) as a teacher, sharing students. I was not his student, and not significantly his junior. He had started teaching in 1963, I in 1965. My relationship with him was somewhat divided on the grounds of the status of humanism. He always listened carefully when I interrogated his position and I speak in that spirit today. There was no guarantee that I could convince him but I always tried as hard as I could. These are the two topics that tied me to him and to which the rest of this paper will attend: 1) public awareness, with reference to post-colonialism; and, 2) teachers and students, with reference to treaties. I will make a somewhat unrelated concluding gesture.

Public awareness and post-colonialism

The brutalities of settler colonialism are writ large in Israel's policy towards Palestine. As such, it is out of joint with the post-colonial, which began in the middle of the last century. Indeed, it may be said that the global part of the Second World War, which started a move towards the end of territorial colonialism; in its European formation began a project of settler coloni-alism in the name of Israel. The parallel with the project, shared by many, including Abraham Lincoln, of deporting all the emancipated blacks to an African location after the US Civil War, is unmistakable.

The depredations of colonialism are shamelessly public. We are grateful to risk-taking investigative journalism for activating this already existing public aspect, less public under contemporary legal structures. It is also true that some effect on policy can be expected if the obvious and typical cruelties of colonial modernity are made clear. The sustained experience of what is called post-colonialism, however, teaches us to ask: who creates public awareness, why, for what public? In the case of Said and those who worked with him, there was no doubt that it was a Palestinian in exile who raised his strong voice on many registers to affect policy on the highest level. Like Socrates, he was a gadfly. We will not consider him typical. We will frame his intervention in its own context and move on to generalizations.

I have for long held that, apart from gendering, the most international post-colonial movement was twentieth-century Pan-Africanism. Aamir Mufti's contribution in this volume enriches our understanding of this. Asked to speak on post-colonialism in France, I wrote an essay on Patrice Lumumba (2014). In its course, I was obliged to distinguish clearly between vestiges of Pan-African post-colonial impulses, among peoples given no chance to practise freedom then and now, and French and Belgian post-colonialisms. The case of Palestine is not analogous. The suppression of the practice of freedom for Palestine is of a more recent date. And the distinction between international and located intervention is perhaps less clear. In addition, the kind of sustained violence that we associate with earlier phases of settler colonialism is rampant in the area today. Asked to go beyond the post-colonial, it is such distinctions that we must foster if we want to locate and consider the subject of social justice rather than insurgency alone.

For, if the declaration of the achieved state is in the future anterior, the post-colonial is either not yet or no longer. This works in two ways: one because the task of developing democratic intuitions in the electorate – systemic institution of the breaking of internal class apartheid to facilitate the securing of the right to learn to *use* the intellect and the imagination for labour specific to it for every child as an implied part of a public rather than a developing private subject – is an indefinitely temporized task learning from necessary and engaged failure, the very name of a just history – the post-colonial not yet. We must remember that this is not just an idealistic philanthropic task; it involves the abstract structures of democracy at the cusp of the public and the private.

And secondly, the no longer post-colonial relates to the fact that that entire political epistemology is tied to the simple past, colonialism as a preterite: it happened. We are here for you were there. This, again, is not 'just philosophical'. Is anything? The post-colonial is predicated on polarizing the colonial and the national. It is interested in the reversal of this opposition, of this predication, which it calls liberation, not its displacement into a revolution. National liberation is not a revolution. My generation, as I have often repeated, spoke of 'post-colonial' ironically because the failure of decolonization seemed to start the morning after. In spite of Edward Said's confidence, 'the history of liberation movements in the twentieth century' does not 'eloquently attest' that 'indeed, the subaltern *can* speak', except in the merely military sense of the subaltern as 'junior officer', nationalist leaders under colonial control, not in the Gramscian sense of those without access to (even a colonial) state, whose history cannot be written (Said 1994: 335). The leaders are usually members, as Lenin correctly opined, of the 'progressive bourgeoisie'.

The *post*-colonial participation of subaltern insurgency in the new nation is almost unheard of. For this we can turn to the South African experience, for today Palestine is under the kind of sustained siege that is more comparable to South Africa under apartheid. None the less, it has to be said that, if we move into globality from failure of decolonization through neo-colonialism, the real problem in Palestine, if we can look forward to that day, will be no practice in the management of capital, combined with the usual lack of experience in the practice of freedom. Who can think of that now? Yet that is part of the definitive timing of the post-colonial – not yet, no longer. And, further, to turn that into the question of social justice, not reliance upon the international civil society's goodwill but sustain the right to intellectual and imaginative labour, connect it to the correct disposition of capital and then delicately open the question of gender that remains today confined to inadequate opportunities for feminist work at the universities – seems just as impossible. If efforts at public awareness are directed towards unaware outsiders, the work for building a will to social justice even in the mindset of the greatest diversity requires focused epistemological mingling with the subaltern and the subalternized. Although theoretically there is nothing to stop the two efforts from coexisting, in fact it is hardly ever the case. It goes without saying that we are not talking about fact-finding trips, but sustained efforts to access the epistemological apparatus of the subaltern victims of violence.

Case by case, nothing is 'just' beyond post-colonial. The relationship between a just fit and justice will take us too far or perhaps not far enough. Let us say that Palestine, caught in the general (im)possibility – there is no contrastive possible possible here – of the *post*-colonial as a just and practical position, just practical, is also prevented to act out the performative contradictions of post-colonialism. It is that limited but crucial impossibility in the narrow sense, that collective preventive detention, that the forever postponed preparation for democracy – every child's right to intellectual labour – works to quell. To 'perform' together works to help, in its place. Raising public awareness, the easiest form of academic activism, travels in a circle, unless the impossibility of post-colonialism is picked up appropriately. Otherwise, we are neither literate enough nor transnational enough to understand that the Indian Chamber of Commerce's unpublicized complaint that the government's brilliantly successful project to provide every citizen with the right at least to manual, if not intellectual/imaginative labour for at least one hundred days in the year is depriving them of skilled labour connects conjuncturally to the London *Times* passage, apparently quoting a florist, representing 'the man on the street' that '[t]here are fears of the consequences of ending Chavez's social spending. "If Capriles end [sic] these programmes, there'll be civil strife", said Dayan Briceno, a florist' (2013). Lack of skilled labour, threat of civil war. Ways of keeping at bay a socialism understood materially as access to manual labour for the worker and/or state-supported welfare. How, beyond the post-colonial, will Palestine fare with this? Only the preparation for the use of the right to intellectual labour for all makes it slip across other borders in globality. Otherwise, we are left with the failures of mere nationalism, class greed subalternizing the poor so the liberated nation can claim development.

On pedagogy and treaties

I turn now to the second stream: teachers and students, with reference to treaties. Part of my point has already been made in my discussion of public awareness. Treaties are made between heads of state. The peace they announce can only be sustained if their inhabitants are trained in the practice of peace, whose instrument is training in the right to use intellectual labour. I repeat what I quoted at the outset:

> The real contribution of artists and philosophers is that they change minds. Art and philosophy, detached from their producers, become instruments for viewer, listener, player, teacher, to be changed from mere self-interest. You notice that word 'teacher', last on the list. I am neither

artist nor philosopher, but I am indeed a teacher of the humanities. It is our task always to work for the future of humankind. The stream of art – within which is included literature and music, today the filmic and the hypertextual – must flow forever; the practice of philosophizing must be passed on from generation to generation, so that the human mind is prepared to use the technological setting-to-work of science for the betterment of the world. Today, this is particularly urgent because the digital has all the power and beauty of the wild horse. Without adroit handling, it can be destructive.

My personal memory is that Edward Said's first personal realization of the distance between the contributions of the intellectual and the making of treaties came with the Treaty of Oslo (1993). In conversation, his irritation was that Arafat had agreed to give Palestine away to be run by committees appointed by Israel, in the interest of a travesty of the Kantian project of peace through commerce. A joint Israeli–Palestinian liaison committee, a Continuing Committee that would decide by agreement on the modalities of admission of persons displaced from the West Bank and Gaza Strip in 1967, an arbitration committee, a joint Palestinian–Israeli Co-ordination and Co-operation Committee for mutual security purposes, an Israeli–Palestinian continuing committee for economic co-operation, and so on.

Yet Said's spirit was continuous with the Treaty of Utrecht, or at least its ideals: peace, security, human rights, multilateralism.[3] I, on the other hand, am with the Voltaire who placed his *Candide* in Westphalia, to mark the distance between treaties and reality – the depradations of rape located in a place hallowed by a treaty that many think was the beginning of modernity – the very modernity that secured our humanism as a weapon against colonialism. We remember that the wise words in that work were spoken by an old woman (a Baubo figure) with only one haunch remaining as part of a punishment. 'The Old Woman says: "A hundred times I have wanted to kill myself, but I was still in love with life"' (Voltaire 1990: 30–1). This is a mature optimism. This is not the Panglossian, clearly irrational formula repeated over and over again. She says, 'Yes, I should end this life, it's so horrible. *No*, I love to be alive.' To live in this absurdity, to adopt the philosophy of the double bind, is a much more robust philosophy than what is being criticized in Pangloss, and I think we should notice that it's in the mouth of this decrepit Old Woman. Speaking with the voice of the improbable old woman then, I say, consider the Treaties of Maastricht 1843, 1992: from unjust partition to failed model of union, of a group of debtor states and creditor states, an expression now widely used, without irony, by everyone, including ministers of European states. Consider the double bind inherent in treaties because they are devised by the vanguard. They cannot operate successfully without their indefinite supplementation by teaching, the teaching of the imaginative activism practised by the humanities as such, upon the polity as such, persistently, generation by generation, to train the future citizen into the double bind. Some here will know my formula: an uncoercive rearrangement of desire. Both Judith Butler and Akeel Bilgrami, in this volume, write of double binds; in binationalism, for Butler; and between liberty and equality, for Bilgrami. I add to them the one between treaties – the implacability of statecraft – and the historical contribution of a teaching that must unravel them in the interest of change when necessary. Butler's discussion of the amphibolic 'two-state solution' in the case of Israel and Palestine shows the virtues of double bind politics. Bilgrami shares my concern for the aporia between liberty and equality that constitutes democracy. But he offers a solution that takes us (academically trained intellectuals) outside of the democratic system into a sort of social behaviour that will not sit well with preserving democracy. He proposes that we usher the Enlightenment away from centre stage and think unalienated life rather than learn to live the double bind of liberty and equality. I invite him to think this as the limits of mere humanism, on the model of Kant's censored work on mere reason. The double bind of liberty and equality is where we work at the persistent movement of the subaltern into hegemony. We should be deeply sympathetic with Bilgrami's attempt to think something new beyond a vexing problem: that liberty and equality will never play together and are dependent upon tremendous efforts at subaltern education that do not seem to be in the world's future. However, his proposed solution may also not be a solution at all. Inevitably, his examples of dissent are all from Britain or northwestern Europe, whereas the assumptions of unalienated life depend upon broad generalizations about non-European civilizations that ignore their historical developments and social stratification patterns; not to mention varieties of rational critique present in such areas. Bilgrami has strong company. Lévi-Strauss after *A World on the Wane* and *A Savage Mind* made such assumptions popular, and objections similar to mine have been made to his point of view as well (the most famous being Derrida 1976: 101–40). If I may place a short self-citation here, indeed from an essay from a volume that Bilgrami is co-editing, I would basically comment on non-European social formations in the following way, even as I sympathize deeply with Bilgrami's sense of the problem:

> Benevolent or malevolent or in-between or indeed not-bothered-to-be-volent-pre-colonial power groups unevenly enriched themselves at the expense of the postcolonial groups inheriting older hierarchies. This gives us a pre-modern clue to the word 'underdevelopment' as it spread to varieties of class-apartheid present in all polities, cutting across gender-apartheid and group-apartheid, where the usual overflowing of something like 'class' in the everyday must be allowed to contaminate the disinfected house of scientific socialism. … Interested underdevelopment rather than development has forever made the world turn, it inhabits the persistent structures of contemporary globality, and rogue

capitalization, as it is now indicated by more and more people at the center, could inhabit those structures not only as rupture but repetition. … If we allow the concept of development to overflow the interplay of capital and colony, we make room for an acknowledgement of complicity – folded-togetherness. … Development as sustainable under-development has a longer history and perhaps this history is beginning to make itself visible as the pattern of globalization explodes economic growth into developing inequality.[4]

The undoing of the colonial narrative from the secret writing of the 'Middle East' with the Sykes–Picot agreement of 1917 has resulted in a messy worldwide situation that seems a blind alley, no alternative to the peculiar constitution of the *via fracta* of social justice. Today we must thicken this with considerations of the new Khilafat movement in Syria.

We must remember that the Sykes–Picot agreement was European. And, whatever the virtue or the virtues of the Treaty of Utrecht in the European context, its contemporary inheritors do not offer a significant exception. This is not my specific field of research. I offer a few random examples to mark the contemporary moment. If this seems irrelevant to the 'European' reader, s/he may be part of the problem. The Netherlands, then, do not seem a significant exception. Just a random passage from a February 2008 report, published by the European Commission against Racism and Intolerance, notes the negative shift in public discourse on immigrants and Islam in the Netherlands, causing a 'worrying' societal polarization and a 'substantial' increase of Islamophobia. The Dutch response to the immigration problem has created new barriers to immigration. A rule was recently enacted that requires future residents (as opposed to citizens) to pass a Dutch language and culture – do you speak English? I myself was asked at the border as I came in – test before arriving in Holland, making it the first country in the world to demand that permanent residents complete a pre-arrival integration course. A local council oversees and tracks the individual. We all know about stop-and-search. Immigrants such as Muslims, Turks and Moroccans are expected to become majorities in a decade in Amsterdam and Rotterdam. These major cities have had huge problems with crime. Much of the crime is blamed on the immigrants in the city. Since 11 September 2001, there has been increased attention and hostility when those perceived as immigrants commit crimes. The welfare system, which is considered generous, is currently undergoing problems because of declining native birth rates (necessary to support the pensions) and increasing need for welfare support by immigrants. Immigrants, especially from Turkey and Morocco, make up a disproportionate amount of the population imprisoned, unemployed or on disability benefit. Once immigrants become residents (not necessarily citizens), they can apply for social welfare benefits (2008: 19). As Julie Roberts reports in her 'Letter from Brussels' in a recent issue of *Frontier*, the situation in neighbouring Belgium has been exacerbated tremendously. In this crumbling of Europe's self-representation as the custodian of peace, security, human rights and multilateralism, we must train our own imagination and the imagination of our colleagues and students and global compatriots, small group by small group, for this faculty of the mind to be able to undertake the counter-intuitive epistemological performance of a complicity that seems unequal or incoherent to a history understood as a linear narrative – political or religious. 'Culture' is a buzzword. Knowing the discontinuous other is easier said than done. How about the non-Abrahamic? How about non-harmonic musical traditions? The questions crowd the landscape.

I go back to Barenboim's words: 'that we can exist together'. What is implicit here is a much broader, indeed global, model of simultaneity: we do exist together; how? Of course, the situation in Palestine is explained in terms that are obviously true to the case. But if I can analogize from W. E. B. Du Bois's analysis of the failure of Black Reconstruction after the US Civil War (1998: 210), I would say that the way to understand what is happening is in terms of the global simultaneity, the simultaneity of global capital, that manages the world. The failed model of the European Union makes visible the successful model of uneven and violent global simultaneity: a dystopian existing together. How does the teacher respond to this?

On simultaneity

History understood as the linear narrative of race has sometimes diagnosed the Du Bois of *Black Reconstruction* as a race traitor. Du Bois wrote to train the imagination to be able to undertake an ungraspable epistemological performance. Describing the question of giving voting rights to the emancipated Negro in the middle of the nineteenth century, he shows how abolition-democracy allied itself with the self-determination of capital. I quote one of many passages:

> In all this reported opposition to Negro suffrage, the grounds given were racial and social animosity, and never the determination of land and capital to restrict the political power of labor. Yet this last reason was the fundamental one. While the South was in suspense, and the abolition-democracy was slowly debating and crystallizing opinion, industry in the North was forging forward with furious intensity: and this movement was foreshadowed and predominant in the mind and vision of living persons in that day. (Du Bois 1998: 186)

The capital-complicity of the global is a lesson in simultaneity. What institutions of tertiary education in varieties of the metropole now have to think about is that globalization has introduced a kind of accessible contemporaneity to us, and placed us within it, which has not taken away, but rendered obsolete, the established ways of knowing the historical. Modernity/tradition methodologies, colonial/post-colonial methodologies remain appropriate in their own place, but are no longer useful to understand this new situation, which seems to lend itself more easily to a quantified, statisticalized, and, in a less rigorous way, simply arithmeticalized approach, democracy computed as supervised safe elections, epistemic claims without reality checks, going hand in hand with a collection of 'global' curiosities as evidence.

Let us rather ask ourselves how *we* must change in response to this challenge to knowing, not how we can add more information and money to the spectacular alternative streams at the edges of disciplines. How can the mainstream of disciplines be rearranged so that we and our students learn to think differently, rather than separate rigorous history and method from the glamour of easy globality. Such challenges have come in history from time to time and intellectual historians as well as students of the history of consciousness have told us after the fact how these changes happened. To that extent, we too must give ourselves over to what we call the future anterior, what will have happened in spite of our best efforts. But at the university, we must also make these efforts – once again, to change ourselves, rather than simply to acquire more substantive knowledge. These general words on teaching can only be fleshed out in diversified classrooms across the world, not just elite universities in the North and South.

Somewhat unrelated concluding gesture

Example one: In March 2013, as a group of academics were going to the campus of Point Loma Nazarene University, one of our hosts mentioned the arrival of the Spanish in the sixteenth century. Another one of us remarked, 'can you imagine anything happening here before the sixteenth century?'

It was an innocent remark. But my imagination, trained to read since 1957, kicked in ... and I began to think, not just of the Maya, the Inca, the Nahuatl in a general way, but also of the Diegueños. I thought of the Kumeyaay nations, the Tipai-Ipai, the Paipai and Kiliwa. Of the Kumeyaays, I learned of the many bands, many with Spanish names, holding an alien history inaugurated 500 years ago: the Barona, the Campo, the Capitan Grande, the Cuyapaipe, the Inaja-Cosmit, the Jamul, the la Jolla, the La Posta, the Coyotes, the Manzanita, the Mesa Grande, the Pala, the Pauma/Yuima, the Rincon, the San Pasqual, the Santa Ysabel, the Sycuan, and the Viejas. I thought that the point is not to say ah but they too were violent, or oh, but they did not develop the land. The point is to remember that they held the land in common, that they loved the land and largely left it alone, did not move recklessly towards the anthropocene. A limit to mere humanism, but not an unalienated choice to avoid the double bind of liberty and equality. I was addressing these words to high school students. I knew that many of them worked already in environmental studies, so they knew the word 'anthropocene'. But to those who had not come across it yet, I said: Google it. I said 'Google it' simply to make it clear that I of course applaud digital resources, if only for the mind trained to 'follow' actively, not simply to listen to advice, real or virtual. Unmediated cyber literacy can produce a simulacrum of the unalienated, forget that the unconditionality of equality is conditioned by many 'liberties'. On Wikipedia one could find:

> The Anthropocene is an informal geologic <u>chronological</u> term that serves to mark the evidence and extent of human activities that have had a significant global impact on the <u>Earth</u>'s <u>ecosystems</u> ... Many scientists are now using the term and the Geological Society of America entitled its 2011 annual meeting: Archean to Anthropocene: The past is the key to the future.

I got the info about the Diegueño Native Americans off the webpage of the University of San Diego, again a digital resource. I found the name of Professor Nancy Carter of the School of Law, who may be a future ally. But in the trace of that history, forgotten by my colleague, there is no access to unalienated life.

Example two: I have been training teachers through teaching elementary schoolchildren among the landless illiterate in a corner of India for the last thirty years. Since I will not last very much longer, I am trying to choose workers who can do the training work in that actively following way that literary reading has taught me. Our goal is not top-down philanthropy for income production – which is undoubtedly a good thing – but to produce the intuitions of democracy in a tiny section of the largest sector of the electorate in India, the world's largest democracy. I quote something I wrote to one of the candidates seeking to join my efforts:

> To make it convenient for you immediately to be able to access the schools is not what we are about. I have been making many mistakes and trying to learn with what instruments those who cannot immediately access a car for convenience learn – believe me, there is a difference – although I cannot write you an ethnographic account right this minute. What I am trying desperately to learn is how to access such instruments with no access to means of convenience to which we have immediate and unthinking access, and I don't know yet. At first, I too used to hire cars, and my associates, including the women (illiterate, therefore not involved in the education) were quite delighted to ride in these wretched cars. But slowly, they began to realize that I was practical *in their own terms*. How I managed to achieve this, I have no idea – but I consider this as one of my major achievements in the field. And then they began to save me

money. This is a complete epistemological turnaround. The first intimations of equality (though not sameness). First they directed me to ride rural buses, sometimes walk – independently of the school walks that I arranged for myself as exercise. Then when I had my shoulder operations and got my spinal disease, only motorbikes. It would be more convenient for me to ride a car. But the work that I am embarked on is not about my convenience, or ours, I repeat. This does not mean an uncritical 'going native.' This is indeed a double bind. There are certain things without which I cannot operate: toilets, clean water, mosquito nets. I offered no explanation but required these without trying to convert. Clean water, of course, is abundantly available through tubewells, so everyone habitually uses clean water. Slowly, on their own, they are beginning to move toward toilets, and therefore over the last two years, I have said that so-called 'my toilets' are in fact everyone's if they are kept as clean as I keep them. So, given that you immediately came up with this convenience of a car, and defended it as only an expression of your admiration for me (which doesn't really make sense), my feeling is, that you will go toward these kinds of solutions on your own when I'm gone. I'm not interested in transforming this undertaking into an NGO-style enterprise. The first thing to learn is how really to teach effectively in this environment, not how to access the schools conveniently. Maybe we can ourselves learn how not to want to put quite so many motor-cars on the road, fight the anthropocene. Given that your control of Bengali is also less good than I had thought, I have decided to let you out of this obligation and, as I mentioned, I will look forward to a long association involving your own research work.

In our everyday, we condition the unalienated, by taking ourselves as representative! Just thinking otherwise will not solve this.

I summarize again: look below, not just away. Supplement vanguardism, rather than taking yourself as an example of the human. Earn the right to join the *local* movements against the unrepresentative gender crimes, and to feel if justified lament over loss of property is necessarily 'ecological'. I end in the name of my friends, Afiya Zia and Rana Husseini, active against faith-based gender oppression in their place (Zia 1994, 2008; Husseini 2009). This is rearguard action, in memory of Edward Said's unforgettable heroism.

Notes

1   Modified acknowledgment speech for Kyoto Prize in Art and Philosophy (2012) (2012 Kyoto Prize Presentation Ceremony is available on YouTube).

2   I have gotten further along in this line in 'Crimes of Identity' (2015).

3   The Wikipedia entry, representing the popular view, emphasizes the end
    of war and balance of power: good things. 'The Treaty of Utrecht, which
    established the Peace of Utrecht, is a series of individual peace treaties, rather
    than a single document, signed by the belligerents in the War of the Spanish
    Succession, in the Dutch city of Utrecht in March and April 1713. They
    marked the end of French ambitions of hegemony in Europe expressed in the
    wars of Louis XIV and preserved the European system based on the balance
    of power.'

4   Spivak, 'Development: A Political Concept', forthcoming in volume edited by
    Ann Stoler and Akeel Bilgrami.

References

Derrida, J. (1976), 'The Violence of the Letter: From Lévi-Strauss to Rousseau'. In
    Of Grammatology, trans. G. C. Spivak. Baltimore: Johns Hopkins University
    Press.
Du Bois, W. E. B. (1998), *Black Reconstruction*. New York: The Free Press.
European Commission against Racism and Intolerance (2007), *Third Report on
    the Netherlands*, http://www.refworld.org/pdfid/47b19c582.pdf (accessed 13
    November 2015).
Hider, J. (2013), 'Insults and Budgies Fly in Fight Over the Soul of Venezuela',
    The Times, 13 April, p. 30.
Husseini, R. (2009), *Murder in the Name of Honor: The True Story of One
    Woman's Heroic Fight against an Unbelievable Crime*. Oxford: Oneworld
    Publications.
King, M. L. (1987), 'Beyond Vietnam'. In Clayborne Carson (ed.) *A Call to
    Conscience: The Landmark Speeches of Dr. Martin Luther King*, Jr. New York:
    Warner.
Roberts, J. (2014), 'Letter From Brussels', *Frontier*, online article published on 15
    January: http://www.frontierweekly.com (accessed 13 November 2015).
Said, E. W. (1994) *Orientalism*. New York: Vintage.
Spivak, G. C. (2014), 'Postcolonialism in France'. *Romanic Review* 104 (3–4):
    223–42.
Spivak, G. C. (2015), 'Crimes of Identity'. In Robert Duschinsky (ed.), *Juliet
    Mitchell and the Lateral Axis: Twenty-First Century Psychoanalysis and
    Feminism*, London: Palgrave.
Voltaire (1990), *Candide and Other Stories*, trans. R. Pearson. New York: Oxford
    University Press.
Zia, A. S. (1994), *Sex Crime in the Islamic Context: Rape, Class and Gender in
    Pakistan*. Lahore: ASR.
Zia, A. S. (2008), *Challenges to Secular Feminism in Pakistan: A Critique of
    Islamic Feminism and Revivalism*. Cambridge: Centre of South Asian Studies.

CHAPTER THREE

Borderless Worlds?

Ankhi Mukherjee

1.

'I have noticed that "border-crossing" has become such an all-purpose, ubiquitous way of talking about translation that its purchase on the politics of actual borders – whether linguistic or territorial – has been attenuated', writes Emily Apter in *Against World Literature* (2013: 100). The catalogue of thematics in post-colonial literature and theory – hybridity, *métissage*, *creolité*, code-switching, Edward Said's 'contrapuntality', Homi Bhabha's advocacy of the in-between position of practice and negotiation, and Gayatri Spivak's delineations of the catachrestic action of seizing the apparatus of value-coding – all seem to uphold cultural border-crossings, cross-dressings and translations as crucial to the constitution of new subjectivities, new positions of identification and enunciation. Mobilizing intransigent and blockaded physical borders, the 'antiborder border', as Emily Apter terms it (2013: 100), I discuss three kinds of borderlessless in this essay, drawing broadly on some of the constitutive ideas and ideals of Gayatri Spivak's and Edward Said's work on the topic, and those informing the Treaty of Utrecht, whose 300th anniversary makes imperative reflections on borderlessness and also on the resistance to its triumphalism and implied transcendence.

The first kind of borderlessness I touch on is related to what Gayatri Spivak, in a talk at the University of Arizona, 'A Borderless World' (2012b), called the 'performative contradiction' of capital, and that refers to the globe as the totality produced by processes of globalization.

So capital is in fact borderless; that's the problem. On the other hand capital has to keep borders alive in order for this kind of cross-border trade to happen. So therefore the idea of borderlessness has a performative contradiction within it which has to be kept alive.

The spatial diffusion and extensiveness of global markets and media give rise to a sense of belonging to a borderless, shared world, when the reality is that such developments lead instead to greater polarization and division of nations and regions. The Pulitzer Prize-winning investigative journalist Katherine Boo's recently published *Behind the Beautiful Forevers* (2012), the latest in a series of narrative non-fiction books coming out of India, reminded me forcefully of Spivak's useful formulation. It is set in Annawadi, a slum located near Mumbai's international airport. Its central characters include Abdul Husain, a garbage sorter, members of his family, and neighbours. This book, which the Nobel-winning economist Amartya Sen's blurb describes as a 'beautiful account' of the 'lives of the precarious and powerless in urban India', sees in the destitute Abdul what Dipesh Chakrabarty calls 'the figure of difference', which fractures from within the very signs that seem to proclaim the emergence of abstract labour, and that governmentality has to 'subjugate and civilize' (2009: 94). Boo offers alternative accounts of 'life, death, and hope', to borrow from her subtitle, which challenge hegemonic understandings of modernity and modernization as linked to the global expansion of the capitalist mode of production: the aberrational form of fiction that is *Behind the Beautiful Forevers* urges a re-examination of the social purpose of the novel form, with its historical commitment to class mobility and social circulation, the redistribution of opportunity, wealth and justice, and its fidelity to equivocal forms of national belonging.

The phenomenological border in Boo's book is not between the slumdogs and the lucky one per cent in the 5-star hotels that loom over Annawadi, a squatter slum comprised mostly of migrants fleeing a crisis-ridden agricultural sector only to find themselves as the surplus of cheap labour in Mumbai. 'For every two people in Annawadi inching up, there was one in a catastrophic plunge' (2012: 24). The border then is between 'the more advantaged poor', the poor, and the 'poorest of the poor', the divisions listed by Mike Davis in his influential *Planet of the Slums* (2006: 43). Abdul gains his sense of upward mobility by contrasting his lot with that of his less fortunate neighbours, miserable souls 'who trapped rats and frogs and fried them for dinner', or 'ate the scrub grass at the sewage lake's edge' (2006: 6).

The poor, shockingly, are territorial, given to in-fighting, and want borders and stratification just like the rich in their unbreached gated communities. It is the construction of a solid wall between two hovels by Abdul's family that precipitates the calamity that destroys both families. One-legged Fatima, Abdul's belligerent neighbour, sets herself on fire – another instance of what Spivak, in 'Can the Subaltern Speak?' (2010), called the rewriting of the social text of sati-suicide in an interventionist way. The protest comes to nothing, and does not better the life of Fatima, as she had intended. A small crowd gathers but does nothing. 'The adults drifted back to their dinners, while a few boys waited to see if Fatima's face would come off' (2010: 98). Trying to take Fatima to the hospital, her husband finds himself rebuffed by auto rickshaw drivers, worried about the potential damage to seat covers. The poor, Boo writes, 'blame one another for the choices of governments and markets' (2012: 254). And the poor take down one another in internal class apartheid, or the intraclass apartheid of the classless, as the world's great unequal cities soldier on in relative peace.

The 'beautiful' of the book's title refers to a hoarding over a concrete wall that repetitively uses the words 'beautiful' and 'forever' to advertise Italianate tiles, and that serves to hide the sprawl of the shanty town from the international traffic down the airport road. The advertisement is a fitting facade of the ideology of third-world urbanization, the 'anthropocentric doctrine[s] of secular salvation' underlying theories of the cumulative growth of science and technology (Nandy 1983: x). Abdul's mother Zehrunisa 'wanted ceramic tiles like the ones advertised on the Beautiful Forever wall – tiles that could be scrubbed clean' (Boo 2012: 83). As usual, the slum poor are peripheral to the existence of the city, the surplus population utterly deprived of social goods or services despite providing the labour critical to the functioning of the service sector in advanced and growing economies. Boo constructs a third person fictional narrative and explains in an interview why she foregoes the first person perspective:

> As a reader, I sometimes find that the 'I' character becomes the character – that the writer can't resist trying to make the reader like him just a little better than anyone else in the book. And I think that impedes the reader's ability to connect with people who might be more interesting than the writer, and whose stories are less familiar.
>
> (behindthebeautifulforevers.com)

This technique can be seen in operation in Boo's portrayal of Abdul, who sells the trash of Mumbai's rich to recycling plants for profit. Despite the fact that it was 'a fine time to be a Mumbai garbage trader' (2012: 6), Abdul wants to escape an identity indistinguishable from the trash he sells – 'some called him garbage, and left him at that' (ibid.) – and dreams not only of survival but of land ownership and full civic participation. It is Boo's task to convey, through 'written notes, video recordings, audiotapes, and photographs', hundreds of interviews cross-checked with 'three thousand public records', this obscure life and its animating narratives (2012: 249–50). 'He wanted to be better than what he was made of. In Mumbai's dirty water, he wanted to be ice', she says of the aspiring Abdul (2012: 218). Unlike the dystopian vision of a work like Mike Davis's *Planet of Slums* (2006), which outlines the catastrophic effects of unlimited capitalism and neoliberalism, Boo neither fetishizes abjection nor engages in escapist fallacy or apocalyptic projections. She strains against metaphorical appropriation or the allegorizing impulse when it comes to representing the poor. As she says in an interview:

> I've been waiting years to run into a representative person. Sadly, all I ever meet are individuals ... [and] qualities that transcend specificities of geography, culture, religion, caste, or class. My hope, at the keyboard, is to portray these individuals in their complexity – allow them not to be Representative Poor Persons – so that readers might find some other point of emotional purchase, a connection more blooded than pity.
> (Q&A with Katherine Boo, behindthebeautifulforevers.com)

Behind the Beautiful Forevers is the culmination of the four years its author spent in Annawadi. Boo, whose revelatory 'Author's Note' comes at the very end of the novel, has said that she aspires to invisibility, as if to confer maximal representation to the visible but unseen lives of the Annawadi 'undercitizens', as she calls them. Her negative capability and cultivation of impersonality, and her careful self-situation and declaration of interest in the author's note reference the function of the analyst, reinventing it for a global capitalist system which, to quote Michael Rothenberg, 'generates dispersed and uneven experiences of trauma and wellbeing simultaneously'. With overworked people, especially boys like Abdul or Sunil, who spent the bulk of their days working silently with waste, 'language tended to be transactional'. 'I came to my understanding of their thoughts by pressing them in repeated (they would say endless) conversations ... often while they worked' (2012: 250). Besides transcribing interior monologues in her case studies, Boo chronicles symptoms of the insidious trauma suffered by the Annawadians. She records a brilliant 'Freud in the slums' scene where Manju, daughter of the slumlord Asha, and pipped to be the first female college graduate to emerge from the slum, copes with her life by 'by-hearting [learning by rote] her psychology notes', and practising the denial they taught her. 'Young men have mostly ambitious wishes. Young women have mostly erotic ones. The ordinary person feels ashamed of his fantasies and hides them' (2012: 179). Manju blocks out painful subjects like her corrupt, degenerate mother, and a failed love affair. Boo observes that 'Annawadians rearranged narratives for psychological solace: giving themselves, in retrospect, more control over an experience than they had had at the time' (2012: 252). They share with her stories of unrecorded tyranny because, she says, they recognize her moral concern for equality and justice in a fast-changing country. 'When I wasn't dredging up bad memories, they liked me fine.' Boo's 'compassionate imagination' – in which, according to Martha Nussbaum, lies the value of literature (Nussbaum 1997: 93) – manifests in her tireless and punctilious recording of the violations of human autonomy and dignity she sees. Kalu's murder, she records, is officially registered as an 'irrecoverable illness' (Boo 2012: 168). Beatings, outlawed in the human rights code, 'were practical', she notes, 'as they increased the price detainees would pay for their release' (2012: 107). And Fatima's death from an infection is quickly hushed up as 'the doctor adjusted the record in the name of hospital deniability' (2012: 114).

2.

In Jacques Derrida's last seminar, *La bête et le souverain*, translated by Geoffrey Bennington as *The Beast and The Sovereign*, Derrida reflects on the 'obscure and fascinating complicity' between beast, criminal and sovereign: 'a worrying mutual attraction, a worrying familiarity, an *unheimlich*, uncanny reciprocal haunting' (2009a: 17). If the beast and the sovereign are antipodal in that one is below the law and the other above it, they are also alike in this exteriority: the beast as king, the prince as wolf. This obscure complicity is relatable to the creaturely, which Eric Santner defines as 'life abandoned to the state of exception/emergency, that paradoxical domain in which law has been suspended in the name of preserving law' (2009: 22), or that which Georgio Agamben called 'the bare life' (1998). Can creaturely life or the bare life offer, to quote Santner again, 'a resource for new kinds of social links' (2009: 30)? The subaltern enjoins a special form of mediation, a physical proximity with the objects of enquiry through sustained and destabilizing encounters. In *Behind the Beautiful Forevers*, Fatima, the one-legged woman, with whom Boo starts her narrative, is 'grievously burned' (Boo 2012: iv). Fatima, the third-person voice states, 'had fair skin, usually an asset, but the runt leg had smacked down her bride price' (2012: xvi). Her Hindu parents, therefore, had taken the single offer of marriage they had received, securing her a groom who was 'poor, unattractive, hardworking, Muslim, old' (2012: xvi). Fatima's promiscuity is a revolt against the normate sexual politics of the slum that doubly marginalizes disabled bodies, rendering them invisible:

> Her abiding interest was in extramarital sex, though not for pocket change alone. That, her neighbours would have understood. But the One Leg also wanted to transcend the affliction by which others had named her. She wanted to be respected and reckoned attractive. Annawadians considered such desires inappropriate for a cripple. (2012: xvii)

'Animalization refers to that indistinct zone of the inhuman where life is rendered brute', observes Kalpana Seshadri (2012: 23). Boo describes what it might be like to be rendered non-sentient creatures, numerical entities that constitute a population, or are forcibly humanized as a spectacle. She also details the process of brutalizing living creatures by power's ability to manipulate the indeterminacy that threatens all identity. In *The Open*,

Georgio Agamben talks about the anthropological machine through which man registers his historicity.

> He can be open only to the degree that he transcends and transforms the anthropophorous animal which supports him, and only because, through the action of negation, he is capable of mastering and eventually destroying his animality. (Agamben 2004: 19)

Instead of the incessant procedure of self-separation, by which the subject humanizes himself or herself through the negation of his or her animality, I am arguing that we see in Katherine Boo's narrative a critique that is kinaesthetic as well as cognitive, embodied if also, ultimately, doomed to be at a critical remove. 'I see so much of myself in the people I write about, whether it's Fatima's fury at being defined by a physical difference or Asha's self-rationalizing or Abdul's fear of losing what he has', Boo writes on her website (behindthebeautifulforevers.com). 'It is easy, from a safe distance, to overlook the fact that in undercities governed by corruption ... it is blisteringly hard to be good' (Boo 2012: 254). For her there is no safe distance, she also seems to be saying.

Gayatri Spivak, writing on *Jane Eyre*, describes the scene where Jane first encounters the white Jamaican Creole Bertha Mason as a situation that deliberately makes indeterminate the difference between human and animal, the narrative register shifting emphasis from marriage and sexual reproduction to 'Europe and its not-yet-human Other' (Spivak 1985: 247). Nineteenth-century feminist individualism could indeed conceive of a greater project than access to the closed circle of the nuclear family, Spivak writes: 'This is the project of soul making' (1985: 248). Evoking the Kantian imperative, the universal moral law given by pure reason, which mandates that every rational creature is an end in himself, Spivak observes that here the native subject is the object of violation in the name of the categorical imperative, or the very scapegoat that will preserve the categorical imperative: '*make* the heathen into a human so that he can be treated as an end in himself' (1985: 248). *Jane Eyre* can thus be read as 'the orchestration and staging of the self-immolation of Bertha Mason as "good wife"' (1985: 248). Spivak's revisionist critique of imperialist axiomatics has been animated by what she calls in her essay 'the intention of saving the singular oppositional', such as the message intercepted in Bhubaneshwari Bhaduri's suicide (2005: 479). 'My modest reputation', Gayatri Spivak is known to say, 'rests on two items – the introduction to Derrida and the commentary on Bhubaneswari Bhaduri's suicide'. The first is Spivak's introduction to *Of Grammatology* and the second item refers to her epochal essay, 'Can the Subaltern Speak?', first published in 1985 in the journal *Wedge* and later reprinted in collections of essays. In it, she describes the circumstances surrounding the suicide of a young Bengali woman that indicates a failed attempt at self-representation. Because her

attempt at 'speaking' outside normal patriarchal channels was not understood or supported, Spivak concludes that the subaltern cannot speak. Her
extremely nuanced argument, admittedly confounded by her sometimes
opaque style, led some incautious readers to accuse her of phallocentric
complicity, of not recognizing or even not letting the subaltern speak.
Some critics, missing the point, buttressed their arguments with anecdotal
evidence of messages cried out by burning widows. Her point was not that
the subaltern does not cry out in various ways, but that if speaking is 'a
transaction between speaker and listener' (Spivak, Landry and MacLean
1996: 289), the subaltern does not achieve this dialogic level of utterance.

But who is the subaltern? Spivak borrows this concept from the
Marxist, Antonio Gramsci, who, in his *Prison Notebooks* (1971), written
during Mussolini's regime, uses the term to mean both subordinate and
non-hegemonic groups or classes. Gramsci refers in particular to disag-
gregated groups of peasants in Southern Italy, who had no cohesive social
consciousness or political programme, and were therefore vulnerable to
the ideas, culture and leadership of the state. Gramsci's account of the
subaltern has been further developed by a group of Indian historians called
the Subaltern Studies Collective. Extending the terms of Gramsci's original
definition, Ranajit Guha defines the subaltern as 'the general attribute of
subordination in South Asian society, whether this is expressed in terms
of class, caste, age, gender and office or in any other way' (Guha 1982:
vii). The historians of the Subaltern Studies Collective argue that India
achieved self-governance without a concomitant social revolution in the
class system and that the concept of the subaltern has tremendous relevance
in addressing the oppression of peasantry, the working classes and the
untouchables in post-independence Indian society. Spivak agrees with the
historical arguments of the Subaltern Studies Collective, but adds that
their classic Marxist approach to social and historical change effectively
privileges the male subaltern subject as the primary agent of change. She
also takes exception to the rigid Marxist categories of analysis deployed by
the collective, which valorize class politics at the expense of other forms of
liberation struggles relevant to Indian social history such as the women's
movement, the peasant struggles or the rights of indigenous minorities.
Spivak's hermeneutics of suspicion extends to methodology itself which, in
the case of the Subaltern Studies Collective, bestows a false coherence on
complex and disparate struggles of specific subaltern groups. The subaltern
studies historians, Spivak warns, are in danger of insidiously objectifying
the subaltern, of controlling 'through knowledge even as they restore
versions of causality and self-determination to him' (Spivak et al. 1996:
210). Spivak's own project as archivist of subaltern selves and texts, she
says, 'is the careful project of un-learning our privilege as our loss' (Spivak
1990: 9). The emancipatory project, Spivak says, foreshadowing the work
of humanitarian fictions such as Boo's, is more likely to succeed if one
thinks of other people as being different, perhaps absolutely different. Not

explaining, but bearing witness: 'Explaining, we exclude the possibility of the radically heterogeneous' (Spivak et al. 1996: 33).

It would be useful to revisit the complex argument of 'Can the Subaltern Speak?' where Spivak reads the radical claims of Michel Foucault and Gilles Deleuze to speak for the disenfranchised against the audacious claims of British colonialism to rescue native women from the practice of Hindu widow sacrifice in nineteenth-century India. Spivak claims that the liberal and left-wing Western intellectual can mistranslate and paradoxically silence the subaltern by claiming to represent and speak for their experience in the same way that the paternalist colonialist silenced the voice of the widow who 'chooses' to die on her husband's funeral pyre. Her critique of Deleuze and Foucault starts from her premise that the structures underpinning aesthetic representation also inform political representation. The difference between aesthetic and political structures of representation is that aesthetic representation tends to be self-reflexive and foregrounds its status as a re-presentation, whereas political representation denies its mediatory implication and poses as a presentation of the real instead. For Spivak, the problem with Foucault and Deleuze is the perennial problem of the mediating intellectual in global alliance politics, the 'first-world intellectual' posing as an 'absent nonrepresenter who lets the oppressed speak for themselves' (Spivak 2010: 263). Despite their rigorous analyses of how subjects are posited discursively through networks of power and knowledge, Spivak argues that, when it comes to discussing real, historical examples of social and political struggle, Foucault and Deleuze advocate a transparent model of representation in which 'oppressed subjects speak, act and know' their own conditions (2010: 247).

When this model of political representation – which is not categorically different from aesthetic representation – is mapped on to the 'Third World', the gap between the aesthetic and the political is even more objectionable. Spivak bristles at Anglo-American feminism's tendency to speak on behalf of 'Third World' women:

> On the other side of the international division of labour, the subject of exploitation cannot know and speak the text of female exploitation even if the absurdity of the nonrepresenting intellectual making space for her to speak is achieved. (Spivak 2010: 258)

It is the guise of nonrepresentation of the Western feminist that silences the voice of subaltern women. If the subaltern cannot speak, the solution does not lie in appointing an advocate to speak for her, affirmative action or special regulatory protection. 'Who the hell wants to protect subalternity? Only extremely reactionary, dubious anthropologistic museumizers. No activist wants to keep the subaltern in the space of difference ... You don't give the subaltern voice. You work for the bloody subaltern, you work against subalternity' (Spivak 1992: 46). Spivak has cited the work of the

Subaltern Studies group as an example of how this critical work can be practised, not to give the subaltern voice, but to clear the space to allow it to speak. 'Subaltern', Spivak insists, is not 'just a classy word for oppressed, for Other, for somebody who's not getting a piece of the pie' (1992: 45). She points out that in Gramsci's original covert usage (being obliged to encrypt his writing to get it past prison censors), it signified 'proletarian', whose voice could not be heard, being structurally written out of the capitalist bourgeois narrative. In post-colonial terms, everything that has limited or no access to cultural imperialism is subaltern: a space of difference. The cultural work of the literary critic is not to speak for a lost consciousness that cannot be recovered, but, as Robert Young says, to 'point to the place of woman's disappearance as an aporia, a blind-spot where understanding and knowledge are blocked' (Young 1990: 164).

Spivak elaborates on the idea of the subaltern through an analysis of the Hindu practice of *Sati* or widow self-immolation and a case study of Bhubaneswari Bhaduri. Drawing from Rig Veda and other Hindu scriptures, Spivak states that while scriptural doctrine mandated that suicide is reprehensible, room was made for certain forms of suicide which, as formulaic performance, lost the phenomenal identity of being suicide. The scriptures sanctioned the practice of widow sacrifice as an exceptional sacred practice, where the widow physically repeated her husband's death in a sacred place. The event of *Sati* was an exemplary moment of woman's free will and moral conduct within Hindu culture – not prescribed or enforced behaviour but an exceptional signifier of the woman's conduct as a good wife. For the British colonial administrators, however, the practice epitomized the abhorrent atavism of Hindu society and the woman's choice to die in *Sati* was expressly re-coded in colonial law as an abdication of her free will. *Sati*, read as a barbaric practice, which was outlawed by the colonial government in 1829, justified empire as a civilizing mission. Spivak's oft-repeated description of this stratagem is: 'White men are saving brown women from brown men' (Spivak et al. 1996: 50).

'Obviously I am not advocating the killing of widows,' Spivak writes in the revised edition of 'Can the Subaltern Speak?' (2010: 55). Spivak's argument is that the British colonial representation of *Sati* overlooks the voice and agency of Hindu women: what the British present as poor victimized women going to the slaughter is in fact an ideological battleground. Between the Hindu patriarchal codes of conduct and the British colonial representation of the *Sati*, between 'two contending versions of freedom' (2010: 55), the subaltern cannot speak. It is not that women cannot speak as such, or that no records of the subject-consciousness of women exist, but that she is assigned no position of enunciation. She isn't allowed to speak: everyone else speaks for her, so that she is rewritten continuously as the object of patriarchy or of imperialism. Spivak's discussion of *Sati* culminates in the case study of a young woman who hanged herself from her father's modest apartment in North Calcutta in 1926. Nearly a decade later it was discovered that she was a member of one of the many groups involved in the armed struggle for Indian independence. Bhubaneswari had attempted to cover up her involvement with the resistance movement through an elaborate suicide ritual that resembled the ancient practice of Hindu widow sacrifice. Bhubaneswari wasn't a widow; the suicide did not take place in the sacred site of a husband's funeral pyre. There is no incontrovertible proof of her actions. Nevertheless, Spivak reads Bhubaneswari Bhaduri's story and that singular inscribed body as an attempt to rewrite 'the social text of *sati*-suicide in an interventionist way' (282): she had no husband, dead or alive, and, in waiting for the onset of her menstruation, as she does, she was reversing the interdict against a menstruating widow's right to immolation. Bhubaneswari had been entrusted with a political assassination which she was unable to confront, and had committed suicide to avoid capture by the British colonial authorities. Bhubaneswari killed herself while menstruating so that she could disprove what she knew would be the conclusion drawn from her hanged body – illicit pregnancy. This model of interventionist practice, of course, is a tragic failure: the subaltern cannot be heard or read in the patriarchal terms of the national independence struggle. Bhubaneswari's act of women's resistance in extremis during the independence struggle in the 1920s, her remarkable, if immediately misunderstood, refusal of victimage, is disguised as an act of suicide, and later decoded as a case of illicit love, a source of shame for future generations of her family.

The relevance of the subaltern in the present discussion is in the context of the 'educative activism' (Spivak 2012a: 429) that the incorporation of this subject position into hegemonic logic enjoins. This is all the more urgent as subalternity does not permit, as Spivak states, 'the formation of a recognizable basis of action' (2012a: 431). The impulse of the human is to turn the trace into a sign, turn the subaltern 'into the humanist figure of the "people"' (2012a: 435), but the trace – the subject consciousness or the voice consciousness of the oppositional singular – fights figuration and humanization. Perhaps the only way out is to give it negative identification, not the negative identification, of course, that haunts the dehumanization associated with racist privations of speech. Derrida's neologism in *The Animal that Therefore I Am* (2009b), is 'l'animot', a singular being which cannot be subsumed under any species concept, and which bears the suffix *mot* that nevertheless brings us back to the word, forcing the vexed question of representation. The frontier between human and animal 'no longer forms a single indivisible line but more than one internally divided line' (2009b: 30). In Katherine Boo's *Behind the Beautiful Forevers*, one-legged Fatima's death marks the subject consciousness of the subaltern, opposable to the human being of Derrida's *Beast and the Sovereign* (2009a) whose propriety is marked by his relation to the *logos*. The confused motives behind Fatima's drastic step forgotten, her act of making her body graphematic came to be 'reconstrued as a flamboyant protest':

To the poorest, her self-immolation was a response to enervating poverty. To the disabled, it reflected the lack of respect accorded the physically impaired. To the unhappily married, who were legion, it was a brave indictment of oppressive unions. (Boo 2012: 178)

As Spivak wrote of the mute and brutish Friday in J. M. Coetzee's *Foe*, the woman/native/other 'is not only a victim, but also an agent' not despite but because of her fatal withholding of her secret, 'a secret that may not even be a secret' in that it could also be read as a category of knowledge, however unrepeatable and non-inscribed (Spivak 1999: 190). The unrecognizable other, Derrida says in his seminar *The Beast and the Sovereign*, 'is the beginning of ethics, of the Law, and not of the human':

So long as there is recognizability and fellow, ethics is dormant. It is sleeping a dogmatic slumber. So long as it remains human, among men, ethics remains dogmatic, narcissistic, and not yet thinking. ... The unrecognizable is the awakening.
  ... what I am doing is simply an almost limitless broadening of the notion of 'fellow' and [...] in talking about the dissimilar, the non-fellow, I am surreptitiously extending the similar, the fellow, to all forms of life, to all species. (2009a: 155–6)

In order for the humanities to instrumentalize the language of the subaltern, in order to bring the subaltern 'from the deduced *subject* of crisis to the logic of *agency*', to quote Spivak (2012a: 436), the organic intellectual will need to set aside her differences and synecdochize herself so that the subaltern, not yet a part of the whole, can one day be free to put aside their differences and synecdochize themselves: 'I synecdochize myself as nothing but the citizen of India, which is where my tribal students, their parents and relatives, and I can form a collectivity, in search of agency,' Spivak states of her experience of teacher-training in the remote reaches of rural Bengal (2012a: 438). 'What would I do, under these circumstances, if I were Asha or Sunil or Meena? That's what I'm always asking myself,' writes Katherine Boo of a relatable and equally performative process of metanomyzation (beyondthebeautifulforevers.com).

3.

In the United Kingdom today, we suffer a peculiar government, which, in the words of Iain Pears:

lambasts people for getting into debt, then forces them to take on much more; which goes on about the need for an educated workforce, then makes that education more expensive; which attacks bureaucracy, then introduces an even more cumbersome system for the transfers of money between individuals, government, and universities. (Pears 2011)

The incoherent mess that is the Coalition government policy of higher education is creating a market in higher education that is not only freeing universities to charge higher fees but is setting quotas for admissions which will eventually make meaningless the Fair Access legislation. What is most insidious of course is the way in which the government is interfering in and regulating research. The Arts and Humanities Research Council, for example, has been instructed to direct a significant part of its funding into six strategic research areas which have been defined for it. One of these areas is 'civic values and active citizenship'. A text published a couple of years ago by the British Academy highlighted a Humanities for Business programme offering modules to companies like Unilever on topics such as 'Machiavelli and entrepreneurial success'; 'Rousseau and modern marketing'; 'Inspirational leadership in Shakespeare's *Henry IV*'. I would argue that the fungible border between humanities research and consultancy work – intellectual gains and that which can be registered on spreadsheets and yoked to direct economic impact – is the corporatized kind of borderlessness that should make us all the more vigilant about re-imagining a different future to come.

The practical criticism Edward Said represented was borderless in three significant and salutary ways. It flouted the old distinction between literature/criticism and social practices, between texts and non-texts, and it was also galvanized by the sense of being between cultures. Said was a great cartographer of theories which travelled to other times and situations. In 'Traveling Theory Reconsidered' he revises the insights of his essay 'Traveling Theory' which had concluded that, despite the beneficial effects of this dissemination and circulation of ideas, an insurrectionary theory in one historical period and national culture could lose strength and political relevance in another, rigidifying instead into an orthodoxy. In the later essay, published in *Reflections on Exile* (2001), Said reflects on Adorno's use of Lukács to understand Schoenberg's place in the history of music and Fanon's dramatization of the colonial struggle in the language of the manifestly European subject–object dialectic that is a legacy of Lukács's *History and Class Consciousness* (1972). Adorno's bleak account of Schoenberg's monadic disavowal of tonality and his embrace of obscurity evokes Lukács's subject–object antithesis only to reject all his laboriously constructed aesthetic resolutions. According to Adorno, Said observes, there is no 'middle-of-the-road synthesis' between subject and object in Schoenberg's technique, between the atomised artistic consciousness and the commercial public sphere in which it must operate (Said 2001: 441). This dialectic between opposed factors does not result in resolution or transcendence, as it tends to do in Lukácsian theory. Similarly, Said sees in Frantz Fanon's last work, *The Wretched of the Earth*, a lusty appropriation of Lukács's subject–object dialectic only to refute the reconciliation of the two opposed zones in the service of a higher unity. These brilliant rereadings invent the other Lukács: 'the theorist of permanent dissonance as understood by Adorno, the critic of reactive nationalism as partially adopted by Fanon in colonial Algeria' (Said 2001: 451). Said enjoins us to think of Fanon and Adorno as not simply coming after Lukács, 'but rather as pulling him from one sphere or region into another' (2001: 451–2). This movement suggests the possibility of actively different locales, sites, situations for theory, 'without facile universalism or over general totalising' (2001: 452). The Saidiean term for Adorno and Fanon's embodied critiques is 'affiliation', that practice of secular criticism which grafts filiative processes to nonbiological social and cultural forms, and that makes of the Lukácsian figure both 'traveling theory' and non-transitive practice.

Edward Said was hopeful about the late twentieth-century ferment in minority, subaltern, feminist, and post-colonial consciousness that resulted in so many salutary achievements in the curricular and theoretical approach to the study of humanities as quite literally to have produced a Copernican revolution in all traditional fields of enquiry. However, the effort to deconsecrate Eurocentrism and Eurochronology or emphasize the heterogeneity of cultures, traditions and situations that constitute American culture, cannot be reduced to an effort to replace one set of authorities and dogmas by another. Tayib Salih's *Season of Migration to the North* (2003) is valuable not simply because it reinvents the Arabic novel at a time of Sudanese nationalism and the concomitant rejection of the West, but because, by deliberately recalling and revising Conrad – an act that would have been impossible for a black man at the time *Heart of Darkness* was written – Salih's masterpiece enlarges, widens and redefines the scope of a narrative form 'at the centre of which', I quote Said, 'had heretofore always been an exclusively European observer or center of consciousness' (Said 2001: 382). While not every reading of a text is the moral equivalent of a war or a political crisis, it is possible to say after Edward Said that 'works of literature are not merely texts' (2001: 384).

References

Agamben, G. (1998), *Homo Sacer: Sovereign Power and Bare Life*, trans. Daniel Heller-Roazen. Stanford, CA: Stanford University Press.

Agamben, G. (2004), *The Open*. Stanford, CA: Stanford University Press.

Apter, E. (2013), *Against World Literature: On the Politics of Untranslatability*. London and New York: Verso.

Boo, K. (2012), *Behind the Beautiful Forevers*. London: Portobello.

Chakrabarty, D. (2009), *Provincializing Europe: Postcolonial Thought and Historical Difference*. Princeton: Princeton University Press.

Davis, M. (2006), *Planet of Slums*. London and New York: Verso.

Derrida, J. (2009a), *The Beast and the Sovereign*, Vol. 1, trans. Geoffrey Bennington. Chicago and London: University of Chicago Press.

Derrida, J. (2009b), *The Animal that Therefore I Am*. New York: Fordham University Press.

Gramsci, A. (1971), *Selections from the Prison Notebooks*. New York: International Publishers.

Guha, R. (1982), *Subaltern Studies*. 7 vols. New Delhi: Oxford University Press.

Lukács, G. (1972), *History and Class Consciousness: Studies in Marxist Dialectics*, trans. R. Livingstone. Cambridge, MA: The MIT Press.

Nandy, A. (1983), *The Intimate Enemy: Loss and Recovery of Self under Colonialism*. New Delhi: Oxford University Press.

Nussbaum, M. (1997), *Poetic Justice: The Literary Imagination and the Public Life*. Boston: Beacon Press.

Pears, I. (2011), 'After Browne', *London Review of Books* 33 (6), http://www.lrb.co.uk/v33/n06/iain-pears/after-browne (accessed 24 February 2015).

Said, E. (1983), *The World, the Text, and the Critic*. Cambridge, MA: Harvard University Press.

Said, E. (2001), *Reflections on Exile*. London: Granta Books.

Salih, T. (2003), *Season of Migration to the North*. London: Penguin Modern Classics.

Santner, E. (2009), *On Creaturely Life: Rilke, Benjamin, Sebald*. Chicago: University of Chicago Press.

Seshadri, K. (2012), *HumAnimal: Race, Law, Language*. Minneapolis: University of Minnesota Press.

Spivak, G. C. (1985), 'Three Women's Texts and a Critique of Imperialism', *Critical Inquiry* 12 (1): 213–61.

Spivak, G. C. (1990), *The Post-Colonial Critic: Interviews, Strategies, Dialogues*. Ed. Sarah Harasym. New York: Routledge.

Spivak, G. C. (1992), 'Interview with Gayatri Chakravorty Spivak'. New Nation Writers Conference in South Africa. By Leon de Kock. *Ariel: A Review of International English Literature* 23 (3): 29–47.

Spivak, G. C. (1999), *A Critique of Postcolonial Reason: Toward a History of the Vanishing Present*. Cambridge, MA: Harvard University Press.

Spivak, G. C. (2005), 'Scattered Speculations on the Subaltern and the Popular'. *Postcolonial Studies* 8 (4): 475–86.

Spivak, G. C. (2010), *Can the Subaltern Speak? Reflections on the History of an Idea*. Ed. Rosalind C. Morris. New York: Columbia University Press.

Spivak, G. C. (2012a), *Aesthetic Education in an Era of Globalization*. Cambridge, MA: Harvard University Press.

Spivak, G. C. (2012b), 'A Borderless World'. University of Arizona, 19 January 2012, https://www.youtube.com/watch?v=E3LYRYR_-XA (accessed 24 February 2015).

Spivak, G. C., Landry, D. and MacLean, G. (1996), *The Spivak Reader*. New York and Oxford: Routledge.

Young, R. (1990), *White Mythologies*. New York: Routledge.

CHAPTER FOUR

Humanities and Emancipation: Said's Politics of Critique between Interpretation and Interference

Jamila M. H. Mascat

'Humanism should be a force of *disclosure*, not of secrecy', writes Edward Said in polemic with the conservative stance that historically dominates the canon of academic humanities (2004: 73). Indeed, Said's exhortation suggests altering the esoteric pattern of the humanities nurtured within university departments and stimulates further questions: can one consider literacy and basic education an elementary practice of the humanities as well as an essential commitment for any humanistic endeavour? What could and should be the connection between the academically circum-scribed *studia humanitatis* and a non-academic *worldly* humanist praxis? What role could *critique*, traditionally conceived of from Kant onward as the core of modern humanities, occupy within this constellation? Can one distinguish a *humanism of critique* (as the prerogative of a small number *enlightened critics*) from a *humanism of education* (democratically addressing an unquantifiable audience – *the people*?) And, in this case, how would it be possible to combine the two projects under the 'least common multiple' of an emancipatory strategy?

This chapter will not provide an exhaustive answer to this range of issues. Rather, it will preliminarily address the peculiar double bind of humanities and critique via Kant (§1) and its posterity (§2). Then it will sketch out an analytical illustration of Said's contribution to the topic, homing in on his complex and multilayered conception of criticism: firstly it will focus on Said's reflection on *humanism and criticism* (§3); subse-quently it will illustrate his *contrapuntal* and *oppositional* critical methods

(§4); and finally it will investigate the *worldly* trait of Said's criticism with respect to the *intellectual's role and function as critic* (§5). In conclusion, after shortly recalling Gramsci's and Spivak's humanistic pedagogies as paradigmatic critical diversions and sabotages of the humanities' patrimony (§6), the chapter will briefly single out the old *querelle* between J. Rancière and P. Bourdieu on the 'vicious circle' of domination (§7) in the attempt to enrich Said's concept of criticism with the perspective of a theory of emancipation.

As Spivak repeatedly suggests, productive undoing must be accomplished 'at the faultlines of the doing, without accusation, without excuse, with a view to use' (2012: 1). Said's idea of humanism can be considered, *entre autres*, as an example of one of those *ab-usive* usages to which Spivak alludes, in so far as it challenges the normative legacy of the canon of the humanities, in turn allowing interpreters to pursue and supplement his intellectual enterprise by pushing it beyond its own boundaries as well as beyond the limits of the academic institutions. For this reason the path followed in the next sections will progressively try to displace the setting of Said's conception of humanist criticism onto his (frequently evoked, although only partially explored) framework of *interference* of the humanities with the world, a framework that he mobilizes against the common trend of '*noninterference* in the affairs of the everyday world' embraced by many of his fellow-humanists, too easily accustomed to apply what Said labels the *laissez-faire* principle – '"they" can run the country, we will explicate Wordsworth and Schlegel' (Said 2000: 144).

1. Humanities and critique: On Kant's public use of reason

In the context of the ongoing debate over the downgrading of human sciences and the marginalization of humanities departments (Nelson 2011) – as a consequence of the massive neoliberal university restructuring offensively taking over the faculties of the Global North – the defence of academic freedom, freedom of speech and the right to dissent often appeals to the notion of *critique* (Butler 2012), this being conceived of as part and parcel of the millennial tradition of Western humanities. Such issues classically resonate with the over-quoted Kantian advocacy of the ancient motto from Horace's *Epistulae* 'sapere aude', which the philosopher restates in his famous 1794 essay 'Beantwortung der Frage: Was ist Aufklärung?'. However, in spite of its manifest encouragement of reason's brave quest for knowledge, Kant's appeal to the *public use* of reason remains perfectly in accordance with Frederick the Great's well-known dictum 'Argue as much as you will and about what you will; only obey!' (Kant 1999: 22).

Actually, Kant opposes censorship by defending the scholars' right to exert their complete freedom in investigating and communicating to the learned public of the world. Therefore it is clear from the outset that the very notion of a *public use of reason* is delimited by a significant restriction: not only is it opposed to the *private use* of reason which remains subject to the control of political authorities, but it also circumscribes the *public* to the capacity of the scholarly community. Accordingly, the notorious Kantian definition of Enlightenment as 'humankind's emergence from its self-incurred minority' (Kant 1999: 21) solicits a question that regards the very limits of mankind: what, then, would humanity consist of?

On the other hand, in Kant's terms the public use of reason corresponds to a peculiar notion of *critique*. In the *Conflict of the Faculties* (a text published in 1798 as a collection of earlier produced writings), Kant describes and analyses the controversies that may arise between what he terms the *higher faculties* – namely theology, law and medicine – and the *lower faculty* – namely philosophy, which actually comprises a broader spectrum of disciplines – 'a department of *historical knowledge* (including history, geography, philology and the humanities, along with all the empirical knowledge contained in the natural sciences), and a department of *pure rational knowledge* (pure mathematics and pure philosophy, the metaphysics of nature and of morals)' (Kant 1979: 45). Kant does not deny each government's legitimate interest in securing obedience to the religious doctrine, to the laws of the State and to medical regulation. He only marks 'a respectful distance' between the empirical domain of application of the higher faculties and the realm of philosophy devoted to the analysis of a priori principles and of the conditions of possibility of every empirically determined entity. In this vein, he argues that the freedom of the philosophy faculty (its 'free play of reason') is beneficial for the advancement of all other disciplines on their way to truth (Kant 1979: 35). He also traces another boundary that separates the status of faculty representatives (scholars) from that of government-appointed officials (clergymen, doctors and legal functionaries): whereas the latter should not express their doubts and objections before the public, which might risk inciting people to disobedience, the former should be allowed to freely examine all the contents of knowledge and morals, as long as they only exchange among 'one another, as scholars, and the people pay no attention to such matters in a practical way, even if they should hear of them' (Kant 1979: 47).

In short, by investigating 'with critical scrupulosity' and evaluating 'with cold reason', 'the lower faculty has not only the title but also the duty, if not to state the *whole* truth in public, at least to see to it that *everything* put forward in public as a principle is true'. Therefore the conflict between the faculties is not a conflict between the faculties and the government – as Kant repeatedly stresses – since the theoretical dispute never pertains to the *civil* community, rather only to the *learned* community of scholars, and – he adds – 'the people are resigned to understanding nothing about this' (Kant 1979: 55–7).

Kant's limited conception of freedom – whereby the 'public use' of reason remains restricted to a selective scholarly public – can be placed at the origin of some of the paradoxes that still traverse the current debates on academic freedom and the role of the humanities (Butler 2012). How are the contours of such freedom to be defined and delimited? Is academic freedom a guarantee or at least a necessary premise for the defence of extra-academic freedom? In the context of an ever-greater privatization of the education system, does not the 'public' (meaning: scholarly) use of reason run the risk of becoming privatized too?

A possible way to indirectly reply to these questions is to reset them in the broader conceptual constellation disclosed by the complex semantics of *Kritik*. This notion, indeed, seems to have been historically inhabited by at least four main basic meanings. Generally speaking, one of these meanings amounts to the Socratic and Cynical *parrhesia* as the *free speech* of those who *must* speak the truth; another can be referred to the Kantian examination of truth and its conditions of possibility by means of reason; a third one can be identified with Marx's immanent criticism of society and the consciousness of its members; and the last one could be described as the Foucauldian *ethos* of insubordination, or the critical attitude to challenging truth and power by questioning their mechanisms of governmentality (Foucault 2007). Thus, drawing on the multilayered semantics of *Kritik*, the concept and the practice of freedom can be expanded far beyond the scope of academia.

2. *Kritik* as critique and criticism

Judith Butler (2009) has aptly remarked on a few significant distinctions that can be pinpointed between *critique* and *criticism* and within the notion of criticism itself. First, Butler illustrates critique as 'concerned to identify the conditions of possibility under which a domain of objects appears' and criticism as an attitude that always targets an object. Secondly, drawing on Raymond Williams in *Keywords* (1976), she recalls that the latter – criticism – has been traditionally and unfairly confined to the activity of 'fault-finding judgment', while another fundamental aspect of its conduct – its being a 'response to cultural works', i.e. a 'practice' (2009: 109) – has almost systematically been overlooked and dismissed (exceptions including Adorno, Williams, Spivak and Foucault among others).

Yet, the German term *Kritik* seems to conflate different meanings in a single ambivalent word. However, these meanings do not merge; rather, as suggested earlier, they coexist within the bounds of one same concept.

In Kant's works, for example, the notions of critique and criticism as defined by Butler are both at work. His *Kritik* defines the *tribunal* (the site of judgement *par excellence*) 'which will assure to reason its lawful claims and dismiss all its groundless pretensions' (Kant 1965: Axi) as well as the enquiry into the conditions of possibility under which something appears and, in the last instance, a practice of freedom (where judgement is nevertheless involved, as freedom evokes 'the power to *judge* autonomously' that is conferred on reason).

In Marx, the notion of *Kritik* is imbued with several distinct nuances. A famous letter that he sent to A. Ruge in September 1843 bears witness to such a variety. Here, critique designates a heuristic exercise that by criticizing the old world leads to the discovery of the new; the 'ruthless criticism of everything existing'; and the task of confronting man's theoretical dimension by 'mak[ing] religion, science, etc., into the objects of our criticism' in order to raise consciousness about their history and their place in society. Yet unlike B. Bauer and the *critical critics*, Marx assumes this task not to be *mere criticism*, but rather the capacity to reconnect a phenomenon to the material conditions of its existence. Moreover, critique identifies with political criticism – which amounts to 'taking sides' and 'entering into the real struggles' – and finally coincides with 'the self-clarification [...] of the struggles and wishes of the age' that Marx also names 'critical philosophy' (Marx 1978: 13–15, transl. modified). Throughout all these occurrences Marx clearly emphasizes the practical vocation of critique's critical enterprise, which by intersecting immanent parameters (the trends of historical development) and transcendent criteria (ethico-political values), synthesizes judgement and clarification, exposition (*Darstellung*) and denunciation, radical theory and radical praxis.

In his 1978 lecture on 'What is Critique?', Foucault's approach to *critique* (which in French as with the German *Kritik* combines both critique and criticism[1]) revisits Kant's stance on Enlightenment – 'What Kant was describing as the *Aufklärung* is pretty much what I was trying [...] to describe as critique' (Foucault 2007: 48). Foucault's positing of such notion in the shape of a question, as in the title of the talk, 'enacts a certain mode of questioning' – Butler highlights – 'which will prove central to the activity of critique itself' (Butler 2001). But most importantly, after recognizing from the outset the polysemy of the concept, Foucault affirms that critique 'only exists in relation to something other than itself', exhibiting an intrinsic dependence on its object(s) that in turn ends up defining the meaning and the orientation of its practice. Being 'a certain relationship to what exists, to what one knows, to what one does, as well as a relation to society, to culture and to others' (Foucault 2007: 42), Foucault's *critical attitude* exceeds the limits of Kant's rational freedom, such to incarnate an *ethos* – namely a more concrete and affective disposition – that also expresses practical and material commitments, as is the case in Marx's multifaceted portrayal of *Kritik* although in a different manner and scope.

Indeed, the *savoir–pouvoir* pair allows Foucault to incorporate truth and power in his conception of critique *qua* 'art of voluntary insubordination': 'If governmentalization is [...] this movement through which individuals are subjugated in the reality of a social practice through mechanisms of power that adhere to a truth, well, then! I will say that critique is the movement by which the subject gives himself the right *to question truth on its effects of power and question power on its discourses of truth*' (Foucault 2007: 47).

The trajectory from Kant to Foucault summarily reconstructed here may be completed by the well-known deconstructive definitions provided by Spivak, who stresses the *double-bind* that intimately connects critique to its object. In her terms critique becomes a *persistent* movement that must be exercised in and against *what one cannot not (wish to) inhabit* (Spivak 1993: 284). Spivak's emphasis on the radical dependence of critique on its addressee resonates with Foucault's idea of critique as a relation to an object. In fact, Spivak also includes the element of *will* (or *wish*) in her formulation: not only does critique always refer to something, but it refers to that something that 'one can not not (*wish* to) inhabit', that 'we cannot not *want*' (Spivak 1999: 110), or to 'things without which we cannot live on, take chances' (Spivak 1993: 4). Her definitions may of course apply to a range of several intellectual constructs – humanism among them – habits and cultural praxes, although they seem less applicable to concrete structures of material oppression and exploitation. In these cases, critique may assume the shape of a critical and struggling attitude to be conducted against things that *we cannot not wish to abolish* in view of emancipation. A politics of critique may well travel on both tracks – *the critique of what we cannot not want* and *the critique of what we don't want* – both of which, once again, take us beyond the boundary lines of Kant's rational freedom.

3. Said and the cunning of critique

Although abundant reflections on the status, the configuration and the limits of the humanities are scattered throughout all his works, it is in the lectures on *Humanism and Democratic Criticism* (a series of talks given by Said between 2000 and 2002 that were published posthumously in 2004) that he condensed his efforts of clarification and his theoretical proposals.

Several interpreters polemically addressed Said's lectures for his alleged methodological vagueness in expounding his conception of the humanities and in providing a consistent illustration of the much hoped-for 'critique of humanism in the name of humanism' (2004: 10) which he ceaselessly invokes. Some scholars reproached him for having ungenerously turned against French Theory, seen as 'flatly contradict[ing] the core of humanistic thought', and not having managed to challenge or dismantle 'that ontologically enabled meaning of humanism [...] that accommodated the other [...] to its invisible *anthropo-logos* [...] within the circle of which the Word of (Western, now American) Man is at the Center' (Spanos 2008: 48). Some others highlighted Said's contradictory compliance with humanism (Radhakrishnan 2008) and the 'a-systemic' character of his approach to the issue that would be responsible for the weakness of his criticism (Robbins 2008).

As Gourgouris (2008: 177) recalls, Said's 'lectures on humanism were met, practically everywhere in American universities, with a sense of betrayal by those who had been counted among his allies in the humanities during the 1970s and 1980s and with a sense of triumph by various adversaries, who had once inaugurated themselves as the defenders of Anglo-American humanist principles against the foreign onslaught'. The controversial reception that the book encountered can be partially explained by the ambivalent (and ambitious) conception of humanism sketched out by Said in his late meditations, a complex discourse that deserves to be carefully examined.

In circumscribing his notion of humanism, Said draws on Vico's well-known principle of *verum/factum* to ground the ever-changing deployment of human matters at the core of humanities and to identify the 'human' as the ensemble of practices and epistemes that account for the making of history, culture and society. Said never attempts to occult the inhuman character of such a human endeavour; however, he suggests embracing the attitude of 'the non-humanist humanist' (Said 2004) who does not only reject what he unrelentingly criticizes. Said's 'antinomian humanism' (Gourgouris 2008: 179) resonates with Benjamin's 'dictum that every document of civilization is also a document of barbarism', and embodies a 'dialectically fraught' attitude that aims at exercising 'a technique of trouble' on the terrain of the humanities themselves (Said 2004: 77).

Critique 'as a form of democratic freedom and as a continuous practice of questioning and accumulating knowledge that is open to the constituent historical realities of the post-Cold War world' proves to be essential to the contemporary humanist enterprise – as Said recalls, '[H]umanism *is* critique' (Said 2004: 21–2) – and so does literary criticism. As the author himself declares, indeed, the main focus of the volume is not 'humanism tout court', rather 'humanism and the exercise of criticism', or in other words 'humanism as it informs what one does as an intellectual and scholar-teacher of the humanities in today's turbulent world' (Said 2004: 2).

If critique pinpoints the self-reflexive gesture that intrinsically characterizes the process of human knowledge and prevents and protects it from dogmatism, (literary) criticism, beyond the boundaries of its disciplinary confinement, defines a peculiarly critical approach that needs to be sustained by determined and convinced efforts on the part of the intellectuals. In his lectures on humanism, Said speaks of 'democratic criticism' and from time to time evokes his early notion of 'secular criticism' (Said 1983). This latter phrase does not simply express Said's notorious aversion to religious closure and fanaticism, against which secularism would stand for disclosure and worldliness, but it also indicates, as Amir Mufti has sharply remarked, a 'practice of unbelief', or a radical scepticism that targets not only 'the objects of religious piety but [...] secular "beliefs" as well' in order to counter and dissolve the reification of cultural paradigms, products and discourses. 'In this sense', Mufti observed, 'the *secularism* implied in secular criticism is a *critical secularism* [...] a constant unsettling and an ongoing never ending effort of critique' (Mufti 2004: 2–3). Secular criticism asserts that 'There is no center, no inertly given and accepted authority, no fixed barriers ordering human history, even though authority, order, and distinction exist'; so the task of the secular intellectual is 'to show the absence of divine originality and [...] the complex presence of historical actuality. The conversion of the absence of religion into the presence of actuality is secular interpretation' (Said 2000: 131).

The adjective 'democratic', on the other hand, highlights the fundamental *openness* that should connote the humanist's conduct: as a 'practice of participatory citizenship', humanism must be 'open to all classes and backgrounds' (Said 2004: 21–2) and its criticism must incarnate 'a force of disclosure, not of secrecy or religious illumination [... It] must excavate the silences, the world of memory, of itinerant, barely surviving groups, the places of exclusion and invisibility, the kind of testimony that doesn't make it onto the reports' (2004: 73, 81) – and, accordingly, make room for them. Said's secular and democratic criticism addresses the canon of Western humanities in order to reject that 'Darwinist' humanism which condemns entire classes and races to an 'eternal backwardness' (2004: 22–3) and challenges orthodox tendencies by adopting a '*paradoxal mode of thought*' (2004: 83) which constantly works to decentre and displace the 'centre' as well as to liberate identities from any identitarian drifts. 'When will we stop' – he asks – 'allowing ourselves to think of humanism as a form of smugness and not as an unsettling adventure in difference, in alternative traditions, in texts that need a new deciphering within a much wider context than has hitherto been given them?' (2004: 55). Humanism appears as a matter of transition – 'it is about transitions from one realm, one area of human experience to another' (2004: 80). Consequently, humanities must travel in space and time, between distant regions and distinct domains, and become – to paraphrase the title of one of Said's old essays (1982) – a 'travelling theory' as well as a self-questioning *travelling practice* with the aim of challenging the 'rigid dynastic formation' of the academic humanistic *cursus* (Said 2000: 137).

But what does it concretely mean to be critical of humanism in a humanistic fashion (i.e. without adopting the anti-humanist attitude of poststructuralist authors)? Said often insists on a number of significant tasks that the intellectual could undertake: fighting against the loss of historical memory and developing counter-memories; disentangling 'misreading and misinterpretations of a collective past and present' (Said 2004: 22);

providing 'alternative narratives and other perspectives on history' (2004: 141); unmasking the cult of specialism and demystifying the myth of *insiders* – namely 'people (usually men) who are endowed with the special privilege of knowing how things really work and, more important, of being close to power' (Said 2000: 119). On this proximity between culture and power – which Said also names 'affiliation' – the critics need to intervene: while 'culture works very effectively to make invisible and even "impossible" the actual affiliations that exist between the world of ideas and scholarship, on the one hand, and the world of brute politics, corporate and state power, and military force, on the other', criticism urges the humanist intellectual to reveal and denounce the presence of such entanglements (2000: 119).

4. Strategies of criticism

In his 1984 essay on 'The Future of Criticism' written to commemorate the death of his colleague Eugenio Donato, Said maintains that 'criticism can be said to have a future in two senses', namely as a literary practice endowed with its own internal norms and performed by the specialists of the field ('experts, coteries, professionals who [...] mold public opinion, make it conformist, encourage a reliance on a superior little band of all-knowing men in power'), and as a worldly practice that addresses and questions society and mass culture and their political aspects. In both cases, Said maintains, *intrinsic* and *extrinsic* criticism take place in a variety of different contexts like classrooms, newspapers and scholarly institutions, but also 'such things as the mind of the age, its taste, political ideologies, national or class structures', i.e. settings that are not spaces and have no definite location (Said 2000: 166).

Moreover, and more fundamentally, one can interpret Said's reflection on the future of criticism as a Copernican overturning of criticism's natural inclination towards the past. Instead, the author argues in favour of its commitment to the future, 'a commitment to appearing in, making a contribution to, or in various other ways forming and affecting the future' (Said 2000: 167). When criticism looks at the future, it operates in an investigative rather than preservative way and enacts its radically secular function: it becomes critical consciousness to counter the threat of 'the institutions of a mass society whose aim is nothing less than a political quiescence assuring the citizenry's "governability" – and turns into "critical practice as a form of resistance"' (2000: 171).

Most of the ambivalences of Said's discourse about criticism arise precisely in the shape of a specific tension between his contrapuntal critical method and the allegedly oppositional stance of humanism *qua* criticism (Arac 1998). On the one hand, indeed, Said frequently stresses the oppositional function of criticism, explicitly affirmed in the introduction to *The*

World, the Text, and the Critic: 'Were I to use one word consistently along with criticism (not as a modification but as an emphatic) it would be oppositional' (Said 1983: 29). With this regard, another telling term used by Said, as recalled by Arac, is 'adversary', when, in the conclusion of *Beginnings*, he describes the efforts made by Foucault and Deleuze in the attempt to 'controvert the dynastic role' imposed on intellectuals 'by history or habit'. For this reason, they belong to 'the adversary epistemological current found in Vico, in Marx and Engels, in Lukács, in Fanon, and also in the radical political writings of Chomsky, Bertrand Russell, William A. Williams, and others' (Said 1975: 378). Lastly, in his introduction to *Representations of the Intellectual* (Said 1994) when referring to the paradigmatic examples of Malcolm X and James Baldwin to characterize the main traits of the intellectual consciousness – 'a spirit in opposition, rather than in accommodation' – Said states that 'the challenge of intellectual life is to be found in dissent against the status quo at a time when the struggle on behalf of underrepresented and disadvantaged groups seems so unfairly weighted against them'. In this sense, for Said, the parrhesiastic attitude of 'speaking the truth to power is no Panglossian idealism: it is carefully weighing the alternatives, picking the right one, and then intelligently representing it where it can do the most good and cause the right change' (Said 1996: xvii, 102).

On the other hand, Said nuances and tempers the oppositional charge of the intellectual's duty. In expounding what he names 'contrapuntal criticism', and more precisely the notion of 'counterpoint' from which it derives, he clarifies that 'in the counterpoint of Western classical music, various themes play off against one another, with only a provisional privilege being given to any particular one; yet in the resulting polyphony there is concert and order, an organized interplay' (Said 1994: 51). Contrapuntal criticism joins and connects, whereas oppositional criticism separates and contrasts. The aim of a contrapuntal strategy is to create fields of coexistence for opposite and rival *récits* avoiding both the 'politics of blame' and 'the even more destructive politics of confrontation and hostility' (Said 1994: 18). Apparently the two methods cannot be reconciled, but on closer inspection the strategy of counterpoint seems to end up incorporating the tactic of opposition, inasmuch as opposing becomes just another way of establishing connections. What Said following Adorno argues about the status of art and its relation to politics provides an incisive illustration of the need for a contrapuntal approach to and within the humanities. For Said art and politics are not one and the same thing; rather they remain formally autonomous in spite of their unavoidable co-presence and their permanent overlaps; they maintain an irreducible distance between themselves that does not allow any artistic expression to be merely reduced to ideological issues. Said thus claims that 'a great work of art is not an ideological statement, pure and simple' and 'no ideological statement, pure and simple, can become a great work of art', remarking that even if according to Sartre 'Paul Valery [...] was a petit bourgeois [...] not every petit bourgeois is a Valery' (Mitchell 1998: 30–3). However, although no immediate link can be established between the sphere of art and the realm of politics, a technique is nevertheless needed in order to enable the grasping of the mutual influences, intertwinings and antagonisms that emerge in the relation between the aesthetic and the non-aesthetic, art-works and society, the literary and the social. Contrapuntal criticism incarnates such a technique, by subsuming, in the last instance, the incompatible polarities generated by oppositional criticism into its manifold play of connections. In so doing, it allows the humanists to sustain the 'fundamental irreconcilability' between the artistic creation and its worldliness – which according to Said constitutes a 'necessary condition' of intellectual work (Said 2004: 62–3) – while at the same time avoiding the mere and simple depoliticization of the humanities. Otherwise – he remarks – 'the consequence is that to deal with literature as well as the broadly defined "humanities" is to deal with the nonpolitical, although quite evidently the political realm is presumed to lie just beyond (and beyond the reach of) literary, and hence literate, concern' (Said 2000: 141).

5. Worldliness and exile

In Said's conception of intellectual work, the autonomy of arts mirrors the *outsiderhood* of the public intellectual that the author sketches out by drawing on the condition of the exile. The exile, he explains, designates 'the state of never being fully adjusted, always feeling outside the chatty, familiar world inhabited by natives' (Said 1996: 53). The figure of the exiled, with whom Said obviously identifies himself, coincides with the heroic model portrayed by Hugh of Saint Victor in his *Didascalicon*, and later celebrated by E. Auerbach (and reprised by Said through Auerbach): it is 'he to whom the entire world is as a foreign place', an individual accustomed to displacement and detachment, trained in the interstitial experience of in-betweenness which ceaselessly crosses borders, lands, languages, forms and fields, an experience rooted in 'unhoused, decentered, and exilic energies'. Said acknowledges that it would be dishonest 'to say that the bravura performances of the intellectual exile and the miseries of the displaced person or refugee are the same' (Said 1994: 332), and therefore focuses on the peculiar consciousness of the exile that belongs to the condition and the position of the humanist as an intellectual (more specifically in the context of American universities).

In fact, the humanist as a scholar is at once the philologist – a specialist, an expert whose philological expertise consists in the capacity to travel across distinct domains ('Between the space of words and their origins and deployments, from text to actualized site of either appropriation or resistance'; Said 2004: 83) – but also the amateur intellectual. This twofold connotation of the humanist as *expert* and *amateur* avoids the apolitical drift towards the ideology of professionalism which argues that 'expertise is therefore supposed to be unaffected by its institutional affiliations with power, although of course it is exactly those affiliations – hidden but assumed unquestioningly – that make the expertise possible and imperative' (Said 2000: 139). Said then argues that, if 'insiders promote special interests', outsider 'intellectuals should be the ones to question patriotic nationalism, corporate thinking, and a sense of class, racial or gender privilege' (Said 1996: xiii). While 'confined to the study of one representational complex, literary critics accept and paradoxically ignore the lines drawn around what they do'; on the contrary, humanist intellectuals examine 'the coexistence of and the interrelationship between the literary and the social, which is where representation – from journalism, to political struggle, to economic production and power – plays an extraordinarily important role' (Said 2000: 141).

Outsiderhood thus appears as a virtue that pertains to both vocations of the Saidian intellectual: to the intellectual *qua* specialist who inhabits the estranged space of academia and the sphere of her scholarly domain, and to the amateur intellectual, for she remains at distance from political parties and institutions maintaining her critical voice without compromise. Indeed, for Said intellectual outsiderhood is an ambivalent trait. On the one hand it designates critical distancing from the institutions of power and becomes another word for disenchantment and detachment; on the other hand, it unequivocally requires responsibility – the intellectual 'is one who believes that by being a responsible and responsive member of the society, one can raise moral questions about the nature of the political' (Jahanbegloo 2012). Said expects the intellectual to be responsible and committed and at the same time demands that she remain estranged and an outsider. But how can responsibility and commitment be reconciled with detachment and freed from belonging in order to embrace a sort of *super partes* and unbound critical stance? Or, in other words, to whom is the intellectual responding and what cause is she ommitted to? For whom and for what is she responsible? Who are the recipients of her words?

Said thematizes these questions adopting a slightly Sartrean register and 'asking *the* basic question for the intellectual: how does one speak the truth? What truth? For whom and where?' (Said 1996: 88). Reflecting on the origins of Reaganism and on the culture of the age, he traverses the history of twentieth-century Anglo-American literary criticism – from 1920s New Criticism to the French-inspired New New Criticism; from F. R. Leavis's school to F. Jameson's academic Marxism – and denounces the limits of the scholarly confinement of critique, once again highlighting the degree to which expertise and specialism run the risk of becoming mere synonyms for the neutralization and depoliticization that are meant to mask a ubiquitous political conditioning.

Like Gramsci, Said rejects the primacy of expertise and specialistic knowledge over critical thinking, but unlike Gramsci he does not embrace or incarnate the prototype of the 'organic intellectual'. Rather, he declares himself 'against conversion to and belief in a political god of any sort', arguing that for the secular intellectual such acts of devotion testify to an 'unfitting behavior' (Said 1996: 109). According to Said, in fact, only freedom from the bonds of authorities and institutions discloses the path to the truth and accounts for the intellectual's 'special duty to address the constituted and authorized powers of one's own society' (1996: 98).

The exiled humanist intellectual thus belongs to no place and has no master; nevertheless, she is morally and politically responsible for communities of resistance in society, for the oppressed and the disenfranchised of the world. Some critics reproached Said for the 'philosophical idealism' upon which his heroic model of the intellectual activist is based, by pointing at 'his unrelenting belief in the power of representation as the site of political and social oppression and/or resistance [...] that supersedes a materialist understanding of people in and of the world' as well as by blaming him for describing the practice of intellectuality as an individual and ultimately 'lonely condition' (Aldama 2008: 74).

Precisely because of his conception of the intellectual as a scholar-in-exile whose main task is *representing*, Said is seen as having opted for a top-down model of political transformation that only criticizes governmental and cultural institutions while confronting the adversary representatives in the academic milieu, instead of raising consciousness at the bottom level of society and engaging with organizing struggles. In this view, Said situated his own polemical discourse within the context of the dominant discourse in the US public sphere. As such, in spite of recognizing that he mostly opposed this discourse, its antidemocratic inclinations and its imperialist ambitions, Said's critics hold that he opted to fight within an infra-hegemonic debate, instead of choosing to build the hegemony of the social group to which he could have chosen to belong as an organic intellectual.

However, the intellectual condition of the exile does not amount to confinement nor to asceticism; rather, it maintains a strong engagement with the world. In this perspective, *worldliness* refers to the being in the world of the text ('"the circumstantial reality" of its creation'; Said 1983: 35), of the reader and of the humanist as a responsible critic. As against the idea of preserving the humanities (their canon and their doctrines) from the influence of the material reality, Said advocates a *worldly* critical perspective, according to which criticism should involve an awareness of the social and political context surrounding the reader, the text, the author and the critic herself. Thus he writes with regard to text: 'whether a text is preserved or put aside for a period, whether it is on a library shelf or not, whether it is considered dangerous or not: these matters have to do with a text's being in the world' (1983: 35). Then, concerning the reader: 'A reader is in a place, in a school or university, in a work place, or in a specific country at a particular time, situation, and so forth' (Said 2004: 75–6). The same thing can be said of the humanist intellectual.

Facing the profound worldly entrenchment of the literary environment, its objects and its actors, humanist criticism operates as a *politics of interpretation* (Said 2000: 118) of the world and becomes a sort of civic commitment which 'is in the last instance reducible neither to a doctrine or a political position on a particular question, and it is to be in the world and self-aware simultaneously'. Said names such a humanist commitment 'interference' and states that 'instead of noninterference and specialization, there must be *interference* as a crossing of borders and obstacles, a determined attempt to generalize exactly at those points where generalizations seem impossible to make' (Said 2000: 145).

The very notion of interference remains open to multiple meanings: one option indicates the perspective of a cosmopolitan intercultural and non-identitarian conception of the humanities; another option, explicitly suggested by Said, describes trespassing across different terrains ('one of the first interferences to be ventured, then, is a crossing from literature, which is supposed to be subjective and powerless, into those exactly parallel realms, now covered by journalism and the production of information, that employ representation but are supposed to be objective and powerful' (2000: 145). And one further option may point at education as a never-ending process that 'involves widening circles of awareness' (Said 2004: 75).

Said never advances 'a fully articulated program of interference' (Said 2000: 146), but it could be imagined and located at the edge of the humanities where enlightenment and emancipation intersect, expanding humanist criticism beyond textuality and representation in the direction of the world.

6. Humanism, humanities and education: on Gramsci and Spivak

To follow Said's invitation to exceed the boundaries of classical humanism and to disclose the enclosure of the humanities in order to bring them to interfere with the world, one may be tempted to pursue the path of education as significant experience of human liberation and social change. One could then distinguish, although not in a rigid fashion, between a 'humanism of critique' conceived of as the intellectual task of speaking truth to power, and a 'humanism of education' conceived of as a pedagogical endeavour whereby humanities becomes just another word for democracy and emancipation. Gramsci's project of the 'scuola unitaria' (common school) in the early 1920s in Italy, and Spivak's analysis and critique of the wheels that sustain the 'teaching machine' (1993) in both the Global North and the Global South, constitute two brilliant – and very different – examples of what a *humanism of education* might be.

In his *Notebooks* Gramsci analyses the peculiar nature of Italian Humanism in the fifteenth and sixteenth centuries, which he describes as a 'contradictory' 'regressive' phenomenon and even as a 'restoration', for it developed as a cosmopolitan and a-national process promoted by intellectual elites that had no connection with the people-nation. Nevertheless, he recognizes that the most interesting aspect of humanism – the 'classicism of the humanists' – aimed at the 'rehabilitation of the human spirit as the creator of life and of history' (Gramsci 2011: 373). For this reason Gramsci himself draws on the legacy of the humanities to elaborate his outline of the 'common school' as a counter-model for the aristocratic reform of the Italian school-system that took place in 1923 (Mussolini called it 'the most fascist of all reforms') and inherited the name of the then-minister of education, the philosopher Giovanni Gentile. Against the logic of setting a divide between schools for the few and the best, and others for *hoi polloi*, Gramsci imagined a comprehensive educational apparatus drawing precisely on the classical humanistic *curriculum*: from the 'purely receptive form of learning' of elementary school through gymnasium to the 'creative' regime of the lyceum (212).

The common school he advocates was designed to develop 'in each individual human being an as-yet-undifferentiated general culture, the fundamental power to think and to find a direction in life', leading as its ultimate goal to the highest humanist values of 'an unlimited intellectual self-discipline' and an equally 'unlimited moral autonomy' (Gramsci 2011: 208, 212, transl. modified). Therefore in Gramsci's conception, anti-specialist humanism, far from some sort of humanistic elitism, constitutes a concrete tool for a non-abstract democratization. Reversing the classical aristocraticism of the humanities – though without questioning their classical Eurocentrism – humanism here becomes a means of intellectual emancipation, and not a marker of election or exclusion or a prerogative of the intelligentsia. In this sense the humanities play an essential role in accomplishing the formation of the intellectual *qua* 'leader (specialist + politician)' who is supposed to be an *organizer* and not just simply an *orator*. For her, in fact, neither *parrhesia* nor free speech suffices, as she must be up to the pedagogical mission evoked by Gramsci's idea of the *permanent persuader* (Gramsci 1971: 11).

In a different register, Spivak's aesthetic education describes a pedagogy for change that weaves together literacy, literature and citizenship by way of imagination. Indeed, its realization consists in the 'displacement of beliefs onto the terrain of imagination', a displacement which is designed to 'train the imagination for epistemological performances' as well as for ethical interventions (Spivak 2012: 10). For Spivak imagination constitutes 'the irreducible element of an *aesthetic education*' (Spivak 2012: 3) that is highly needed when desires have been trapped in reflexes and teleologies that must be transformed and deactivated. As she explicitly claims, education does not *right wrongs* in the name of human rights nor does it consist of indoctrination in nationalism and identitarianism. On the contrary, it operates at the level of desires, attempting their *'uncoercive* rearrangement' through a patient and site-specific exercise (2004: 526). Education, in fact, teaches how to learn and how to unlearn, but it does not teach the same way everywhere it teaches.

In the context of the Global South, torn by both the heritage of colonialism and the unevenness of the present, a humanistic education amounts, well beyond literacy and numeracy, to teaching a culture of responsibility in order to activate democratic habits. It aims, in other words, at 'nurturing the capacity to imagine the public sphere and the fostering of independence within chosen rule-governance' which according to Spivak is 'the hedgehog's definition of democracy' (2004: 558). At the opposite spectrum of the planet, instead, metropolitan humanities – 'an arena of cultural explanations that question the explanations of culture' (Spivak 2006: 160) – run the risk of being caught between the institutional defence of their own survival, on the one hand, and 'the tremendous exploitable energy of the freshman English machine as a panacea for social justice' on the other (2006: 148). Spivak's old adage, 'unlearning one's privilege as loss' (1990: 9), describes precisely the process of dismissing 'the conviction that I am necessarily better, I am necessarily indispensable, I am necessarily the one to right wrongs' (2004: 532); such a learning-to-unlearn should make up part of humanities teaching in the tertiary education of the Global North. In this setting, imagination, trained through literary reading, allows one *changing reflexes* (Carvalho and Spivak 2010) and 'suspending oneself in the text of the other' in the attempt to avoid the trap of 'cultural relativism as cultural absolutism ("American-style education will do the trick") and to prevent the drift toward a simple "(corporatist) benevolence"' (Spivak 2004: 532).

Nevertheless Spivak suggests that 'literature is also not "political" in the narrow sense', since reading and acting do not share the same temporal alignment. She also eventually adds as a memento that 'you don't *do* politics in the classroom, but you sharpen the ethicopolitical instrument' there, because 'the political requires a *lifelong* preparation that goes along with the short term call to action' (Carvalho and Spivak 2010: 326–7). Accordingly, humanities only provide the propaedeutic training that sustains political action, and precisely on this terrain imagination qualifies a gap, the 'irreducible difference between *what we need* and *what we can do*' (Spivak 2012b). This is why Spivak affirms that 'the humanities are without guarantees' (2004: 537).

7. A humanist politics of critique in the light of emancipation

Unlike Gramsci and Spivak, in his discourse on humanism Said seems to privilege criticism over education. However, the two approaches that have been mentioned – a 'humanism of education' and a 'humanism of critique' – do not actually exclude nor oppose each other; actually, they may be mutually complementary. In the attempt to outline such a horizon of complementarity, it could be useful to address, via Rancière, the issue of emancipation as a supplement to the very notion of critique, namely as the supplement that converts critique into a critical praxis.

Indeed, although it entails no immediate and simple synthesis, emancipation helps us to sketch out a political perspective that combines pedagogy and criticism providing a different framework for rethinking the relationship between Said's categories of outsiderhood and insiderhood, interpretation and interference. In his polemic with and against Bourdieu, Rancière (2004) reiterates the criticism he had already expressed against his mentor L. Althusser regarding the opposition of science and ideology, truth and illusion, knowledge and ignorance, along the lines of the Marxian division between mental and manual labour, that is between intellectual-thinkers and social actors (Pelletier 2009).

Rancière identifies in Bourdieu's works (1979, 1984, 1990) the consolidation of the anti-emancipatory schema of his vicious circle of domination, which the philosopher incisively summarizes as follows: 'The truth that everybody knows is a truth that hides the fact that it is concealed' (Rancière 2004: 170). In a similar vein, commenting on Bourdieu's analysis of the statistics of the French higher education system (Bourdieu and Passeron, 1979, 1990) he observes: 'School therefore eliminates by dissimulating that it eliminates. Which of course implies another trick. In order to perfect the system it must eliminate in order to dissimulate the fact that it eliminates while pretending not to eliminate' (Rancière 2004: 172). Hence, mis-recognitions and illusions seem to condemn the masses to perpetual ignorance, by keeping society separate from its apparently unretrievable truth.

For Bourdieu, from Bourdieu's perspective the role of the scholar – namely the sociologist, and in Rancière's words *le sociologue roi* – is to highlight the gap existing between science and representation, and to explain how the latter prevents access to the former. Emancipation thus becomes a question of scientific knowledge while everyday practices, struggles and resistances remain simply caught in the eternal yoke of illusion and ineffectiveness. As Rancière explains: 'On this basis, emancipation was no longer conceived as the construction of new capacities. It was the promise of science to those whose illusory capacities could be nothing but the reverse side of their real incapacity.' Additionally, he remarks, 'the very logic of science was that of an endless deferment of the promise. The science that promised freedom was also the science of the total process whose effect is endlessly to generate its own ignorance' (2009: 43–4).

Whereas Bourdieu presents himself as the champion of the outsiderhood of critique, stressing its exteriority and distance as the main grounds of its efficacy, Rancière valorizes the immanent character of the emancipatory praxis enacted by the insiders-dominated, namely by the actual practitioners of *disagreement* whom the critical theorists have to give voice. Said's portrait of the exiled intellectual only superficially resembles Bourdieu's conception of the critic, in so far as Said repeatedly rejects the myth of specialism and professionalism while passionately pleading for the intellectual's social commitment and responsibility, far beyond the scope of scholarly analysis and theory production. On the other hand, Said's notion of criticism as 'interference' could be expanded and supplemented by Rancière's 'affirmative critique' (Sonderegger 2012), consisting in the 'critical investigation of practices' that aim to retrieve, circulate and share fights and strategies of insubordination, promote dissent and foster emancipation as a core form of the political. In this regard, emancipation, conceived of in Rancière's term as 'the collectivization of capacities invested in scenes of dissensus' in contrast with the melancholic impotence of the critics' expertise (Rancière 2009: 37, 49), may provide the proper terrain where the only partially exploited practical inclinations of Said's worldly criticism could be rethought and enacted. This, in turn, could mark the first step towards a *politics of critique* yet to invent at the intersection between the humanists' complementary tasks indicated by Said of critically *interpreting* the world and critically *interfering* with it.

Note

1   Actually in both German and French the words *Kritizismus* and *criticisme* indicate the philosophical approach inaugurated by Kant to overcome the dualism of empiricism and dogmatic rationalism. Nevertheless the multiple meanings associated with the English term *criticism* – as for example the scholarly investigation of literary or historical texts, the analysis and judgement of the merits and faults of a literary or artistic work, the expression of disapproval of someone or something on the basis of perceived faults or mistakes – are expressed respectively with the words *Kritik* and *critique*.

References

Aldama L. (2008), *Why the Humanities Matter. A Commonsense Approach*. Austin: University of Texas Press.

Arac, J. (1998), 'Criticism between Opposition and Counterpoint'. In P. A. Bove (ed.), *Edward Said. A Special Issue*, Boundary 2, 25 (2): 55–69.

Bourdieu, P. (1984), *Distinction: A Social Critique of the Judgement of Taste*. Cambridge, MA: Harvard University Press.

Bourdieu, P. and J.-C. Passeron (1979), *The Inheritors: French Students and Their Relation to Culture*. Chicago: University of Chicago Press.

Bourdieu, P. and J.-C. Passeron (1990), *Reproduction in Education, Society and Culture*. London: Sage.

Butler, J. (2001), 'What is Critique? An Essay on Foucault's Virtue', *transversal – eipcp multilingual webjournal*, issue 'Borders, Nations, Translations', http://eipcp.net/transversal/0806/butler/en (accessed 17 February 2015).

Butler, J. (2009), 'The Sensibility of Critique: Response to Asad and Mahmood'. In T. Asad, W. Brown, J. Butler and S. Mahmood, *Is Critique Secular? Blasphemy, Injury, and Free Speech*. Berkeley: Townsend Center for the Humanities, University of California, 101–36.

Butler, J. (2012), '*Critique*, Dissent, Disciplinarity'. In R. Sonderegger and K. de Boer (eds), *Conceptions of Critique in Modern and Contemporary Philosophy*. New York: Palgrave Macmillan, 10–29.

Carvalho E. J. and G. C. Spivak (2010), '"Changing Reflexes." Interview with Gayatri Chakravorty Spivak', in V. Cohen (ed.), *The New American Movement: An Oral History*, Works and Days 28 (1–2): 325–45.

Foucault, M. (2007), 'What is Critique?'. In *The Politics of Truth*, Los Angeles: Semiotext(e), 41–82.

Gourgouris, S. (2008), 'Rethinking Humanism'. In M. Karavanta and N. Morgan (eds), *Edward W. Said and Jacques Derrida: Reconstellating Humanism and the Global*. Newcastle: Cambridge Scholars Publishing, 174–98.

Gramsci, A. (1971), *Selections from the Prison Notebooks of Antonio Gramsci*. New York: International Publishers.

Gramsci, A. (2011), *Prison Notebooks*, vol. II. New York: Columbia University Press.

Jahanbegloo, R. (2012), 'Edward Said's Conception of the Public Intellectual as an "Outsider"', http://jahanbegloo.com/content/edward-saids-conception-public-intellectual-outsider

Kant, I. (1965), *Critique of Pure Reason*. New York: St. Martin's Press.

Kant, I. (1979), *The Conflict of the Faculties*. New York: Abaris Books.

Kant, I. (1999), *Practical Philosophy*. New York: Cambridge University Press.

Karavanta, M. and N. Morgan (2008), *Edward W. Said and Jacques Derrida: Reconstellating Humanism and the Global*. Newcastle: Cambridge Scholars Publishing.

Marx, K. and F. Engels (1978), *The Marx-Engels Reader* (ed. by C. Tucker). New York and London: W. W. Norton & Company.

Mitchell, W. J. T. (1998), 'The Panic of the Visual: A Conversation with Edward W. Said'. In P. A. Bove (ed.), *Edward Said. A Special Issue*, Boundary 2, 25 (2): 11–33.

Mufti, A. R. (2004), 'Critical Secularism: A Reintroduction for Perilous Times'. *Critical Secularism*, Boundary 2, 31 (2): 1–9.

Nelson, C. (2011), *No University Is an Island. Saving Academic Freedom*. New York: New York University Press.

Pelletier, C. (2009), 'Emancipation, Equality and Education: Rancière's Critique of Bourdieu and the Question of Performativity', *Discourse: Studies in the Cultural Politics of Education*, 30 (2): 137–50.

Radhakrishnan, R. (2008), 'Edward Said's Literary Humanism'. In M. Karavanta and N. Morgan (eds), *Edward W. Said and Jacques Derrida: Reconstellating Humanism and the Global*. Newcastle: Cambridge Scholars Publishing, 88–115.

Rancière, J. (2004), *The Philosopher and His Poor*. Durham, NC: Duke University Press.

Rancière, J. (2009), *The Emancipated Spectator*. London and New York: Verso.

Robbins, B. (2008), 'Said and Secularism'. In M. Karavanta and N. Morgan (eds), *Edward W. Said and Jacques Derrida: Reconstellating Humanism and the Global*. Newcastle: Cambridge Scholars Publishing, 140–57.

Said, E. (1975), *Beginnings: Intention and Method*. New York: Basic Books.

Said, E. (1983), *The World, the Text, and the Critic*. Cambridge, MA: Harvard University Press.

Said, E. (1994), *Culture and Imperialism*. New York: Vintage.

Said, E. (1996), *Representation of the Intellectuals*. New York: Vintage.

Said, E. (2000), *Reflections on Exile and Other Essays*. Cambridge, MA: Harvard University Press.

Said, E. (2004), *Humanism and Democratic Criticism*. New York: Columbia University Press.

Sonderegger, R. (2012), 'Negative versus Affirmative Critique: On Pierre Bourdieu and Jacques Rancière'. In R. Sonderegger and K. de Boer (eds), *Conceptions of Critique in Modern and Contemporary Philosophy*. New York: Palgrave Macmillan, 248– 64.

Spanos, W. V. (2008), 'Edward Said's Humanism and American Exceptionalism: An Interrogation after 9/11'. In M. Karavanta and N. Morgan (eds), *Edward W. Said and Jacques Derrida: Reconstellating Humanism and the Global*. Newcastle: Cambridge Scholars Publishing, 24–54.

Spivak, G. C. (1990), *The Post-Colonial Critic. Interviews, Strategies, Dialogues*, ed. Sarah Harasym. New York and London: Routledge.

Spivak, G. C. (1993), *Outside in the Teaching Machine*. New York and London: Routledge.

Spivak, G. C. (1999), *Critique of Post-Colonial Reason. Toward a History of the Vanishing Present*. Cambridge, MA: Harvard University Press.

Spivak, G. C. (2004), 'Righting Wrongs', *The South Atlantic Quarterly*, 103 (2/3): 523–81.

Spivak, G. C. (2006), *In Other Worlds. Essays in Cultural Politics*. New York and London: Routledge.

Spivak, G. C. (2012a), *An Aesthetic Education in the Era of Globalization*, Cambridge, MA: Harvard University Press.

Spivak, G. C. (2012b), 'Un/learning With Gayatri Chakravorty Spivak: An Aesthetic Education in the Era of Globalization', Center for the Humanities, CUNY, April 27, http://vimeo.com/49844501

CHAPTER FIVE

Not Yet Humanism
or
the Non-Jewish Jew Becomes
the Non-Humanistic Humanist

Paul Gilroy

Humanism is about reading, it is about perspective, and, in our works as humanists, it is about transitions from one realm, one area of human experience to another. It is also about the practice of identities other than those given by the flag or the national war of the moment.

SAID (2004: 80)

Among the most testing and difficult subjects associated with the intellectual legacy and political example of Edward Said is the issue of his staunch humanism. This is far from being a narrowly academic matter. It was a passionate feature of Said's combative life and articulates his work as a scholar, an intellectual and a political advocate for Palestine. His humanist position is both distinctive and complex. It does not derive simply from the philosophical anthropology of the early Marx with which it intersects via the work of Lukács, Gramsci, Williams and the other twentieth-century radical humanists like C. L. R. James with whom Said was familiar. He was at pains to explain that it had an older lineage deriving in part from eighteenth-century Europe's 'efflorescence of secular anthropology' (Said 1994: 44). Fundamentally, it is warranted by the writings of Vico, counterpointed by Fanon's audacious call for a renewal of humanism in the light of anti-colonial revolution, and anchored in the cosmopolitan, multilingual and comparative excursions of philolog's like Auerbach and Spitzer who steered a similar course to the one pursued by Said through the critical, historical study of language and literature during the emergencies and conflicts of 'the century of camps' (Bauman 1995: 192). The central conditioning factor in its development is, however, the unfolding of decolonization. Behind that, or perhaps beneath it, stands a critical antipathy to the languages of race and type which have the power to occlude, corrupt and banish the Human entirely.

One wise commentator said recently that all that has been needed in order to appear radical during the last few decades is to stand firmly in the same place while the profane forces of privatization, militarization and financialization churn destructively around you. This acute observation about the retrenchment of global capital and the tempo of triumphant neoliberalization also captures something useful in exploring the case of Said. While not wanting to play down the extent or the sophistication of his utopian and political imaginings, in particular his loathing of arbitrary power and colonial governance, it is difficult to contain his outlook simply beneath the conventional headings of the left. Perhaps his oppositional disposition and his eloquent dissent were not straightforwardly chosen. They seem to have resulted from a commitment to cultivate the courage and solitary practice of the dissident intellectual, fountain pen in hand, poised anachronistically over a fine sheet of vellum, hoping for but anticipating no other reader beyond themselves. Rather than a righteous reflex, Said's perspective seems instead to have been a formation that grew organically from the need to observe and then rethink scholarship, culture and criticism in response to conjunctural events – often, though not always, centred on the predicament of Palestinians.

Though audible, his distaste for contemporary capitalism is therefore one muted note in a louder, dissonant chord. Indeed the distinctive blend of themes and perspectives that he exhibited poses an important question about the relationship between radical politics and varieties of philosophical, critical or aesthetic conservatism in this particular historical setting.

Speaking of Raymond Williams in a discussion of the limits of 'the old Second International base-and-superstructure model', Said outlined what he takes to be some of the interpretative advantages of being a reflective critic rather than a committed revolutionary (1983: 239). This advantage was notable not only where what he calls secular criticism identifies the religious eschatology secreted inside much contemporary theory. Its value increased as old lines of enmity dissolved and new possibilities emerged to challenge outworn conventions and to prompt new modes of understanding and resistance that surpassed the left/right divide. Said often acknowledged his deep debt to Williams who was determined to refute the charge that his own intellectual and political project could be easily assimilated back into a 'humanist essentialism' (Eagleton 1976: 22). Drawing strength and insight from the sage of the Black Mountains borderland, Said opts to drive home a challenge to 'theory' by demonstrating why something like an immanent critique of humanist customs and habits remains not only an essential source of hope but a practical, political tool in a range of post-colonial conflicts.

If this appears to be a provocation rather than a principled commitment, it should be emphasized that Said's humanism was an extended reaction to the history of colonialism and to the decolonization struggles of the twentieth century, both thwarted and successful. Though post- and trans-humanism are now the order of the day, his thoughtful responses should not be dismissed as a reactionary residue at odds with his essaying of a *democratic* criticism and a deeply democratized world – even when he describes them as part of his own culturally conservative outlook (Viswanathan 2001: 145). They are certainly tied to a great love for the moral pedagogy and autopoiesis made possible by the academic humanities but they are not reducible simply to those passions or to the Europe-centred cosmopolitics that so often inheres in them. This democratic humanism is part of Said's defence of critical thought and of the mission of the university as well as the responsible political pedagogy that could once be cultivated there. It is recognizably the humanism of dedicated, tireless intellectual labour, often against the epistemology that underpinned imperialist rule and exploitation. It is also a humanism that was bravely articulated in opposition to war, nationalism, racism and ethnic absolutism. That stance had been explicit in *Orientalism* which is, regrettably, seldom read as a text that registers the importance of racial hierarchy and speaks to the political tangle deriving from racism and a political ontology of race that encompassed not just Negroes and Jews but Arabs and Whites. Said asks:

> Can one divide human reality as indeed human reality seems to be genuinely divided into clearly different cultures, histories, traditions, societies, even races, and survive the consequences humanly? (Said 1979: 45)

In asking that question, his not-yet humanism is revealed to be in harmony with the anti-colonial and 'human rights' struggles of the twentieth century. He underscored this in one of his many reflections on Auerbach's life and scholarly project where he emphasized that the German had provided an important precedent and illustration of where national and ethnic particu-larity came into conflict with other obligations and potentials:

> The heart of the hermeneutical enterprise was to develop over the years a very particular kind of sympathy toward texts from different periods and different cultures. For a German whose specialty was Romance liter-ature, this sympathy took on an almost ideological cast, given that there had been a long period of historical enmity between Prussia and France,

the most powerful and competitive of its neighbors and antagonists. As a specialist in Romance languages, the German scholar had a choice either to enlist on behalf of Prussian nationalism (as Auerbach did as a soldier during the First World War) and study 'the enemy' with skill and insight as a part of the continuing war effort, or, as was the case with Auerbach and his peers, to overcome bellicosity and what we now call 'the clash of civilizations' with a welcoming, hospitable attitude of humanistic knowledge designed to realign warring cultures in a relationship of mutuality and reciprocity. (Said 2004: 93)

The history here is too compressed. However, even in impacted form it can be illuminating. Belligerence and nationalism are vanquished through a variety of intellectual labour in which human curiosity and the attachment to culture surpass loyalty either to the national state or to the mechanisms of absolute ethnicity with which one finds oneself entangled. This stance will always be regarded as a kind of treachery but it points to higher or deeper loyalties than can be specified by merely national citizenship. There are echoes of Freud's First World War disillusion here and they should be amplified even if the political geometry of the later twentieth century is more forbidding than the shocking environment that had shaped his Viennese disenchantment and distaste for belligerent group identification (Freud 1957: 279–80).

Said was frank about the fact that his own humanist disposition had been affected not only by his life as an exile but also by what he took to be the distinctive cultural pluralism created in the United States by the after-effects of its colonial past, its immigration history and the country's distinctive legal relationship between race, settlement and citizenship. That diverse, demotic formation remains an index of how the country was changing as it evolved from the world's most successful instance of settler colonialism towards a perilously unstable version of multiculture that enjoys few historical precedents. No progressive outcomes could be guaranteed but it did appear to be incubating an intensive plurality that called for a new kind of cosmopolitan attachment. That outlook might even be thought compatible with the finest promises of its republican, civic traditions even though they were betrayed routinely each day in the deficits generated by racial hierarchy and segregation, securitocracy, consumer imperialism and corporate populism. Important lessons as to how to negotiate these conditions lay, he felt, in the earlier history of the Americas which indicated a general strategy for the humanistic politics of knowledge, reading and interpretation.

[G]reat anti-authoritarian uprisings made their earliest advances, not by denying the humanitarian and universalist claims of the general dominant culture, but by attacking the adherents of that culture for failing to uphold their own declared standards, for failing to extend them to all, as opposed to a small fraction of humanity. Toussaint L'Ouverture is the perfect example of a downtrodden slave whose struggle to free himself and his people was informed by the ideas of Rousseau and Mirabeau. (Said 1991: 31)

The democratic humanism that could be deduced from this impasse was, according to Said, equally at odds with, on one side, the conservative defence of a disinterested, elite humanism proposed by civilizationist culture warriors, and on the other the empty radicalism favoured by their foes: the apostles of a formulaic 'multiculturalism' that abjured the question of value – aesthetic and cultural – in favour of identitarian logic and ethnic absolutism fixated on interpersonal relations and framed by an intractable commitment to groupness. When those straw figures of multiculturalism and political correctness are invoked as a bogey, particularly by critics on the left, it can be difficult to know exactly what the speaker has in mind. In Said's case, the summoning of those spectres seems to be more than a device to make his own position immediately identifiable with a central course between unsatisfactory extremes. It is also a way to highlight what he thought of as the theological residues pending in the reduction of modern intellectuals to the status of clerics employed to organize the comforting rituals of absolute identity that complicate his distinctive use of the word secular (Said 1983: 292).

Said described his opposition to those options in a short Raritan essay on 'The Politics of Knowledge' where his perplexity at the symbiosis established between different sorts of critics emerged as a frame for his own choices and he voiced his critique of the limited approaches to the epistemology of imperialism that aspired not only to deconsecrate Eurocentrism but to replace it with Afrocentric or Islamocentric approaches. Those perspectives also stand accused of the crime of glorying in marginality and homelessness (Said 1991: 17–31). This is an odd charge with which to cement the dismissal of political correctness particularly given Said's own repeated account of himself as, in effect, a rootless cosmopolitan whose heroic, interpretative positioning as a critical, militant intellectual was not only exilic but reliant upon itinerancy and a principled refusal to hold any ground whatsoever: 'I don't own any real estate. The flat I live in is rented. I see myself as a wanderer. My position is that of a traveler, who is not interested in holding territory, who has no realm to protect' (Viswanathan 2001: 457). The advantages of peregrination aside, the variety of humanism he favours can be shown to enjoy a distinctive relationship with two other important formations. The first is the history of modernism while the second is the development and appreciation of certain kinds of musical creation which, by being implacably at odds with the historical circumstances in which they appear, require from us a distinctive critical orientation.

Said's intellectual and literary engagements with Conrad and, above all, Adorno mediate these problems. The German setting of the latter's work constitutes another important general connection with the effects of ultranationalist and imperialist politics of the twentieth century and to the dialectic of enlightenment that becomes unavoidable through the rational irrationality of the Third Reich even though it has a much longer colonial history. The racial elements in that worldly narrative are absolutely crucial. However muted they sometimes become in Said's own work, thanks, in particular, to his deployment of Fanon's insights, they provide a licence to roam into the dangerous territory that his advocacy of a novel humanism requires him to occupy. The fruits of that bold positioning were evident in the optimistic pages of *The Question of Palestine* where Said proposed a reconciliation between Israelis and Palestinians based upon a 'human rights view of their common situation as opposed to a strictly national perspective upon it' (Said 1992: 52).

The meaning of that 'human rights view' had been transformed three decades later and Said's more detailed, late account of his humanism goes to some lengths to make clear that it was not tailored to the contours of the sovereign subject that defined the bourgeoisie in its emergent phase. That figure eventually found its historic counterpart in liberal political theory animated by the thought experiments which had been conducted in imagined colonial environments: the America of Locke, the Caribbean of Rousseau and Voltaire, and of course, Robinson Crusoe's tropical island. Said's ambitious counter-anthropology notes the historic epiphany of that violent subject and grasps the full significance of its religious and racial shadows but, in refusing dualistic styles of thought, this revised humanism cannot be content with simply reversing the unacceptable polarity of European domination. Instead, drawing upon resources that descend from ancient sources via a distinctive, 'rescuing' reading of Europe's enlightenment – again centred on the contributions of the autodidact Vico – it seeks to precipitate a new set of habits outside of any Manichaean code.

After 1945, the obligation to explore the forbidden zones of humanism had been endorsed by seeing the problem of the human in the light of industrialized genocide warranted by racism and, as Césaire's post-Second World War writing had insisted, as a transplanted colonial *and* post-colonial phenomenon.

Said's account of the formation and character of his humanist disposition is most fully sketched out in *Humanism and Democratic Criticism* (2004). There, setting out the parameters of his final intervention, he cautiously accounts for the emergence of academic anti-humanism and provides an explanation of its particular appeal in the context of North American university life. It should be understood, first of all, as part of a generational response to the war in Vietnam, and, secondly, as a symptom of the impact of identity-centred social movements upon the wilfully innocent habits of the academic humanities in 'the West'. Thus an avowedly radical kind of anti-humanism emerged not as a clever rhetorical strategy for slyly engendering its opposite but as an unthought common sense tailored specifically to the multicultural exigencies of US campus life. I hope it is not reckless to suggest that this tendency, augmented by bastardized Lukácsian episte-mology and bolstered further by the ethnic absolutism espoused by 'identity politics', has proved to be an enduring voice. It remains intact even now inside the clamour for intersectional sensibilities that has allowed sover-eignty over experience to remain within the grasp of those who can police it most effectively – usually on the Internet where social networks and the clusters they create are so regularly misrecognized as political movements. The power and radical credentials of this perspective are only gradually being queried. Mostly that has been done by polite voices delivered either from the global South or from far outside the citadels of overdevelopment (Ahmad 2006). However, we should not overlook the clamour from inside the fortifications made by those who act in solidarity with Southern struggles or have been working towards new kinds of humanism. These attempts have sometimes been based upon indigenous cosmologies. Many of them have been prepared to articulate themselves in response to the democratic claims of feminism as well as to answer the technological revolutions in warfare and warcraft that have attended the inauguration of the great global counterinsurgency and what Said, writing after September 11, 2001, memorably called 'the clash of ignorance' (Said 2001).

I've said that Fanon, to whose political geography we are being returned by recent events in North Africa, plays an especially important role in consol-idating Said's humanism. The broadly-defined Pan-African movement, in which the Martiniquean psychiatrist stands, represents the paradigm of post-colonial politics in the twentieth century. He spoke for many of his peers in that endeavour when he concluded that the new humanism they sought was not only possible but desirable for Europe as well as for the continuing struggles against epidermalization, racial-corporeal schemata and various structures of colonial domination. The problem of humanism had become directly relevant to his critique of nationalism and his view of militant, revolutionary struggle in securing the psychological and cultural transformations required by liberation from the colonial yoke.

Among the most accessible and important writings that assist in assessing the vitality and trajectory of this subaltern variety of humanist thinking were provided by the Trinidadian revolutionaries C. L. R. James and George Padmore. James's path-breaking study of the Haitian revolution had, as a subtext, a great deal to say about the functioning of political movements and the character of insurrectionary leadership. His schoolmate Padmore is a much less celebrated figure and had a longer and deeper, though certainly critical, association with the orthodox communism of the Soviet Union. Like many of their political generation, both men invested a great deal of hope in the opportunities for change that commenced with the establishment of an independent Ghana under the leadership of Kwame Nkrumah (Hooker 1967). That newly independent state would constitute the institutional hub of a Pan-African movement which could provide a political alternative not just to the polarized options of the Cold War phase, but to the oversimple opposition between tradition and modernity. Padmore's essential survey of their conjuncture, Pan-Africanism or Communism, took its epigraph from Rabindranath Tagore and concludes thus:

> In our struggle for national freedom, human dignity and social redemption, Pan-Africanism offers an ideological alternative to Communism on one side and Tribalism on the other. It rejects both white racialism and black chauvinism. It stands for racial co-existence on the basis of absolute equality and respect for human personality. (Padmore 1956: 379)

The humanistic tone conspicuously evident there represents more than just a faint echo from the influential rhetoric of the United Nations declaration on human rights which would be taken up later by anti-colonial groups like the Rastafari in their pursuit of equality and justice. It is an effect of the commitment to struggle explicitly against racism, race-thinking and racialized hierarchy. Similarly universalistic language was a feature of the writing of many others who foregrounded those battles. It is clear that this disposition links Said not only to Fanon but also to Césaire, Léopold Sédar Senghor and Amilcar Cabral as well as to a host of more ephemeral anti-colonial sources. Their sometimes lofty, sometimes eschatological but always doggedly non-racial humanisms are extremely significant, though they are now likely to be regarded as too crude: an embarrassment to the more abstract, sophisticated and scholastic contemporary versions of post-colonial theory.

The central point is that all these humanistic speculations bear a precise, negative imprint of racial systems of thought and power. The specific commitment to overthrow racism and ethnic absolutism endows in them a distinctive quality which is not shared by state-centred, top-down, anti-racist universalism of the basic UNESCO variety, even when their respective rhetorics seem to overlap. The same unruly tone is audible in the post-colonial writing of figures like Nelson Mandela, Albert Memmi and, above all, Said's close friend and interlocutor, the Pakistani, Eqbal Ahmad. Their contributions to the emancipation of former colonies and the consolidation of independent political life were bolstered by a common desire. They wanted to elevate the struggles of colonized people to a universal level while simultaneously holding on to the historical and cultural specificity of the particular groups involved – an approach pioneered, at least as far as political theory is concerned, by Senghor, who, interestingly, credited the influence of African American writing on these topics in his own development (Sénghor 1964: 84–6).

These difficult commitments were especially pronounced among those who had served in the European armies and resistance movements during the struggle against Fascism and who tried, as a result of their experience in combat, to adapt the ethical and political analyses of evil, racism and democracy found there to the different cause represented by decolonization.

The insights bequeathed by this group of thinkers, particularly by Jean-Paul Sartre, Fanon and Senghor, were decisive in generating a distinctive voice for post-colonial theory after the creation of the United Nations. Sartre built upon Richard Wright's view of the Negro as 'America's Metaphor' and Simone de Beauvoir's parallel sense of woman as a social rather than a natural entity, to create a more general and historical theory of racial ontologies. For all of them, the infrahuman objects of racial hatred were generated by the dominant group. The dominated were, as Fanon would show, victims of colonialism's racial hierarchy. Unable to enjoy the more authentic modes of being in the world that could develop an account of their racial difference with reference to the future, they were condemned to live out an 'amputated' humanity within the restricted categories afforded by the nomos of epidermalized social life (Fanon 1986: 84). For these thinkers, there were strong historical and political connections between the genocidal racism of the Nazis and the racisms securing colonial rule in Indo-China and Algeria where Nelson Mandela and other South Africans had gone to undertake military training.

Césaire had confronted these issues in his 1955 *Discourse On Colonialism*. He was one of the first theorists of post-colonial social and political order to argue for an interpretation of the industrial killing of Europe's Jews and other minorities as an amplified and relocated instance of the routine brutality of colonial government. This genocidal style of political administration had, he suggested, looped back into the core of European civilization from the colonial killing zones. As a result, he argued, for the European bourgeois class, Hitler's unforgivable crime was not a crime against man as such, but rather

> the crime against the white man, and the fact that he applied to Europe colonialist procedures which until then had been reserved exclusively for the Arabs of Algeria, the Coolies of India, and the blacks of Africa. (Césaire 1972)

There are now many versions of this chilling proposition. It has received support from historians of the concentration camp – a political technology that emerged from colonial wars – as well as from some of the survivors of the Third Reich. Today, post-colonial theory mobilizes all these seemingly discrepant historical and ethical resources and places them in a challenging dialogue. Primo Levi wrote about the components of the racialized terror he knew in ways that were not prescriptive and invited thoughtful comparison across historical and cultural distances without being drawn into a competition over the relative dimensions of different histories of suffering. Most notably, in his theoritcally rich discussion of the experience of being an intellectual in an Auschwitz lager, Levi's fellow inmate, the Austrian phenomenologist and philosopher Jean Améry, identified Fanon's work on violence as one place where he had been able to find an analysis that could help restore physical and metaphysical dignity to the damaged body and being of the tortured prisoner (Améry 1980: 91).

These connections had been fostered because, after 1945, the evolution of post-colonial theory took place in a special atmosphere shaped by widespread condemnation of the Third Reich not merely as evil incarnate but as a racial regime. To understand the development of Said's work, we must appreciate that the political analyses that resulted can be triangulated by several interrelated political developments tied to the decomposition of the British Empire. The cataclysm of 1948 saw the partition of India, the institution of Apartheid in South Africa and the reparative establishment of the state of Israel in Palestine as well as the state of Pakistan (Devji 2013).

Edward Said's work of critique and exposition represents the moment in which the history of Palestine entered fully into this larger conversation and took its place after the moral and political conflicts opened up the struggle against Apartheid. Said does not always seem to have found the comparison of Israel and South Africa very helpful (Said 2001: 450–1), but in a 1984 essay 'Pioneering in the Nuclear Age' his collaborator, Eqbal Ahmad, drew attention to the geopolitical potency then still bound up with the Palestinian cause. Circumstances today are somewhat different but there is still a significant store of moral and political authority associated with

> a people's quest for a home, the right to live outside refugee camps free from the daily terror of settlers and soldiers; of the persistence of a people's inalienable claim to dignity, equality and self-determination … the Palestinian experience like the South African affects a majority of mankind at a deeper, more primordial level. Our painful colonial past, neo colonial present, and the dangerous perspective for our future converge on the question of Palestine. (Ahmad 1984: 301)

Like his interlocutors in the development of post-colonial analysis, Said's views of politics and culture, their relationship and their necessary differentiation had been enriched by formative experiences of migration and exile, cultural plurality and hierarchy, as well as by the everyday complexities of social life under race-conscious, post-colonial rules. His work exemplifies the way in which the immediate progenitors and earliest practitioners of self-consciously post-colonial thought have in different ways promoted a refined sense of culture as a political and para-political field, creating a broad critical enterprise that has, at its best, spanned academic and political concerns.

That dialogue, oriented by *Orientalism*, was often lodged, with varying degrees of discomfort, in US institutions of higher education. Its intellectual energy was directed towards analysing some especially difficult problems: the residual potency of colonial arrangements in constraining nominally independent states, the specific power of racism which tied colonial history to the lives of immigrant/settlers and deformed the polities of nations that had benefited from a colonial phase, the difficulties which the ex-colonies discovered in the process of forming new governmental arrangements undamaged by their histories of brutal rule, and so on. Thanks to Said's efforts, the problem of Palestine became increasingly prominent in all these deliberations.

Opposition, first to the wars in Algeria and Vietnam and then to South Africa's undeniably racialized government, dominated post-colonial theory during the period of its emergence. In particular, South Africa became the object of an unprecedented international movement of resistance in which the campaigns for disinvestment and a sporting boycott were notable. The one country in which the political force of racial hierarchy could not be disputed supplied a moral and methodological test to all would-be analysts of the distinctive patterns of statecraft found in post- and neo-colonial regimes (Fanon 1965: 29).

The interventionist projects pioneered by the migrant thinkers that followed on from the generation of political leaders dominated by Second World War combatants laid foundations for their ever more scholastically inclined successors, many of whom were interested in understanding the post-colonial articulation of culture and politics through rapidly-expanding global circuitry while not being actively committed to the profane political causes of the national liberation movements involved.

Following the publication of *Orientalism* in 1978, attention to the historical, cultural and philosophical formations that had produced the Orient as an object of knowledge and power began to generate an expanded sense of the imperial and colonial politics of race and ethnicity. This was augmented by the history of immigration into the old imperial heartlands by formerly colonial peoples and by their own, unruly interpretations of their political fate and duty in circumstances where having access to formal citizenship did not mean either that equality could be taken for granted or that complacent democracy would be capable of setting aside its historic associations with *cultural* racism. This was the stage in which post-colonial analysis began to be consciously undertaken from literary and historical, if not yet social scientific, perspectives.

Said reconsidered some of the foundational issues associated with the significance of race in his autumnal *Freud and the Non-European*. Without giving much ground to psychoanalysis as a system, he used aspects of its history to underscore the impossible pursuit of purity and the ironies that flow from the mythic founding of political communities by aliens and foreigners (Honig 2001). His luminous exploration of the limits of sameness suggested fruitful directions for 'a secular intellectual tradition that sees in unafraid and unapologetic critique the path to human freedom' (Said 2000). That noble aspiration provides a thread running through the wonderful book of interviews with Said, edited by Gauri Viswanathan (2001). The volume concludes monumentally with a paragraph in which Said provocatively identified himself as 'the last Jewish intellectual ...

a Jewish Palestinian'. Perhaps with this conclusive, irony-laden joke in mind as a supplement to Isaac Deutscher's arguments which had meant so much to him, Said conjured up the possibility of imagining 'paradoxi-cally a non-humanistic humanist, someone given neither to piety nor to tiresome and inconsequential word-spinning'. His abiding commitment to that evasive, heroic possibility now corresponds to a number of new issues. Considered after the end of natural evolution, in the era of genomics and in the face of irreversible climate change that will enforce its own regime of social and economic differences beyond the institutional and imaginative grasp of national states, it prompts the possibility that his Adornian concept of 'lateness' might somehow be extended beyond the arc of individual creative lives and pressed artfully into an account of our diverse cultural habits as a species that differs from itself. That precious insight might then contribute not merely to what has been termed a re-enchantment of the human by rendering aesthetic service as a critical apparatus, but also to a morbid relocation or restaging of our always vulnerable humanity in the waiting room of death, that is in relation to the horizon of our omnipresent but disavowed mortality. There is an obvious echo of Giacomo Leopardi's cosmic, materialist pessimism in this stubbornly secular prospect and it is that horizon, rather than the history of the concept of extinction so deftly eviscerated by Sven Lindqvist, that holds the most promising possibilities for the future of the humanities (Lindqvist 1996: 101–33).

It seems to me that Said used citations from the poetry of W. B. Yeats repeatedly to specify this very option. Whatever Freud may have contributed to understanding the upper floors of the structure of our ontology cum sociogeny, Said is now focused tenaciously upon the non-negotiable predic-ament of human being in the body. He calls it, following Yeats's poem 'The Magi', 'the bestial floor'. This is not for him the bedrock of something like bare life which would be instantly recognizable from this perspective as Agamben's eccentric alternative account of the ways that racial orders have functioned over time. Wrenched out from any holy setting, Said employs Yeats's brief, challenging poem to anchor an unsettling decolonial commentary and to raise a confrontation with not only theology but all theologically-derived approaches to criticism centred upon what Lewis Gordon has referred to as the 'theodicy of the text'. The bestial floor is revealed to be a necessarily contested locus. It is neither the exclusive dwelling place of cattle nor the ground zero of Messianic incarnation. The territory Said invites us finally to join him in holding turns out to be a poeti-cally, heuristically and agonistically identified, universal space of human becoming. Yeats's words associate that difficult location with mystery. In Said's act of profanation, humanity thus reduced, presents an interpretative puzzle that assumes narrative shape and that cannot be allowed to remain under the monopoly of the sacred. Inquiries into the character of human being are not, after all, to be merely the transcoded puzzle of god incarnate.

The human can become bestial – to be a beast among other beasts is no doubt better than being an object among objects. Some posthumanists will doubtless discover a welcome measure of liberation in that very possibility. However, if we are to accept that the decolonization of the world was a primary historical event that still requires our time and attention, we have work to do. We must show, for example, how and why the reduction of human beings to the infrahuman condition that Du Bois associated with that of the 'tertium quid' – lodged but not lost between the animal and the human – matters again now in the age of human rights that Said defined through the trope of 'bewildering interdependence'. It would seem that time is also now the era of apparently endless war.

References

Ahmad, E. (1984), Available online at http://cup.columbia.edu/book/the-selected-writings-of-eqbal-ahmad/9780231127103

Ahmad, E. (2006), *The Selected Writings of Eqbal Ahmad*, Carollee Bengelsdorf, Margaret Cerullo, Yogesh Chandrani and Noam Chomsky (eds). New York: Columbia University Press.

Améry, J. (1980), *At the Mind's Limits*. London: Granta Books.

Bauman, Z. (1995), *Life in Fragments: Essays in Postmodern Morality*. Oxford: Blackwell.

Césaire, A. (1972), *Discourse on Colonialism*, J. Pinkham (trans.). New York: Monthly Review Press.

Devji, F. (2013), *Muslim Zion: Pakistan as a Political Idea*. London: Hurst.

Eagleton, T. (1976), *Criticism and Ideology*. London: Verso.

Fanon, F. (1965), *A Dying Colonialism*, H. Chavalier (trans). New York: Grove Press.

Fanon, F. (1986), *Black Skin, White Masks*. London: Pluto Press.

Freud, S. (1957), 'Thoughts for the Times on War and Death', Part 1, 'The Disillusionment of the War'. In *The Standard Edition of the Complete Psychological Works*, trans. and ed. James Strachey, vol. 14, 1914–16. London: The Hogarth Press, 279–80.

Honig, B. (2001), *Democracy and the Foreigner*. Princeton: Princeton University Press.

Hooker, J. R. (1967), *Black Revolutionary: George Padmore's Path from Communism to Pan-Africanism*. London: Pall Mall.

Lindqvist, S. (1996), 'Exterminate All The Brutes'. In J. Tate (trans.), *One Man's Odyssey into the Heart of Darkness and the Origins of European Genocide*. New York: The New Press.

Padmore, G. (1956), *Pan-Africanism or Communism?*. London: Denis Dobson.

Said, E. (1979), *Orientalism*. London: Penguin.

Said, E. (1983), *The World, The Text and The Critic*. London: Faber.

Said, E. (1991), 'The Politics of Knowledge', *Raritan* 11.

Said, E. (1992), *The Question of Palestine*. London: Vintage Books.

Said, E. (1994), *Culture and Imperialism*. London: Chatto and Windus.

Said, E. (2000), 'Heroism and Humanism', MLA presidential address. *PMLA* 115 (3): 28–291.

Said, E. (2001), 'The Clash of Ignorance', *The Nation*, 4 October.

Said, E. (2004), *Humanism And Democratic Criticism*. New York: Columbia University Press.

Senghor, L. (1976), 'Edward Wilmot Blyden Precursor of Négritude'. In H. R. Lynch (ed.), *Selected Letters of Edward Wilmot Blyden*, xix. Millwood, NJ: Kraus Thomson International Press.

Viswanathan, G. (ed.) (2001), *Power, Politics, and Culture. Interviews with Edward W. Said*. New York: Vintage Books.

CHAPTER SIX

The Political Enlightenment: A View from the South

Akeel Bilgrami

Edward Said's most celebrated work (*Orientalism*, 1978) is known for its exposure of the distortions in the West's (now more usually called the North's) understanding of distant lands that were once called 'the Orient' (and are now more often called 'the South'), a distortion that comes from refusing to acknowledge the privilege of the metropolitan location from which that understanding is articulated, a privilege derived not from intrinsic qualitative sources but rather by the brute as well as the commercial force of imperial conquest and its accompanying posture of a cultural superiority. This broad exposure was extended by him to the distortions of the *self*-understanding in those distant lands induced by the cognitive enslavement of the colonized mind and its acquired mimicry of its masters.

This remarkable and by now utterly familiar critique of what the cultures and ideas of the South looked like from the perspective of the metropolitan North made it possible for others to ask a question that even the long histories of resistance that led to decolonization were not, just by themselves, able to give one the confidence to ask – the question: what do the ideas of the metropole look like from the perspective of the South? Not the metropole's ideas of the Orient or the South, but just simply the ideas of the metropole in its *own evolving self-understanding*. How do these appear from the perspective of the South? And not how do these appear from the perspective of the South that has been cognitively shaped by the metropole, but rather from the point of view of the traditions of thought and culture in the South that remained relatively uncontaminated by that shaping.

I want to now briefly pursue that question, at least to the extent that it is possible, in terms that are entirely earnest and without irony, resisting the pressures to think at the outset that there can be no perspective of the South on metropolitan ideas any longer that has not itself been formed by the metropole. If there is any such inevitable forming of it, even in what I in this exercise am trying to do, I want that to be presented not *ex ante*, before the deliverances of the exercise, but at its end, in assessing its intellectual outcomes. Those outcomes, though I will present them initially as what things look like from a distant perspective of once colonized lands, will turn out to have deep affinities with *dissenting* voices in the intellectual history of the metropole itself, voices which, however eloquent and powerful once, *lost out* in that intellectual history.

If, as I suspect, the very fact that they lost out will give the impression that my efforts here are naïve to those who are perpetually and alertly poised to find in every intellectual exercise of this kind the pitfalls of nostalgia, there is nothing to do but to acknowledge that that might be so and proceed. The project that many pursue which seeks formulations of what has come to be called 'alternative modernities' would be silenced if one were to be inhibited from so proceeding by such up-to-the-minute form of sneering about nostalgia. Of course, ignoring this sort of complacent sneering does not mean that in the project of seeking these alternative formulations one ignores just how defective the traditions of the South may be (for example, in some of their 'feudal' aspects, to use a vastly summarizing term on which we have all been brought up), or how admirable certain dissenting voices in the West had been and are to this day. Even within the weight and preponderance of one's sense of critique of metropolitan privilege, it is an obligation of no small counterweight to be selective in what one repudiates from the frameworks of the North, and what one invokes from within the perspective of the South. So long as the criteria by which one is selective are not arbitrary and are theoretically and politically well-motivated, there is no reason to be stopped by anxieties that the alternative formulations of modernity that they yield will seem to some to be out of step with what is possible for one's time, defined as that is upon the modernity that we are already landed with. One might take comfort in the fact that creative efforts of the Renaissance were likely accused of something like a nostalgia for a classical period by some of the more complacent scholastic orthodoxies of the mediaeval period.

What follows, then, braids what I have called the perspective of the South with the dissenting critiques in the intellectual history of the North.

A good place to begin, it would seem, would be to look, from the perspective of the South, at the most central political ideals that define the modern period of the North, the ideals of liberty and equality. How do these seem from such a conceptual distance, a distance at which those ideals have never really had a distinct centrality, at any rate not in these explicit terms? The first thing that would come into view I think is a bizarre development. Virtually as soon as these ideals were first articulated, they began to be elaborated in theoretical and methodological developments in such a way that they were chronically (and acutely) at odds with one another. Why, one would ask, if one was not oneself in the midst of the outlook, does an outlook, describing itself in such self-congratulatory terms as 'The Enlightenment', declare and (rightly) cherish two remarkable ideals and yet immediately come to understand them so that they are in a sort of zero sum tension with one another, such that increasing one seems always to be accompanied by the necessity to decrease the other. A distant observer would notice this peculiar phenomenon entrenched and everywhere in the philosophical and political arguments, with the rhetoric of cold war disputation as only a very late and very crude manifestation of the tension that has existed between these two ideals for well over two and half centuries.

So, I repeat: why should a tradition of political thought theoretically frame its two chief ideals in such a way that they are pitted against each other? That is a question which cannot possibly get an answer that leaves out the much larger context of the sort of political economy that had developed in Europe and the effect it had on political thinking in and since the Enlightenment. I cannot pursue that context and its effect in a brief chapter, the main theme of which lies elsewhere. I cannot, in fact, do much more than mention one or two features of the political theorizing that produce this tension between its two ideals and convey how – given the deep roots that these features have taken in our sensibility and our practice – we have come to see it as virtually impossible to question these features without seeming to be pursuing quite unintuitive or outdated lines of thought.

One feature is too well-known and well-mined to bear much more than the most minimal mention, and that is the linking of the notion of property to a notion of the personal liberty which its ownership bestows on one, a liberty that is carried in a 'right' and therefore enshrined in the law of the land. How the possession of private property, when seen in these terms of liberty, undermines equality in the economic sphere (and therefore in other spheres) has been the subject of extensive commentary; and Marx was, of course, only its most famous and most powerful critic. Less explicitly theorized is another feature, which I will call the 'incentivization of talent'. It seems to us the most natural thing in the world to think that someone's talent should be acknowledged as *hers* and that it is s*he* who should be praised and rewarded for it. We think it a failure to respect someone's individuality to fail to do so. Take any example of a poem or a scientific discovery or a fine test century ... We praise individuals for such things and other such products of individual talent and expect them to be rewarded, whether it is a poet or a scientist or a batsman or ... We don't simply admire the zeitgeist for such productions, we admire the particular individuals and we think the rewards they get for it are deserved. Notions such as 'dessert' thus are also linked to one right possessed by individuals. This is so deeply entrenched in our thinking that it is likely to be considered an hysterical egalitarian ideologue's artifice to deny it. Denying it seems to fly in the face of our intuitive understanding of what it is to be an *individual* (rather than just a symptom of the zeitgeist in embodied human form), it violates what we conceive to be the *liberty* of an individual to reap the rewards of the exercise and efforts of his talents, not to mention the liberty of *others to enjoy* the productions of these efforts at their most excellent because they are *incentivized* in these ways to be as excellent as they can be. But, like the liberty attaching to possession of property, this way of thinking of liberty as attaching to talent also promotes social and economic inequality. This feature is less structurally central to our culture than the liberty that is tied to property, but it perhaps goes even deeper psychologically and the dichotomy it generates with equality is, therefore, more subtly troubling; and it seems just as impossible to overcome.

I mentioned these two sources of the tension only to give a completely familiar sense of how far such thinking has gone into our sensibility, how entrenched it is in the very way we deploy these terms, and how, therefore, it would seem almost to change the semantics of the terms if we were to think that the tension could be removed or resolved. That is to say, if we managed *per impossibile* to see them as not being in tension, it would only be because, as Thomas Kuhn might have put it, we have changed the *meanings* of the terms 'liberty' and 'equality', not because we have produced an improved theory or politics *within* the framework of the Enlightenment. Within that framework things are, on this score, unimprovable. In other words, what I mean by framework here is perhaps one of the (diverse) things that Kuhn meant by his term 'paradigm' (Kuhn 1962) and, if so, clearly we need to shift to another framework if we are ever going to remove the tension between these two notions. In such a new framework, neither 'liberty' nor 'equality' would *mean* what they mean in the framework of Enlightenment thought, no more than 'mass' in Einstein's physics meant what it meant in Newtonian mechanics, if Kuhn is right.

How might such a shift in framework be sought? To do so directly, by brutely re-defining the terms or announcing a new term (Balibar's neologism 'equaliberty' (2014), for instance) might come off more as a valiant act of semantic stipulation. But the worry is that it may be an act in vain. This sort of wilful dictation of nomenclature seldom works, except perhaps in purely classificatory exercises, which do not pretend to theory. To say, 'From now on, I will use the word "..." as follows ...' with a view to presenting an alternative theory, is to place the cart ahead of the horse. *Discourse* about human concerns should be posterior to a natural outgrowth of a prior *conceptual* understanding; it cannot by itself declare new forms of understanding into existence. What makes language so central to our human concerns is not that it can in itself dictate how we think but that it is the repository of how we think and how we have thought. So new frameworks for thought must be constructed first and this may then have the effect of revising the meanings of terms by situating them in a new conceptual framework.

In keeping with this obvious suggestion, here is how I have allowed myself to think of it. There is no improving our understanding of these notions of liberty and equality – as they stand – so as to resolve the tension between them. So let's as a start usher them off stage entirely. If this is to disinherit the entire tradition of liberal thought of the Enlightenment, so be it. Once these are exeunt, we need to replace them on centre stage with a third, more primitive, concept; that is to say, a concept more fundamental to our social and political life than even liberty and equality. And this is to be done with the idea that 'liberty' and 'equality' may *subsequently* be introduced once again – by the back door, as it were – but now merely as necessary conditions for the achievement of this more basic ideal that occupies the central position. So re-introduced, there is reason to think that these terms may have undergone substantial revision in their meaning, and thus may not any longer express concepts that are at odds with one another.

We need, then, to fasten on an appropriately more fundamental concept. To be more fundamental than concepts such as liberty and equality which have been so central to our theoretical understanding of politics, it would have to track something not necessarily older and more traditional in our political understanding so much as something that speaks more immediately to our experience and our ordinary lives. And here, if we continue to keep firmly in mind that we are engaged in an exercise finding a view from the South that has not been wholly dominated by the metropolitan frameworks, the folk and spiritual and popular traditions of the South outside the orbits of that framework, the concept and ideal that is most naturally on offer is the concept of an *'unalienated* life'. And I think that the perspective of several traditions of the South from which it might seem as if the ideal of an unalienated life could be extracted as the most fundamental goal of politics would find deep affinities in a long tradition of dissent in the North, dissent from its own orthodox and dominant framework – starting with the early prescient radical sects of the English revolution well before the Enlightenment, and a whole range of subsequent scientific dissenters against the wilful exploitation of science for profitable gain, through some canonical romantics, and then Ruskin, Morris, Thoreau, the so-called 'early' Marx, all the way down to Heidegger and to Horkheimer and Adorno. I will not spell out the affinities between them and the Southern perspective, but instead let me just try and put an *analytical framework* on what the *sources* of alienation appear to be from this perspective, with a view to approaching some broad conclusion about what the notion of an *un*alienated life would then be seeking to address.

From the popular rather than the elite and imitative traditions of the South, it would seem that something like the following very general question might be initially fruitful in expressing their puzzlement about what they see from such a distance: *How, and when,* they might ask, *did it come to pass in a whole dominant part of the globe that the 'world' came to be seen not merely as a place to live in but a place to master and control?* This question gives a very primitive and premonitional sense of the sources of alienation but, posed in just these terms, it is so omnibus that it is hard to know how to go about addressing it. At this level of generality perhaps all one can do is to see what sort of issue is being raised in raising it. Thus consider a development in high philosophy from within which the genealogical dimension of the question's point comes more into focus. The South's more philosophical observers would notice, for instance, that in the North philosophers have for some 2,000 years recurringly raised in epistemology sceptical questions about our knowledge of the external world. But sometime in the seventeenth century, primarily in the hands of Descartes, a new conclusion was drawn: if one can doubt our knowledge of the external world, quite possibly the external world *does not exist*. No sceptic in the tradition ever drew this conclusion till Descartes. The Ancients who formulated sceptical doctrines never concluded that the world may not exist from their assertion that there was no knowledge of it. Why not? Because they did not assume that the only way to relate to the world was via knowledge. They took it for granted that if one were to doubt the possibilities of knowledge that would do nothing wholesale to undermine the more ordinary relation we bear to it, of merely *living in it*. It was Descartes's innovation, one that expressed a transformation in his time whose legacy is that of an increasing detachment of outlook towards the world we live in, elevating the idea of living in it *itself* into some highly cognitively mediated relation that *underlies* the mastery and control we are trying to genealogically diagnose.

But much more breakdown of the question is needed if we are to go beyond this generality to some more detailed analysis. Bringing in broader observational perspectives from the South than purely philosophical ones, four further breakdown questions might help to make more vivid the sources of the alienation. They are:

> How and when did they transform the concept of *nature* into the concept of *natural resources*?
> How and when did they transform the concept of *human beings* into the concept of *citizens*?
> How and when did they transform the concept of *people* into the concept of *populations*?
> How and when did they transform the concept of *knowledges to live by* into the concept of *expertise to rule by*?

And the reason why each of these questions – which you will recognize as echoing at a more specific and tractable register the more general question – hints at an underlying source of alienation is that each of them tries to genealogically uncover an increasing detachment or disengagement in the way one approaches its chief subject, whether it be nature or humanity or knowledge.

In a brief paper, I am going to speak only, and that too very briefly, to the first two of these four questions, before concluding with some very rudimentary remarks indeed about what an ideal of an unalienated life that seeks to overcome these two sources of alienation might in its most crude and sloganized form look like from the traditional perspective of the South.

Within the outlooks of that traditional perspective, nature was not equated with natural resources almost always because the tradition took nature to be *sacralized*, a built-in constraint against seeing it as a mere resource, even if one lived on and by it, and this is just how much of *popular* Christianity conceived of nature in the Early Modern period in Europe (sometimes this was described as a modified neo-Platonism in popular Christianity by intellectual historians). Thus, for instance, the radical puritan sect, the Diggers, among several others in England, resisted the system of enclosures because it was transforming something sacred, something to live in, to make a life in and to respect, into a resource and a site for an early form of agri-*business*. Not the new science itself, but the *outlook* that was emerging around the new science of that period was precisely keen to undermine these sacralized conceptions so as to remove all conceptual obstacles to predatory commercial extraction from nature, and the mandarins of the Royal Society in England and its counterparts somewhat later in the Netherlands and then the rest of Europe were aligning themselves with commercial interests and with *High* Christianity (in England this was the established Anglican orthodoxy which opposed the 'neo-Platonism' of the popular Christianity of the radical sects as dangerous 'enthusiasm') to make this possible. These are the developments that, if one were to see them as alien to the perspective of the South, one would find that perception anticipated pervasively among the *dissenters* of the late seventeenth century and early eighteenth century in Europe who fought against such a desacralization of nature. These dissenters appealed to the neo-Platonism of the earlier radical sects as a form of resistance to the emerging outlook wrought by the new science that was (with the alliances it had formed with commercial interests) transforming the local, egalitarian, collective agrarian life – the transformation of merely *living* in nature to its mastery and control for large-scale profit and gain; and these agricultural surpluses would, in turn, feed into the creation of large metropoles, further destroying the life of agrarian communities.

Much of this was consolidated in the systematic *political thought* of the North by a widely influential methodological development that posited a conjectural past in which contracts, social contracts, were said to have been generators of norms and principles to live by. Thus, for instance, in one dominant familiar strand of this contractarian tradition (going from John Locke to Robert Nozick – there are other strands that are not relevant to what I am presenting), we are told this: suppose that we start in the state of nature. And suppose that there are as yet no policies or laws to live by. Nor is there any sort of institution of property. Then suppose that some of us join and come up with an agreement with which we resolve to keep faith, an agreement about rules for the private appropriation of property out of the common. We agree that if someone comes upon a stretch of ground, fences it, and registers it with a primitive form of bureau that we also set up, then it becomes his or hers. And (this is the punchline) we then say to ourselves that this may be *only done if, by doing so, no other is made worse off than they hitherto were – and we elaborate this crucial proviso by saying in particular that, if one were to hire others at wages which enable them to live better, they would in fact be better off than they were in the state of nature.*

The underlying claim of these theoretical posits of a contract (in all versions and strands of it) is to show one thing: how come we are, as a result of the contract, better off than we were in a state of nature. In the strand that I am focusing on in particular, the assessment of political principles by such a conjunction of mutual advantage in aggregative ameliorative conditions, both for possessors of land and those who worked on it, becomes the cornerstone of the economic outlook of liberalism even through a later period of industrialization when industrial capital rather than land was at stake. In its historical context, what this contractarian notion consolidates and justifies is the system of enclosures, which, though it had begun fitfully a century earlier, had set in deeply and systematically in society only in Locke's time and led to the thoroughly predatory commercial attitudes towards nature and its bounty as well as to a very specific conception of governance and law to support them. The Lockean social contract, as a bit of political theory-construction, both *explains* these developments, while, in a carefully constructed *normative* façade, presents them as moral and political *achievements*. The entire doctrinal outcome of such a theorization appealing to a conjectural past is thus presented as having *both* an historical inevitability *and* a rational justification – with an appeal, therefore, on two quite different registers, the descriptive and the normative. The historical embedding of social contract theory is more fully revealed if we take a look at some of its arguments and assumptions via criticisms implicitly found in the range of dissenters and 'enthusiasts' I have mentioned above.

Let's return to the punchline of the familiar contractarian scenario. This is what I had said in the exposition: 'We agree that if someone comes upon a stretch of ground, fences it, and enters it into a register in a primitive form of bureau that we also set up, then it becomes his or hers. And (this is the punchline) we, then, say to ourselves that this may be *only done if, by doing so, no other is made worse off than they hitherto were – and we elaborate this crucial proviso by saying in particular that, if one were to hire others at wages which enable them to live better, they would in fact be better off than they were in the state of nature'.*

The radical critique of this imagined scenario would then go something like this. Such a contractual outcome as is expounded here has what might be called, what economists call, an 'opportunity cost'. What is that? An *avoided* benefit when you make a choice is counted as an opportunity *cost* of your having made that choice. This idea applies straightforwardly to our case. What the radical critique says is: Because the land is thus privatized we cannot set up a system for working the land in common and as a commons. *Thus, even though we agree that we are all better off than we* were *in the state of nature, it is still perfectly possible for us to say that we are worse off than we* **would have been** *had the private economy not been established.*

This is a simple and obvious enough counterfactual claim but it has a very significant and less than obvious theoretical result – it philosophically transforms the very notion of consent to something that is not even so much as recognizable from within the contractualist tradition. Consent, once this counterfactual is in place, should be viewed instead as a more complicated act than might otherwise seem in that tradition. It should be viewed as follows: whether someone can be said to have consented is not necessarily to be viewed as this contractualist tradition proposes but rather it may be a matter of what he or she **would** *choose in situations that do not obtain* – in which case the entire Locke-to-Nozick tradition of thought may be assuming or inferring that we have implicitly rationally consented to something which we in fact have not.

Such a revisionary understanding of the notion of consent can be understood as offering a counterfactual manoeuvre in order to *improve* upon the normative ideal that this tradition of contractualism offers, or if you find that a tendentious way of putting things, then, at the very least, to offer an *alternative* normative ideal. But really the point I am insisting on is that this entire line of criticism is, in any case, not just an idle theoretical counterfactual exercise at improving the normative ideal, because *history* gives considerable support to the counterfactual by recording a tremendously active and vocal dissenting tradition in the Early Modern period against these incipient liberal ideas about the economy and polity. Some of these dissenters – the early ones – were not targeting Locke, since they in fact pre-dated Locke. I include them even so because the counterfactual I have presented should not be thought of as an argument from anachronism. It is counter to fact as counterfactuals are, but the point is that it is not counter to all facts, it is counter only to facts which came to be because *others very much in the air* did not survive for reasons that need not by any means be described as having the force of rational necessity about them. Their failure to survive, far from being determined by rational force, was a matter of the success of particular worldly alliances that I mentioned, which were formed, consciously and unconsciously, at a particular period of time and which managed to silence a lively and systematic resistance to them by quite different dissenting ideas, a silencing that owed nothing to rational superiority but rather to the greater force of worldly organization of elite interests on the victorious side.

The dissenters – such as Winstanley and Walwyn, for instance, to name just two – gave serious elaboration of the ideas contained in the counterfactual I have proposed, ideas about precisely what might be possible for the economy and polity if one did work the land in common, and indeed not just theoretical elaboration but in the case of the sect known as the Diggers, even implementation, in local experiments thereby raising, at least briefly for a period of a dozen years in mid-seventeenth-century England, the possibility of preempting the entire trajectory of doctrines that Locke's theoretical construct of the social contract was intended to generate.

If I am right, then this counterfactual with its own historical instances detectable in the dissenting traditions of the time shows that the normative ideal found in the very idea of a 'social contract' are not only merely consolidating of the orthodox liberal doctrines that eventually won out, but it shows also first that the doctrines are (presented via the social contract) as having *a historical necessity and inevitability*, which, if the dissenting critique was right, they do not possess, and second (presented via the social contract's aspiration to a normative ideal) as possessing the right of a *rational* force and conviction, that they need never be granted as possessing.

I am keen to put on record an entire historical dissenting tradition in the Early Modern North so as to see how closely they are echoed in struggles in the contemporary South. Consider the following report from the *Kolkata Telegraph* (7 January 2012) of what Mr P. Chidambaram from his perch in the Indian cabinet had declared:

> Union home minister Chidambaram today called for a rejection of the *counterculture* against the use of natural wealth, pitching the development debate as a choice between museums and modern societies at a time several mining and power projects are held up because of protests. 'I don't think we should allow the counterculture to grow, a counterculture which says that people in these areas should live as they lived 300 or 400 years ago. We are not building museums here, we are building a modern society, a modern state,' Chidambaram told the inaugural session of the Northeast Business Summit here.

The purpose is clear. Those people who protest that the natural environment (and the people who 'live in' it and are sustained by it in the modest ways that allow it too to be sustained) was not a mere resource for 'development' had no future in what India is to become. An entire point of view and the people who propagate it are thus made inconsequential, a people without any place in a blueprint of the future as drawn up by 'experts' at a 'Business Summit', a people reduced to not mattering for where the North had gone and where India was to go. This is the ultimate form of detachment: to remove a people by the stroke of an ideological declaration from a position of corporate and governmental power, a form of rarified, cognitive (rather than bodily) genocide in the name of the forward march – or perhaps 'the end' – of history.

One might think: this is just to cite a minister with a mission of 'development', but why attribute this outlook to an accumulating wider elite sensibility as I have been doing rather than merely to the state that promotes such 'development' on the part of the corporations it serves. But there is plenty of evidence of the outlook's widespread elite subscription. Even one of the most humane of contemporary economists, Amartya Sen, has written against those who protested about the dispossession of agricultural land (for corporate 'development' projects) from those who worked on it, that England went through its pain to create its Manchesters and Londons, and India will have to do so as well. Such a claim, which appeals to an historical analogy, is remarkable for omitting the entire historical context about which it speaks, one which reveals Sen's analogy to be grossly imperfect. Those who were dispossessed from their land and way of life by the 'primitive accumulation' of an earlier period in England moved in great numbers across the Atlantic to America. There is no place for the dispossessed of, say, rural Bengal to go, except to the already glutted cities and their slums, creating heightened forms of urban immiseration.[1] When the mobility of labour had some sort of parity with the mobility of capital, remarks such as Sen's may have had a point. When there is complete disparity between them, with immigration laws on the one side constraining labour's mobility and the dismantling or re-mantling of the Bretton Woods institutions on the other side, releasing capital for far greater mobility than it ever had, Sen's remark comes off as being quite of a piece with Chidamabaram's remarks, and shows how entrenched the attitude is among the intelligentsia.

So far, in charting early sources of alienation, I have stressed the transformation of the concept of nature and its effects on generating ruthless, dispossessing forms of extractive *political economy*. But, as I had said earlier in posing the four deeply related questions from the Southern perspective, as well as from the dissenting point of view of the North, these issues of nature and political economy are inseparable from questions of political governance.

On the question of the transformation of human beings into citizens, the issues are ripe for misunderstanding, given what seem to be honourable commitments to many Enlightenment ideals, but let me present some aspects of these commitments as they might appear from a perspective from the South as it views their genealogy.

From this distance, it would seem that Europe, in the late seventeenth century, as a result of some of the changes already mentioned above, had come to find outdated its earlier forms of legitimation of the state which had appealed to the divine rights of the monarch who occupied it. It, therefore, had to seek new forms of justification for the state and the power it exercises. And (since the Westphalian Peace) it sought this justification by a quite different strategy, by looking to modern social psychology rather than to a God-given right of the tenant of an exalted office. The strategy was complex. The state was now to be seen as one half of an undecouplable conjunction with a new form of entity. This entity that came to be called the 'nation' could not sufficiently be defined in purely territorial terms and borders. If it was conceived merely territorially, it could only justify the state in terms of the power it needs to protect it from other such entities, but that would not justify the state's power and authority over its own 'population'. A further element was needed, then, a commitment drawn from the populace. Contractualist accounts were presumably relevant to this commitment too, basing themselves on a conjectural fiction about an originary past of a willed, conventional compact among human beings, an act by which they were transformed into citizens. But this was high theory. A yet further and far more crucial element would have to be less fictional and less hypothetical, more grounded in an actual political psychology that had to be generated in this emerging 'citizenry'. The populace had to be made to develop a *feeling* for this new kind of entity, the nation; and because the latter was understood as being inseparable from the state (the 'nation-state'), the feeling for the first half of this hyphenated conjunction would confer a justification upon the second half, which had no longer any independent significance except as part of this conjunction with the first, and which *because* of its conjunction with this abstracted ('imagined') entity took an increasingly *centralized* form unlike earlier forms of power which were relatively scattered. In due course, this psychology of feeling would come to be called 'national*ism*', understood in terms that were at odds with the traditional perspective of the South that I am stressing, which often sought to define nationalism as wholly synonymous with 'anti-imperialism' and emptied of these historical European connotations.

These points are so familiar that they might seem innocuous even when viewed from the South, until something equally familiar comes into view when one asks: *How* did post-Westphalian Europe go about generating this legitimating political psychology, this feeling to be instilled? All over that continent, it was done by a method whose notoriety only came to be fully understood by Europeans in the middle of the last century as a result of developments in Germany in the 1930s and 1940s, but which, if viewed from a sufficient distance as the South offers, will be seen to have much deeper historical roots. This was the method of finding an external enemy within the territory and the 'population' and despising them as the 'other' and subjugating 'them' (the Jews, the Irish, Protestants in predominantly Catholic countries, Catholics in predominantly Protestant countries ...) and thereby instigating a feeling among the rest of the population of a sense of privileged possession of this new entity, the nation, as 'ours'. Later, when numerical forms of discourse emerged and statistical methods in the social sciences were applied, categories such as 'majority' and 'minority' would be deployed to describe this, and such a method of generating a feeling for the nation and thereby legitimating state power would come to be called 'majoritarianism'. From the perspective of some parts of the South, one could only hope that this entire trajectory by which Europe came to be what it is, an assembly of modern 'nation-states', should not be imitated even as it fell into nationstatehood after decolonization. This was how 'citizenship' began in the North and it is to *repair* the ravages wrought by this method that the North had to adopt various civic measures and ideologies such as 'secular*ism*' (a political doctrine, something distinct from the larger social, cultural process of 'secularization'), and later 'multicul-turalism'. Where (and only where) such damage had *not* already occurred and become entrenched in the South, rather than adopt secularism in an act of pointless mimicry it would be better instead to disallow that damage to occur among its own people in the first place. My caveat (where and only where those conditions are entrenched) may be quite unnecessary by now in many parts of the world. Still, it would be a worthwhile scrutiny that establishes first where the conditions do exist, if one is not simply to indulge in the adoption of doctrines and policies that have no point and no local historical evolution.

Citizenship as it came to be consolidated in notions of rights and in constitutional codes, for all that is rightly celebrated as worthy in them, had other genealogical aspects too that one might only notice if one had a distant enough perspective as I am trying to seek from the South. This genealogy goes back to notions of civility that emerged in the same period in which I have been locating the fault line. There has been fine and detailed study of the rise of notions of civility in the work of such intellectual histo-rians as Norbert Elias (1969) and more recently Keith Thomas (1983) and Peter Burke (2000). In some of their descriptions one can gather a certain *semantics* that was essential to how the notion was characterized in this period. Civility, which consisted in a range of things from comportment to dress and speech, was said to be a property of the lifestyles of the monarch and his courts who were often said to rule over a brute populace by analogy with (indeed as a mundane version of) a distant and removed, an exiled, Newtonian God, a clock winder, controlling a now *desacralized* and brute and material and inert universe (Newton in his *Opticks* (1704/1998) had called nature and matter 'stupid'). And so, correspondingly, in this semantic stipulation, civility was contrasted with 'cruelty' which was the property of the lifestyles and behaviours of the rude populace. When I call this a semantics, I mean to suggest that this distribution of locations for civility and cruelty respectively had nothing to do with empirical concerns of evidence and observation. These were *stipulations* of how these words were to be used and internalized, independent of the *facts* of behaviour at either location. And the effect this usage had was remarkable, one of a deeply imbibed self-deception, a fact that the intellectual historians I mentioned do *not* register, though they are central to how the culture of liberal democracy would appear to a perspective from the South. The self-deceptive effect of the semantics was to create a screen that hid from the European monarchs and their courts the cruelty of their *own* perpetration on the brute populace, who alone were counted, by the semantics, as capable of cruelty.

And from the Southern view, in the modern West or North this screen of self-deception morphed over from the notion of civility into the more abstract domain of rights and constitutions and codes, whereby cruelty came to be understood by nations who possessed such rights and constitutions as only occurring in nations that do not possess them. Thus the cruelty perpetrated by the former on the distant lands of the latter was hidden from the perpetrators because cruelty can only really happen in lands without rights and constitutions – an attitude quite prevalent to this day, when it is still pervasively assumed that cruelty can only really happen, say, in Mugabe's Zimbabwe or Saddam's Iraq but not in the metropolitan West. There is, I believe, no understanding the phenomenon of Guantanamo without this self-deceptive function that rights have come to have, no matter how rightly celebrated rights are for the great good that they have done where they have been adopted. Torture of that sort cannot be located on American soil because 'we don't do torture', since cruelty only happens in other sorts of places. If the South in some of its traditions shows a studied indifference to rights and constitutions and the very idea of citizenship, it should not be because it repudiates the good that these may bring but because it is able to see these other aspects of it as emerging from these links with expert knowledges of codified rule whose self-deceptions had a genealogy in an earlier period of elite lifestyles and aspirations to civility.

Turning now, with all this observed as the genealogical sources of alienation in the North (and threatening now, as we just noted, to a vision of where the South should be headed), how might the promise of a shift in framework that I had proposed at the outset be sought, even in the broadest outline from within the resources of the South?

Let us observe first that in this Southern genealogy of the sources of alienation in the North, the fault line of the increasing detachment of outlook that sets us on its path is the desacralization of our conception of nature; and even if we cannot in the historical present of the North easily conceive of a return to sacralized nature to overcome this source of alienation, we nevertheless have a more *secular* conceptual repertoire by which to think of what it might be to 're-enchant' the world, including nature. For it is arguable, I think, that the more general, the deeper and more underlying fault line is not desacralization but the evacuation of *value* from the world (including nature). That the divine should have once widely been believed to be the ultimate source of value in nature does not require us to conceive of value today as having no other source than the divine. Indeed, there is no reason to think that value cannot be simply self-standing, that it has no source whether divine or any other. To think otherwise is to invite a stunning fallacy to which developments in the Early Modern North that I have been genealogically tracing, fell prey: if value cannot any longer be said to have a divine source it must be that nature has no value properties since, once desacralized, the only way to characterize nature is as containing only those properties which the natural sciences study. In other words, since the natural sciences do not study the sacred and since they do not study value either, nature must be evacuated of value as well as God. You cannot concede that there is a God delusion in your understanding of nature without also conceding that there is a value delusion. It is this characterization of nature as 'that which the natural sciences study', which is the genealogical *starting*-point of the detachment of outlook that my four questions (really five, if you count the broadly general question that the other four specify) have identified as pervasive; and as a characterization of nature, it is nothing less than a *superstition of modernity*. By 'superstition' I just mean a belief so accepted in the wider belief community that we take it on trust and forget when or how it was proved and why and in what ways it helps us to live. Among the dominant intellectual classes, it is a dogma that has been maintained by sheer intellectual browbeating, dismissing all denials of it as an expression of an unscientific mentality. But there is nothing unscientific whatever about denying it. One can only be unscientific if one denies or contradicts some proposition in some science – and no science contains the proposition that the natural sciences have full and exhaustive coverage of nature. To declare this to be a superstition is *not*, therefore, to express any phobia against science itself. It is rather to protest and resist an outlook promoted by the *mandarins around science* via alliances they had formed with commercial and orthodox interests in the modern period of the North, an outlook of detachment (that the four questions tried to convey) and whose alienating social and political effects we have tried to diagnose.

If I am right, then the most general and underlying conclusion of the diagnosis is that the ideal of an unalienated life, at least in our relations with nature, derives most generally and most fundamentally from the idea that nature contains the sorts of things (values) that make normative demands on us, and when we exercise our subjectivity and our agency to be in tune with these demands, we are in an unalienated relation with nature. If one wanted an encapsulated form of the ideal, here is a slogan:

> To be unalienated from nature is *for our subjectivity to be in sync with the normative demands upon it coming from the value properties of nature.*

To try and achieve such a relation with nature would be to begin to confront some of the effects of the transformations that the perspective of the South identifies in the self-understanding of the North. The thought encapsulated in the slogan needs much further elaboration than I can give here, but it is the most fundamental thought that can make for a sane relation to the environment and the world we inhabit. The idea that we can come to a satisfactory relation simply by invoking elements entirely from within our own interests and utilities and moral sentiments, independent of *normative demands from nature itself*, is not merely shallow. It is a false optimism that makes no dent in the framework that has landed us with the forms of alienation, whose genealogy I have been sketching.

I had given a slogan to capture what it is to be unalienated from nature. Is there a corresponding slogan for what it is to overcome the more social forms of alienation? From the folk and popular spiritual traditions of the south that I have kept implicitly in mind, without much naming of them, a matching sloganized ideal might be extracted as simply (breathtakingly simply and much in need of eventual elaboration) this:

> What we aspire to when we seek a socially unalienated life is the realization of the ideal that *nobody in a society or group is well off if someone is badly off*.

As I said, such a thought is embedded in diverse popular understandings of social and communal life of the South. Let me conclude this chapter with just a preliminary and promissory hint of some of the complexity behind this deceptively simple thought by considering an objection to it that might come naturally to mind. It is tempting to say about this slogan: this just *is* the idea of equality, so why was I so keen on saying at the outset that I would construct a framework in which equality would not be on centre stage but a necessary condition for some other ideal that was on centre stage such as the ideal of the unalienated life? All I have done, it might be said, is simply *equated* the social aspects of being unalienated with the idea of equality. I have not done the more complex thing that I had set out to do.

This response misses what the slogan is seeking to convey. What it misses is that the entire point of the slogan was to assert the importance of equality only at *second remove*. In a situation where some are well off and others are not, the idea of the slogan is not merely to say that this is a bad thing (as an assertion of the importance of equality that is *not* once removed would), but rather to say that even those who in a situation of inequality are *well* off are *in fact not so*. That distinction makes all the difference. Given that someone is badly off, the sense in which therefore *no one* is well off *is just what the social aspect of alienation amounts to*, a form of malaise that affects all until necessary conditions of other ideals are met. It is a generalized unease of the mind or, as metaphysicians like to say, of *being*, which affects all social relations. In a society where some are not well off, all feel and partake of this alienation, even those who are well off. Often people do not know the cause or the grounds of the malaise as having its roots in a society characterized by discrepancies in well-offness. Yet the malaise is manifest in a variety of different behaviour of theirs. Thus it is a subjective state of felt experience that can be said to have an objective presence in the minds of people whenever they live in societies with such discrepancies. Though I will not try and present it here, the empirical correlation between such discrepancies and the behaviour that reflects this malaise is extremely well established. Of course, the behaviour which reflects the malaise is bound to be very different in those who are well off than it is in those who are not, and it takes some careful psychological integration of theory and evidence to show how these are both symptoms of the same malaise; but that ought not to be an insuperable difficulty.

Where does all this leave us with how to think of the slogan's ideal of an unalienated life? To put it in a word, what the ideal expresses is just the kind or form of mentality in which this kind of malaise is entirely *absent*.

Let me conclude, then, with a few general integrating remarks to pull some strands of the discussion so far together. Though, as I said, I cannot possibly spell these things out much beyond the slogans and negative formulations I have offered so far, a rough sense of this *dialectic*, within which any *further* spelling out would have to be pursued, can be roughly conveyed.

The unalienated life that came with the sense of *belonging* that was made possible by the social frameworks of a period prior to modernity was, as is well-known and widely acknowledged, highly limited by the oppressive defects of those social frameworks. (To say 'feudal' to describe that oppression would be merely to use a *vastly* summarizing category that we have all been brought up on.) It is precisely those defects that the sloganized ideals of the Enlightenment, Liberty and Equality, were intended as *directly* addressing. And I have argued that, since the methodological and theoretical framework within which those two concepts were then developed made it impossible to so much as conceive how they could be jointly implemented, we should no longer see them as something to be *directly* approached, but rather as indirectly approached by the direct construction of something quite else, the ideal of an unalienated life, thereby theoretically trans- forming the concepts of liberty and equality. Now, if the achievement of an ideal of an unalienated life were to bring, in its wake, *indirectly*, condi- tions of liberty and equality (however transformed), it is bound to be very different from the unalienated life which is acknowledged to have existed in times prior to modernity because the conditions in which it existed then were also acknowledged to be acutely *lacking* in, precisely, liberty and equality. Thus, given this rudimentary conceptual/historical dialectic, what we need to show is how a new framework that breaks out of the dialectic would solve for *three* things at once – a transformed notion of liberty and equality, as I have said from the outset, but also it would now seem a transformed notion of the unalienated life. So, this is to be conceived as a holistically triangular transformation – we overcome a certain historical and conceptual dialectic and in doing so together and at once transform all three concepts that feature in the dialectic.

If this is the highly ambitious theoretical challenge to have emerged from our dialectic, how might we begin to think of this triangulated boot- strapping transformation of the notions of liberty and equality and the ideal of an unalienated life in concert, all at once? The complexity of the dialectic within which this ambitious task emerges suggests very general further questions to be asked and answered. We have to ask, first, what can be retained of the general idea of social 'belonging' of an earlier time in any revision of the idea of an unalienated life for our own time. We know from the other elements of the dialectic that the social belonging of an earlier time was marred by the defects of acute and chronic lack of liberty and equality, but we also know from the labours of this chapter's analysis that the attempts to directly overcome those defects were, in turn, marred by the fact that liberty and equality flowered in conception within a social framework in which deep forms of, precisely, alienation and non-belonging developed, and these in turn were of a piece with the theoretical and methodological developments that generated a highly *individualized* notion of liberty that attached to property and talent in the ways that made for liberty's conceptual incoherence with equality.

It would seem, then, that one place to begin the search for a concerted and triangulated transformation of all three notions is to look to a conception of more *collective* forms of liberty. If liberty resides in self-governance or the possession of the power to make the vital decisions that shape the material and spiritual aspects of our lives, collective liberty (something which, as I said, would not generate inequalities) would consist, it would seem, in approaching these decisions in such a way that we make them not primarily with our own interests in mind but the interests of everyone in society. The last few words of that last sentence express something that is utterly and entirely familiar, almost a cliché, a piety. The critique of self-interest has long been with us. If there is going to be novelty in the pursuit of this, then, it is only because it is to be essentially connected to the first part of the sentence – for it is far less well known and hardly at all theoretically developed that what such a critique of self-interest amounts to is the construction of a notion of *liberty*. Why is that so little known and developed? Because self-governance (which is essential to how we conceive liberty to be) has for so long been viewed in individualist terms.

The world, both the natural and the social world, as I had said earlier, makes normative demands on us as individuals. That has been central through the entire long passage of this paper's argument. And to be unalienated, I have also said, is for our agency to be in responsive sync with these demands. To see these demands from the world (capaciously conceived in both natural and social terms) *for what they are*, our own orientation to the world has to be to something that goes beyond the orientation in which individual interests are primary (consider – a physical analogy that should be extrapolated to the social – how when we drive a car we orient ourselves to the road not from the point of view of *our own body* but from the point of view of the *car*). That orientation, even though it may involve the mentality of individuals, because it exercises *liberty* from the point of view of a more collective orientation of each individual to the world (i.e. of the interests of all and of nature), is bound to *internally* cohere with equality in its outcomes. Equality would, thus, not be seen as something *extra*, it is *built into* the deliverances of the exercise of liberty, when the exercise of liberty is the exercise of a mentality in unalienated responsiveness to the 'world' free of the effects of a detached outlook to that 'world' which this chapter has tried to genealogically diagnose.

I need hardly repeat that these closing remarks are the most elementary gestures in the direction of what it takes to pursue the tasks that emerge from the dialectic that this chapter has set up. That will be painfully obvious to any reader. But I hope something of the *significance* of what might be achieved if we pursued those tasks along this direction comes through from the elaboration of this background dialectic derived from a view of the South in which I have situated them.

Note

1   See Prabhat Patnaik (2011) for an extended criticism of the sort that I am presenting very briefly here. For Sen's elaboration of the analogy see his 'Prohibiting the Use of Agricultural Land for Industry is Ultimately Self-Defeating' (2010).

References

Balibar, É. (2014), *Equaliberty: Political Essays*. Durham, NC: Duke University Press.

Burke, P. (2000), *A Social History of Knowledge*. Cambridge: Polity Press.

Elias, N. (1969), *The Civilizing Process*, Vol. I. *The History of Manner*s. Oxford: Blackwell.

Kuhn, T. S. (1962), *The Structure of Scientific Revolutions*. Chicago: University of Chicago Press.

Newton, I. (1704/1998), *Opticks*. Palo Alto: Octavo.

Patnaik, P. (2011), 'Globalization and Social Progress', *Social Scientist,* 39 (1–2): 47–59.

Said, E. (1978), *Orientalism*. London: Vintage Books.

Sen, A. (2010), 'Prohibiting the Use of Agricultural Land for Industry is Ultimately Self-Defeating', in *The Telegraph*, Kolkata, 23 July.

Thomas, K. (1983), *Man and the Natural World: Changing Attitudes in England, 1500–1800*. London: Allen Lane.

CHAPTER SEVEN

'We Belong to Palestine Still': Edward Said and the Challenge of Representation

Robert J. C. Young

1.

Edward Said's preoccupation with humanism and the human is often seen to be provocatively at odds with the intellectual tenor of his own times, where humanistic enquiry seemed to have moved on to other questions, such as those of citizenship or the Anthropocene. Said's repeated affirmations, however, should be seen less from the perspective of contemporary academic concerns, than in terms of his pursuit of an absence, of his seeking to invent the status of something that remained lacking. Just as Aimé Césaire and Frantz Fanon had proclaimed the need for a new humanism that would include all those people of colour in the world who had hitherto been excluded from the realm of the fully human, so Said sought to affirm the existence of a people whose right to exist was permanently in question, whose name was disallowed, whose conditions of existence, in refugee camps around the Middle East and in isolated diasporas around the world, meant that very many of their lives were lived beyond the pale of humanity and all the personal, social and political conditions that such a term implies. Said's contestation of this situation meant that his central concern was, literally, with putting Palestine and Palestinians on the map, with making the invisible visible, with reshaping a forgotten or discarded people so as to return them to the recognized realm of the fully human. But how do you represent the invisible? How do you represent a place which is no longer there?

In July 1917 a slim pamphlet called *Two Stories* was sent to 134 private subscribers in London. It was the first publication of the Hogarth Press, typeset by hand and bound by Leonard and Virginia Woolf. It contained a short story by each of them. Virginia's was called 'The Mark on the Wall' and has been almost continuously in print since the day that it appeared in 1917. Leonard's, by contrast, has never been commercially republished. It was called 'Three Jews'. Written in 1915, it tells the story of a Jewish Londoner like Woolf who wakes up one morning on the first day of spring. Feeling restless, he takes himself off to Kew Gardens for a walk. Afterwards, he wanders into a teashop garden for a cup of tea. While he sits there, another man walks in and, since all the other tables are taken, asks if he can join him. He says he doesn't mind at all, though as the man speaks, the narrator notices what he describes as 'the slight thickness of the voice, the over-emphasis, and the little note of assertiveness in it'. Seeing the man's dark head against the delicate apple-blossom and the pale blue sky, he smiles.

> 'You are amused', [the man] said … 'I believe I know why.'
> 'Yes,' I said, 'you knew me at once and I knew you. We show up, don't we, under the apple-blossom and this sky. It doesn't belong to us, do you wish it did?'
> 'Ah', he said seriously, 'that's the question. Or rather we don't belong to it. We belong to Palestine still, but I'm not sure that it doesn't belong to us for all that.'
> 'Well, perhaps your version is truer than mine. I'll take it, but there's still the question, do you wish *you* belonged to *it*?'

The conversation concerns their mutual sense of being outsiders, of not belonging, socially and physically – 'We show up, don't we, under the apple-blossom and this sky' – and the inevitable question that follows, where they do belong to? While the story hovers ambivalently around the question of whether they belong to 'it', that is, to the unnamed England, the second Jew repeats the refrain: 'we belong to Palestine still'. He then tells another somewhat inconsequential story of a third Jew, a cemetery keeper who 'belongs to Palestine too'. What interests me here is not just the uncertainty the men feel about belonging to England, but also the insistence, repeated across the story of the three Jews, that they belong to Palestine 'still'.

The question is particularly interesting in that the story was published in July 1917, just four months before the British Foreign Secretary, Arthur James Balfour, wrote the letter to Baron Rothschild, for transmission to the Zionist Federation of Great Britain and Ireland, which came to be known as the 'Balfour Declaration'. Predating the Declaration, the story suggests a scenario that the Balfour Declaration, despite its qualification with respect to 'the civil and religious rights of existing non-Jewish communities in Palestine', transformed dramatically. In practice it ended the particular configuration of identity that Woolf evokes. Today, the phrase in the story, 'we belong to Palestine', is striking, so different from 'Palestine belongs to us', a sentiment already invoked in the second Jew's ambiguous use of 'it' which semantically at that point means England, but grammatically, within the sentence, Palestine: 'We belong to Palestine still, but I'm not sure that it doesn't belong to us for all that.' We could say in fact that the whole history of the Middle East in the twentieth century has revolved around that semantic reversal from 'We belong to Palestine' to the exclusivist claims of 'Palestine belongs to us'. If the Arab and Jewish population of Palestine had been able to think their relation to Palestine in terms of the first kind of belonging rather than the second, then Israel/Palestine might now be a country of peace rather than the unhappy, divided and violent entity that it has become. Woolf's phrase, 'we belong to Palestine', seems to envisage a Palestine in which diaspora Jews in London, Mizrahi Jews and Arabs in Palestine, can all belong to the same place, be part of a shared space to which they all belong, just as today Londoners or New Yorkers, in their extraordinary ethnic, religious and cultural diversity, all feel that they belong to London or New York. Woolf, we might say anachronistically, envisages a one-state solution, assuming the mixed, diverse cultural environment that was in fact already there at the time that he wrote his story, the norm in a Middle East at that time still populated by the diverse cultures of the Ottoman Empire, not only in Palestine, but in Smyrna, Alexandria and elsewhere, the 'land without borders' hauntingly re-imagined by Raja Shehadeh in *A Rift in Time: Travels with My Ottoman Uncle* (Shehadeh 2010). All of that was irrevocably lost when the principles of nationalism were enforced by the Great Powers in 1922, after which the human and humane fluidity and open borders of the Ottoman Empire were gradually frozen into the boundary prisons of the modern nations or non-nations of the Middle East.

The shrinking remains of that earlier world was the milieu in which Edward Said grew up, and it was his sense of 'belonging to Palestine still' that would fuel the focus and commitments of his life in a time when the very question of whether he, or other Palestinians, belonged to Palestine had become a contested issue. As he grew older, Said was translated into an era when even to cite the very name of Palestine bizarrely became a heretical act: in 2001 the then British Foreign Secretary, Jack Straw, found himself in the middle of a political storm on a tour of the Middle East because he had used the term Palestine. Ariel Sharon responded by refusing to meet him, clearly unaware of the historical irony of his outrage at a British Foreign Secretary daring to use the P word. The attempt to erase the very word Palestine was a kind of negative metonymy that points to a much larger, material, cultural and human erasure.

The Palestine to which the earlier British Foreign Secretary, Balfour, had referred 84 years before had disappeared, no longer existing even in name. It is that evanescence of a place, its identity, its communal life and the fate of the majority of its Arab inhabitants, that was to preoccupy Said, whose courageous stubbornness, we might say following Shehadeh (1982) *summud*, was to insist on using that anachronism, the word Palestine, the Palestine to which he had belonged, and which he continued to claim that he belonged to, even if it no longer existed and he was told that he had no right to belong to it. The question that Said could not avoid was, given the official disappearance of Palestine, what or where *did* he belong to? The protean boundaries of Palestine have changed throughout history, but rarely as often as in the second half of the twentieth century: in Said's lifetime, in less than fifty years, the former territory of Palestine under the British Mandate under which he grew up was transformed three times, in 1948, in 1967 and in 1995. The Oslo agreement in particular, with its 'Palestinian administered territories' and strange Bantustan-like scattering of a myriad of tiny Palestinian areas within a West Bank still occupied by Israel, was perhaps the most bizarre development of all in terms of the memory of an actual Palestine. For Said, Palestine had been indisputable, real, but it existed no longer, though the physical place where it had been was still somehow there.

How does a country disappear? How can a country disappear? How do you represent the country to which you belong but which is no longer there? How to represent a country which had been there since before Roman times but had never been a country as such in the modern sense of the word, and which in the twentieth century became another country altogether? How to represent what was once there, is still there and is no longer there? These are the issues that Said grappled with all his life, which is why the question of representation was so important to him, and at the same time is why representation always seemed to him so unsatisfactory. 'I've always been interested in what gets left out', Said remarked in 1999. 'I'm interested in the tension between what is represented and what isn't represented, between the articulate and the silent' (Bayoumi and Rubin 2000: 424). What is represented and what is not, who creates the representations and who does not, what gets left out of representations, contemporary and historical, 'the places of exclusion and invisibility' (Said 2004: 81), remained the intellectual focus of Said's life and grounded the link between his political and theoretical interests. The disappearance of the representation of Palestine on the map formed part and parcel of the process denying sovereignty and political representation to its people. In his discussion of the question of representation at the beginning of *Orientalism*, Said cites Marx's dictum from the *18th Brumaire*, 'sie können sich nicht vertreten, sie müssen vertreten werden'.[1] In the case of the Palestinians, however, Said would later argue, not only do they appear not to be able to represent themselves, but the imperative has been that they must not be represented. The lacuna articulated by Marx within the question of representation was always the central issue for Said and explains his lifelong preoccupation with issues of representation in all their possible ramifications.

At a theoretical level, this began with the question of how representation works – both in itself, since representation is always already riven internally, and in the tense relation between the word and the image and the actual 'exterior' thing, person or scene that it represents. This is doubtless why Said, for a while at least, found Foucault so compelling, particularly his book *Les mots et les choses* which Said felt explored the tensions implicit in his own historical situation (Foucault 1966). For Said, representation was never simply a problem of epistemology. It was always also a political problem, as in the fundamental question with which he closes *Orientalism*: 'How does one *represent* other cultures?' (Said 1985: 325). More urgent than that, however, in Said's case, was the question that precedes it, namely how does one represent one's own culture?

In 1975 Said characterized the representational relation between words and things, its gaps and uncertainties, with the unexpected term 'molestation': 'Molestation', he explained 'is a consciousness of one's own duplicity, one's confinement to a fictive, scriptive realm ... And molestation always occurs when novelists and critics traditionally remind themselves of how the novel is always subject to a comparison with reality and thereby found to be illusion' (Said 1975: 84).[2] It is hard not to link the odd use of this word to the sense that Said was always haunted by his consciousness of exile which enforced a sense of molestation in the relation between representation and reality, but more specifically, in its aura of victimage and violence, in relation to Palestine. Palestine had been real, but its historical and continuing reality now could not be represented. Perhaps that was one reason why Said could not offer the counter-representation to orientalism for which he was unjustly much criticized. For with Palestine the actuality was both there and not there anymore. The place was also somewhere else, the people who had lived there for the most part dispersed, and initially left without even a way of describing who or what they had been. Said's lifelong preoccupation with the question and problems of representation and its conceptual limits can be framed and rethought from the perspective of the complex intertwining of memory with the trauma of loss and the oblivion of the Palestinian people. Representation thus always proved more than a theoretical or philosophical problem for Said; for him it was always animated, as he put it in *After the Last Sky* (1986), by 'the problem of writing about and representing – in all senses of the word – Palestinians'.

2.

In 1983 Edward Said commissioned an exhibition of Jean Mohr's photographs of Palestine at the United Nations. The UN, however, then prohibited any writing, that is written texts or captions, from accompanying the photographs. Said's *After the Last Sky* formed a response to that injunction against a scriptory Palestine, and developed into his first autobiographical account that sought to retrieve in writing and images a living actuality in the cultural memory of Palestine. The prohibition against attaching any words to the images at the UN exhibition staged in a bizarrely dramatic form the severance between representation and the real. Words were not allowed to point to images which might point to things. Said's response, to write *After the Last Sky*, offered the beginning of a process by which he succeeded, with other Palestinians, in creating or recreating Palestine and Palestinians in their own imagination and in the imaginary of the world. In the need to stake a claim for the existence and identity of Palestinians who, in 1986, remained for the most part an unacknowledged people, Said was obviously attracted to the photograph because of what Roland Barthes calls the indexical quality of the image, the fact that the representation correlates to a moment of the actual that was once there. Barthes is taken by the way that the photograph holds forever a Proustian moment of the actuality of lost time. But for Said the exile, the dispossessed, the photograph involves a double loss: of time and of place. The photographs had been commissioned to bring the reality of Palestinians to life, to make it real. Each photograph shows the everyday details of Palestinian life 'not simply there but represented by photographs as being there – saturated with meaning and memory, and still very far away' (Said 1986: 30–1). Said, however, feels uncertain that photographs of Palestinians can fulfil their usual documentary role. 'I do not know', he said, 'whether the photograph can, or does, say things as they really are. Something has been lost. But the representation is all we have' (1986: 84). Paradoxically, however, Said suggests that such photographs can also produce the loss of memory:

> There is little that I can truly remember about Jerusalem and Nazareth, little that is specific, little that has the irreducible durability of tactile, visual, or auditory memories that concede nothing to time, little … that is not confused with pictures I have seen or scenes I have glimpsed elsewhere in the Arab world. (1986: 30)

Instead of providing the actuality that Said seeks, photographs seem almost to take it away, to usurp the memories of the past with their own reality.

How, though, to photograph 'Palestine': do you photograph the place or the people of whom the majority have become separated from their origins? The book is subtitled *Palestinian Lives* and the photographs that Said chose are for the most part of people, so that the book itself brings together a scattered, now-imagined community: we see Palestinians not only in former Palestine, the West Bank, Gaza, but also all over the Middle East and Europe. Drawing the photographs together with his moving and evocative commentary, Said creates a kind of third space out of the crucible of Palestinian dispersion, its possibility drawn from the void of its non-existence, rather like Ireland's imagined fifth province: a dream of Palestine. In Israel/Palestine each side dreams of a different past. Among the many ironies and reversals surrounding the history of Palestine, the forced exchange of the dream of Palestine is amongst the most poignant: this dream of Palestine bizarrely mirrors the Zionist dream of Israel, which began as a dream of a lost past but then succeeded in establishing itself in reality by evacuating the majority of Palestinians from their homeland, turning what had for generations been a reality for them into the dream of the lives that they had lost. An exchange of dreams and an exchange of diasporas.

What is most noticeable in *After the Last Sky* is Said's sense of an emptiness in what constitutes 'Palestine' and Palestinians. He complains that the Palestinian has no cultural capital, no Freud, no Einstein, no Rubinstein: it's a kind of empty space – a void. How can we be a people if we don't have a culture that we can point to? Said asks. This lack of cultural resources, Said clearly feels, is a particular vulnerability given that one of the arguments deployed against Palestinians is that they don't exist. In Golda Meir's well-known words, spoken two years after the 1967 war:

> When I came to Israel in 1921 there were no such thing as Palestinians. When was there an Independent Palestinian people with a Palestinian state? It was either southern Syria before the First World War, and then it was a Palestine including Jordan. It was not as though there was a Palestinian people in Palestine considering itself as a Palestinian people and we came and threw them out and took their country away from them. They did not exist. (Meir 1969)

Golda Meir was clearly not a reader of Kant, who uses the term 'Palestinians' to describe the Jews in his *Anthropology from a Pragmatic Point of View* (1978: 101).[3] 'We belong to Palestine still': in English the word Palestinian has been used to describe natives of Palestine, both Jewish and Arab, since 1583 (OED). The term Palestinian therefore already foreshadows the inextricably interwoven history of Jews and Palestinians who both 'belong to Palestine'. In the twentieth century, however, even the word itself has been denied.

'Do we exist?' Said asks in the face of Meir's challenge; 'What proof do we have?' (Said 1986: 34). His underlying project in the book is a simple one: to prove the existence of Palestinians by representing them. They must be represented. Their identity is by no means accepted within the West: Meir's argument can still be found in many forms today. Take, for example, the following entry to be found on 'Answers.com', a website with 86 million visitors a month, no. 20 in the USA and no. 33 worldwide:

> If those Arabs wish to call themselves Palestinians – that is their right, but they are not a distinct people any different in language, culture or any other measure, than the inhabitants of Jordan, and to a certain extent, Syria and Lebanon.

... Palestine is a foreign word, first invented by the Romans, after whom it was never used until the 20th century by natives of the country.

To go back far into the annals of History, of the peoples who inhabited this land in the 2nd millennium BC – Israelites (Jews), Edomites, Nabateans, Philistines, Phoenecians [sic] and Canaanites – only the Jews still exist to this day as a nation (Definition of a nation = common culture, language, geographical connection and in the case of the Jews, a common religion). These other peoples no longer exist to claim the country as theirs.

... Never did Moslems refer to the land as 'Palestine' before 1919.[4]

If you are surprised to find such assertively particular views on Answers. com, then look up Answers.com on Wikipedia, and you will find the following information: 'The website is the primary product of the Answers Corporation (previously GuruNet), an Israel-based Internet reference and Q&A company with offices in New York City and Jerusalem, founded by Bob Rosenschein in 1999'.[5] The link to Bob Rosenschein tells us that he is an American Internet entrepreneur who moved to Israel in 1983.

Similar statements about Palestinians can be found on many more overtly pro-Israel websites. What's striking is that they share certain misapprehensions that from a historical perspective, particularly from those schooled in the history of colonialism, seem scarcely credible today. Despite the appeal to ancient history, their preconceptions are entirely modern. There are two key issues: the first is obviously the curious suggestion that only people who lived in Palestine in the second millennium BC have the right 'to claim the country as theirs'. It is interesting to think what would happen if that logic was put into practice everywhere in the world (for example, the USA). The second is the implication that the idea of a nation has remained consistent from the second millennium BC to today, which shows little historical understanding of the evolution of the idea of the nation into its relatively recent political institution of the post-Westphalian nation-state. Meir's statement implicitly raises Renan's question – what is a nation? What is a people? The definition that wiki-answers.com offers of a nation is, improbably, derived from Joseph Stalin's *Marxism and the National Question* (1913), where we read 'A nation is a historically constituted, stable community of people, formed on the basis of a common language, territory, economic life, and psychological make-up manifested in a common culture' (Stalin 1935: 8) – to which is added in Wiki-answers 'and in the case of the Jews, a common religion'. What Answers.com leaves out, however, is the idea of 'a historically constituted, stable community of people', that is that a nation has a common history of people living in a particular territory over an extended period of time. While all the other people from the second millennium BC, it is argued, 'no longer exist to claim the country as theirs', bizarrely no one who has lived in Palestine in the 4,000 years since the second millennium BC is allowed to have a claim to the territory either.

When she said 'there were no such thing as Palestinians', at one level Meir may have been technically correct, in the sense that the identity of Palestinians as Palestinian in the way that the word is used today is relatively recent. You could equally well say there were no such thing as Israelis in 1921 either – 'Israelis' did not come into being until 1948 (OED). However, the logic of the idea that the Palestinians have no right to be a nation because they did not formerly call themselves Palestinians under Ottoman or British rule would apply to most peoples around the world who lived under colonialism – as in the case of the Palestinians, it was very often colonial rule in its various forms that forged and produced the nation. There were no 'native Americans' or 'First Nations' in Canada before settlers arrived from Europe – but just because they did not call themselves that does not mean that they were not there and do not belong there. Colonialism created new formations of indigenous people who arose in the context of shifting boundaries and forms of sovereignty but who constituted themselves by virtue of their culture, ethnicity and the historical locality of where they lived. Meir's argument in fact repeats exactly the kind of argument made by all colonizers against the claims to sovereignty by indigenous inhabitants. If Palestine had simply become an individual, separate state after 1945 in the same way as the other provinces of the Ottoman Empire that had been carved up by European powers over the course of the nineteenth and early twentieth centuries, then Palestinians would have become Palestinians in a more regular way. They did not get that option. But they became Palestinians anyway, via a different, far more painful route.

The Palestinians, Answers.com informs us, 'are not a distinct people'. The assumption that the people of Palestine were just Arabs who could easily assimilate elsewhere in the Arab world when expelled from Israel was, undoubtedly, the major conceptual mistake made by Zionism and Israel in its military and political strategies. More charitably, you could say that they were seduced by the claims of Pan-Arabist ideology. What happened in 1948 was, in itself, by no means unique. There was plenty of historical precedent for expelling people from their land – think of any settler colony – so it could be argued that the Israelis were only following a well-established procedure, and not just that practised in settler colonies such as Algeria, America or Australia, but also in England in the enclosure movements, in Scotland in the depopulation of the Highlands, in the eighteenth century, or in Ireland in the nineteenth. Relatively close by and more recently, there had been the mass expulsions of Greeks from Turkey and Turks from Greece in 1923, to say nothing of the Armenians during the First World War, or of course European Jews from Germany. In 1947 there was the semi-forced exodus of millions of people between India and Pakistan. The twentieth century was the century of the managed mass transfer of millions of people in order to create nation states that conformed to the racial and cultural ideology of nationalism. The, for the most part,

internationally-sanctioned population transfers of the twentieth century
were deemed to be workable (as well as morally acceptable) because
those who were expelled, let's say Muslims from Gujarat or the Punjab,
notionally had somewhere to go to, a homeland, even if they had never had
any connection with it before, namely in that case Pakistan. The mistake
of Zionism was to assume that the inhabitants of Palestine were simply
Arabs who did not need their own homeland in which they were living, and
that as Arabs they were disposable people who could easily be deported to
another Arab country where they would fit in indistinguishably. In fact, as
we know, the majority of the refugees from the newly created state of Israel
did not assimilate into other Arab countries, but ended up in vast refugee
camps on the West Bank and Gaza. The rejection of the Palestinians by the
Arab states, clearly not welcomed on the grounds of their being generically
'Arab', was what enforced the Palestinians' sense of themselves. In that
sense, it was, in fact, Israel itself that in a sense created the Palestinians
by expelling them, while it was the Arabs' defeat in 1967 that created the
breach, the historical crucible from which the Palestinian people developed
self-consciously as Palestinians.

Even if there were no Palestinians using the name Palestinian, therefore,
there *were* people who lived in Palestine and these people 'belonged to
Palestine still'. Their lack of a constituted national identity in modern
terms, however, initially made it hard for them to make any claims. It is
this gap between a felt and a provable identity on which Said reflects and
broods in *After the Last Sky*. How can he represent, or make a representation of, a people who lack a proven empirical identity? The problem is
similar to the problem of land claims where the owner owns land because
his or her family or people have always owned it, for so long that there is
no legal written document answering to the requirements of modern times
to prove it. Said's book is haunted by the intractable problem of having
an identity that lacks an empirically provable identity, a place that lacks a
representation, a people who have no cultural capital to claim as their own
with which they can identify, and no documented history that they can lay
claim to. 'Do we exist? What proof do we have?' Said asks. 'The further
we get from the Palestine of our past, the more intermittent our presence.
When did we become "a people"? When did we stop being one? Or are we
in the process of becoming one?' (Said 1986: 34). His answer is that the
people displaced from Palestine did not in a sense become Palestinians until
1967, when in a kind of Freudian *nachtraeglichkeit*, or deferred action,
1967 created the meaning and the collective memory of 1948 and precipitated the Palestinians into a national consciousness. There is no better
example of this deferred action than Edward Said himself, who became a
Palestinian activist after 1967.

3.

Asking the question about who the Palestinians are was, in fact, already part of the answer, part of the process of the development of a national culture that could be self-consciously represented and projected: as Frantz Fanon argued, 'To fight for national culture means in the first place to fight for the liberation of the nation' (Fanon 1965: 187). The national culture *is* the struggle, or as Said put it: 'Our literature in a certain very narrow sense *is* the elusive, resistant reality it tries so often to represent' (Said 1986: 38). Ever since, Said and other Palestinians have been producing a body of writing and cultural production, cinema, art, that both defines themselves as Palestinians, and proves it to the world, even the Israelis. Today the lack around Palestinian identity, cultural and historical, that Said laments in 1986 is no longer there – in no small part thanks to Said himself. That generation of cultural capital shows why initiatives such as the West-East Divan orchestra were so important.

In the 1999 interview about the problem of what gets represented and what gets left out, from which I have already cited, Said continues as follows:

> In the particular case of the Palestinians, one of our problems is that we don't have any documents to substantiate what we said happened to us. Take one of the Israeli new historians, Benny Morris, for instance. He's very literal-minded, and he's done very important work, but his assumption is that he can't say anything about what happened in 1947–48 unless there's a document to show for it. I say, well, why not try to animate that silence? ... Why not go through the process of trying to reconstruct out of the silence what was either destroyed or excluded? (Bayoumi and Rubin 2000: 424–5)

That lack of representation has been increasingly answered: for example, the documenting of the Nakba by the historian Ilan Pappe in *The Ethnic Cleansing of Palestine* (2006), Ahmad Sa'di and Lila Abu-Lighod's *Nakba, 1948, and the Claims of Memory* (2007), Nur Masalha's *The Palestinian Nakba* (2011), and the remarkable archive photographs published in Arielle Azoulay's *From Palestine to Israel: A Photographic Record of Destruction and State Formation, 1947–1950* (2007). Whereas in 2001 Gabriel Piterberg could suggest that the claim that there had been an ethnic cleansing of Palestine was still a matter of debate, it has become ever harder to deny.[6] Representation no longer seems so distant from historical memory, the concerted attempt since 1948 to make Palestinians unbelong at every level has become ever more fully documented, and is now of course commemorated, every year, around the world on 15 May: *Yawm an-Nakba*, the day of the catastrophe. And as with the forbidden writing at the UN that produced *After the Last Sky* which will be read for generations, the more the commemoration is forbidden, the more it will be remembered.

In the same way, whereas in 1986 Said cites what he regards as the tentative beginnings of the literary representations designed 'to restore Palestine', by the end of his life, he was able to go much further – the remarkable outpouring of Palestinian literary writing since the 1980s which amounted to a kind of artistic, cultural intifada, allowed Said in his posthumous work, *On Late Style* (2007), to make the remarkable claim that, by virtue of being 'late' – 'Late works are the catastrophe' he says, citing Adorno, and it is impossible that in doing so he did not intend to add the Palestinian resonance – Palestinian literature had become more powerful than Israeli literature.

> In the twentieth century great art in a colonial situation always appears in support of what Genet ... calls the metaphysical uprising of the natives ... In Palestine the same is true, since the radical, transformative, difficult, and visionary work comes from and on behalf of the Palestinians ... not from the Israelis. (Said 2007: 87)

So representation, which for Said seemed so inadequate in many ways, nevertheless in the end after 1987 did increasingly work successfully as self-representation for Palestinian identity and history in the fight for a national culture, even if what Said calls the Palestinian dream, which was also of course his dream – 'the perfect congruence between memory, actuality, and language' (Said 1986: 75) – remains as far away as ever. The great achievement, however, is that against all odds, all attempts to expel them physically, culturally, historically, personally, Palestinians do belong to Palestine still – even if Palestine does not belong to them – not yet.

Notes

1   Cf. Gayatri Chakravorty Spivak's formulation with respect to the indissociable but problematic relationship between *Darstellung* and *Vertretung* in Spivak 1988: 271–313, and 1999: 257–66. For an analysis of both Said and Spivak's use of Marx, see Larsen 2001: 59–66.

2   The discussion of 'molestation' was originally published in Said 1971. Said's essay was included in this collection on the suggestion of Paul de Man (J. Hillis Miller, personal communication, April 2011). For an earlier discussion of Said's use of 'molestation' see Young 2012: 39.

3   Kant 1978: 101. My thanks to Etienne Balibar for pointing this out to me.

4   http://wiki.answers.com/Q/Why_did_the_Jews_believe_that_Palestine_belongs_to_them (accessed 4 May 2013).

5   http://en.wikipedia.org/wiki/Answers.com (accessed 4 May 2013).

6   Thanks in part of course to Piterberg's own work: Piterberg 2001: 31–46.

References

Azoulay, A. (2007), *From Palestine to Israel: A Photographic Record of Destruction and State Formation, 1947–1950.* London: Pluto Press.

Bayoumi, M. and A. Rubin (eds) (2000), *The Edward Said Reader.* New York: Vintage.

Fanon, F. (1965), *The Wretched of the Earth* [1961], trans. Constance Farrington. London: MacGibbon & Kee.

Foucault, M. (1966), *Les mots et les choses: une archéologie des sciences humaines.* Paris: Gallimard.

Kant, I. (1978), *Anthropology from a Pragmatic Point of View*, trans. Victor Lyle Dowdell. Carbondale: Southern Illinois University Press.

Larsen, N. (2001), *Determinations.* London: Verso.

Masalha, N. (2011), *The Palestinian Nakba.* London: Zed.

Meir, G. (1969), 'Interview with Frank Giles', *The Times* (London), 15 June; rpt. as 'Golda Meir Scorns Soviets: Israeli Premier Explains Stand on Big-4 Talks, Security', *Washington Post*, 16 June.

Pappe, I. (2006), *The Ethnic Cleansing of Palestine.* Oxford: Oneworld.

Piterberg, G. (2001), 'Erasures', *New Left Review* 10: 31–46.

Sa'di, A. and L. Abu-Lighod (2007), *Nakba, 1948, and the Claims of Memory.* New York: Columbia University Press.

Said, E. W. (1971), 'Molestation and Authority in Narrative Fiction'. In J. H. Miller (ed.), *Aspects of Narrative. Selected Papers from the English Institute.* New York: Columbia University Press, 47–68.

Said, E. W. (1975), *Beginnings. Intention and Method.* New York: Basic Books.

Said, E. W. (1985), *Orientalism: Western Representations of the Orient* [1978]. London: Penguin.

Said, E. W. (1986), *After the Last Sky.* London: Faber and Faber.

Said, E. W. (2004), *Humanism and Democratic Criticism.* New York: Columbia University Press.

Said, E. W. (2007), *On Late Style: Music and Literature against the Grain.* New York: Vintage.

Shehadeh, R. (1982), *The Third Way. A Journal of Life in the West Bank.* London: Quartet Books.

Shehadeh, R. (2010), *A Rift in Time: Travels with My Ottoman Uncle.* London: Profile.

Spivak, G. C. (1988), 'Can the Subaltern Speak?'. In C. Nelson and L. Grossberg (eds), *Marxism and the Interpretation of Culture.* London: Macmillan, 271–313.

Spivak, G. C. (1999), *A Critique of Postcolonial Reason: Toward a History of the Vanishing Present.* Cambridge, MA: Harvard University Press.

Stalin, J. [1935], *Marxism and the National and Colonial Question.* New York: International Publishers.

Young, R. J. C. (2012), 'Edward Said: Opponent of Postcolonial Theory'. In

T. Döring and M. Stein (eds), *Edward Said's Translocations: Readings, Ruptures, Legacies*. New York: Routledge, 23–43.

CHAPTER EIGHT

'Where Am I Supposed To Go Now?'

Ariella Azoulay

Yet, for all the writing about them, Palestinians remain virtually unknown. Especially in the West, particularly in the United States, Palestinians are not so much a people as a pretext for a call to arms.

EDWARD SAID (1986: 5)

To the Israelis, whose incomparable military and political power dominates us, we are at the periphery, the image that will not go away.

EDWARD SAID (1986: 5)

Prologue – thus the insider becomes outsider

Only two years ago, after the death of my father, and by sheer accident, I learned the proper name of my paternal grandmother. On her occasional visits with us from France, to where she emmigrated in the early 1950s, we, her grandchildren, called her 'gran'mere'. As we didn't know French at the time, we mistook the French noun for her proper name. I never had the opportunity to hear her name – Aysha, a common Arabic first name – in my father's voice. My father did everything he possibly could to remove and deny Arabs traits and attributes that would impede him from inventing himself as a French immigrant in Israel, *un ancien combattant*, who fought with the Allies during the Second World War to liberate Europe and, in 1949, joined the Jewish soldiers in Israel to defend their country against Arab invasions. My father decided to stay in Israel and marry the woman he met there – my mom. Even though in 1949 she had been (officially) an Israeli for less than a year and a Palestinian for all her nineteen years (until the founding of the state), in her own eyes and for my father, who always kept his French allure, she embodied Israeliness. We, the generation born after Palestine was ruined and transformed into Israel, were expected to be born Israelis, embodying the natural and historical rights that made us Israelis as they were narrated in the fable that is the Israeli *Declaration of Independence*, and to protect these rights from our co-citizens, the Palestinians, who constantly threaten our right to have those rights to ourselves. Earning those rights solely for ourselves was conditioned by the eviction of their eviction from the meta-narratives around which the different spheres of our life were organized. It required one dramatic reversal – to displace Palestinians to an outside so that we occupy the inside exclusively for ourselves, and constitute the body politic and its institutions to enable us to act and speak from this inside. We were 'overwhelmingly threatened' by Palestinians and Arabs in general, constantly invading our land and infiltrating our borders, undermining our sovereign rights to defend ourselves. Palestinians wanted their homes back and we memorized and recited that it was our natural and historic right to build our national home in and over their homes. We were born citizens of the State of Israel, we didn't know we were born citizens-perpetrators, i.e. that our citizenship is the key to the non-citizenship of Palestinians, to the infinite reproduction of this constitutive reversal. Once we began to narrate our life from a non-Zionist point of view, we were not satisfied by 'solutions' for the 'Palestinian Question', we wanted to re-think the question of Palestine – and its destruction – altogether and to make it our own problem too. Reading Said was not just reading 'Zionism from the Standpoint of Its [Palestinians] Victims' but reading it from the standpoint of our possible common future, based on an actual common past to be reconstructed from the time before the dramatic violent reversal was imposed, legalized and recognized internationally.

Overwhelmingly threatening

'Despite our subordinate status, our widely scattered exile, our reduced circumstances, our extraordinary military weakness relative to Israel,' Edward Said writes in *After the Last Sky*, asking 'how is it that we appear so overwhelmingly threatening to everyone?' (Said 1986: 110). This is one of many rhetorical questions that punctuate Said's book and assist him in making a point. Following a brief summary of Ghassan Kanafani's novel *Men in the Sun*, in which three refugees concealed in the belly of a tanker truck die of suffocation, Said asks: 'Why didn't you bang the sides of the tank? Why? Why? Why?' (1986: 32). Or elsewhere in the book, he asks: 'Do we exist? What proof do we have?' (1986: 34). What Said terms 'the remarkable epistemological achievement' of Zionism, the despairing trait of Palestinians' life – no matter what Palestinians will do to change their condition, they will be deprived of the potency to anchor their narratives, initiatives, actions and endeavours in lasting facts, that can be recognized and solidified – brings Said to formulate his questions in a rhetorical way. In 1979, in his *Question of Palestine*, where he used this term, he articulates this despair: 'I use the philosophical term because there is no other one adequate to expressing the sheer blotting out from knowledge of almost a million natives' (Said 1992: 23). At moments, Said – as do Palestinians in general – believes in the possibility that once the evicted narrative of the eviction will be open, its presence will matter, and the day after it should not be told anew, as if it had never been told before. 'The PLO', he writes, 'have reopened for Israeli Jews the file closed in 1948 when Palestinian society was destroyed' (Said 1986: 113). With each and every expellee who sought ways to return home, the 'file closed in 1948' was re-opened for a moment, but it did not cease to be re-opened every time anew, as if it had never before been re-opened. Regardless of being Palestinian or Jewish Israeli, under the Zionist regime it is simply impossible to truly open the file of 1948. The fact that a catastrophe of such magnitude as the destruction of Palestine is made a Palestinian problem, and not the problem of the Jewish Israeli perpetrators, assumed insignificant to them or even advantageous to them, reinforces the constitutive principle of this regime based on this constitutive difference between those two populations. Under the Zionist regime, Jewish Israeli citizens' actions are necessarily those of 'insiders', identified with and represented by the Zionist regime and 'protected' by it. As long as the Zionist regime exists, Jewish Israelis can experience themselves either as 'overwhelmingly threatened' or as perpetrators, doomed to perpetrate the dispossession of Palestinians and take advantage of what is not theirs.

Said's 'epistemological achievement' does not account for the recurrence of this achievement. In order to account for the persistence of this constitutive reversal – insider/outsider – and for the constant closing-up of the 1948 file that is constantly re-opened, I propose to shift from epistemology to phenomenology. The 'blotting out from knowledge of almost a million natives' was never a merely epistemological achievement. The Palestinian had to be literally 'blotted out' in order to be 'blotted out' from knowledge. Here it is in a nutshell, in Moshe Dayan's words, quoted in Said's book:

We came to this country which was already populated by Arabs, and we were establishing a Hebrew, that is a Jewish state here. In considerable areas of the country [the total area was about 6 per cent] we bought lands from the Arabs. Jewish villages were built in the place of Arab villages. You do not even know the names of these Arab villages, and I do not blame you, because these geography books no longer exist; not only do the books not exist, the Arab villages are not there either [...] There is no one place built in this country that did not have a former Arab population. (Said 1986: 14)[1]

But, as is widely known, even if this fact had to be repeated every time anew, the Palestinians were not completely blotted out either from the land or from knowledge. In response to the recurrent claim, by Dayan or Golda Meir, that the Palestinian people never existed, a group of Palestinian cinematographers in a refugee camp performed their existence and shot a film: *They Do Not Exist*.[2] The total domination of the political language of the nation-state imposed as a standard part of ending the Second World War, enabled the sewing together of the standard political vocabulary of liberation (of the Jews from the British mandate), self-determination, sovereignty, rule of law, etc., with the fabricated phenomenal field based on the transformation of the Palestinian insider into an outsider, no matter where she or he are literally and actually present. Thus not only the insider became an outsider, but the phenomenal field became the reflection of the fabricated body politic. Thus, since 1948 the Palestinians have existed in this 'visible invisibility' (Chung 2005: 3), a political regime that evades any stable differentiation between what is and what appears, what is known and what is said and between fact and fiction. Said often continues to engage in the discussion of these points made by these rhetorical questions, but never in the form of sealing them with an answer. Not only can such questions not have concise and satisfying solutions and answers, such questions should in fact pose a problem, the problem of the legacy of colonialism and its violent tools to determine the fate of people, to evaluate their ability and maturity to enjoy self-rule, to reduce or partition their territory, to deprive them of their rights to their property, lands, resources and wealth, etc. 'When did we become "a people"?' (1986: 133) Said asks, and continues by questioning this lethal question that enabled the Jews to be 'elected' as more fit for the task of self-rule than the Palestinians – whose refusal to discuss their political life with the Anglo-American delegation to Palestine leading to the UN partition resolution, decided their fate: 'When did we stop being one? Or are we in the process of becoming one?' (1986: 134).

What is it you Palestinians want?

By posing these rhetorical questions, Said transforms them into pertinent ones not only to those who were made their objects – 'the Palestinians' – but to everyone implicated in the colonial legacy, i.e. to everybody. It is not the particular nature of the Palestinian people that should become others' problem, but the colonial legacy that transforms people into 'a people' whose history begins to unfold separately from and as a problem for that of others, as performing the proof that this people is unfit to partake in the general progress of peoples and nations. 'People ask us [Palestinians],' Said writes, 'as if looking into an exhibit case, "What is it you Palestinians want?" – as if we can put our demands into a single neat phrase' (1986: 33). And yet another question, this time not his own, but one he heard from a man in the audience in yet another conference where the Palestinian question or problem was addressed, 'with reconciliation high on the agenda': 'I am a Palestinian, a peasant. Look at my hands. I was kicked out of 1948 [the area that became the State of Israel] and went to Lebanon. Then I was driven out, and went to Africa. Then to Europe. Then to here [the US]. Today [he pulls out an envelope], I received a paper telling me to leave this country. Would one of you scholars tell me please: Where am I supposed to go now?' (1986: 32). Said doesn't bring this question up in the perspective of finding individual solutions. As I said, the rhetorical question is an opportunity for Said, and for those engaged in the conversation he opens, to question the political questions, to question their temporality, the speaking position and their addressees. Even though the use of the 'now' in this last question invites one to address it as reflecting the contemporaneous conditions of the person who raises it, we have to remind ourselves that this question is not asked just now for the first time. Not only from his condensed story can we assume that he himself already asked it several times, every time he had to leave the place where he began to install himself; we can also assume that each and every Palestinian uprooted from her or his home has asked it with the same despair and urgency.

The urgent question – 'Where am I supposed to go now?' – asked by Palestinians would not have become a rhetorical one if those whose citizenship is the pre-condition for its recurrence – Jewish Israelis – were to contest the nature of their citizenship and claim their right to be governed not as the guardians of others' deprivation. It is the Israeli citizenship – based on keeping Palestinians outside of the borders imposed from within upon their homeland – that isolates this question and makes it the personal problem of the individual who asks it, not the common concern of those it implicates, Palestinians and Jewish Israelis alike. With the help of Said's rhetorical questions we can relate to the year 1948 not as a distant past separated from the political space in which we act and interact with others, but as an open political space whose dividing lines are still malleable and can be shaped by our actions and interactions. The year 1948 is a non-geometrical political space in which the question 'where am I supposed to go now?' is not heard as a weak voice from an accomplished past irrelevant to our present, but rather as an urgent call open to our response, to the way we will hear it, to the meaning we will endow it with, to the way we view its speaker as an interlocutor, recognize the plausibility of her or his claim. What is at stake, what Said's rhetorical questions imply, is not only the nature of the concrete solution to be found for that individual as a place to go to. It is the political space that will be shaped through the nature of the response to his call. It is not solely about him, it is also about us, about who we are – revealed by the way his call is heard. 'I would like to think,' he writes in the last paragraph of this book,

> that such a book not only tells the reader about us, but in some way also reads the reader. I would like to think we are not only the people seen or looked at in these photographs: we are also looking at our observers [...] We do more than stand passively in front of whoever, for whatever reason, has wanted to look at us. If you cannot finally see this about us, we will not allow ourselves to believe that the failure has been entirely ours. Not any more. (1986: 166)

With this final note of Said's book and from the non-geometrical political space, I propose to re-visit some of the moments of *failure* that Said accounted for earlier in the book. These 'failures' – moments in which Palestinians acted to showcase their cause, to affect the discourse related to them, to voice their claims – should not be discussed as isolated cases nor should they be attributed to their protagonists. These failures, like the recurrence of the same urgent question, are the symptoms of the political regime that deprives Palestinians, keeps them outside and dooms their civil actions to be either 'overwhelmingly threatening' or failures.

Invisible visibility

In his keynote lecture in 2003 at the Palestinian Film Festival, Said went back to his own experience presenting an exhibition of photographs taken by the Swiss photographer Jean Mohr in 1949 at several refugee camps in Gaza, Jordan, Egypt and the West Bank.[3] In 1983, on the occasion of the International Conference on the Question of Palestine (ICQP) in Geneva, Said, acting as a consultant, wanted to present Mohr's images at the United Nations hall in Geneva. 'Something unexpected happened,' Said recalls. 'The photographs were shown in the hall, but only very limited captions were permitted' (Said 1986: 2).

This led Said in the mid-1980s to collaborate with Jean Mohr on *After the Last Sky* in which, surprisingly, none of those early photographs are included.[4] This incident led Said to say:

> it became obvious to me that the relationship of Palestinians to the visible and the visual was deeply problematic. In fact, the whole history of Palestinian struggle has to do with *the desire to be visible*. Remember the early mobilizing phrase of Zionism: 'We are a people without a land going to a land without a people'? It pronounced the emptiness of the land and the non-existence of a people. (1986: 2)

Said didn't leave his argument as is – a structural argument on the conditions of visibility of the Palestinians – but provided it with a short history of this quest for visibility, the accuracy of which he himself seems to doubt. According to this historical narrative, the 1960s, with the emergence of the PLO as 'legitimized representative' as well as of 'emblematic figures' such as Arafat, were a turning point. Arafat was able to 'gather the shards of Palestine and give the whole a form and cohesion it never had. Our case, he seemed to us to be saying, is formulable,' and even, 'it can be represented in the forums of the world' (1986: 122). Arafat, Said continues, 'made it impossible to see the Middle East in general, and Israel in particular, without also seeing the Palestinians' (1986: 121). A few lines further down the page, Said overtly shares with his readers his scepticism regarding his own narrative and its construction around the visibility/invisibility dichotomy. 'Too many of us', he writes, 'feel that we have gained representation and media visibility at an exorbitant cost. We became known as hijackers and terrorists, and our much-vaunted "armed struggle" landed us in the chambers of the United Nations, in debate for a full decade now, with dwindling attendance, and regrettably constant results' (1986: 121).

This discussion is accompanied by another photo by Jean Mohr, taken in one of the United Nations halls in New York, on the occasion of the annual

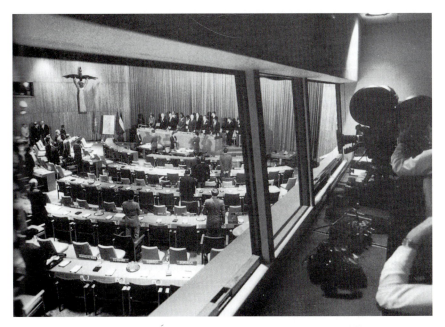

FIGURE 8.1 *Jean Mohr, 'New York, Nearly empty room at United Nations Day with the Palestinian People, November 29, 1983' [original caption by Edward Said, p. 123 in the book he authored with the photographer Jean Mohr:* After the Last Sky, *New York: Columbia University Press, 1986]*

'Day with the Palestinian People', 29 November 1983. The photograph, taken from behind the glass of the journalists' lounge, captured the contrast between the stage crowded with Palestinian representatives and the vacant seats of the United Nations delegates. The caption, written by Said, makes the point: 'Nearly empty room'.

Even when the hall was full, and Arafat gave his memorable speech in 1974 in the United Nations General Assembly hall about 'The difference between the revolutionary and the terrorist', Israel did everything possible to transform this moment into a failure. With the new science titled 'counterterrorism', Arafat's words about the PLO's 'dreams and hopes for one democratic state where Christian, Jew and Muslim live in justice, equality, fraternity and progress' were transformed into proof of terrorist motivation. 'Israel has promoted,' Said writes,

> a rather fictitious group called 'the terrorists,' who mechanically contain within themselves not merely an identity but a whole systematic discipline of nefarious practices. A veritable industry – operating from institutes in Tel Aviv and Washington for the study of terrorism, furnished with experts, seminars, and endless documents – now churns out a 'science' called counterterrorism, the product of an appalling doctrinal reductiveness applied to an already scandalous dehumanization of the Palestinian. This has justified Israeli mass terror against even the idea of Palestinian nationalism. (1986: 113)

Not only did Israel create the 'overwhelmingly threatening' Palestinian, argues Said, but it also laid the foundation for a new science and vocabulary that asserts the existence of its creatures – 'counterterrorism'.

Said is right to link the tragedy of Palestine to the problem of visibility, but the latter cannot be formulated along a single line moving from invisibility to visibility. Palestinians were never really invisible, and visibility cannot be equated with success, nor invisibility with failure.[5] The expulsion of 750,000 Palestinians from Palestine in 1947–9 cannot be depicted as an invisible event. Their expulsion followed the massive expulsion of approximately 15 million Europeans of different nationalities in 1945–7, with the implementation of a new world order imposed as part of ending the Second World War. The European waves of forced migration are very poorly documented compared to the Palestinian exodus, only recently beginning to be discussed, and always in terms of a fait accompli. Dozens of photographers and cameramen together with international delegates of the United Nations, International Red Cross and other organizations, were in Palestine and recorded the expulsion with their pens and cameras. Hundreds of thousands of Jews were there too, attending the horrifying spectacle of Palestinian expellees in processions and the destruction of their beloved country – Palestine – for the sake of providing the Jews with a new state – Israel.[6] After all, Palestine was the beloved country of Jews who immigrated to it or were born there, before it was transformed into the taboo name of a place that should never exist. The lasting presence of Palestinians in refugee camps cannot be framed as invisible either. The tragedy of Palestine is perpetuated not because the Palestinians failed to be visible, but because the meaning of their visibility was prevented from being produced in common and their misery was made their own, as if what was done to them can be secluded from the history of those who dispossessed them, or more broadly, from the history of the aftermath of the Second World War. Among the millions of expellees after the Second World War, the Palestinians voiced the most assertive refusal to acknowledge the meaning that was imposed upon their deportation and to accept it as a policy necessary for the preservation of world peace.

What should be studied, however, are the conditions under which the visible destruction of Palestine and the imposition of a totally new reality on this place did not emerge as a universal catastrophe but was made a 'Palestinian catastrophe'. One of the major characteristics of a totalitarian regime, according to Hannah Arendt, is that 'whenever it rose to power, it developed entirely new political institutions and destroyed all social, legal and political traditions of the country' (Arendt 1979: 460). The destruction of Palestine was the destruction of its social fabric, its diverse populations, its body politic, its languages, its names, its symbols, its political and social institutions, its legal system, its traditions, its culture, its architecture, its landscape, and their replacement by new social, legal and political struc-tures. The suspicion that it is a totalitarian catastrophe is enticed by the fact that part of it was the imposition of its meaning as a non-catastrophe or, at best, a catastrophe of a people who were made superfluous – the Palestinians. They were removed from the future of Palestine, enclosed in a past that was made irrelevant, while the Jewish Israelis had to move forward, ignore the destruction of the society of which they were part and celebrate its replacement by a new one. From that moment on, the experience of Palestinians and Jewish Israelis had to be kept incommen-surable. This could be achieved only by making the Palestinians outside intruders, and the Jewish Israelis natives, regardless of the historical facts. If the Israeli political regime is made of elements of totalitarianism, these cannot be reconstructed from what the regime does to Palestinians, i.e. from certain actions or policies that target them, but rather from what the regime renders unimaginable in the present, in the future but also as the past, affecting the entire population – Palestinians and Jewish Israelis alike. The possibility that Jewish Israelis and Palestinians can live equally and share a common space as co-citizens is foreclosed from any imagination: it is a constitutive element of the actual regime, key to its reproduction, and guarantees that the meaning of the catastrophe suffered by Palestinians will **not** emerge as catastrophe.

In the last chapter of her *The Origins of Totalitarianism*, Hannah Arendt doubts that 'elements of totalitarianism' will disappear with the collapse of

Nazi Germany or the death of Stalin. 'It may even be', she writes, 'that the true predicaments of our time will assume their authentic form – though not necessarily the cruelest – only when totalitarianism has become a thing of the past' (Arendt 1979: 460). The element of totalitarianism in the Israeli regime is not 'the cruelest', but it is certainly the longest ever to exist. For over sixty years, every time a Palestinian claim recurs, it elicits the same Jewish Israeli response as if it were by definition 'overwhelmingly threatening' and a violation of Israel's right to exercise its sovereignty. The truth is that Palestinian claims are 'overwhelmingly threatening to Israel's rights to exercise its sovereignty' since this sovereignty is devoid of legitimacy as long as Palestinians are made non-citizens in their homeland by this particular sovereignty.

In Said's seminal text *The Question of Palestine*, published in 1979, he argues that the 'almost total silence about Zionism's doctrines for and treatment of the native Palestinians' is 'one of the most frightening cultural episodes of the [twentieth] century' (1979: 113). 'My task', he writes there, 'is to present the Palestinian story; the Zionist one is much better known and appreciated' (1979: 118). Said's book is not only what it was meant to be; it is at the same time an eye-opening story of Zionism, different than those known and available at the time of its writing. It is certainly one of the first stories of Zionism written from a non-Zionist point of view. This point of view is Palestinian, but it should not be identified solely with Palestinians if one seeks to see beyond the phenomenal field constituted and imposed by Zionism. The frightening cultural episode Said refers to cannot, as I showed earlier, be studied solely as silence or invisibility regarding *what was done to* the Palestinians, including the 'irrefutable evidence' of 'Israeli preventive detention, torture, population transfer, and deportation of Palestinian Arabs' (1979: 113). The frightening thing about this 'frightening cultural episode' was that it was not conducted in silence or invisibility, but was rather immersed in verbosity and was always visible in its invisibility. It was 'frightening' because its meaning was never allowed to be produced through an open deliberative process, but rather always under the command of the constitutive reversal of the 'insider who was made outsider', meaning imposed from above and maintained through good citizenship.

Those 'doctrines for [the] treatment of the native Palestinians', known from the long history of colonialism, were embedded in the Israeli political regime without detracting much from its functioning as a democratic sovereign state in the eyes of its own citizens as well as in the eyes of the entire international community. If there is any sense in speaking of silence or invisibility, it is only in relation to the particular phenomenal field created by the political regime – and as the political regime – along the three dividing lines that constitute it: spatial – between what is included and what is outside; temporal – between the reality of pre-1948 and the reality constituted after the creation of the state; and body politic – between citizens and

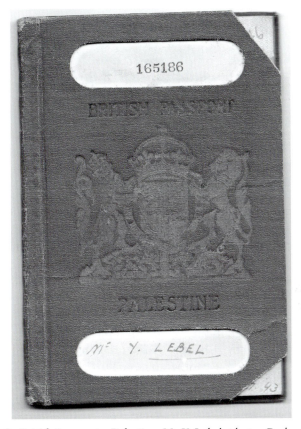

FIGURE 8.2 *British Passport – Palestine, Mr Y. Lebel, photo: Graham Simpson*

the others. The meaning of whatever was done to Palestinians since 1948 and on cannot be seen or heard within it as a common universal meaning acknowledged by others. This phenomenal field is in accordance with the model of differential body politic, the signature of colonialism and modern nation states. This silence, that I propose to call the meaning of catastrophe, is, therefore, not only about what was done to Palestinians, but also about what the perpetrators did. It is the meaning of the actions of those who became perpetrators and who under the current regime have lost their right not to be perpetrators and release themselves from this inherited position, deprived of the capacity to acknowledge this harm of *becoming perpetrator*. The denial of the catastrophic meaning and its mis-recognition go so deep as to deprive most Jewish Israelis of their right to imagine a future where the exercise of more violence to maintain what was achieved through violence is no longer required, a right to restore their – or their ancestors' – homeland: Palestine, where once upon a time, before the creation of the State, they had found hospitable neighbours, a home, a shelter, a future,

FIGURE 8.3 *The archive From Palestine to Israel: A Photographic Record of Destruction and State Formation, 1947–1950. The Mosaic Rooms, A. M. Qattan Foundation, London, 2011, photo: Graham Simpson*

where they participated in the creation of a mixed and open society whose daily life was guided by coexistence rather than violence.

In 2009 I assembled a photographic archive – entitled *From Palestine to Israel* – documenting the constitutive violence by which the Jewish State was established in 1948.[7] In and through this archive, whose photographs I discuss here, I sought to reconstruct not only the catastrophe that affected Palestinians, the direct victims of that constitutive violence, but also the traces of the transformation of the catastrophe into a Palestinian-only catastrophe, i.e. an event conceived as a catastrophe from 'their' point of view, which for Jewish Israelis has become a completed past that should never be approached without sovereign and military precautions.

Thinking about the catastrophe as a solely 'Palestinian' matter implies the acceptance of partition – of the land and of one's phenomenal field – at one and the same time as a fait accompli and as an inevitable, almost natural fact, forgetting that it is an outcome of the same violence that generated the catastrophe and that was used to suppress the opposition to partition by the majority of those living in Palestine at the time. With time, the compliance of the perpetrators and their descendants with the destruction of Palestine in 1948 as a non-catastrophe required no special effort, not even what Ann Stoler calls 'hindrance ignorance'.

Official forms, history books, landscape, memories, everything began to reflect the phenomenal field, and 'thus', Said writes, 'the insider becomes the outsider', and writing in official forms that a person was born in 1936 in Israel, or history classes of 3,000 years of history of Israel, do not sound like aberrations or lies. The phenomenal field is the common denominator of the regime, and hence people can enjoy freedom of speech, debate and argue, hold different opinions and even represent the Palestinian point of view, provided what they say is nourished by and based on this fabricated phenomenal field. Not only can the Palestinian cause not be acknowledged and the Palestinian transformed from claimant to threat, the Jewish Israeli cannot be a perpetrator, but is righteous and acts within the law.

Reading the photographs as bearing testimony for the fate of Palestine and its inhabitants – Palestinians and Jews alike – made it clear that the unproblematic adoption of the term 'war' to describe 1948 is in itself the unproblematic adoption of the narrative of the vanquishers. The war as the apex of a long-lasting 'Israeli–Palestinian conflict' eliminates the complex variety of exchange and interactions between Arabs and Jews in Palestine, replacing them anachronistically with the outcome of that period – partition, separation, and a seemingly unavoidable 'national conflict'. The historiography of the period continues to describe the series of events that occurred in Palestine in the late 1940s as a transition from 'war' to 'State'. Thus the exercise of systematic violence to create a clear Jewish majority that would correspond to and justify the formation of a Jewish state and the Judaization of state organs is still conceptualized as part of an unavoidable war between two nations – not as violence exerted against the many who insisted on continuing their life without necessarily taking sides in the 'national conflict' that was imposed as the sole tolerated description of reality.

The unquestioned adoption of military terminology, e.g. 'battles' and 'operations', made insignificant the wide range of roles the army played in violating the hundreds of civil alliances among Palestinians and Jews achieved in 1947–8. The civilian population can by no means be classified and identified as one of the fighting sides in a war, and the violent policies seeking to transform the politico-demographic reality in order to establish a new regime in Palestine cannot be described as a war against another army. From the photos that I included in the section headed 'military governmentality' one can reconstruct the systematic organization of expulsion and the successive phases of its completion. The selection of population – separating the old from the young and the men from women and children – is repeated in photos from various localities; the photos also indicate that in various places the army supplied the buses – they are marked 'Army' – and made sure they reached the newly established border. In a photo from Haifa, soldiers even accompanied individuals to make sure they reached the port. At Ijlil or Atlit, the army functioned as a construction contractor, imprisoning Palestinians and exploiting them as a labour force. The new and varied forms of violence exercised by the army of the newly established regime must be taken into account and weighed against the scattered battles and violent clashes between armed forces before one calls the period from November 1947 to March 1949 a 'war'.

From the photographs one can reconstruct the new regime's efforts to undermine the possibility of a common world and civil life shared by

Arabs and Jews, the entire citizenry of the land. This destructive effort was part of a whole system of 'military governmentality', i.e. managing the civilian population – the Palestinians, certainly, but the Jews as well – with military logic. The symbiosis of military logic and civil order has characterized the Israeli regime ever since its inception, and cannot be restricted to the Palestinian sector. Freedom of movement was denied Palestinians, but was controlled and administered for Israelis as well. The caption for a photo taken in Jerusalem describes it as 'curfew', when in fact what we see is a lost woman, presumably Jewish, looking for answers, and as the city is under curfew she addresses the soldier who now controls the public space and allegedly provides her security. The transformation of public space into a space mastered by military logic did not just suddenly happen. The first day of conscription to the IDF was not really a success and was, therefore, followed by a huge operation code-named 'Beser', whereby 3,200 soldiers fine-combed Tel Aviv with dogs and conducted a careful house-to-house search to flush out those who were already termed 'draft dodgers' (*mishtamtim*).[8] Careful reading of these photographs – not restricted to what the picture is supposedly 'about' – shows that military presence always means the end of civil life, for Jews as well as for Arabs. Citizens quickly accepted and adopted the constraints imposed by the military on public space and the boundaries it allocated for that space. This can be illustrated, for example, by a photo from the Jaffa ghetto indicating that, while Palestinians were being trained to become inmates in public space, Jews across the road were trained to live in the presence of people enclosed in a ghetto just because they were Arabs.

The more deeply I viewed photographs from that period, all the less plausible became the use of 'war' as the general organizing category of the photographed situation. The term itself has gradually revealed itself as an effect of the regime's power to impose its unifying logic of national enmity upon complex civil relations. But the Nakba appeared insufficient historiographically and could not frame the reading of these images of violence. It presupposes and reproduces the split between the two populations and preserves the catastrophe of 1948 as an object for Palestinian history and concern, as if Israeli Jews can proceed with their life without accounting for these dramatic events in their own history. The Nakba framework places all Jews on one side and all Palestinians on the other, ignoring the role of the Nakba in creating the national rift as well as its destructive effects within the Jewish population.

By viewing the protagonists depicted in the photos as opposing 'sides' in a conflict, one ignores two important things: first, this view fails to account for the considerable history of common civil resistance to the violence of war all over Palestine until the very end of the 1940s. Second, one ignores the force it took to silence attempts among Jews to acknowledge and condemn – or at least problematize – the overt violence of expulsion and destruction depicted in the photos. The division between Arabs and Jews as ruled and rulers did not happen all of a sudden. Look at this photo from al-Nasirah. The city had been captured the day before the photo was taken. Women, children and the elderly remained in their homes under curfew. The elderly Palestinian man seems hesitant. He stands shrinking in his suit while the two Palestinian women openly and vigorously gesture to the soldier. They are telling him they do not understand the curfew, fearlessly demanding their right to be there. Although armed, the soldier, too, does not react as one who clearly knows how to respond. Otherwise the Palestinians would already have been forced to return to their home and the soldier alone would dominate the public space. The women and the soldiers are learning their new positions, roles and functions.

The expulsion, destruction and dispossession we are looking at should be questioned as affecting the entire population, victims and perpetrators alike, as well as generations of later spectators. For this, a new type of visual grammar is needed, an exercise in active/passive modes of viewing in a way that anything that can be said about Palestinians – for example, the statement 'they *were deported and deprived of citizenship*' – should be made inversely about Jewish Israelis: '*they deported* Palestinians while establishing their own citizenship'. Only with this to-and-fro movement could a common ground be possible out of which a potential history can be drawn.[9]

Thus, when photographs of the violence of 1947–8 are carefully read, both protagonists appear as part of the same history that cannot be narrated separately. Both appear in their mode of becoming – becoming victims or perpetrators. From this perspective, their fateful trajectories appear inseparable, and the partition of their history into two national narratives becomes an unproblematic acceptance of partition not merely as a political fact but also as an unsurpassable historiographic framework. Constitutive violence cannot be undone without redeeming both victims and perpetrators, which the present regime keeps producing as readymade positions for Palestinians and Jewish Israelis.

Let us live together

In 2007, in Yael Bartana's *Mary Koszmary (Nightmares)*, a Polish intellectual addresses the Jews, calling to them: 'Come. Let us live together, let us be different but not harm each other.'[10] In his speech, Slawomir Sierakowski emphasized the nightmares that have haunted Poles ever since their land was ethnically cleansed of Jews.

The possible return of Jews to Poland is not merely the renewed possibility of Jewish life in Poland but rather the renewed possibility of life-together revived out of the ruins of ethnic cleansing. The rejection of ethnic cleansing is to serve as a basis for new partnership. Although this work focuses on the Jewish/Polish context, its scope is wider by far. Ever since I heard it, this speech has haunted me relentlessly with its ramifications on other political contexts and most particularly the local context of Palestine. It resounded in my head until, one day, it emerged in my own language as an address to Palestinians:

> Only with you, Palestinian women and men – by force of our common demand to be governed equally – can the state embody its proper, favorable dimensions: a neutral framework upheld by the governed and for their sake. Neither negotiations nor conditions, neither 'peace' treaties nor transition phases but a basic demand – by the governed and by those who have been expelled from the sphere of governance – to be counted and be a part, to become citizens, imagining their future, reinstating political partnership.

'Palestinian women and men', I repeated in my imagination until a certain day it was no longer a matter of imagining a future but of reconstructing it from the past that had to be imagined anew. This happened when – while trying to locate in the archive a single civil contract between Jews and Palestinians mentioned in a single line of a book Benny Morris published in 1989 – I was greatly surprised to find hundreds of documents recording such contracts, signed in Palestine in the years 1947–8.[11]

I learned that intense civil activity had taken place throughout the country at that time, and was completely ignored by historians. Its removal from historical narratives supported the retroactive depiction of the 1948 war as the culmination of a long-lasting national conflict. This civil activity whose

FIGURE 8.4 *Still from Civil Alliances, Palestine 47–48, a documentary by Ariella Azoulay, 2012, 48 min (see: https://youtu.be/lqi4X_ptwWw)*

amplitude I had just begun to reconstruct included urgent encounters, some short and spontaneous, others planned in advance and carefully designed in detail – whose Palestinian and Jewish participants raised demands, sought compromises, set rules, formulated agreements, made promises, asked for forgiveness, made efforts to reconcile and compensate – and did everything possible not to allow violence to take over their lives. They did their utmost to halt the violence that national and military forces were intent on igniting, and negotiated with each other in order to create mutual civil alliances. This tremendous civil effort continued during the constitutive violence that was practised in Palestine between 1947 and 1949, making obsolete the efforts of citizens to imagine their future outside the dictates of the nation-state.

In the nascent global order consolidated and implemented in the final months of the Second World War, such civil activity was doomed, outcast and replaced by a nation-state member of the United Nations Organization. The pairing up of citizenship and national self-determination with forced migration and the creation of non-citizens and impaired citizens was presented as necessary means to reduce the prospects of new national conflicts and was part of the new international order that emerged from the Second World War. Unsurprisingly, as these 'solutions' were conceived and achieved by international organizations, resolutions and state powers,[12] in almost any geographical territory where such a 'solution' was implemented, the conflict that it was supposed to pacify was either generated by such implementation or enhanced and exacerbated.[13]

The pile of documents I found in the Haganah archive, relating to the period between November 1947 (the Partition Plan ruled by the UN) and May 1948 (the official founding of the State of Israel), emerged slowly, not only as a missing chapter of local history, but also as traces of its missing geography. The map these documents help one reconstruct differs from those relatively familiar maps of Palestine before the Nakba, where Palestinians' towns and villages are represented almost exclusively; it is, rather, a map of the mixed and shared space cohabited daily by Palestinians and Jews, which the constitutive violence systematically ruined. The destruction of Palestine included the erasure of this shared map. Its reconstruction had to rely on scattered information drawn from what came to be two different and parallel geographies. When I began to locate the places where these Jews and Arabs met and talked in urgent ad hoc encounters, or in others, planned in detail and well in advance, I realized that these places were ubiquitous, spreading all over Palestine – but it took many hours of pains-taking research to determine the exact location of all these meeting places.

I then invited twenty-five Arabs and Jews of varying age groups, each of them capable of speaking both Arabic and Hebrew, to gather around the reconstructed map and recite these encounters, reiterate the language of the agreements reached and promises made by our ancestors in hundreds of villages and towns during this period. Their conflicting desires and dreams, their strife and miseries, their conflicts and disagreements, emerge, and in the absence of a sovereign, they were compelled to use language differently, to use it with a civil grammar, the grammar that precludes exclusion.

Those vehement joint efforts of Jews and Arabs to preserve their shared life, find peaceful solutions to conflicts and disputes, reach compromises, be mutually attentive to needs, make agreements and promises – all these did not cease once violence erupted. These efforts lasted even while some of the agreements were not observed. In most cases – Deyr Yassin might be recalled as an example – promises were broken not by the inhabitants themselves but rather by members of national militias who tried to impose a new political reality upon the land. In May 1948, the founding of the State of Israel put an end to this mutual recognition by Jews and Arabs of their responsibility for their shared life. The new sovereign rule replaced the old civil rules of the game with new – national – ones. The end of this activity should be compared to the violent end that Robespierre, with his reign of terror, brought to the *sociétés populaires* where an alternative political organization was budding. Not only the similarity between those French societies and local activities in Palestine justifies the comparison, but also the power of terror to make such rich and pertinent activity disappear at once. Numerous were the measures that were taken in order to prevent Palestinians and Jews from gathering together, assembling, speaking to each other, solving their conflicts, cooperating, improving their life or imagining other forms of exchange. Arendt's description of the Jacobin persecution of those societies reads as if it was written about the local context. 'Theoretically,' she writes, 'this was the fight for a unified public opinion, a "general will", against the public spirit, the diversity inherent in freedom of thought and speech; practically, it was the power struggle of party and party interest against *la chose publique*' (Arendt 2006: 245). The stunning similarity is not accidental, as what took place in Palestine in 1948 is the recurrence of the same constitutive event where, in Arendt's words again, is the fight of 'the nation-state against the first beginning of a true republic'.[14]

With the gradual erasure of Palestine, the refusal to let the expellees return, and the consolidation of the violently constructed phenomenal field as origin of the political life in the new state, this struggle became totalitarian. Under the new rule the civil life in Palestine, including this chapter, was erased or made insignificant. The little that was known of efforts to promote civil treaties was presented in a negative light, in the ruling perspective through which civil partnership appears as 'collaboration', namely an act of national treason. A civil reading of documents recording the mutual efforts, collected in the Haganah archive, yields a complex, vital picture full of hope and faith in the power of shared life. This picture cannot be reduced to the national narrative that began to be constructed from May 1948 and projected hopeless polarity and hostility onto the past.

During those numerous encounters and negotiations the participants raised demands, sought compromises, set rules, formulated agreements, made promises, sought forgiveness, made efforts to compensate and reconcile. Their shared purpose was to keep violence from taking over their lives. They sought to protect the common world of their life in Palestine and salvage it from those who wished to destroy it. In over one hundred documented encounters – and probably many more whose records have yet to be restored – they promised themselves and each other the continuation of their shared lives.

This archival material foregrounded by the film has been kept dormant in State archives. The film frames these documents as an important chapter in local history and geography that has been erased from history books to enable the hegemonic historical narrative of an enduring Arab–Jewish conflict. Gathered together, these stories are presented for the first time as significant common civil efforts of Jews and Palestinians. The presence of two cameramen mingling with the speakers and filming them, being captured by a third camera fixed in the ceiling, embodies the fact that these were exciting news developing and persisting day after day for half a year, and their outcome was not foreknown. The film ends as the map is covered by hundreds of white dots embodying the extent of the agreements spread throughout Palestine.

It rejects the narrative of inevitable war between two homogeneous sides and insists on reproducing numerous, rich models of conflict resolution that were practised in Palestine until shortly before the creation of the State, also contradicting the image of communities whose sole interest is to dispossess each other and risk their lives in a spiraling escalation of violence. The film reconstructs the historical moment when Palestinians and Jews together, as equal partners, sought ways to maintain and protect their shared life in the same territory and when local conflicts eventually emerged they found ways to solve them.

To Edward Said's formulation of imperialism as theory and colonialism as practice, 'differential citizenship' should be added as historiography and a vantage point. Much has been written about the theory and the practice, about colonialism being a lever for acquisition of more and more land, money and manpower. Too little, however, has been written about differential citizenship that dictated colonial historiography and to a large measure also shaped the horizon of the anti-colonialist position. This historiography is based on the national–sovereign delineation that dictated the boundaries of narrated history as national history, often demarcated from the geopolitical context in which it unfolded. Thus, for example, for about two hundred years the French and American revolutions were studied as national events, isolated from the Atlantic context in which they took place. While the history of the State of Israel has been written as detached from Palestinian history, as though the Nakba – the Palestinian catastrophe – happened by itself and is an internal Palestinian affair, and as though the declaration of the State of Israel, the violence that became law, indeed created a distinct time–space unit whose Jewish Israeli rulers can also rule the history that will be told of and about it.

Out of such historiography, peoples – and their international supporters – wishing to be liberated from the bonds of colonialism, could hardly imagine liberation that does not entail national self-determination and the replication of the sovereign citizenship model. If totalitarian regimes of the first half of the twentieth century sought 'world domination', as Arendt argued, with the dissemination of the model of nation-state based on differential bodies politic, world domination gets a different meaning. The violence required to create and maintain non-citizens and non-governed within differential politic bodies is made into an implementable legal policy, and its outcome – dispossessed citizens – are what Arendt termed 'superfluous', sundered from the violence involved in their fabrication, and their claims are meaningless for the good functioning of the political regime. The omnipresence of the differential body politic, its world domination, makes of the phenomenal field it creates to emerge as the order of things, the common standard.

Time has come for Palestinians to return to Palestine. Time has come for Jewish Israelis to join the Palestinians and claim pre-partition Palestine as their lost country. It is time for Jewish Israelis to cease the reproduction of violence, maintaining the consequences of the constitutive violence of 1948 that made them citizens, and Palestinians non-citizens, of their homeland. Time has come for Jewish Israelis to recognize the constitutive disaster – the Nakba – not only as a Palestinian catastrophe but as a catastrophe in the production of which they are implicated on a daily basis.

Time has come for the second and third generations of perpetrators – descendants of those who expelled Palestinians from their homeland – to claim *our* right, *our* fundamental and inalienable right: *the right not to be perpetrators*. Without this fundamental right one can never be a citizen governed equally with others.

Notes

1   The original quotation from Dayan is from *Ha'aretz*, 4 April 1969.

2   A film by Mustafa Abu Ali (1974) https://www.youtube.com/watch?v=2WZ_7Z6vbsg. The film disappeared with the disappearance of the PLO cinematic archives in 1982 during the Israeli invasion to Lebanon (see King and Extras film on the loss of these archives, by Azza Al-Hassan).

3   Jean Mohr took these photographs for the Red Cross in the late 1940s.

4   On this book as a photo-essay see W. J. T. Mitchell (1994), 'The Photographic Essay: Four Case Studies'. In *Picture Theory*. Chicago: Chicago University Press.

5   See Ariella Azoulay (2011), 'Photography without Borders'. In Thomas Cushman (ed.), *The Routledge International Handbook of Human Rights* (London: Routledge), on the transformation of Palestine into a borderless photographic studio.

6   See the last section of photographs of Ariella Azoulay, *From Palestine to Israel: A Photographic Record of Destruction and State Formation, 1947–1950*. London: Pluto Press, 2011.

7   All the photos discussed here can be viewed in the book in which this archive is materialized (Azoulay 2011) and in the later exhibition I curated based on its materials and other photographs under the title 'Potential History'. The additional images can be seen in 'Potential History' (2013), *Critical Inquiry* (39 (3)): 548–74.

8   Reconstructing the itinerary of the 'Beser' operation, Tomer Gardi counted one soldier stationed every 14 metres from the north end of Tel Aviv to the south (Gardi 2011).

9   This notion of common ground guided Hilal and Petti in their collaboration with Eyal Weizman on the project 'De-colonizing Architecture'.

10 Excerpt of Bartana's film can be watched here: https://www.youtube.com/watch?v=3-53eGNNZSA

11 In his book on the Palestinian Refugee Problem, published in 1989, Benny Morris mentioned the existence of a civil agreement between the inhabitants of both the Palestinian village Deyr Yassin and the nearby Jewish neighbourhood Giv'at Shaul. This line haunted me for years, as Deyr Yassin was the place where an atrocious massacre had taken place. Not surprisingly, no historian wrote about this or any other agreements achieved between the Jews and Palestinians. (See Benny Morris, 2003. *The Birth of the Palestinian Refugee Problem revisited 1947–1949*, Cambridge: Cambridge Middle East Studies.)

12 'Thus all appeals on behalf of Zionism were international appeals perforce. The site of Zionist struggle was only partially in Palestine; most of the time until 1948 – and even after – and Weizman's own work is the best case in point – the struggle had to be waged, and fueled, and supplied, in the great capitals of the West' (Said 1979: 23).

13 On the creation of the Palestinian–Jewish conflict by the constituent violence exercised following the partition plan see Azoulay 2011.

14 The 'spectacular success of the party system', Arendt continues, 'and the no less spectacular failure of the council system were both due to the rise of the nation-state, which elevated the one and crushed the other' (Arendt 2006: 247).

References

Arendt, H. (1979), *The Origins of Totalitarianism*. New York: Harcourt.
Arendt, H. (2006), *On Revolution*. London: Penguin.
Azoulay, A. (2011), *From Palestine to Israel: A Photographic Record of Destruction and State Formation, 1947–1950*. London: Pluto Press.
Azoulay, A. (2013), 'Potential History', *Critical Inquiry* 39 (3): 548–74.
Chung, W. (2005), *Control and Freedom*. Boston, MA: MIT Press.
Gardi, T. (2011), *Stone, Paper*. Jerusalem: Hakibbutz Hameuchad.
Morris, B. (2003), *The Birth of the Palestinian Refugee Problem revisited 1947–1949*, Cambridge: Cambridge Middle East Studies.
Said, E. W. (1979), *The Question of Palestine*. New York: Times Books.
Said, E. W. (1986), *After the Last Sky*. New York: Columbia University Press.

CHAPTER NINE

The Missing Homeland of Edward Said

Aamir R. Mufti

1.

Edward Said died on 25 September 2003 at the Long Island Jewish Medical Center, where he had received periodic treatment for the rare form of leukaemia from which he had suffered for over a decade. We may consider it the final paradox of his life that on the death certificate his place of birth is identified as 'Jerusalem, Palestine'. In death, it seems to me, this son of a Jerusalemite and a Nazarene, who was born in 1935 in Jerusalem, raised there and in Cairo, educated in both those places and in Massachusetts and New Jersey, and who restlessly travelled the four corners of the world while making his home for the last four decades of his life in Morningside Heights in Manhattan – in death, this man may be said to have found his missing homeland.

Palestine is in a strong sense a non-place, constantly required and repeatedly failing to prove its existence (Cleary 2002). Take the revealing case of Elie Suleiman's *Divine Intervention*, an avant-garde film about life under the occupation, structured as a series of vignettes largely without dialogue, which was denied the right to compete in the 'best foreign film' category of the Academy Awards in 2002 as the entry for Palestine on the grounds that such a place did not exist. The work of the imagination in fashioning its own collective and communal vectors is itself erased in this demand before the fact, before even its existence can be acknowledged, that the work of art prove that it in fact comes from *somewhere*.[1] Palestinian works of art, Said often pointed out, experience the judgement that they come from nowhere as an *internal* pressure and anxiety, not just as an external act of censorship and repression. The strange life of the name itself in world politics over the last several decades is testimony to the unreal reality of this non-place. Unlikely though this seems, George W. Bush was the first sitting American president at least since the 1950s to use the name by itself in public: Palestine. Even in the public discourse of the Clinton administration, which is generally thought to have brought at least the Fatah movement in from the cold, 'Palestine' could only ever occur as a qualifier for something else: 'the Palestinian Territories', 'the Palestinian Authority', 'the Palestinian people', even 'a future Palestinian state' – but not *Palestine*. The name of this non-place, however, has many other lives, distinct from, though never quite untouched by, the language of geopolitical power – as 'the inside' (*al-dākhil*) for Palestinian communities dispersed across the world, above all, but also in the political imagination of the Arab world more broadly, and in many places in the Third World, from its resonant appearance in Urdu poetry in India and Pakistan, to the so-called *Palestinos* in Havana, migrant workers from the Cuban countryside living in impoverished, refugee-like conditions (*The Economist* 1997).

In this essay I attempt to examine Palestine as image and idea in order, first, to produce an inventory of some of its modes of signification and circulation in our worlds. My ultimate goal, however, is to suggest some ways of understanding the uses of Palestine as historical experience for critical thinking in our times. To this end, I shall turn to the elaboration of Palestine in Said's oeuvre, which undertakes, I argue, a radical refashioning of the meanings of homeland. In such works as *The World, the Text, and the Critic, After the Last Sky*, 'Reflections on Exile', the memoir *Out of Place*, and a polemical exchange with Michael Walzer on the meanings and uses of the Exodus narrative, Said reflects explicitly on the possibility of criticism and its relationship to homeland, that is to say, to a matrix of ancestral places and meanings. 'The strength of the Canaanite position, that is, the exile position', he writes in critique of Walzer, 'is that being defeated and "outside," you can perhaps more easily feel compassion, more easily call injustice injustice, more easily speak directly and plainly of all oppression, and with less difficulty try to understand (rather than mystify or occlude) history and equality' (1986a: 105). If 'secular criticism' entails for Said, as I have argued elsewhere, a dialectical disturbing of location and connectedness, of nothing less than our habitual modes of inhabiting the world, then Palestine provides for it the image of the appropriate forms of *attachment* to place and people, of ties to the (missing) homeland (Mufti 1998).

As Judith Butler has argued in *Parting Ways: Jewishness and the Critique of Zionism*, Said refashions an earlier tradition of exilic thinking, which was of course significantly informed by Jewish historical experience, into a way of thinking about cohabitation in historical Palestine between Jews and Arabs. Far removed in its affective and conceptual investments from the *cosmopolitanism* that has become prominent in some recent discussions in the humanities, secular criticism is in the end more an exercise in anguished and failed attachment than one of sanguine detachment. The homeland of criticism is, for Said, a *missing* homeland. Above all, however, I am interested here in the troubling question raised by the disappearance of Palestine itself: what does it mean to come from, or even to be 'inside' or 'outside'(*al-dākhil* or *al-khārij*) a place that does not exit? Said raises these resonant terms of the everyday Palestinian lexicon, I shall later argue, to the level of conceptuality in order to explicate the relation of criticsm to place and world.

The Palestinians emerged in the postwar era as the quintessential stateless population, marked by displacement and exile, uprooted from home and ancestral places and meanings, from state and nation, from the most basic political and civil rights, and from visibility itself. I take the emergence of the figure of stateless Palestinian as my starting-point in order to examine the very possibility in our times of thinking of, with, and for one's homeland. How and when did this figure emerge? What does it do to us and for us? What meanings does it carry, what warnings and portents, in those battered pieces of baggage it carries as it rushes yet again towards the imagined promise of relief across some border or boundary, or is expelled from one country or territory to another, only to end up in a no-man's-land that is at once territorial, juridical, political and symbolic? I shall be concerned with questions such as these in what follows. But this globally recognizable figure is also given to stubborn, even irrational acts of resistance, both inside and outside this place that does not exist. Starting in the last years of the 1960s, regionally and globally dispersed communities of Palestinians underwent a historical transformation that was simultaneously political, social and cultural in nature. The Revolution (*al-thawra*), as it was called, lasted nearly two decades and produced one of the most iconic political figures of the second half of the twentieth century – the Palestinian fedayee – a figure of planetary scope and reach. The fedayeen as a whole constitute one of the least documented and least understood of the many vanguards of the global 1960s and 1970s.

This internationalism of the Palestinian national movement in the decades of its emergence is well known but little understood. The fedayeen came to be at the forefront of the worldwide culture of anti-imperial solidarity of these decades, drawing to their ranks supporters and sympathizers from across the formerly colonized world. In the Revolution, anyone could become a Palestinian, as Jean Genet observed in *Le captif amoureux* (1986); and the fedayeen as a social group marked the very antithesis of identitarian rigidity. They were thus one of the most visible icons of the global anti-colonial struggle, at the forefront of the dispersed political culture whose development we now generally associate with the long aftermath of the conference of Asian and African states held in 1955 in the Indonesian city of Bandung (see Lee 2010). Their presence in the city of Beirut turned it into the international centre of anti-imperial resistance, thrusting it relatively suddenly into a geopolitical role that no city of comparable size and history could have long withstood. The ability of the movement to draw to its cause militants from places as far afield as Japan, German and Venezuela; the appeal of the movement to intellectuals and writers in places as diverse as Pakistan, France and South Africa; its ability, at least for a while, to strike with seemingly equal facility inside Israel, in the Jordanian desert and in European cities; and the ostentatious, *sexy* and often reckless braggadocio inherent in the reputation of the 'stateless' Palestinian fedayee slipping in and out of countries and travelling across the world on multiple passports – all point to an orientation towards the larger world that marks, at the very least, a paradox, coming as it does from the sons and daughters of either the peasantry or what had been just two generations earlier a local and utterly provincial petty bourgeoisie in terms of the larger Ottoman cultural system (see, for example, Sayigh 1979). The very choice of the international jetliner, the icon of a newly promised mobility on a world scale, as the stage for the performance of political actions draws our attention to this worldly orientation.

The Israeli invasion of Lebanon and the siege and bombardment of Beirut in the summer of 1982 were aimed at destroying this vanguard and therefore also the larger historical possibilities associated with it, not just those in Palestine. So in decimating this anti-imperialist vanguard, the Israeli state was serving the purposes of the wider Global North and of global capitalism as such. The summer of 1982 is thus a crucial moment in the historical process of the establishment of the neoliberal order, the process that culminated in 1989 in the collapse of the Berlin Wall. In other words, it was not the collapse of the Soviet Union that vitiated the historical possibility of anti-imperialist emancipation in the decolonizing world, but rather the latter that opened the road to the former.

Said, who belonged exactly to this generation of Palestinians – he was a year older than Ghassan Kanafani and Waël Zuaiter, for instance, both assassinated by the Israeli secret service in retribution for the deaths of Israeli athletes at the 1972 Munich Olympics during a botched German attempt to rescue them from their Black September hostage-takers – is a late figure of this historical constellation. He embodies *the late style of Bandung*, we might say, bringing a sceptical historical epistemology to the double task of re-examining the historical modes of imperialization of the world and re-envisioning the possibilities of emancipation from them in our times. This concept of 'lateness' is of course influenced by Said's own reflections, following Adorno, on those 'late works' in the career of some artists and authors that reject synthesis and convention, including those that have been internal to and associated with the individual career, offering instead ruminations on a lost and unredeemable totality (Said 2006; Gourgouris 2005). But here I emphasize the lateness of a career project as a whole within a larger historical – social, cultural, intellectual and political – constellation. The particular Palestinian historical experience of dispossession and disappearance thoroughly infuses Said's criticism of the dominant forms of Western humanism as well as his attempt to formulate the terms of a humanism of the dispossessed and disappeared, a new mode of critical thinking, humanistic in its ambition and yet skeptical and alert to the particularity and locatedness of any supposedly universalist claim about human experience.

2.

In a brief and well-known passage in the pivotal ninth chapter of her magisterial work, *The Origins of Totalitarianism*, Hannah Arendt has given us a way of thinking about the new world, the global system of nation-states, that was only beginning to emerge at the time of its writing from the ashes of the European genocide and the coming collapse of the colonial empires. I quote the passage in full:

> After the war it turned out that the Jewish question, which was considered the only insoluble one, was indeed solved – namely, by means of a colonized and then conquered territory – but this solved neither the problem of the minorities nor of the stateless. On the contrary, like virtually all other events of our century, the solution of the Jewish question merely produced a new category of refugees, the Arabs, thereby increasing the number of the stateless and rightless by another 700,000 to 800,000 people. And what happened in Palestine within the smallest of territory and in terms of hundreds of thousands was then repeated in India on a large scale involving many millions of people. Since the Peace Treaties of 1919 and 1920 the refugees and the stateless have attached themselves like a curse to all the newly established states on earth which were created in the image of the nation-state ... For these new states this curse bears the germs of a deadly sickness. (Arendt 1979: 290)

That the Zionist presence and project in Palestine are in a full sense colonial in nature is stated in a matter of fact manner, as directly observable fact, and Arendt places the destruction of Palestinian society within a larger, global colonial frame, identifying a structural link between the destruction of Palestine and the dissolution of society in the subcontinent that is known as the partition of India – two events that took place over almost exactly the same stretch of time in the late 1940s. She identifies the knot of a global crisis in the emergence of the post-colonial system of nation-states: the impossibility of assimilating the world's diverse societies and civilizations into the emerging nation-state system without massive rearrangement, the uprooting and displacement (and even annihilation) of the populations newly defined as non-national peoples and minorities.[2] More broadly, therefore, Arendt's analysis foregrounds the fate of these non-national populations, which form for her the ground of statelessness as a 'symptomatic' political experience (Arendt 1979: 272). Nation, minority, partition, statelessness – along with the notion of the right to have rights, this conceptual constellation forms the armature of Arendt's understanding of the political crisis of the modern age, at whose centre she places the history, and the mode of resolution in Palestine, of the European Jewish Question.

Even more decisively for our purposes here, Arendt also articulates an early perception of one of the most stark facts of the political history of the postwar world: the transfer of the problem of statelessness (and of minority as such) at mid-century from European to Third World, and more particularly Palestinian, populations. When we encounter stateless refugees in the 1930s and 1940s, these are primarily Europeans and disproportionately Jewish. From the 1950s and 1960s onward, the term evokes only colonial and post-colonial peoples. The relevant agencies of the League of Nations dealt largely with displaced Europeans; those of the United Nations have dealt overwhelmingly with Third World populations. This transition parallels at the political level what the invention of the welfare state has meant for 'white' Euro-American populations at the socioeconomic level: access to a minimal level of safety and security compared to the rest of humanity. To say the very least, the Palestinians have played an iconic role in this historical transition and transformation.

The most well-known elaboration of the stateless Palestinian in literature is perhaps to be found in *Men in the Sun* (*Rijāl fī al-shams*, 1963), the well-known novella by Kanafani, which Said often described as the quintessential narrative of post-1948 Palestinian experience (1986b: 36). It was published three years after Kanafani's arrival in Beirut, at the end of a trajectory that had taken him from birth and childhood in Acre in Palestine, to a refugee camp in Damascus, where he grew up, and to Kuwait, where for a while he worked as a teacher. In Damascus, Kanafani had become involved with the Arab Nationalist Movement under the mentorship of Dr George Habash, and as the group around Habash morphed in 1967 into the Popular Front for the Liberation of Palestine (PFLP), Kanafani, then only thirty-one years old, emerged as one of the leading intellectuals in the revolutionary PFLP, founding and editing its weekly organ, *al-Hadaf* (*The Goal*) and serving as its public spokesman. He was a prolific novelist, short-story writer, critic, historian, educator, and journalist, widely recognized in his own short lifetime as one of the leading Palestinian writers. Kanafani was killed in 1972 at the age of thirty-six with his young niece, when a bomb rigged to his car by Mossad agents exploded under them, one in a series of assassinations of Palestinian intellectuals in retaliation for the Munich Olympics killings – including Zuaiter, whose life and death in Rome that same year are the subject of a remarkable work of installation art by Emily Jacir.[3]

The novella tells the story of three Palestinian men of different ages, each trying to cross the border from Iraq into Kuwait in search of employment, and the water tanker driver, also Palestinian, who undertakes to smuggle them across together inside his empty tanker. The existence of Palestine as a *place* is very much in question in the story, and Said's own reflections on the idea of place are pertinent in this context. For Said, the modern experience of place is fundamentally linked to a 'proprietary' notion of culture, to 'culture as possessing possession' and thus to 'the idea of the nation, of a national-cultural community as a sovereign entity'. The sense of place is thus a social artefact, a symbolic fabrication that ensures the determination of 'what is *extrinsic* or *intrinsic* to the culture' (emphasis added). I want to suggest that Said's language here is resonant with the colloquial Palestinian notions of 'outside' and 'inside', and I shall return to that important and fascinating question in some detail shortly. Here we might just note that this series of concepts points towards and culminates in the concept of the state – place, nation, culture and state – as Matthew Arnold, Said notes, already understood. Culture is thus 'a system of discriminations and evaluations ... for a particular class in the State able to identify with it; and it also means that culture is a system of exclusions legislated from above but enacted throughout its polity' (1984: 9). Against these settled 'hierarchies' of culture that are inherent to its life in the state, Said attempts to develop an epistemology of *homeless* social experience (1984: 11).

In Kanafani's novella all the normalized determinants and markers of place are missing. It opens, for instance, with an interior dialogue of Abu Qais, the oldest of the three refugees, as he wakes up on a damp piece of earth unable immediately to determine the identity of that piece of earth as place, wondering if he is on his land a thousand miles and more than a decade away. Even his eventual recognition that he is on the bank of the Shatt al-Arab outside Basra returns him to his former village and a school geography lesson he once overheard describing this river on the Iraq–Iran border, formed by the confluence of the Tigris and the Euphrates. Palestine is thus in at least one concrete narrative sense a *non-place* in the story – the action in the present is located entirely in Iraq and just inside Kuwaiti territory, hundreds of miles and a decade away from historical Palestine, which now seems to exist only in fragments of memory for a few of the individual characters. In other words, 'Palestine' is not just an imagined place in this passage, an imagination of place as such, it is also a different time. Hence the allegorical significance of the death of the three refugees being smuggled from Iraq into Kuwait in the belly of the empty water tanker. The men die after the tanker has left Iraq but before it has been granted legal entry into Kuwait, suffocating inside the tanker under the blistering desert sun as the tanker driver and part-time smuggler is delayed by the minor officials at the border post who engage him in light banter. Their death occurs, in other words, between two nation-states, that is, in a sort of no-man's-land, a strip of land that belongs to no one state and therefore may be said to belong to all those who have no state or place of their own. No-man's-land is in fact a recurring image in the literature of the historical transition I am exploring here, for instance in the literature of India's Partition. Saadat Hasan Manto's iconic Urdu short story 'Ṭōbā Ṭēk Siṅgh' is a well-known case in point – in which the title character, an inmate of a mental hospital whose population is being divided by the two post-colonial states along religious lines, dies on no-man's-land rather than make the choice that is being offered him by the emergent nation-state system in the subcontinent – but there are numerous other instances, by Manto and others (Mufti 2007). But in Kanafani's story the border and no-man's-land play a somewhat different role, with the novella exploring one of the most often recurring experiences associated with post-1948 Palestinian life – the sudden emergence of a population stuck at the border between two political and territorial entities, as seen once again in our own times at Iraq's border with Syria in the aftermath of the Anglo-American invasion of the former country in 2003, and in the densely populated wasteland separating Gaza from Egypt after the Israeli closure and siege of Gaza following Hamas's electoral victory in 2006.

Finally, as Said has noted, the question that Kanafani's story confronts is that of representabilty itself, 'the almost metaphysical impossibility of representing the present' (1986b: 38). The question that confronts the Palestinian work of art, in other words, is how to represent a non-place. 'Return' (al-'awda) is of course one of the master concept-metaphors of Palestinian political life. But regaining 'Palestine' is in no simple sense a question of land and territory in Kanafani's novella, it having become in the process of its disappearance a signifier that attaches itself to too many things, places and memories, generating an excess of meanings. Behind all this of course lurks a sense that the Palestinians, the victims of the quintes-sential victims of fascist militarism in Europe in the first half of the century, have become precisely like those Jewish victims in their homelessness, and both the iconic figure and historical agents of a new internationalism. The story's famous and controversial ending – the tanker driver Abul Khaizuran reproaches the dead men for dying silently and not banging on the walls of the tanker as the heat became unbearable, but leaves their bodies in the end on a garbage heap outside Kuwait City – also carries echoes of the experience of the death camps: before dumping the corpses, he searches them carefully and removes their few valuables.

At one level, of course, the nation-states in play here, and the border whose crossing is a matter of life and death for the stateless refugees, must be understood as signifiers in their dense historical particularity. Iraq and Kuwait, carved out as distinct political territories by the colonial powers out of the collapsed Ottoman Empire in the post-First World War years, largely in line with the terms of the Anglo-French Sykes–Picot Agreement, which was secretly signed by the powers in 1916 and exposed for the first time by the Bolsheviks after the war, mark in the story the colonial *partitioning* of Arab society in the southeastern regions of the Ottoman sphere and the installation of a system of rival polities whose destructive legacy it fell to pan-Arabism to try, unsuccessfully in the end, to confront and overcome.[4] The continued working of the historical trauma attached to 1922 may be gauged by its repeated manipulation in the discourse of militant jihadism today, including the very recent revival of the terms *khilāfa* (caliphate) and *khalīfa* (calif) – the latter being the title of the Ottoman Sultan in his claimed role as the head of global Sunni Islam until the institution was abolished by Turkish Republicans – by the so-called Islamic State in Iraq and Syria. At another level, the story's very delinking of the question of Palestine from territory – the refugees are not attempting to return to their own historical homeland – points it towards larger questions concerning the political landscape of the twentieth century, making of the story a parable about the notion of homeland as such, about the characteristic political form of the modern era – the nation-state – and 'the curse', to recall Arendt's mixed metaphor, that attaches itself to it 'like the germs of a deadly disease'. It draws attention to the hugely unequal distribution of the ability to cross international borders that is a constitutive feature of the global system of nation-states. More specifically, it highlights the perils and the maddening paradoxes of any attempt at mobility if in fact you come from *nowhere*.

3.

It is these many paradoxes and the fragmentedness and discontinuities of Palestinian experience that Said takes as his subject in *After the Last Sky*. There is, to say the least, something curious about the place of this book in Said's oeuvre as a whole. It contains some of the most powerful language he ever wrote, and yet it continues to be one of the least commented upon of his works. It is a declaration of love for a globally dispersed agglomeration of communities and ways of life only tenuously tied to each other, with almost none entirely free of the threat of annihilation and yet somehow confident of their mutual connections, affiliations and responsibilities. An encounter with its prose, open-ended and bleeding on each page into Jean Mohr's remarkable photographs, is always a compelling experience – but whether this effect is primarily aesthetic, ethical, political, all of these together, or something else altogether, remains far from clear in the end. Any attempt to capture and fix its argument, claims or 'message' about an external reality in propositional terms seems to fail miserably, turning its words to ashes before the reader's eyes. And yet, the language itself makes it impossible for a reading of it to be merely a contemplative or formalist experience. Is it polemic or is it literature? In this sense, this work of Said's can be compared to some of the most complex and avant-garde examples of the essay form in the Western languages in the twentieth century – including Benjamin in *One-Way Street*, for instance, but more proximately, perhaps, John Berger's works, especially *A Seventh Man*, also a collaboration with Mohr, which served Said as a model for his own collaboration with the photographer.

Said's own comments about the language of the essay, however, seem strangely schematic at first:

> [The book's] style and method – the interplay of text and photos, the mixture of genres, modes, styles – do not tell a consecutive story, nor do they constitute a political essay. Since the main features of our present existence are dispossession, dispersion, and yet also a kind of power incommensurate with our stateless exile, I believe that essentially unconventional, hybrid, and fragmentary forms of expression should be used to represent us. What I have quite consciously designed, then, is an alternative mode of expression to the one usually encountered in the media, in works of social science, in popular fiction. (1986b: 6)

'Style' *and* 'method'. What does it mean *programmatically* to write a 'fragmentary' narrative? What is the nature of this voice that reflects upon its own programmes and procedures in this manner? Does it stand outside of, and exercise command over, that experience of dispossession and 'that alternative mode of expression'? What this passage reveals is a dimension of hybridization in the event that is this text – a dual performance as artist and critic, narrative and criticism. Locked in embrace with Mohr's photographs, Said's text offers glimpses of ways of inhabiting the world that, as he puts it in the polemic with Walzer, are 'unredeemed, strange, displaced and outside moral concern' from the perspective of power and possession and seeks to establish their indispensability to the possibility of critical thinking itself (1986a: 105). In a powerful essay on the art of Mona Hatoum, Said lays out in startling terms the stark choice confronting a critical and creative intelligence when faced with the force of conformism in the world: either the intransigence of Jonathan Swift, whose 'profanity is incurable', or the mourning and restoration in T. S. Eliot, who offers 'a totally redeemable home after the first one expires' (2000a: 15). The formal and stylistic complexity of *After the Last Sky* is thus equally an inscription of a 'belligerent intelligence', a term Said uses to characterize Swift's very different formal and narrative strategies.

Said's book is of course a hybrid work in a more immediate sense as well, since it consists precisely of both language and images, or, more precisely, of both verbal and visual texts. As W. J. T. Mitchell has noted, the always tense and ambivalent relationship between photography and language – is the photograph structured like, or subject to, the codes of language, or is its primary feature an uncoded, indexical relationship to an event? – appears in an even more intense form in the photo-essay as a hybrid form (Mitchell 1994: 281–322). And in *After the Last Sky*, language and image are placed in a shifting and dialogic relation to each other, with the pictures appearing now as illustration, now as occasion, for the writing. Above all, the photographs become in the book a means of exploring the complexities of *figuration* itself, as the text works through the tension within them between a person or event, on the one hand, and figures of various sorts, on the other.

One of the moments where this tension between language and photographic image rises to the surface and becomes the explicit concern of the text comes in the chapter called 'Interiors', arguably the most important in the book. It is also the occasion for the most sustained engagement with gender anywhere in Said's writing. The image in question is a close-up of an older woman, face deeply lined, wearing thick glasses, and smiling, with what looks like a hairnet on her head. Said's initial remarks on this photograph – 'a face, I thought when I first saw it, of our life at home' – are interrupted with the intimation that the author's sister had interrupted this process of figuration with the reminder that the subject of the picture was one 'Mrs. Farraj', a distant relative of the family's living in Amman. As Mitchell observes, the passage marks an acknowledgement of Said's larger 'ambivalence toward the associative complex, Woman/Image/Home, a confession of his complicity in the sentimentalizing of women and of the lost pastoral homeland that fixates the imagination of the Palestinian male' (1994: 318). This anxiety finds a profoundly more painful expression in the retelling of the story of his mother's loss of identity on getting married in Mandate Palestine: the British colonial official who tore up her passport because she would now travel on her husband's, noted that this would further the cause of Jewish immigration into the country by creating bureaucratic room for one more immigrant (1986b: 85, 84, 77–8). The mother's loss is inscribed into this story of the family's very origin, with the author, as a male Palestinian, coming to recognize and acknowledge the guilt of his own formation in this complicity between native and European patriarchy and the project of colonial usurpation.

Women thus play a central role in the exploration of the elusive Palestinian notion of 'the inside' (al-dākhil), to which the chapter 'Interiors' is dedicated, but which is one of the more fascinating and compelling facets of the book as a whole. At one level, al-dākhil registers the fluctuations and inversions in meaning that result from the steady expansion of the Israeli state's control over communities and places once part of Palestine: 'It refers, first of all, to regions of the interior of Israel, to territories and people still Palestinian despite the interdictions of the Israeli presence. Until 1967, therefore, it meant the Palestinians who lived within Israel; after 1967 the phrase expanded to include the inhabitants of the [occupied territories].' Before this expansion, to be min al-dākhil ('from the inside') was an abject condition, a life lived most directly under Israeli domination and cut off completely from the wider currents of the Palestinian and Arab worlds. After the incorporation of the West Bank and Gaza as well into the sphere of Israeli sovereignty, to be inside, already inside, as it were, is a sort of privilege to be envied, the 'privilege of obduracy' (1986b: 51, 68). After the Israeli invasion of Lebanon in 1982, which destroyed organized Palestinian political life in that country and dispersed its remnants to a beach in North Africa, the focus of Palestinian life, Said suggests, is turned from outside to inside. The most dramatic sign of this shift is of course the mass uprising, the intifada, which broke out in 1987 in the territories twenty years after their occupation, leading to Yitzhak Rabin, later a Nobel Peace Prize winner and now an almost mystically revered martyr for peace, instructing the armed-to-the-teeth soldiers of his occupying military force to 'break the bones' of the adolescent boys throwing pebbles and stones at them.[5] If the fidayee was once the icon of Palestinian rebellion 'outside', the icon of the 'inside' is now the young body, arms stretched and tracing an arc through space that ends with the release of a stone in the direction of heavily armed soldiers, soldiers with the explicit instructions to "break" that body. Said's own infamous performance of the act of stone throwing at the Israeli border with Lebanon was thus in a precise sense a gesture of solidarity from the politics of the outside towards the politics of the inside.

But at another, more expansive and more elusive level of meanings, Said notes, al-dākhil points to those zones of the private and interior that emerge wherever Palestinian lives are lived – zones of mutual encounter, recognition, conflict, solidarity, and above all coded exchanges. This 'second meaning of al-dākhil is slightly more complicated than the first. It refers to privacy, to that region on the inside that is protected by the wall of solidarity formed by members of the group, and the hostile enclosure created around us by the more powerful.' For those in the diaspora, the challenge, we might say, is thus how to live on the outside as if on the inside and within hearing of outsiders, many resentful and frequently outright hostile. It might even be possible to say that this paradox comprises one of the book's central preoccupations – the myriad ways in which beleaguered and globally dispersed populations produce and reproduce a sense of commonality but also a relationship to a place that is, in the dominant languages of politics and power, as I have tried to argue, a non-place. The force of exile (manfā) and estrangement (ghurba) is so powerful and all-encompassing in Palestinians' lives, Said suggests, that wherever they encounter one another, they seem to recreate 'Palestine', or at least an 'inside', however tenuously and for the moment. And present in the background of any account of the inside is the figure of woman as custodian of the interior, its memories, and inheritance. Thus, despite the 'crucial absence of women' in the public life of Palestinian communities, Said notes, nevertheless 'I can see the women everywhere in Palestinian life, and I see how they exist between the syrupy sentimentalism of roles we ascribe to them (mothers, virgins, martyrs) and the annoyance, even dislike, that their unassimilated strength provokes in our warily politicized, automatic manhood' (1986b: 52, 51, 77).

For Said, therefore, this everyday and seemingly trivial feature of Palestinian speech practices concerning origins, past and present location, and the gendered nature of place itself represents a profound exploration of Palestinian historical experience – the dialectic of belonging and uprooting, departure and arrival, immediacy (or intimacy) and estrangement, nation and dispersion, centripetal desires and centrifugal existence, self and other, and concreteness and abstraction. In *After the Last Sky*, 'Palestine' thus points to an indeterminate and shifting set of referents – country, nation, place, society, cause, memory, idea, or frame of mind – none of them able to achieve a settled signification. But while 'Palestine' functions as an unstable signifier, it is by no means, Said insists, chaotic or without form. This question of the possibility of *homelessness as form* or, conversely, the possibility of form without recourse, as he puts it elsewhere, to 'the quasi-religious authority of being comfortably at home among one's people', is in fact at the centre of this photo-essay (1984: 16). But it is by no means unique to this work alone within Said's wider oeuvre. It constitutes a preeminent and recurringly articulated preoccupation of his work as a whole, appearing in various and more or less mediated forms throughout his writings.

There is perhaps no more decisive a place to look for the inscription of Palestinian historical experience in Said's critical practice than his description of 'the cooperation between filiation and affiliation that is located at the heart of critical consciousness' – or, to be more precise, the *dialectic* of filiation and affiliation – in the remarkable introductory essay in *The World, the Text, and the Critic* (see also Mufti 1998: 111–12), perhaps the central programmatic text of his entire critical oeuvre. Said identifies a 'three part pattern' in bourgeois modernity in which received and traditional forms of authority, which claim an organic connection to the subject, are repeatedly upended by non-organicist, historically contingent and seemingly voluntaristic forms of connectedness to culture and society. But this displacement, which is experienced as a moment of emancipation, then reverses itself in replicating the very forms of authorization associated with the former/earlier moment. Said calls the first moment and mode filiation, and the second affiliation, drawing, among other things, on the German sociological tradition, above all the distinction between *Gemeinschaft* ('community') and *Gesselschaft* ('society') that is derived from the work of Ferdinand Tönnies, though we may also recall Georg Simmel's analysis of primary and secondary groupings in society. At the level of the individual, and sociologically speaking, one may be said to be *filiated* with those things that seem so primary and defining of the self that the person appears to have been born into those forms of connection. And she is *affiliated* with those groupings, projects and meanings that she has in some sense acquired or achieved in the course of her life in society, which can therefore presumably be acquired and achieved again and differently. But each moment of emancipation carries the potential of its own reversal, and the work of the critic is to interrupt this process of reversal in which forms of affiliation come to replicate the modes of authorization of culture and community associated with the forms of filiation. At the same time, it is a fundamental task of the critical consciousness to seek to turn the filiative relationship to the 'natal culture' itself into an affiliative one, a *re*attachment that takes as its very condition of possibility a prior detachment and displacement from it. Speaking with reference to Arnold's 'assimilation of culture to the authority and exterior framework of the State', Said attributes to the work of culture as such 'the entire matrix of meanings we associate with "home," belonging and community'. And 'outside this range of meanings ... stand anarchy, the culturally disenfranchised, those elements opposed to culture and State: the homeless, in short' (1984: 11, 16). Said seems here to have reinscribed the social situation of the Victorian industrial working class, its potential for Arnoldian 'anarchy' – that is, its potential disruption of bourgeois social relations – as predicated itself on a certain form of homelessness, a suggestive innovation with as yet unexplored consequences for the very concept of proletarian consciousness and its relationship to the national frame in social and cultural terms. Said's account of the dialectic of filiation and affiliation is therefore an account of the dialectical production of place and home as the predicates of social relations, and the interruptive role of critical thinking in their elaboration.

Said's elaboration of exile as consciousness thus departs in significant ways from those dominant and conventional versions that view exile entirely in terms of loss. Exile as a social experience is structured around a fundamentally dialectical logic: it 'is predicated on the existence of, love for, and a real bond with one's native place; the universal truth of exile is not that one has lost that love or home, but that inherent in each is an unexpected, unwelcome loss. Regard experiences then *as if* they were about to disappear' (1993: 336). In speaking of 'exile's intellectual mission', in bringing the problem of exile in articulation with that of the possibilities of critical consciousness, Said insists on turning exile, which could be the most devastating and abject experience, into an *enabling* life condition: 'The exile knows that in a secular and contingent world, homes are always provisional. Borders and barriers, which enclose us within the safety of familiar territory, can also become prisons, and are often defended beyond reason or necessity. Exiles cross borders, break barriers of thought and experience' (Said 2000b: 185). This internal awareness of exile, this 'belligerent intelligence' which seeks to transform the looming possibility of social death, to say nothing of physical annihilation, into the condition of possibility of an embracing of life, is furthermore an *imputed* consciousness, a concept in Lukács's *History and Class Consciousness* to which Said repeatedly returned. Lukács speaks of 'proletarian consciousness' as a form of knowledge of the social process as a whole which may be imputed to the proletariat as a specific location within that social process. It may not always be empirically achievable, and may be objectively blocked due to the structure of specific conjunctures, but it is the ultimate task of all political activity – and Lukács is thinking above all of the vanguardist party as such – to seek to bring about its realization within the historical consciousness of social collectivities. Despite the vastly different constellations and political contexts of their thought, I think it is credible to see Said drawing on Lukács here, *imputing* a specific form of historical intelligence to the social and political conditions of exile, displacement and dispossession.

'Exile' or 'homelessness' as Said articulates them in the works I have been drawing upon here are already abstractions from the myriad and concrete minutiae of the historical experience of variously (and differently) dispossessed communities, whose gathering and collation is, we might say, the work of aesthetic practices. But although, as we have seen, Said goes even further in the direction of conceptualization (and thus abstraction) in his discussion of filiation and affiliation, the concept in his elaboration retains a visible and vibrant trace of the particular historical condition and thus of particularity as such. What Said reveals explicitly in *After the Last Sky* is thus the historical reality in dialectical relation with which he develops an epistemology of dispossession, or, to be more precise, *an epistemology of the missing homeland*, the *concrete* experience in constitutive tension with the *abstraction* whose conceptual elaboration is spread out across a range of his works from at least *Beginnings* onward. In other words, Said *translates* a distinct spatial element in Palestinian language and culture, that is, in the historical experience of being Palestinian after 1948 – 'inside' versus 'outside' – into the language of Euro-American criticism, which is as a result itself *disaffiliated* from those cultural and civilizational moorings or filiations and made available for a broader and less partial critique of the structures of power and subjugation in our world. Said's signal achievement therefore may be that he extracts from the everyday Palestinian lexicon a far reaching theory and critique of location and locatedness, an epistemology of the missing homeland that is distinct from both cosmopolitan detachment and the particularist and local forms of belonging – to race, ethnicity, nation, gender and sexuality – that have been privileged in recent decades in a range of critical and political projects.

For Said the Palestinians became the exemplary figure of exile for our times because (in part) of the paradox that 'they have been turned into exiles by the proverbial people of exile, the Jews' (2000b: 178). To be a Palestinian is thus a doubly displaced and doubly vulnerable condition. To 'belong' to Palestine, a non-place, thus implies a uniquely restless imagination, always oriented at an angle to received and congealed social and cultural forms. Put differently, Palestinian historical experience uniquely exemplifies the possibilities of 'Canaanite reading', as Said calls it in his exchange with Walzer: 'Canaanite', in the sense of those who – he quotes Walzer here on the Exodus narrative – 'are explicitly excluded from the world of moral concern' but who necessarily (adds Said) 'resist and try to penetrate the walls banning them from the goods of what is, after all, partly their world too' (1986a: 105). Furthermore, the life and history of 'Palestine', that is, the place that is the missing homeland, is now inextricably tied to that of 'Auschwitz', that is, to the place that marks the history of Jewish annihilation and thus to the enormous cultural archive in the West that contains portents and traces of that inferno. Thus, while the purely 'national' approaches to knowledge of Palestine might be both understandable and conjuncturally necessary, they are hardly sufficient to the complexities of its history, which calls for, Said noted, an 'ironic double vision' that can retain the thought of both of these catastrophes in a single act of thinking (1979: xiii).

In her recent book examining the relationship of Jewishness to Zionism, Butler adopts this double vision but from the other historical direction, arguing that the question of the possibility of Jewish existence in our times, a possibility questioned with massive brutality in the twentieth century by dominant forces in European society, is now inextricably linked with the question of the imperialization of the world in the modern era and the worldwide history of struggle against it, bringing Arendt's argument from mid-century a step further and into our times (2012). This book may even be viewed as a response to *After the Last Sky*, in a discontinuous and discordant conversation out of place and out of time, and it may well be the most important work of cultural and philosophical criticism concerned with the question of the inhabiting of historical Palestine to appear since Said's.

4.

As is well known, in the last decade or so of his life, Said adopted a largely binational position in the Israeli–Palestinian conflict as the only properly *secular* solution to the conflict – the term he actually uses is 'the one-state solution' – first outlined in a *New York Times Magazine* article in 1999. This turn is most meaningful if understood in the context of the historical shift of the focus of Palestinian political life from 'outside' to 'inside'. Speaking of Jews and Palestinians as 'two communities of suffering', Said argued that both 'must resolve that their existence is a secular fact and that it has to be dealt with as such'. To act and think in accordance with this secular condition of social life entails the dismantling of exclusivist narratives of possessionn – of the land, of suffering, of historical memory – in both communities:

> [It means] being willing to soften, lessen and finally give up special status for one people at the expense of the other. The Law of Return for Jews and the right of return for Palestinian refugees have to be considered and trimmed together. Both the notions of Greater Israel as the land of the Jewish people given to them by God and of Palestine as an Arab land that cannot be alienated from the Arab homeland need to be reduced in scale and exclusivity. (Said 1999)

First of all, we may note that binationalism appears here neither as an a priori principle, nor as an empirical matter of political expediency, but rather as a continuous *process* involving mutual adjustments and reorientations that are 'social' in the full sense, that is, incorporating the social imaginaries that both emerge from and inform social relations themselves.[6] Second, this process is a 'secular' one precisely because it rejects the transcendental, absolute and exclusive nature of narratives of national-social cohesion. The movement proposed here is the quintessentially secular gesture in the Saidian sense. It should not be confused with simply give-and-take or compromise in the empirical sense. What is called for instead is the transformation of the very modalities for the making of national-historical claims in contingent, conjunctural and immanent terms.

Said's rethinking of the binational idea, which is part of a larger contemporary recognition of the de facto existence of a single – though extremely polarized and unequal – political and social entity from the Jordan River to the Mediterranean, draws on the Zionist binationalists of the early and mid-twentieth century, but is nevertheless distinct from their formulations, rejecting any notion of a *redemptive* tie or return to the land. It above all carries the insistence that the return to a territorial form of the question of Palestine – as in the now hegemonic 'land for peace' formula – not be allowed to freeze historical possibility into a nationalist frame, even a *binationalist* one. Already a decade earlier in *After the Last Sky*, Said had expressed misgivings about the possible direction of politics and culture in an autonomous Palestinian future, repeatedly cautioning against the danger of replicating the terms of the Zionist solution of the so-called Jewish Question: 'Better our wanderings, I sometimes think, than the horrid clanging shutters of their return. The open secular element, and not the symmetry of redemption' (1986b: 150). His subsequent call for a 'one-state solution' sought to bring the insights of diaspora and dispersal, now an irreducible element in the history of both peoples claiming a homeland in historical Palestine, to the question of the establishment of a homeland and a state: *one* state and *one* society, of *two* exilic and diasporic peoples. Said's binationalism implies that the two hostile societies are now also already one, inextricably intertwined in their inseparable histories of exile and uprooting, the life of the one depending irreducibly on that of the other.

In other words, Said envisions a state, not of *national*, but *exilic* and homeless peoples and attempts to transform the Palestinian attempt to wrest a state from the global system of nation-states into a permanent rebuke to this system itself – an exilic state, as it were, not a nation-state. This is of course a position formulated from and with the experience of those 'outside', but it also reveals the profoundly dialectical nature of the production of outside and inside. For one of the most elusive and bitter ironies of the contemporary Palestinian configuration is that those Palestinians most fully 'inside' – that is, those constituting Israel's violently redefined 'Arab sector' – are also those who are most 'outside', distanced and decentred from a collective Palestinian and Arab existence, having become an alien presence in their own disappeared homeland without having been physically displaced from it, but placed under the permanent, constitutive threat of uprooting and dispersal, a threat made repeatedly by not only right-wing politicians and senior cabinet ministers but also such liberal intellectuals as Benny Morris. To call for an exilic perspective from 'outside' is therefore also, paradoxically, to call for responsibility to the historical experience of these Palestinians who are supposedly 'inside'. Only the fragmentary perspectives of exile (*manfā*) and its attendant forms of estrangement (*ghurba*) can make possible now an attitude of attentiveness to the totality of Palestinian (and Jewish-Israeli) experience.

As the possible refuge of two homeless peoples, the missing homeland of Edward Said is thus a place like those domestic environments in Hatoum's installations where 'the past is not entirely recuperable', a place that is not overdetermined by a redemptive 'return or real repatriation'. In other words, in its complex and contradictory reality it emerges for Said as a secular place, a place that 'travesties the idea of a single homeland', despite being overloaded with religious expectations and meanings, or perhaps precisely because of this excess of millennial meanings. It is a place of habitation marked by 'the precarious humanity we share with each other' rather than the bluster and triumphalism of possession (2000a: 17). In Said's writing, therefore, Palestinian historical experience – the experience of a missing homeland – is placed in a dialectical relation with the possibility of a new humanistic practice, an articulation and elaboration of human possibility from the margins of the world system.

Notes

1   The Academy reversed its decision the following year.

2   For a fuller analysis of this historical conjuncture, see Mufti (2007).

3   On the emergence and early years of the various components of the Palestine Liberation Organization, see Khalidi (2006) and Cooley (1973); for Kanafani's political life, see Siddiq (1984); For the Jacir installation, see *The Hugo Boss Prize 2008* (New York: Guggenheim Museum, 2008).

4   The classic historical work by a participant in the Arab national movement is Antonius, *The Arab Awakening: The Story of the Arab National Awakening* (1969).

5   We are indebted to Jacqueline Rose for reminding us of the place of this remarkable pronouncement in the psychology of Zionism as a whole. See Jacqueline Rose, *The Question of Zion* (2005), ch. 3.

6   On the ethico-political dimension of mutual 'accommodation' in the modern state, see Mufti (2007: 171–6).

References

Antonius, G. (1969), *The Arab Awakening: The Story of the Arab National Movement*. Beirut: Librairie du Liban.

Arendt, H. (1979), *The Origins of Totalitarianism*. New York: Harcourt.

Butler, J. (2012), *Parting Ways: Jewishness and the Critique of Zionism*. New York: Columbia University Press.

Cleary, J. (2002), *Literature, Partition and the Nation State: Culture and Conflict in Ireland, Israel and Palestine*. Cambridge: Cambridge University Press.

Cooley, J. K. (1973), *Green March Black September: The Story of the Palestinian Arabs*. London: Frank Cass.

The Economist (1997), 'Deporting the Palestinians', 15 May, http://www.economist.com/node/149441 (accessed 8 April 2015).

Fromkin, D. (1989), *A Peace to End All Peace: Creating the New Middle East 1914–1922*, London: Deutsch.

Gourgouris, S. (2005), 'The Late Style of Edward Said', *Alif: Journal of Comparative Poetics* 25: 37–45.

Khalidi, R. (2006), *The Iron Cage: the Story of the Palestinian Struggle for Statehoood*. Boston: Beacon Press.

Lee, C. J. (ed.) (2010), *Making a World after Empire: The Bandung Moment and its Afterlives*, Athens, OH: Ohio University Press.

Mitchell, W. J. T. (1994), *Picture Theory*. Chicago: University of Chicago Press.

Mufti, A. R. (1998), 'Auerbach in Istanbul: Edward Said, Secular Criticism, and the Question of Minority Culture', *Critical Inquiry* 25 (1): 95–125.

Mufti, A. R. (2007), *Enlightenment in the Colony: The Jewish Question and the Crisis of Postcolonial Culture*. Princeton: Princeton University Press.

Rose, J. (2005), *The Question of Zion*. Princeton: Princeton University Press.

Said, E. W. (1979), *The Question of Palestine*. New York: Times Books.

Said, E. W. (1984), *The World, the Text, and the Critic*. Cambridge, MA: Harvard University Press.

Said, E. W. (1986a), 'Michael Walzer's "Exodus and Revolution": A Canaanite Reading', *Grand Street* 5 (2): 88–106.

Said, E. W. (1986b), *After the Last Sky: Palestinian Lives*. New York: Pantheon.

Said, E. W. (1993), *Culture and Imperialism*. New York: Knopf.

Said, E. W. (1999), 'The One-State Solution', *New York Times Sunday Magazine*, 10 January, http://www.nytimes.com/1999/01/10/magazine/the-one-statesolution.html?pagewanted=all (accessed 29 April 2015).

Said, E. W. (2000a), 'The Art of Displacement: Mona Hatoum and the Logic of Irreconcilables'. In *Mona Hatoum: The Entire World as a Foreign Land*. London: Tate Gallery, 2000.

Said, E. W. (2000b), *Reflections on Exile and Other Essays*. Cambridge, MA: Harvard University Press.

Said, E. W. (2006), *On Late Style: Music and Literature against the Grain*. New York: Pantheon.

Sayigh, R. (1979), *Palestinians: From Peasants to Revolutionaries*. London: Zed Books.

Siddiq, M. (1984), *Man Is a Cause: Political Consciousness and the Fiction of Ghassan Kanafani*. Seattle: University of Washington Press.

CHAPTER TEN

Versions of Binationalism in Said and Buber

Judith Butler

It is inadequate only to affirm that a people was dispossessed, oppressed or slaughtered, denied its rights and its political existence, without at the same time doing what Fanon did during the Algerian war, affiliating those horrors with the similar afflictions of other people ... This does not mean a loss in historical specificity, but rather it guards against the possibility that a lesson learned about oppression in one place will be forgotten or violated in another place or time.

EDWARD SAID, *AFTER THE LAST SKY* (1986: 44)

It would be easier for me to broach this question of binationalism if it were already discussed widely and we might call upon a shared understanding of its history and its impasses. My sense, however, is that this older idea has yet to be heard. Does binationalism mean that there should be two states, Palestine and Israel, or does it mean that there should be one state which includes equally two peoples? In short, what do we mean by binationalism in the context of Israel/Palestine, a place whose very name is already politically contested. Perhaps there are both one-state and two-state versions of binationalism, or perhaps binationalism describes a condition that is separate from state formation, even at odds with the notion of the nation-state. I pose these questions not because I can, or will, answer them in this text, but rather to make two more limited suggestions: first, that traditions of binational thought have been occluded by the changing history of the meaning of Zionism, even though binationalism named an important strain of Zionist thinking throughout a good part of the twentieth century; and secondly, following Edward Said, that there can be no conceptualization of a workable binationalism within the ongoing terms of settler colonialism. This last seems crucial to consider in the light of debates about 'the one-state solution', for Netanyahu and others would very much like a single state, Israel, which would include what they, invoking biblical claims, call Judea and Samaria – the building of the wall along the Palestinian border with Jordan seeks to materialize that very claim. That version of the one-state solution would absorb Palestine into Israel where, as we know, Palestinians would either remain second-class citizens or have no recognizable citizenship – only residency papers. That version of the one-state is very much in tension with another that would require equal rights of citizenship for all inhabitants of the land, or with legitimate claims to the land, and the eradication of all laws and policies that legitimate illegal land seizures, expulsions, and colonial rule and expansion. If the only way to guard against the first version of the one-state solution is through the establishment of an independent Palestinian state (and so, a two-state solution), would that spell the end to binationalism? Binationalism also works in at least two ways. The increasing number of settlers in the West Bank with full rights of citizenship and on land illegally seized live in proximity with Palestinians who are living under occupation. One could say that Israeli Jews and Palestinians 'live together' there, and that a certain version of binationalism holds. And yet, as long as those forms of proximate living rely upon ongoing forms of structural domination and dispossession, they cannot constitute a form of legitimate binationalism. Even on those occasions where settlers and the colonized live together without explicit violent conflict they remain differentially saturated in power, organized by asymmetrical relations that are suffered and protested against by those living under colonization. Such forms of 'coexistence', which some cynically call 'peace', do not qualify as forms of legitimate political binationalism since they continue colonial rule and, as a result, fail to incorporate principles of democratic equality. So before we commit ourselves to binationalism as such or to a one-state or two-state solution, let us be clear about what we mean by such a term, which versions we accept, which we oppose, and why.

I have found that being able to work in two directions at the same time is obligatory as one tries to think about the very form of relationality designated by binationalism. To follow diverging and converging paths is not the same as vacillation, ambivalence or contradiction; rather, it is an effort to move beyond and against the limits of a single, defining frame and a way of thinking of time as unilinear to pursue an understanding of political complexity and its more promising dynamics. One can go back to the time in which binationalism was actively debated or one could start with the wretched forms of binationalism that have become part of the colonized condition, but in the end it turns out to be obligatory to do both in order to understand what possible and effective notions of the binational are available to critical thought now.

So, starting off from one direction I propose to address a version of binational thought that emerged within Jewish intellectual life, one that was actually a recognized part of Zionism for several decades, and that has disappeared from the semantic reach of political Zionism as we know, reemerging now as an emblem of anti-Zionism. From another vantage point, I want to give some indication of why that historical notion of binationalism developed within Zionist thought proved to be inadequate. In short, even its best versions, in my view, did not adequately call into question Zionism as a settler colonial project. Nevertheless, I want to suggest that some aspects of that tradition of binationalism bear important similarities to the late binational vision of Edward Said or, at least, that these are views that can speak to one another – a comparative approach to binationalism thus enacts one of its possible trajectories at a theoretical level. Said clearly understood this resonance between his view of binationalism and the one formulated within early Zionist debates – but he also underscored the points of divergence between those views and his own.

Said and binationalism

Asked in an interview in 1999 whether his 'vision of inclusion and the one-state solution actually resonates with one of the old streams of Zionism' (Said and Barsamian 2003: 7–8),[1] Said responded that he had read the early traditions, including the early documents of B'rith Shalom, and the plans for federated authority proposed by Ichud, the political party vanquished when Ben Gurion came to power in 1948. Said continues:

> There were people of a fairly important caliber, such as Martin Buber, Judah Magnes, who was the first president of Hebrew University, Hannah Arendt, and a few others who were not so well-known, these are the international luminaries, who realized that there was going to be a clash if the aggressive settlement policies and the unreflecting ignoring of the Arabs pressed ahead. (ibid.)

And yet, Said then makes clear that much of this discussion of binationalism within Zionism, for instance, was part of an 'intra-Jewish debate' taking place 'within the Zionist or Jewish camp'. He continues: 'there were attempts to reach Palestinians. But the situation was overall so polarized, and the British were playing such a Machiavellian role [in 1948], and the leadership of the Zionist community … were also such clever politicians that these individuals, who in the end were individuals, really didn't have much of a chance' (2003: 9). He goes on to say 'it was a rather restricted debate. I don't think one should overemphasize it' (ibid.). And yet, in his essay, 'Truth and Reconciliation', Said revisits this same history a few years later, but now with a greater sense of hope. Let me cite it for you here:

During the inter-war period, a small but important group of Jewish thinkers (Judah Magnes, Buber, Arendt and others) argued and agitated for a binational state. The logic of Zionism naturally overwhelmed their efforts, but the idea is alive today here and there among Jewish and Arab individuals frustrated with the evident insufficiencies and depredations of the present. The essence of that vision is coexistence and sharing in ways that require an innovative, daring and theoretical willingness to get beyond the arid stalemate of assertion and rejection. Once the initial acknowledgment of the other as an equal is made, I believe the way forward becomes not only possible but attractive. (Said 1999)

The second quotation does not fully vitiate the first, but it does open up the question of how to think about associated terms like coexistence, cooperation, cohabitation and even binationalism. What distinguishes the form of binationalism that Said is prone to accept is the reciprocal recognition of equality. A certain circularity emerges here that, in my view, cannot be avoided. It goes like this: one might say that the acknowledgement of the other as equal precedes the radical structural changes at the level of the state that are necessary for substantial forms of cohabitation, for binationalism itself. Or one might say that only once those structural changes, including the end to settler colonialism and the establishment of a constitution, have been made will acknowledgement of equality become possible. At stake is the difference between models of coexistence that assume continuing colonization, and others the realization of which presume its end. What is most important at this juncture is Said's insistence, repeated in *Freud and the Non-European* (2003), that the Jewish tradition includes an experience of diaspora that is crucial for the project of political equality in Palestine. What is that relationship between diaspora and political equality?

At various points in his career of political writing, Said makes a significant distinction between a 'self-segregating' trend in Jewish life, and a diasporic one. As early as 1968 in 'The Palestinian Experience', Said marks the triumph of the former tendency within Zionism, one that 'overrode its own moderates in establishing a form of nationalist segregation that refuses any counter-claim to territory or political rights of self-determination' (Said 1994: 17). He will later argue, in *Freud and the Non-European*, that the diasporic condition of both people, however historically distinct, forms the condition for acknowledgment and alliance between them. As early as 1968, he writes, 'the main characteristics of the Arab Palestinian's life since 1948 have been peripherality, isolation, and silence – all of those are conditions of displacement and loss'. And then within parentheses, he writes, '(It cannot fail to escape the Palestinian's notice, by the way, how much their experience begins to resemble that of the Diaspora Jew)' (1994: 18). And then again, in *After the Last Sky*, his memoir published in 1986, he writes:

I do not like to call it a Palestinian diaspora: there is only an apparent symmetry between our exile and theirs. Besides, the Diaspora no longer exists spiritually and culturally as it once did in Central Europe, with tragic figures like Kafka, Schoenberg, and Benjamin at its core. Today's diaspora is represented centrally by American Zionism, a far different phenomenon ... I find it much easier to debate with an Israeli than an American Jew. (Said 1986: 115)

Later, however, in *Freud and the Non-European*, he will draw implications from this resemblance, emphasizing the 'unhoused and diasporic character of Jewish life' that aligns it 'in our vast age of population transfers' with 'refugees, exiles, expatriates, and immigrants' (Said 2003: 53). He proposes again that this diasporic character of Jewish life is in tension with its self-segregating tradition. In some of his work on binationalism, he refers to Israel and Palestine as two peoples 'irrevocably' bound together. And in that context, he suggests as well that 'Israel and Palestine are parts rather than antagonists of each other's history and underlying reality' (2003: 55).

Said knows exceedingly well that these are distinctly different histories of displacement, and that there is no absolute structural analogy to be drawn between them. After all, it is most often the case that the displacement of the Jews which led to the establishment of Israel was the cause of the dispossession of the Palestinians. Can there still be a way of pursuing the analogy without forgetting the causation here, and what sensibility, what practice of translation, is required for such a task? The establishment of Israel as a sanctuary for European Jewish refugees produced a new refugee problem, that of the Palestinians, which means that a refugee problem continues to be reproduced in the twentieth century up until the present. A comparative approach to the refugee problem (Said was importantly a Professor of Comparative Literature, a field that fosters the recognition of uneasy or unexpected parallels between different texts and contexts, or that regularly undergoes shifts in frame) becomes possible only when the vision is widened to include several instances (Arendt's approach in *On Totalitarianism*, 1951, for sure).

In drawing the analogy between Jews and Palestinians (significantly distinct from any analogy between Israelis and Palestinians) Said is seeking to widen the lens on the refugee problem, mobilizing the potential for a diasporic understanding between those in the diaspora or whose diasporic past continues to inform their ethical and political sensibility. 'Diaspora' is not foregrounded as the aim or goal of politics nor can it possibly describe a fixed location. It is, rather, proposed as a critical perspective on forms of political nationalism that have required repeated expulsion of those perceived as non-national and, in the case of Zionism, those who favour expulsion are understood as 'self-segregating', continuing a form of settler colonialism that is bound up with the historical and ongoing dispossession of Palestinians from their homes, and the building of dwelling structures on those appropriated lands (such as is currently happening under the Prawer Plan which is destroying the homes of 60,000 Bedouins, Palestinians who live in the Negev, and forcing them to leave the area).[2]

Political forms of binationalism either presume that the social or ethical grounds for cohabitation is possible or think that the political form can gradually produce the ethos that makes its implementation possible and sustainable (citing post-apartheid modes of coexistence in South Africa or the state formation in postwar Bosnia-Herzogovina). Said is not being naïve about the possibilities of cohabitation or coexistence. His formulation suggests only that when what he calls 'processes of identity enforcement' (Said 1994: 356) are challenged, and heightened forms of nationalism are put in check (1994: 16), that another understanding can emerge, one that draws upon, and elaborates, a diasporic sensibility drawn from different histories and anticipated by new political forms.

There are, as we know, many sceptical questions that attend any suggestion of this kind. First, the very reason for the analogy between Palestinians and Jews is traced to the fact that Israel forced the expulsion of nearly 900,000 Palestinians in 1948, causing the very dispossession they suffer. This means that Palestinians listening to Said's suggestion are asked to consider that they suffered something that is comparable to what their oppressors have undergone. Palestinian resistance to the analogy is under-standable on such grounds, especially when their oppressors do not seem to draw the analogy themselves. Of course, the Naqba, and the successive expulsions of Palestinians from their lands, are not precisely the same as the expulsion of the Jews from Europe under fascism, and the analogy is made all the more complicated by the fact that it was the Zionists, often those who had been expelled or needed to flee, who then expelled the Palestinians. For Said, then, to ask Zionists to embrace the diasporic character of their own history and ethical sensibility is, at the same time, to ask them to come to terms with their own policies that forced another people out of their homes and off their homeland into an unchosen diasporic condition. We should not underestimate how very difficult it is to narrate and to show the history of the Naqba, as we saw when in the Spring of 2012 right-wing Zionists violently interrupted the efforts of Zochrot to commemorate the Naqba in what has become Israeli public space.[3]

My sense is that in this writing Said is quite mindful of this difficulty, and is seeking recourse to the diasporic trend in Jewish cultural self-understanding precisely to heighten, and to generalize, a commitment to the rights of refugees. It is only consistent for a people to affirm their own rights to be relieved of statelessness, their rights to sanctuary under conditions of persecution, and to make that case by establishing the general and trans-posable character of such rights. And even if the historical conditions of displacement differ, and even if one people – or its emerging and continuing state apparatus – is responsible for the displacement of another, reparation begins precisely through a recognition of the general and transposable character of the rights of the stateless to the political conditions of belonging – whether that is considered as a right to citizenship within an existing state, a right to form a new state, or another exercise of political self-determination that may or may not take state formation as its *telos*.

Second, to be 'against nationalism' seems commendable, if not necessary, but if a people are deprived of the fundamental conditions for national belonging and political self-determination, does nationalism not take on a different valence? A national liberation struggle for basic rights of citizenship is not quite the same as the nationalism of a nation-state that continues to exercise colonial control over a population deprived of full rights of political self-determination. Even as we know that the first kind of nationalism can convert into the second, they remain analytically distinct. And even though the nationalism of a militarized and occupying nation-state is not the same as the nationalism of a people developing a unified resistance to the condition of damaged rights, occupation, dispossession and expulsion, there still may be reasons to be wary of both kinds of nation-alism. Under certain conditions every form of nationalism can convert into that heightened and destructive form. Indeed, is binationalism the linking of two nations and two nationalisms or can the ethos and practice of bination-alism operate as a check on heightened nationalism? Is it the presumption of two equal nations, or is it a critical relation to the nation-state and that form of nationalism? One can emphasize the 'bi' of binationalism, or the 'hyphen' that sometimes enters between the 'bi' and the 'national. Even the proposal of a relative autonomy of both nations within a single state or administrative structure that establishes equality presumes that the one is next to the other, that the very boundaries established between the two are already part of the very definition of each one. There is no autonomous space without a border that has to be negotiated, which means precisely that there is no autonomy without a negotiated relation to the other, and that that relation essentially conditions the very notion of autonomy. So even separation, as we know from other domains of catastrophic intimacy, is usually a way of having a very long-lasting relationship – and often not on the best of terms.

Said is of course not the only referent in the Palestinian history of binationalism. In the 1930s and 1940s, some Palestinians became interested in binationalism in order to establish a firmer framework for entrepreneurial alliances with Jewish settlers in an effort to extend their markets throughout the region.[4] The idea was to link authorities mainly for the purposes of strengthening market partnerships. The point was not political self-determination, but economic collaboration, and so that version might well count as non-nationalist undertaking. In a different vein, Lama Abu-Odeh has argued in 'A Defense of Binationalism' (2001/2) that Palestinians would be brought into a one-state structure that would appeal to international law rather than political rights of self-determination. Palestinians would be required, in her view, to give up their status as 'independent national subjects' and become citizens of greater Israel. That view then relies on a rather substantial intervention by international law into Israeli constitutionalism. Would such an Israel still be based on principles of Jewish sovereignty? Would Palestinians still have to swear allegiance to Israel as a Jewish state? Would they, like contemporary Palestinian Israelis, suffer second-class citizenship, yielding housing and education rights to Jewish citizens, especially those who served in the army? And would they continue to have their rights of mobility and expression restricted? Lastly, would the State of Israel ever agree to a one-state solution that would surely imply the loss of Jewish demographic advantage? It is doubtless important to remember that Netanyahu also wants a one-state solution, one that would lay claim to the entirety of the West Bank as part of Greater Israel and establish cantons on the model of South African Bantustans.

Odeh's proposal only makes sense if the constitutional state she imagines is one that can guarantee equality for all citizens, and that would require the full undoing of Jewish sovereignty and colonization as the basis of the state itself. She calls such a state 'Israel' but she does not exactly lay out what Israel would need to do in order to become such a polity based on constitutional principles of equality.

Salim Tamari has argued in 'The Double Lure of Binationalism' (2000) that binationalism names a wish and an aspiration, the end-result of a political struggle, but without a clear understanding of how such a wish might ever be realized. For Tamari writing in 2000, binationalism remains a wish precisely because it does not include a set of programmatic proposals for its realization. Although that diagnosis remains largely true more than a decade, it is also the case that the 'one-state solution' has become precisely what Israel proffers in a sense that most radically undermines the political claims of decolonization and equality implied by the Palestinian sense of the phrase. As a result, it is important to note that neither a one-state nor a two-state solution can be built on the unaltered ground of colonization. If colonial rule, including its securitarian and military powers, its practices of indefinite detention, expulsion, and its war practices, becomes the basis of either state, then colonial relations are ratified by state formation itself, and the state or states become alibis for the continuation of colonial rule. So before any substantial debate on the one-state or two-state solution can proceed, it is crucial that decolonization is understood not only as a precondition, but as a goal supported by a workable programme. Who would undertake decolonization? Could it be undertaken together, through different means, inside and outside of the existing borders? And how would that work?

Although I am unfortunately not in a position to lay out such a programme (nor should it be my task), I do think that the above framework starts to illuminate why forms of cohabitation based on equality are very different from forms of coexistence that disavow and, hence, ratify forms of colonial rule. In his early political writings, Said made clear that it would not be possible for Israeli Jews and Palestinians to enter into *cooperative* arrangements under conditions in which colonization continues to be the ongoing and unaddresssed condition of that form of cooperation. This point is an important one, since it brings us to the broader question of the conditions of a livable cohabitation, a non-wretched form of binationalism. In 'The Palestinian Experience' Said referred to a condition that 'could not be borne easily', namely, 'to believe in a democratic, progressive multi-confessional [multi-denominational] Palestine and yet to be forced to live "cooperatively" under Israeli domination' (Said 1994: 23). Here Said refers to the numerous cooperative associations that were set up after 1948 to establish cultural good will with Palestinians who had remained within the borders of 1948. Shortly thereafter, in the early fifties, came the Israeli land redistribution laws, the time in which Palestinians were given no rights to vote, had their mobility and their access to employment restricted; as well, they were separated from family and kinship members who had been pressured and forced to leave. In this context, Said poses the question, what does it mean to enter into cooperative ventures that depend upon, and ratify, continuing dispossession, political disenfranchisement, and coloni-zation? If cooperation presumes continuing colonization, or retrenches forms of structural inequality, then the subjugated who cooperate ratify the status quo of their own subjugation.

Of course, the apparent alternative to cooperation would be resistance, that is, resistance to the status quo of subjugation, dispossession and occupation. Solidarity within a resistance struggle is thus different from those forms of cooperation that presume and reproduce the terms of subju-gation itself. My tendency is to distinguish coexistence from cohabitation along these lines: the former accepts the colonial structures that condition living in proximity; the latter names those joint struggles for decoloni-zation. How do we understand Said's formulation of coexistence within this framework? It seems clear that whatever is meant by both coexistence and binationalism in Said's writings from the late 1990s into the early 2000s is something other than this form of 'cooperation' he places within quotation marks, something other than accepting the status of a good colonial subject, something other than affirming dispossession and disenfranchisement with some measure of fatalism, and developing a depressed and abased mode of sociability within its terms (assisted, no doubt, by forms of impressive gallows humour). Of course, there are now cooperative enterprises, mainly within the State of Israel, that continue to believe that the small, incre-mental steps taken by communities of Palestinian Israelis and Jews will be part of the organic development of larger, more encompassing forms of living together, whether understood as part of a two-state or one-state solution or, as some anarchists prefer, a non-state centred form of ethical sociability. But even within contemporary Israel, I believe we can only find a very few schools that are committed to bilingual education. If anything, the pressure has been increased on Palestinian Israelis to work and live in

Hebrew, to learn English, and to allow Arabic to become a private – and certainly never a national – language. This is, I would suggest, in line with the broader cultural meaning of the loyalty oath that Palestinian Israelis are now obligated to perform, one in which they pledge their loyalty to a state conceived as Jewish and democratic, one that contorts, if not eviscerates, their very existence as political actors and citizens.

The idea of small communities developing binationalism in an organic way was always considered by Martin Buber and others as a way to establish a cultural understanding that was a precondition for a political form of cohabitation – in Buber's case, a federated authority. He was one of those Zionists between the 1920s and the 1950s who argued for agrarian cooperatives that would engage Jews and Palestinians in working the land and developing forms of coexistence (these continued the tradition of market-driven binationalism). And yet, for Buber, working within practices organized by a colonial imaginary, it was the European Jew who was more fully 'developed' than the Palestinian, so the point of the alliance was, in part, to accelerate the Palestinian entry into modernity. Indeed, the settler project was, for Buber, a civilizing project, one that presumed a develop-mental cultural difference between Zionists, conceived as Ashkenazi, and Palestinians, conceived as backward. Moreover, the idea of labour that was at the centre of such imagined ventures was one that belonged to a colonial understanding of property. The settler – and let us remember that settlement has been the model of land appropriation since 1948 and before – mixes his labour with the earth and derives rights of property according to a Lockean logic. In 1929, Buber wrote an essay entitled 'National Home and Policy in Palestine' (see Biemann 2002) in which he delineates one major reason why, in his view, 'the Jewish Nation' has a right to return 'to its country', a form of land acquisition that he insists 'will always be a perpetual good for all humankind'. In addition, he writes that prior to Zionist settlement the country was 'a wasteland', and now it is a 'settled country' achieved through 'years of labor'. The right deriving from creation and fertilization (*Recht der Produktivität*) is in fact the right of settlers. Hardly a stone's throw from Herzl at this moment, Buber confirms the right of the settler colonizer whose work on the land produces an over-riding right to the land. Indeed, in this context he uses the term *kolonisatorisches Recht*. It does not matter that prior contracts or rights of ownership are nullified in the process, or that prior forms of working the land by Palestinians, attentive to the needs of those groves of olive and lemon trees, have been undermined or overridden.

And so we can begin to see an alarming paradox at the heart of some of the traditional models of cooperation, suggesting that deriving contem-porary and future political ideals from this history will not be easy. In my view, this does not mean that all efforts at cohabitation are doomed; it means only that we are perhaps under some obligation to understand the reasons why those forms of 'cooperation' could only exist in scare quotes.

Indeed, it is something of a risk to couple Said with Buber, since those two families briefly crossed. Buber lived at 10 Brenner Street in Jerusalem owned by Boutros Said, Edward Said's father's cousin, and the Said family reclaimed that dwelling when they returned from Egypt in 1942 after a legal dispute. Buber moved to Talbiyeh in 1942. Although I do not know the details of the dispute, it seems that Buber's claims to stay on the property were not legally recognized (something that would have been hard to imagine post 1948 when land redistribution accelerated).

Most people know the name of Martin Buber in relation to his ethics of *I and Thou*, or at least the book by that name (first translated into English in 1937). His was an ethics that claims that one human should treat another not as an object, but as someone who can be addressed directly, and with whom a form of communication considered spiritual might take place. If Kant thought people should be treated not as a means to an end, but as an end in itself, Buber recast that particular ethics in terms of the scene of address. A person should be someone who is addressed, that is, who is considered to be addressable, one to whom I can and would direct my speech, and one who is in some sense acknowledged by that very address as someone who deserves to be addressed.

Buber wrote a rather remarkable essay, 'Zionism and "Zionism"' (see Biemann 2002) in May of 1948, two weeks after David Ben Gurion declared the independence of the State of Israel and became its head of state. Scare quotes once again. In this essay, he is distinguishing himself from Ben Gurion and the political Zionists of the time. In a manner reminiscent of Said, Buber writes – and here I quote – 'From the beginning modern Zionism contained two basic tendencies which were opposed to each other in the most thoroughgoing way, an internal contradiction that reaches to the depths of human existence' (Biemann 2002: 220). He explains that 'one can comprehend the two tendencies at the origin as two different interpretations of the concept of [national] rebirth' (ibid.). The first tendency, he tells us, understands rebirth as requiring the return to, and restoration of, what is called 'the true Israel'; this would involve a return from exile for the Jewish people; accordingly, rebirth would be understood as the renewal and unification of the people as they build their common life with one another; this building or formation process is likened to building a home, but also to giving birth, though these remain for the most part metaphors in his text. According to this first tendency, then, the point is not simply to secure 'the existence of the nation' but to pursue what he called 'fulfilment' understood as a spiritual reawakening or, indeed, renewal.

The second tendency, the one that Buber will clearly oppose, grasps rebirth as 'normalization' (ibid.: 221), and holds that Jewish spiritual renewal requires 'a land, a language, and independence'. Renewal, conceived as normalization, pursues all these goals as 'commodities', assimilating to existing notions of property and the nation-state. It is here that Buber's ethical question emerges in the midst of his political problem with Ben Gurion's declaration of the principle of Jewish sovereignty as the legitimating ground for the State of Israel. He re-poses questions that he understands Ben Gurion to have refused to answer, 'How will people live with each other in this land? What will people say to each other in that language? What will be the connection of their independence with the rest of humanity?' He notes that the advocates for normalization are not interested in such questions. And he imagines the riposte of his Zionist opposition in a mocking way: 'Be normal [a state], and you've already been reborn!' (ibid.: 221).

As early as 1919, Buber became a leading voice in the Jewish renewal movement, one that objected to the dominance of Talmudic studies and Rabbinic Law. He distinguished between religion and religiosity, contrasting the former, understood as the ritualistic observance of law with a living, authentic and creative practice. He was not alone throughout the 1920s as the Jewish renewal movement grew. He turned away from the Talmud, though not entirely, to mine the resources of Hasidic stories, and he developed a notion of living dialogue which, for him, was derived from, but exceeded, the practice of Talmudic disputation. Renewal was associated with reeducation, but also with a renewal of the Jews as a people. In 1925, he was part of a group called B'rith Shalom that was dedicated to 'absolute political equality of two culturally autonomous peoples'. And then later, in 1942, he became part of Ichud, a party whose name translates as 'union' which focused on forms of social and cultural union between Jews and Arabs. Ichud opposed the partition plan, preferring federated models and joint government. But in the political manoeuvring of May 1948, Ben Gurion's Yishuv vanquished Ichud. For Buber, this was the beginning of the end of Zionism as he had known it.

But from the beginning he was concerned to provide an alternative to nationalist understandings of the Jewish people by turning to the idea of a living commitment to dialogue. In 1938, forced to leave Germany, he emigrated to Palestine where he took up residence in Jerusalem in that building on Brenner Street. In the ten years prior to writing 'Zionism and "Zionism"', he found himself in several conflicts with the Orthodoxy on the grounds that his religious writings were heretical, but also with the nationalists, whose views he regarded as dangerous for Zionism. In May of 1948 when he wrote this small essay, Buber supports the idea of the rebirth of the Jewish people only three years after the end of the Nazi genocide, but he worries that the project of rebirth has been stolen and renamed by those who have deprived Zionism of its ethical and spiritual meaning. He objects, for instance, to the 'crude forms of nationalism' indulged by his political opponents, which includes compulsory forms of assimilation for recent immigrants and settlers from Europe. And at one point in this rather short and angry text, he offers the following reminder to Ben Gurion and his followers: 'This land is not, today, devoid of inhabitants, as it was not in those times in which our nation trod upon it as they burst forth out of the desert. But today we will not tread upon it as conquerors ... Today we are not obliged to conquer the land, for no danger is in store for our spiritual essence or our way of life from the population of the land.' And then he goes further: 'today we are permitted to enter into an alliance with the inhabitants in order to develop the land together and make it a pathfinder in the Near East – a covenant of two independent nations with equal rights, each of whom is its own master in its own society and culture, but both united in the enterprise of developing their common homeland and in the federal management of shared matters' (Biemann 2002: 222). Finally, then, Buber sounds off against the very principle of Jewish sovereignty – the normalizing view of Zionism that he opposes asks only for sovereignty for the Jewish people and fails to accept the importance of two peoples, Jews and Palestinians, on that land; in other words, the declaration asserts sovereignty at the expense of cohabitation, and Buber finds that unjust. He writes, 'in contrast to this [his own] view of Zionism, the "protective" tendency makes only one demand: sovereignty' (ibid.). 'If only we can attain sovereignty!' he writes in a sardonic tone, referring to the Palestine Partition Plan that established the borders of 1948: 'The life-concept of "independence" was replaced by the administrative concept of "sovereignty".' For Buber, the success of Zionism as a sovereign state outside of a binational and federated authority constituted the defeat of Zionism. It did not imply that Zionism came to an end, but only that one tendency triumphed over the other, and that Zionism would from that point on become associated exclusively with Jewish sovereign rule. What Buber valued as Zionism slowly, and indeed most certainly, became a thing of the past. He looked upon Israel with what he calls 'a torn heart', only two weeks old, as a small state built precisely during a time when the sovereignty of small states was diminishing (ibid.: 223). He understood that the basis of this founding implies that Israel will be always endangered because it 'stands in perpetual opposition to its geopolitical environment and must apply its best forces to military activity instead of applying them to social and cultural enterprises'. But it was clear to him, as it was to Hannah Arendt at the time, that Israel would be bordered in part by a Palestinian population who had been deprived of their rights to land, forced to leave their homes and their homeland, or asked to submit to a new state not of their making.

In her incisive chapter, 'Zionism as Psychoanalysis', Jacqueline Rose in *The Question of Zion* (2005)[5] includes other writers from this period, Hans Kohn (2005 [1983]) and Ahad Ha'am, both of whom lamented the loss of the binational version of Zionism and the triumph of the sovereign one. 'Today,' she writes, 'theirs is the still resonant, melancholic, counter-narrative to the birth of the nation-state' (Rose 2005: 70). Rose points out that Buber, in his participation in Ichud, went further than some in supporting equal political rights (not just religious or civil equality), and that he countered the idea of 'partition' with the idea of a 'covenant' between two peoples (ibid.: 75). Pursuing a psychoanalytic thesis that the dream of national independence does not take account of what and who must be excluded for its realization, Rose suggests nationalism is a destructive fantasy that has to be countered by another form of nationhood. She writes of the 'dialogic space' that includes Buber, Arendt and Kohn, in which an alternative historical development is conjectured: 'Zionism might have created a form of nationhood that would slash away at politics, face its own dark beast, make room for the foreigner in its midst (or, even more radically perhaps see itself as the stranger for the Arabs in Palestine' (ibid.: 86). For Rose, the 'dark beast' is the political unconscious, those strains of aggression and violence that are regularly disavowed and preserved forms of heightened nationalism and its self-righteous implementation of exclusionary and appropriative policies and forms of statehood.

Rose calls upon the writings of Ahad Ha'am, one of the earliest critics of Zionist nationalism, for whom identity, including religious and political identity, must not make the error of understanding itself as the sovereign centre of its world. Rose concludes that for him, it would not do to accept 'dispersal' or 'self-effacement' (ibid.: 99) as the defining conditions of the Jewish people, nor does it work to establish a position characterized by a self-deluded and destructive sovereignty (ibid.: 101). The self-idealizing tendencies of Jewish nationalism not only acted as if there were no other inhabitants of the land, but ended up realizing that fantasy in explicit policies of expulsion.

So you might wonder, what should we learn about this brief period of a counter-narrative, this old and largely forgotten version of binationalism wrought within a Zionist perspective? Rose gives us an eloquent articulation of what a counter-nationalism might be. But that articulation involves a two-step process of recovering a forgotten or repressed history and transposing and revising that counter-nationalism for the contemporary scene. It is useful to remember that the position that Buber held at the time was a highly debated form of Zionism, though today, if one were to take his view, one would be considered a post-Zionist (someone who was schooled in Zionism but has forsaken the Zionist position) or an anti-Zionist (someone who opposes Zionism altogether, since Zionism is now fully identified with Jewish state sovereignty). Indeed, I want to suggest that when we engage in debates about Zionism today, we have to ask ourselves, which version of Zionism is at issue among us? For instance, if you are asked, 'are you a Zionist?', that usually now means, 'do you accept the right of Israel to exist?' Implicit to that question, but never articulated, is the notion that the historical grounds of Israel's founding were legitimate ones. In other words, if you criticize those grounds, you are not a Zionist.

If you are Buber, you probably would have replied in 1948 that, given that there are two populations on that land, only a form of Zionism that guarantees sovereignty and equality for both populations is legitimate, so that the rights of the one people are linked of necessity to the rights of the other. But versions of political equality such as these are no longer part of a 'legitimate' Zionism; indeed, the question of legitimacy is precisely bracketed by the question, 'are you a Zionist?' This means that Zionism has historically become a discourse in which the question of legitimation cannot be discussed. So the question, 'are you a Zionist?', asks only if you accept the principle of sovereignty, and whether you are willing to suspend any discussion about its legitimacy. It does not ask whether you sustain a commitment to political forms of cohabitation that require decolonization and the realization of political equality. In the very posing of the question, 'are you a Zionist?', a certain oblivion is reconstituted. In other words, the very question, its urgency and tenacity, is precisely the instrument by which the history of a possible political equality among peoples is vanquished once again into the domain of the unthinkable, the forgotten. Indeed, when one thinks that the question, 'are you a Zionist?' means, 'do you believe that the Jewish people have a right to exist (not just the state based on principles of Jewish sovereignty), then we can see that the alternative to Zionism presumes that political equality (the forgotten and unthinkable alternative) is the same as genocide (the ultimately traumatic spectre). How are any of us supposed to think and listen under such discursive conditions?

The question of anti-semitism, or learning how to listen

Let us stay on this point for a moment, since it may help to show why we might read figures like Martin Buber, Hans Kohn, Ahad Ah'am or Hannah Arendt at this particular point in time when debates about Zionism seem particularly confused and vexing. One reason it is so hard to talk about Zionism is that most people believe they know what it is, and even why it is so important. In contemporary discourse, if you ask someone if they are a Zionist, you seem to be asking whether that person believes that the State of Israel has a right to exist. If you say yes, you are understood not only to affirm the right of existence for that particular state, but that state *as it is currently constituted*. If you say that you are *not* a Zionist, it seems that you are saying that the State of Israel as it is currently constituted has no right to exist, and should be dismantled or destroyed.

But this last implication does not follow, and it keeps us from having a broader discussion about what would constitute the legitimating ground of a state that would represent all the inhabitants of that land (including the dispossessed who have rightful claims). 'Destruction' is a strong word, as we all know, since it seems to imply a violent destruction, and it seems to echo with 'the destruction of the Temple' or 'the destruction of the Jewish people' especially if we accept the idea that the State of Israel represents the Jewish people – itself a controversial and debatable claim. Now it may be that someone claims not to be a Zionist (in its contemporary meaning) because they are in favour of an alternative or new conception of the state, one that would be peacefully and democratically achieved and that would establish equal rights for all of the inhabitants of the land, one that would not restrict rights of political self-determination or mobility for any inhabitant of that land, and that would be committed to cohabitation on the condition that colonial rule in the form of the occupation has come to an end, that laws no longer discriminate on the basis of race, religion, or ethnicity, and that the rights of the dispossessed are substantially addressed. Indeed, if those are the goals of someone who says no to Zionism, it is hard to understand how that affirmation of democratic ideals implies a kind of destruction, or is motivated from hatred or even anti-Semitism. But it is important to note that even the struggle to transform the structure of the state in a way that would approximate Buber's federal proposal is sometimes understood as the destruction of the state. Now some philosophers, like Hegel, might say that yes, transformation does involve destruction of a certain kind, but not a violent form of destruction (a view that bears some similarities to a notion of non-violent destruction in the work of Walter Benjamin). But I am not sure we even need to go down that path. For if we affirm a transformative process whereby an existing state structure is transformed into another in order to realize democratic principles more fully, then certainly, yes, some parts of one structure fall away as another structure ascends, but that does not imply a complete levelling. After all, new state structures are recrafted in part from existing structures, as we see right now in Egypt. So the accusation of 'destruction' with its many resonances should perhaps be considered more carefully, so that we know what kind of argument is being made, and what is not.

For Buber, there was a Zionism that could provide a perspective by which the state as it is currently constituted could be held to be illegitimate, prizing the sovereignty of one people over the shared sovereignty and equality of both peoples. For Buber at the time, cohabitation could not happen within the framework of Jewish sovereignty, but had to become the overarching principle of a polity in which sovereignty would be shared. This is a difficult and interesting issue, one that has recently been promoted by Yehuda Shenhav in *Beyond the Two State Solution* (2012). Indeed, the situation of Palestinians within Israel, and the situation of Arabs and Jews within Israel, both provide ways of thinking about Jewish–Arab cohabitation that already exist. Given the discrimination against both groups, however, one cannot look to those situations to find ideal forms for cohabitation. However, the struggle against those forms of discrimination and abjection should be based on principles of political equality that should, under ideal conditions, become the basis for political rights extended to all Palestinians (Shohat 2003).

If one holds that changes in the basic laws of the state, or even a new constitution guaranteeing rights for all citizens on equal terms, for instance, which would establish a state that has greater legitimacy than a state without those two legal foundations, does it follow that one thereby pursues a path of destruction?

If Israel is a Jewish nation and is understood to represent the Jewish people, then any call for the dismantling of the current political form of Israel seems, to some, to imply or convey a call to destroy the Jews. This means that the opposition to Ben Gurion's notion of Jewish sovereignty, for instance, would be identified within this framework with a genocidal project, and that that accusation would be equally levelled against Buber himself. Within this logic, either you are a Zionist in the restricted and normalizing sense or you are in favour of genocide, which means that Buber's version of Zionism would now be cast into that second category. Let us note the irony that his vision of shared sovereignty and cohabitation is identified with genocide. What a terrible impasse, when living with others on the grounds of equality is understood to be a way of ushering in a genocide! For the Zionist who believes that, then living on grounds of equality is death, and only colonial rule spells life, colonial rule and inevitable resistance are permanent features of the political landscape. How did we get locked into this framework according to which the failure to embrace Zionism in its 1948 version is equivalent to the call to destroy the Jews? How might any of us climb out of this terrible bind?

If the Zionist who wants not only to assert Israel's right to exist but to strengthen the grounds that establish the legitimacy of that state, wants to see certain fundamental changes in order to strengthen that claim of legitimacy, which changes would those be? And if the non-Zionist (anti- or post-) who opposes physical acts of destruction and practises non-violence, wants to see fundamental changes in the state and constitutional structure, the conditions of citizenship, or even a new state structure based on formal and substantial equality, how do we understand that list of changes? Where does the second list converge with the Zionist who wants to see changes of a democratic kind that would establish legitimacy for the existing state? If seen this way, there are pivotal changes that one group wants to see, and the other group does not. But there is also a spectrum of views among Zionists, and a spectrum of views among non-Zionists, that overlap to some degree. And this means that the debate about what a legitimate and democratic state would look like, one-state or two-state, could potentially take place without threats of violence and fears of destruction.

If my description of this hegemonic mode of Zionist political discourse is right, then an acceptance of the contemporary version of the State is held to be the only defence against genocide for the Jews. This view is related to yet another one, namely, that the fear of a return of 'genocide' constitutes the rationale for Israeli military actions, including their wars, and excuses all the injustices committed by that state. And yet, it is precisely this logic that embroils the State of Israel in perpetual military conflict. What if living on conditions of equality is the best way to minimize violence for everyone? What enormous cultural struggle is necessary to establish this particular linkage as thinkable?

One problem that follows from the belief that defending the indefensible State of Israel is the only way to ward off another genocide, is that those who find the State of Israel indefensible become cynical about the invocation of genocide itself. So one reason not to use the spectre of genocide for unsound political reasons is that it strengthens the view that reference to the 'holocaust' is always a ruse for military aggression. This conclusion, in my view, is unacceptable. Even though the Nazi genocide against the Jews (which was a genocide against the gypsies, communists, homosexuals, political dissidents and the disabled, to name but a few targeted populations) has clearly been instrumentalized to produce a legitimating effect for the existing state of Israel, that is surely no reason to treat references to that genocide or to anti-Semitism within the debate as if they can only be covers or ruses for colonial expansion and military and legal dispossession. The Nazi genocide against the more than 6 million Jews who died and another 4–5 million gypsies, homosexuals, communists, the disabled and the ill, has to be documented and memorialized and known. At the same time, the political exploitation of the Holocaust to justify unjust practices has to be opposed, but so, too, the cynical rejection of the Holocaust as no more than a rhetorical cover for Israeli aggression. Both of these problems have to be kept in mind at the same time, but I think we need a complex enough picture of things to do precisely that. Morally, we can maintain that it is absolutely necessary to oppose all forms of anti-Semitism and all forms of racism, including state-sponsored racism, and also maintain that the contemporary formation of Zionism is not the best possible safeguard against anti-Semitism. Indeed, what is sometimes called anti-Semitism seems to be a struggle against colonial rule, so that produces quite a bind, if the struggle for basic political freedoms is understood as an expression of anti-Semitism. Much is to be said here, but it cannot be the case that a specific set of oppositions to the State of Israel are by definition anti-Semitic, since the State of Israel and the Jewish people are, indeed, two very different phenomena, and the differences between them are expanding all the time. There are many reasons to affirm that disjunction, but one of those reasons is that Judaism has conventionally valued emancipation from unjust rule, and that this principle of emancipation cannot, ought not, to be restricted to the Jewish people alone.

My own view is that even as we must refuse any effort at revisionism in relation to the Nazi genocide against the Jews along with all the other targeted populations, that does not mean that there is only one way to tell that history. That history did not have to culminate in the political triumph of Ben Gurion which established the State of Israel on the basis of Jewish sovereignty rather than shared rule and federated authority. Any thorough historian of the years 1944–8 will know that Buber's opposition to Ben Gurion is but one of many political positions circulated at that time. Indeed, prior to 1948, and even prior to 1967, it was possible to view Zionism itself as a field of conflicting positions which included various versions of binationalism. And yet, one had to take very seriously the link between the Nazi genocide and the founding of the State of Israel. But for many, the atrocities of the Holocaust did not lead inexorably to the founding of Israel on the terms that Ben Gurion articulated. Indeed, the most active debates on federated authority and binationalism took place precisely between the years 1944 and 1948.

Even among Jews who arrived during the Second World War or after, many were communists, anti-Zionists, socialists and binationalists, and they were not always in accord with the political purposes to which their presence contributed. Indeed, even within the deportation camps, there were strong struggles over Zionism, especially among the communists. Socialists were divided between those who wanted to try out the Kibbutz movement, and others who wanted to reinvigorate European syndicalism or move to the United States, the UK or Australia. Sometimes those fights within the deportation camp over where to go, and why, even became physical (Grodzinsky 2004).

There is yet one more argument I would like to make with respect to anti-Semitism, and it is this: that for many Palestinians living under occupation or in exile or in a condition of damaged rights within the existing borders of Israel, the opposition to the Israeli state is primarily a political opposition to a form of settler colonialism, one that has dispossessed them of homes, of basic human rights and political self-determination, has exposed them to bombings, indefinite detention, injury and devastating loss. And yet, this opposition to continuing military and colonial occupation is often taken to be anti-Semitism. The hideous anti-Semitic rhetoric of Hamas has fuelled this conclusion, to be sure, and that has to be unequivocally opposed. As a result, a terrible logic takes hold in which the only way for a Palestinian to prove that he or she is not anti-Semitic is to accept the legitimacy of the Jewish state, which is to accept ongoing colonial rule. But if one opposes colonial rule, or if one says that recognition of your state depends upon your recognizing my state or my rights to political self-determination, then that invocation of reciprocoty exposes the speaker to the charge of anti-Semitism. What is ruled out from this closed circle is precisely the recognition of legitimate resistance to colonial rule. Moreover, the logic assumes that defending Israel and defending colonial rule is the same as defending the Jewish people, which means that the Jewish people are allied with inequality and colonial rule as well – this negative view of the Jewish people is spawned by the logic itself! It is one reason increasing numbers of progressive Jewish organizations seek to articulate Jewish values that counter those exemplified by the Israeli state, such as democracy, equality, cohabitation and non-violence.

In any case, as one way of battling the conceptual confusions that block the way to thinking, hearing and remembering, it seems crucial to tell the difference between a Palestinian opposition to the State of Israel and a form of anti-Semitism. Only when we accept the claim of the State of Israel that it represents the Jewish people (exclusively and comprehensively), that an opposition to Israel can be construed as an opposition to the Jews as such. To accept this definition, however, is to dismiss the diasporic Jewish tradition and to reject the internal ethnic, religious and racial diversity of Israel as it is currently constituted. Is there a way to break out of this closed logic in order to think about new possibilities for cohabitation?

Dispossession and cohabitation

In 1999, Said maintained the necessity of a constitutional democracy, but also a way of reconciling the right of return (for Jews) and the law of return (for Palestinians). He also wrote that 'the beginning is to develop something entirely missing from both Israeli and Palestinian realities today: the idea and practice of citizenship, not of ethnic or racial community, as the main vehicle for co-existence'. For Said, this meant recognizing that Palestinians and Israelis (including Palestinian Israelis) are bound together, irrevocably connected, but also that self-determination has to be exercised in a substantial way. So the political task is precisely to forfeit neither self-determination nor cohabitation. Clearly, Said was not just talking about modes of citizenship for Palestinians living within '48, but for all the dispossessed. And this meant a certain exercise of citizenship even prior to its institutionalization. At the same time, he recognized that without political change, including the end to colonizing practices, there could be no substantial citizenship. One can work from one end or the other, but the work has to depart from both perspectives. Some of the arguments that contrast the Boycott, Divestment, and Sanctions movement with coexistence projects seem to be caught up precisely in arguing about these two different ways of proceeding. They are not exactly the opposite of each other. Either we seek to start on smaller scales to support modes of cohabitation or we claim that colonization must come to an end before any form of coexistence is possible. But, in fact, the path of organic change can only work if colonization is also contested; and the modes of solidarity that BDS invites, including with Jewish Israelis, constitutes an organic form of working together on the grounds of equality and for the realization of substantial political equality. Organic movement and structural transformation have to go hand and in hand, no matter what the starting point.

Cohabitation, anyone?

I read Said and Buber as asking a common question: how is it that any of us address and receive another. Neither took the fact of communication for granted. But for communication to happen, there has to be a world in which you can hear, an audible world, whether that is something that your ears let you do or a set of technologies enable for you. There may have to be a translation from one language to another, and so an able translator. If we cannot seek recourse to receive another's words, then there is no I and no you, and certainly then no possibility for union, for cohabitation, much less binationalism.

As you know, on this topic, it is often quite literally impossible to hear what another says. We think, oh, if another has that view, I cannot hear what that other says (the view can be Zionism or anti-Zionism, since there are people on both sides who shut out any discourse that is perceived to belong to the other). Finding a way to speak and a way to hear is essential to any deliberate and reflective consideration of this issue, and yet, in speaking about this issue, one runs into a crisis of speakability and audibility all the time. What can be spoken and still heard? What is permitted, and what is censored? How is the sphere of audibility restricted, so that when I hear certain arguments, I must literally leave the space of that speaking in order to feel okay again, or I must invoke a law to stop that speech? We all have our limits, to be sure, but sometimes a space is opened in which one can come up against those limits on hearing or receiving, abide by the anxiety it produces without reaching for the censor.

So part of what I have been doing here is simply to note that Zionism has a history, has itself undergone several transformations. So when we quickly presume that Zionism seems to be confirmed or refuted on the basis of the question 'do you believe Israel has the right to exist?' that history is forgotten. One important dimension of the history of Zionism is precisely an active set of debates about the grounds that would legitimate such a state. In 1929, Buber wrote an essay entitled 'Zionism and Nationalism' in which he tried to distinguish the one from the other. Although that essay has its limitations, it does include the following imaginary dialogue with a nationalist:

> You might object: if we do not participate in the necessary politics of power, how can we secure ourselves? How will we secure this settlement, the beginning *Volksland* in Palestine? To this I reply, 'No conceivable security is as real as this: to become a power in spirit that can sustain the forms of life among the nations, that can become a living example of relations between the nations, that can help prepare a true covenant between Orient and Occident and from there, on the basis of this work, form an alliance with the future elements of all nations.' (Biemann 2002: 278)

I want to point out the difficult balance conveyed by Buber's statement, namely, the idea of 'a living example of relations between the nations'. In other words, he is not speaking about an exemplary nation, but a living example of a set of relations, suggesting that what is most living and most exemplary is inter-relationship. He shifts the emphasis from the nation to its inter-relations, and in that sense stands for what we might call 'the between' of nations. Binationalism, in this view, is not simply the conjoining of one nation with others, but the active and exemplary enactment of the relation that holds among them.

In 1929, Buber confessed upon return from a trip to Palestine:

> Let us beware of regarding and treating as inferior what is foreign to us and not sufficiently known! Let us be careful not to commit ourselves to what has been committed against us! And let it be said again that while self-assertion is a natural precondition of all our actions, it is not enough. It also requires imagination, the ability to imagine the soul of the other – of the stranger – from within the reality of our own. I must not hold back a confession: It was appalling to me to see in Palestine how little we know of the Arab man. (ibid.: 278)

Yet, Buber's notion of imagining the other is not quite the same as a dialogue, recapitulating what Said has called 'orientalism'. Whatever local dialogues took place with Palestinian cooperative councils failed to call into question the settler project itself, and Palestinians were regularly regarded as not measuring up to the task of dialogue (we see this continued in the orientalist discourse that claims that there is no partner on the Palestinian side for a dialogue on peace). And this inability to stop and reverse the the appropriation of Palestinian lands and the dispossession of its people remains an abiding limit and failure of Buber's analysis. Moreover, as if his call for 'A Land of Two Peoples' Jews and Arabs are two distinct and homogeneous groups. But 30 per cent of Israeli Jews are from Arab descent, and another 20 per cent of Israelis are non-Jewish Palestinians. How do we understand the opposition between Jew and Arab within this contemporary demographic situation? This means that a good half of Israel is not from European descent, which suggests in turn that the distinction between Arab and Jew rests on a misunderstanding of who is Arab (some Jews are) and who is Jewish (some Arabs are). Secondly, the Palestinians are themselves diverse, made all the more so by virtue of their own scattered condition, nearly five million now living in exile from the lands they once owned, and where they lived for decades, if not centuries. So does it make sense to talk about 'two peoples' as if they each were distinct and internally homogeneous?

Is the notion of a federated or binational state practical for this time? Interestingly, many of those Palestinians who actively argue for a one-state solution are precisely the ones who are committed to living side by side with the Jewish population, and yet the one-state solution is clearly feared by those who think either (a) it will produce an Arab demographic majority and dissipate the Jewish character of the state or (b) (on the other side) it will produce one greater Israel and destroy Palestinian aspirations for political self-determination.

But the most basic limit of Buber's analysis is that he was not able to grasp the colonial dimensions of Zionism, the notion that settlements and settlers have been, from the start, a way of taking over land that was either legally or conventionally the arable land of Palestinians. As a result, he did not understand that a workable binationalism would only be possible on the basis of an end to settler colonialism and a workable plan for reparations. Similarly, we see today how the issue of Palestinian statehood is often debated without considering whether an independent state for Palestinians will be built within the military and economic structures of occupation, which is one form in which settler colonialism continues in and through the state apparatus. If a Palestinian state incorporates and sustains the occupation, then it is a client state, at best, or an administrative arm of a continuing colonial power. This is not an argument against statehood, but it does raise the question, on what grounds statehood? What would make for a democratic and legitimate state? This question is one that can and must be asked of both Israel and Palestine, of any proposal for a one-state solution, or for a federated polity, or one based on a notion of shared or dispersed sovereignty. It is not a problem to ask this question – it is a necessity. So when we are asked to accept the legitimacy of a state without asking for its reason, we should wonder what has happened to our discourse such that we no longer have access to what establishes legitimacy to begin with. Indeed, any democratic state has to be able to establish and communicate the conditions of its own legitimacy, and showing and communicating that legitimacy is precisely an obligation of a state to its own people and to all people. Granted, there are always limits to that demonstration, since it is probably not possible to offer a fully comprehensive and transparent account of the legitimacy of a state. And, as we know, narratives of history become intertwined with political arguments, and those hybrid forms of narrative and argument are reproduced and transmitted as legitimating stories. But if we retell the history of 1948 such that we see how one group of refugees achieved sanctuary by producing another refugee class, then we move towards a more complex history. And if we think about the debates about state structure that took place prior to the rejection of federated authority, there seems to be a prehistory to Zionism that might well be useful as its posthistory is, and must be, imagined.

For Buber, the 'I' only knows its world because there is a 'you' who has consciousness of that world. The world is given to me because you are also there as one to whom it is given. The world is never given to me alone, but always in your company. Without you, the world does not give itself. I am worldless without you.

Who is this 'you' without whom I would be worldless? The particular you, the human one that you are, is only part of the 'you' to whom I am bound and upon whom my sense of world depends. Since in addition to you over there are a countless number of yous, and some link between all of you seems to exceed the particular yous that you are. How do we understand that which links all the 'yous' who I address and by whom I am addressed? What is this relation, and how does it relate to the living and exemplary relation among nations to which Buber referred in the 1920s? Is that a human relation or is it divine? For Buber, it is a divine link, to be sure, but this divine link does not only bind together those who already belong to the same religion or already share the same history. Rather, it links the 'I' to those who happen to inhabit the same world, and those for whom that world is also meant, that is, equally meant. We could say that the world is equally given to all humans, but Buber's point is that where there is no equality among humans, there is no world – a point that is resonant with Arendt. So if we live under conditions of inequality, we are to that extent world-less. This would mean that the Jewish God for Buber does not appear as a man or as one kind of people, but, rather, persists in the relations between nations, and that would include the Jewish people and all the non-Jewish peoples of the world. This is one reason why for him, if Zionism were to signify spiritual renewal or rebirth, it would have to take the political form of a binationalism for one that would affirm the equality of all people, regardless of their religions, even as it recognizes the cultural specificity of each people. For Buber, a Jewish ethic has to be Jewish and non-Jewish to be ethical at all. It implies living in proximity with others on a condition of equality and difference. If I cannot live in the world without you, according to Buber, then my life is bound up with yours, and we lose our world when we lose each other. That condition of reciprocal dependency is the very condition of renewing, and repairing, the world.

Said noted in 1999, 'I see no other way than to begin now to speak about sharing the land that has thrust us together, sharing it in a truly democratic way, with equal rights, for each citizen. There can be no reconciliation unless both peoples, two communities of suffering, resolve that existence is a secular fact, and that it has to be dealt with as such' (Said 1999). We can surely talk about what he means by secular in this instance, but I take it that it is a way of claiming that two populations, whatever their differences, are already there, bound together on a land that needs to be shared in equal ways and governed by democratic means. But how to get there? It is fair to say that Said was often the one to say that the sphere of culture has to be separated from the sphere of politics – he savoured the paradoxical and unpredictable character of musical performance, and he understood these features of art to be quite different from political debate and negotiation. But perhaps politics is also a field in which unpredictable moments emerge, challenging us to sense and feel in new ways. For Said, certain forms of dialogue, even possibilities for friendship and musical collaboration, constitute 'small acts' in Paul Gilroy's terms, that show that one person can offer an unanticipated form of acknowledgment to another, despite the political barriers and the structural conditions of their exchange. In other words, modes of acknowledgement can take place that are not fully deter-mined in advance by structural conditions such as ongoing colonization. An appeal can be made that seeks to bring the other into a relation of equality that, in turn, can begin to instantiate those forms of equality that most become the political basis for any legitimate form of cohabitation. In Said's formulation, 'you are here, we are here', there is a practice of linguistic solicitation to something new – no one is being asked to leave, only to live together in a way that does not refuse that already existing fact of cohabitation on that land. As a form of direct address, it seeks to open up a dialogic form. The formulation does not install or prize dialogue as the substance and ultimate aim of politics; and it does not mean that those who were forced into exile are not also 'here' or 'there' in a way that needs to be substantially redressed (made so explicit in Darwish's poetry).[6] Rather, it accepts the linguistic and political condition of a demographic proximity, a border that divides and joins, while rejecting the principle of demographic majority, and the historical and contemporary practices of dispossession. On the one hand, a radical structural change is necessary – a constitutional basis for the state, a right of return reconciled with the law of return, the end of settler colonialism, which includes the occupation and continuing land appropriations, and the restitution of the rights of Palestinians from their damaged state – for any kind of cohabitation, and for a just form of binationalism. On the other hand, that change happens sometimes through the smaller acts that build forms of solidarity that keep cooperation from becoming an instrument to ratify the status quo. Can we think and practice a binationalism that moves in at least two directions at once, allowing the binational to become upended and redefined within a shifting set of frames? How to distinguish among those small acts that devastate the colonial structure and those that ratify its reproduction and augmentation? The task remains, how to produce forms of solidarity that have as their aim the resistance to settler colonialism, that is, forms of solidarity that contain within them, and begin to articulate, forms of cohabitation that would start to realize a legitimate binationalism?

Notes

1   See also Said 1994.

2   For a summary of the Prawer Plan, see Adalah website, http://adalah.org/eng/?mod=articles&ID=1589.

3   The successes of Zochrot in holding a public conference in Tel Aviv on 'The Right to Return' in November 2013 are a significant exception, since even after threats of violence and censorship, the event did happen, and now claims a significant Internet audience.

4   See Raz-Krakotzkin 2012.

5   Jacqueline Rose, *The Question of Zion*. Princeton: Princeton University Press, 2005.

6   See Mahmood Darwish, 'Who Am I, without Exile?', 2007.

References

Abu-Odeh, L. 'The Case For Binationalism: Why One State – Liberal and Constitutionalist – May Be the Key to Peace in the Middle East', *Boston Review* 4–7 (December 2001 – January 2002).

Adalah – The Legal Centre for Arab Minority Rights in Israel, 'Demolition and Eviction of Bedouin Citizens of Israel in the Naqab (Negev) – The Prawer Plan', http://adalah.org/eng/?mod=articles&ID=1589 (accessed 7 January 2014).

Arendt, H. (1951), *The Origins of Totalitarianism*. New York: Harcourt Brace Jovanovich.

Biemann, A. (2002), *The Martin Buber Reader*. New York: Palgrave Macmillan.

Buber, M. (1937), *I and Thou*. New York: Charles Scribner's Sons.

Darwish, M. (2007), 'Who Am I, without Exile?'. In *The Butterfly's Burden,* Copper Canyon Press, http://www.poetryfoundation.org/poem/236748 (accessed 7 January 2014).

Grodzinsky, Y. (2004), *In the Shadow of the Holocaust: The Struggle Between Jews and Zionist in the Aftermath of World War II*. Monroe, ME: Common Courage.

Kohn, H. (2005 [1983]), 'Zionism is not Judaism'. In P. Mendes-Flohr (ed.) and M. Buber, *A Land of Two Peoples*. Chicago: University of Chicago Press.

Raz-Krakotzkin, Amnon (2012), 'Exile and Binationalism: From Gershom Scholem and Hannah Arendt to Edward Said and Mahmoud Darwish'. Berlin: Wissenschaftskolleg zu Berlin.

Rose, J. (2005), *The Question of Zion*. Princeton: Princeton University Press.

Said, E. W. (1986), *After the Last Sky*. New York: Columbia University Press.

Said, E. W. (1994), *The Politics of Dispossession: The Struggle for Palestinian Self Determination, 1969–1994*. New York: Pantheon Books.

Said, E. W. (1999), 'Truth and Reconciliation', *Al-Ahram Weekly Online*, 14–20 January, issue no. 412, http://weekly.ahram.org.eg/1999/412/op2.htm (accessed 7 January 2014).

Said, E. W. (2003), *Freud and the Non-European*. New York: Columbia University Press.

Said, E. W. and Barsamian, D. (2003), *Culture and Resistance: Conversations with Edward W. Said*. London: Pluto Press.

Shenhav, Y. (2012), *Beyond the Two-State Solution: A Jewish Political Essay*. Cambridge: Polity Press.

Shohat, E. (2003), 'Rupture and Return: Zionist Discourse and the Study of Arab Jews', *Social Text*, 75 (21/2): 49–74.

Tamari, S. (2000), 'The Dubious Lure of Binationalism', *Journal of Palestine Studies* 30 (1): 83–7.

CHAPTER ELEVEN

Further Reflections on Exile: War and Translation[1]

Étienne Balibar

I am not entirely sure of the exact definition of the concepts that I am using here. This definition is part of the problem. To place 'translation' in a symmetric place with respect to 'war' is not only a way to modernize traditional antitheses such as 'war and peace', 'war and diplomacy', 'war and commerce', in a world that is increasingly characterized by multiculturalism and multilingualism, it is also a way to *displace them*, so that their complexity becomes apparent. War and translation are *different* categories, in theory and in practice, they oppose each other, but they also *penetrate* each other. Edward Said's contribution, as a critic, a cultural historian, a political analyst, is especially illuminating here. Being permanently concerned with the role of war in politics and the extent to which politics models itself on war,[2] Said is also one who reflects on the importance of translation, both in the strict philological sense and in the sense of establishing reciprocities, or challenging cultural hierarchies and relationships of domination which unequally distribute the 'hermeneutic function'. These two concerns constantly interfere: it appears that the politics of translation are involved in the waging of wars and it appears that strategies, if not actual operations of combat, are involved in the construction of the models of translation and interpretation on which our culture relies, especially in the humanities. For this reason, Said is crucial to the project of comparing or articulating war and translation as political models, which I sometimes call the 'polemological' and the 'philological' model.[3] He occupies the place of their necessary inter-ference. In that location, we also find some representatives of the so-called 'post-structuralist school', particularly Lyotard and Derrida, with whom I will attempt a kind of virtual dialogue, in spite of their well-known differences and disagreements. Allow me to call this an exercise in contra-punctal criticism.

I begin with two quotations from Lyotard's *The Differend*.[4] They refer to the tradition of opposing war and commerce, which also indicates their common element, namely the idea that *alternative forms* of sociability, offering *a transcendental choice* to politics, are centrally concerned with representations of the *stranger* and the institution of the *border*. I start with the second one:

> A phrase, which links and which is to be linked [to others], is always a *pagus*, a border zone where genres of discourse enter into conflict over the mode of linking. War and commerce. It's in the *pagus* that the *pax* and the pact are made and unmade. The *vicus*, the *home*, the *Heim* is a zone where the differend between genres of discourse is suspended. An 'internal' peace is bought at the price of perpetual *differends* on the outskirts ... This internal peace is made through narratives that accredit the community of proper names as they accredit themselves. The *Volk* shuts itself up in the *Heim*, and it identifies itself through narratives attached to names, narratives that fail before the occurrence and before the differends born from the occurrence. Joyce, Schönberg, Cézanne: *pagani* waging war among the genres of discourse ... (Lyotard 1988: §218, 151)

What is crucial here in my opinion are two things: one is the absolute reciprocity of the issues of interior vs exterior and the dilemma of war and peace, which itself is interpreted in terms of establishing or inter-rupting the possibility of commerce, exchange, reciprocity. The other one is the fact that, in order to 'politicize' the 'differend' (or difference without a common genre) or to express the immanent *political* character of a differend, which he has defined in very general terms as a relationship of incompatibility among 'phrases', Lyotard must have recourse to the *terri-torial representation* of the political institution: its way of assembling and separating collectives through the establishment of the border. This is a very classical problematic that has been associated with the constitution of nation-states and the juridical categories of sovereignty and territory as the 'normal' basis for the institution of collective identities. What is 'critical' or 'deconstructive' in Lyotard's way of alluding to this classical problematic is indeed his way of relating distributions of self and other within separated territorial entities to the invention of *narratives* (therefore 'phrases'). These narratives are typically national or nationalistic, but they are also *imperial*, or perhaps they relate in a generic manner to the imperial element that is always already involved in the figuration of national states as sovereign entities. The aesthetic examples of Joyce, Schönberg and Cézanne are invoked as metaphors of the failure, the limited power of these narratives for regulating the heterogeneity of phrases, analogous to an insurrection or a partisan war that blurs the distinctions between genres, spaces, states of normality and states of exception.

In another passage, which technically refers to the interpretation of different genres of discourse within Kant's philosophy, namely the scientific or 'cognitive' and the ethical or 'normative', Lyotard invokes a very different scheme for the imagination of the 'differend':

> Each genre of discourse would be like an island; the faculty of judgement would be at least in part, like an admiral or like a provisioner of ships who would launch expeditions from one island to the next, intended to present to one island what was found (or invented …) in the other, and which might serve the former as an 'as-if intuition' with which to validate it. Whether war or commerce, this interventionist force has no object, and does not have its own island, but it requires a milieu – this would be the sea – the *Archipelagos* or primary sea as the Aegean was once called. (1988: 130–1)

What is interesting here is that, by transferring the issue of crossing the borders from a 'continental' imaginary to an 'oceanic' one, thereby invoking a different kind of narrative of the imperial nation (let's suggest a reference to Conrad rather than Kipling or even Joyce), Lyotard is not only stressing the reversibility of the operations called 'war' and 'commerce', which belong to the same world and the same political regime, he is also drawing the attention to the strategic function of translation and its obstacles. What is suggested is not only that the borderline is disputed and uncertain, but that the border itself ultimately cannot be found or located: no fixed line can be inscribed in the marine element unless it is inscribed virtually by a map. Similarly, we have a distinction between the two opposite political notions of war and commerce which is destined to remain uncertain. Indeed, it is particularly in the marine element that one finds the hybrid figure between the trader (*le commerçant*) and the warrior, namely the *pirate*, a public enemy of all States except when they utilize him in order to 'illegally' combine war with commerce. The 'insular' character of the phrases separated by the differend is a metaphor of the *untranslatable* character of the phrases, but it also indicates that what is impossible cannot be avoided, or *must be attempted*. In Lyotard's terminology: one must 'link onto' another phrase, which remains heterogeneous. In particular one must 'translate' heterogeneous phrases *as if* they were translatable: *this* is the wager of judgement, or the wager of politics.

The opposition of war and commerce is always susceptible to being inverted, made into a complementarity, or even made to express a fundamental identity. This is why its alternate formulation – war and peace – becomes so problematic in the modern era. From Augustine to Kant, political philosophy has reflected this ambivalence. Sometimes it sees peace, in the heart of an empire, or within the framework of an 'international order', as the condition of possibility for commerce. At other times it sees in commerce a moral and material factor for the establishment of peace.[5] However, the peaceful essence of commerce remains eminently dubious. It is not only that there are hybrid forms (such as piracy or the *guerre de course* [*privateering*]). But these roles are exchanged in certain circumstances, perhaps inevitably: there are commercial wars and above all there are *wars for commerce*, to impose its 'freedom'. This ambiguity was immediately seized upon by thinkers such as Kant, who referred to the combination of reciprocity and antagonism that constitutes the 'motor' of historical progress as an 'unsocial sociability' (*ungesellige Geselligkeit*). Marx also identifies this ambiguity when he insists on the two sides comprising the extension of commodity circulation: on the one hand, the creation of a cosmopolitical 'universality' through the institution of a *general equivalent* that measures all values, and homogenizes all 'social labour'; on the other hand, the *violent dissolution* of traditional communities and their corresponding cultures, as their commodity exchanges with the exterior intensify and are monetized. In *Provincializing Europe*, Dipesh Chakrabarty (2000) adopts this schema to describe two models of 'translation' and thus two modalities of relation to language and to the diversity of languages.

Let us now return to Lyotard. The notion of a 'differend' (*le différend*) around which he organizes his book gradually elaborates on an experiment in thought which concerns the absolute 'wrong' (*tort*) suffered by victims of extermination processes and, more generally, 'universal suffering' (an expression that refers to the proletariat in Marx's early writings). One such demonstration is as follows:

> The plaintiff lodges his or her complaint before the tribunal, the accused argues in such a way as to show the inanity of the accusation. Litigation takes place. I would like to call a *differend* the case where the plaintiff is divested of the means to argue and becomes for that reason a victim. If the addressor, the addressee, and the sense of testimony are neutralized, everything takes place as if there were no damages. A case of differend between two parties takes place when the 'regulation' of the conflict that opposes them is done in the idiom of one of the parties while the wrong suffered by the other is not signified in that idiom. For example, contracts and agreements between economic partners do not prevent – on the contrary, they presuppose – that the laborer or his or her representative has had to and will have to speak of his or her work as though it were the temporary cession of a commodity, the 'service,' which he or she putatively owns. This 'abstraction,' as Marx calls it … is required by the idiom in which the litigation is regulated ('bourgeois' social and economic law). In failing to have recourse to this idiom, the laborer would not exist within its field of reference, he or she would be a slave. In using it, he or she becomes a plaintiff. Does he or she also cease for that matter to be a victim? (Lyotard 1983: 24–5; 1988: 9–10)

This demonstration is followed by another soon after:

> Would you say that interlocutors are victims of the science and politics of a language understood as communication to the same extent that the worker is transformed into a victim through the assimilation of his or her labor power into a commodity? ... To give the *differend* its due is to institute new addressees, new addressors, new significations, and new referents in order for the wrong to find an expression and for the plaintiff to cease to be a victim ... No one doubts that language is capable of admitting these new phrase families or new genres of discourse. The differend is the unstable state and instant of language wherein something which must be able to be put into phrases cannot yet be. This state includes silence, which is a negative phrase, but it also calls upon phrases which are in principle possible ... What is at stake in a literature, in a philosophy, in a politics perhaps, is to bear witness to differends by finding idioms for them. (Lyotard 1983: 29–30; 1988: 12–13)

There are many ways in which these formulations turn around the problem of the 'untranslatable'. They suggest a much broader use of the notion of translation, and consequently of language (or *idiom*) than that which is officially received. The 'borders' in question here are not purely 'national', they could be *social*, or *moral* or *religious*.[6] The differend itself, in other words *the absence of the possibility to discuss*, and first of all 'to respond' or 'to present one's case' to the other, comes first. Differends are induced within one language – in the official sense of the term – just as they are among *different languages*. But Lyotard complicates this analogy by inverting it. He argues that it is possible *in language*, through the invention of new idioms that make 'translatable' what was not, to express all conflicts based on an absolute or radical 'wrong' (*tort*), a 'wrong' that somehow excludes from humanity or community those who suffer. Obviously, to say that differends can be expressed does not mean that they are thereby 'resolved'. Rather, as demonstrated at the end of the statement quoted above, it means that these differends *can become the object of a politics*, and generate 'subjects' for this politics, with the help of literature and philosophy.

I want now to move to Said's own analysis of the regimens of phrases, translations and interpretations, and its relationship to an understanding of the political. There is no suggestion here that Said and Lyotard think the same thing but express it in different words, as if they were not separated by different attitudes with respect to modernity, and in particular the function of the 'narrative' which constructs collective identities. But I will argue that we can retrieve from their work a similar way of problematizing the political meaning of the activity of translation and its association with an intrinsic ambivalence of the political institution, blurring the separations between states of war and regimes of commerce, or more generally reciprocity. Admittedly, Said's critical analyses are less allegoric. They refer to a precise historical background in the construction of narratives, the 'orientalist' framework that interweaves culture and empire. But they also force us to consider the task of the translator as one that is simultaneously impossible and necessary.

Said's way of articulating the models of war and translation is particularly explicit in his reading of Fanon, to whom he would return several times in his life. They also support his analyses of 'hegemony'. For Said, 'hegemony' (a notoriously ambivalent notion itself, even in its Gramscian sense, denoting at the same time the institution of the universal and the expansion of domination to the cultural sphere) is linked in particular to categories of interpretation that allow for *one-sided*, or historically *dissymmetric* 'translations' between cultures – a production that is linked in turn with the development of philological *disciplines*, therefore institutional *dispositifs* of 'power-knowledge' in the Foucauldian sense. Its ultimate result is a historical development of 'communities of interpretation', which could be considered the *political subjects par excellence* in Saidian criticism, or better, its *quasi-subjects*, since they are pictured as inherently unstable, contradictory even when they are violently imposed on the world. As a consequence, Said analyses interpretation as a practice with a dialogical but also a coercive internal dimension. This was the central orientation in *Orientalism* (1978), a guiding thread for the book's reconstruction of Europe's projection of its Other. But it became even more insistent, in a political environment which evolved towards new forms of imperialism, as Said was discovering that models of interpretation are not only a matter of *representations* (and conflicts of representations, or conflicts between *representing* and *being represented*), but also involved a crucial 'performative' dimension. To represent the other as *absolute* other is not only to presuppose a basic impossibility to translate or to communicate on an equal footing; it is also *to create* that impossibility. In a disturbing manner, this performative aspect of interpretation also allows for the possibility of mimetic reversals, as illustrated by the way in which a nationalistic discourse of resistance to Empire, and above all a certain Islamic political theology, would appropriate the 'orientalist' idea of the absolute incommunicability of the West and the East, in order to make it a weapon against the cultural domination of the Empire.

In *Culture and Imperialism* (1993), Said writes the following *a propos* of Fanon's relevance to understand the tragic conflicts which developed in post-independence Algeria, culminating in the quasi-civil war of the 1990s between a military government and a militant Islamic opposition:

> In his chapter on 'the pitfalls of nationalist consciousness' in *The Wretched of the Earth*, Fanon foresaw this turn of events ... His theory of violence is not meant to answer the appeals of a native chafing under the paternalistic surveillance of a European policeman and, in a sense, preferring the services of a native officer in his place. On the contrary, it

first represents colonialism as a totalizing system nourished in the same way ... that human behaviour is informed by unconscious desires. In a second, quasi-Hegelian move, a Manichean opposite appears, the insurrectionary native, tired of the logic that reduces him, the geography that segregates him, the ontology that dehumanizes him, the epistemology that strips him down to an unregenerate essence. 'The violence of the colonial regime and counterviolence of the native balance each other and respond to each other in an extraordinary reciprocal homogeneity' (Fanon, *Wretched of the Earth*, p. 88). The struggle must be lifted to a new level of contest, a synthesis represented by a war of liberation, for which an entirely post-nationalist theoretical culture is required. (Said 1993: 267–8).

Several pages later, we read these remarkable formulas:

One has the impression in reading the final pages of *The Wretched of the Earth* that having committed himself to combat both imperialism and orthodox nationalism by a counter-narrative of great deconstructive power, Fanon could not make the complexity and anti-identitarian force of that counter-narrative explicit. But in the obscurity and difficulty of Fanon's prose, there are enough poetic and visionary suggestions to make the case for liberation as a *process* and not as a goal contained automatically by the newly independent nations. Throughout *The Wretched of the Earth* (written in French), Fanon wants somehow to bind the European as well as the native together in a new non-adversarial community of awareness and anti-imperialism. (1993: 274)

It would not suffice, it seems to me, to attribute such considerations to a desire to retreat from an antagonistic view of the imperial relationship. I prefer to read them as part of an attempt to elaborate a truly dialectical picture of that antagonism. So, as expressed in the title of a previous section, 'there are two sides', there is domination and there is resistance (cultures of resistance and resistance through culture), but in *the process* of their antagonism, it can be the case (and probably it must be the case) that the language, the interpretive patterns of domination, become reproduced and replicated, 'translated' as it were within the language of resistance. In other terms, after *Orientalism* had powerfully elaborated the critique of the *representative* construction of the non-Western Other, which reduces him either to the figure of the 'exotic object' for a naturalistic description or to the 'native informant' whose discourse always needs a translation that he/she cannot provide, a new context now leads Said to a *dialogic* understanding of the conflict of interpretations, whereby not only the line of demarcation between 'self' and 'other' and the associated relationship of power and resistance becomes *more uncertain*, less and less resembling a 'borderline' (however imaginary), but room has to be made for a consideration of the *feedback effects of representation and interpretation*. Said does not position himself *outside* of this game of translations and counter-translations, as if enjoying a privilege of objectivity or externality by virtue of his intellectual commitment to *understanding*. He is within the battle, not only as combatant, but doubly so because he is a combatant whose discourses can become used in unexpected and unwanted ways. However, not to be outside is not the same as fully *identifying* with the representation that the camps opposed to one another. It should be possible, perhaps necessary, also to introduce a degree of critical distance with the very cause one is defending in order to preserve its future. It is tempting to link this with Said's insistence on the function of 'exile' – to which I will return – and his sense of the possibilities, as well as the uneasiness, opened up by the condition of being 'out of place' in life and politics, especially from the point of view of the national order. That is, neither inside nor outside.

But before turning to this 'subjective' dimension of the reflection on translation, we must read some passages from another crucial essay, called 'Knowledge and Power', which features as a conclusion to the volume *Covering Islam* (published in 1981 and in a revised edition in 1997), with the subtitle *How the Media and the Experts Determine How We See the Rest of the World*. It is divided into section I, 'The Politics of Interpreting Islam: Orthodox and Antithetical Knowledge', and section II, 'Knowledge and Interpretation'. Said would begin with a demonstration that to interpret another culture is always a function of definite power interests, articulating the opposition between the two regimes of interpretive activity which work as *hegemony* and *dissent*: on one side there is the tradition of orientalism, which essentially *speaks for others that it defines itself*, by claiming a monopoly of interpretive activity (Said 1997: 143 sq.). On the other side, we may identify the figures of 'antithetical interpreters' (1997: 157 sq.), a heterogeneous group of scholars, writers and activists who in various ways challenge this monopoly, essentially through a deconstruction of the *disciplinary metalanguage* (or 'framework', 1997: 163) conferring upon it the appearance of the only possible 'intellectual idiom'. But then, in the second part of his essay, Said comes to an affirmative presentation of the *conditions* under which the interpretive activity of 'knowing another culture' could actually blow up the 'framework', in other terms escape the narcissistic self-identification of a community through the imagination of its other and its enemy. There are two main such conditions, which one is tempted to identify as 'objective' and 'subjective', except that once again these polarities dialectically penetrate each other. The first condition is a 'non-coercive contract' among the dialogic agents of the process of interpretation. The second is 'self-consciousness about the interpretive project itself' (1997: 150), which means a reflective practice of interpretation, and in practice a deconstruction of the dominant 'interpretive community' (or *affiliation*, a key word as we know in Said's theory of criticism).[7] We understand that this deconstruction amounts to an infinite task of *translation of oneself*, not in the sense of assimilating all the products of other cultures, but just the opposite: in the sense of *estranging one's own culture* through the encounter with others who are *real*. In many ways, this is what Said himself never tires of attempting anew in his critical essays on philosophy and literature. Read now the striking lines on pages 164–5, featuring a veritable 'discourse on method' (more Vichian than Cartesian, as we know):

> Interpretation is first of all a form of making: that is, it depends on the willed intentional activity of the human mind, moulding and forming the objects of its attention with care and study. Such an activity takes place perforce in a specific time and place and is engaged in by a specifically located individual, with a specific background, in a specific situation, for a particular series of ends. Therefore the interpretation of texts, which is what the knowledge of other cultures is principally based on, neither takes place in a clinically secure laboratory nor pretends to objective results. It is a social activity and inextricably tied to the situation out of which it arose in the first place, which then either gives it the status of knowledge or rejects it as unsuitable for that status ... Every reader, in other words, is both a private ego and a member of a society, with affiliations of every sort linking him or her to that society. Working through national feelings like patriotism and chauvinism to private emotions like fear or despair, the interpreter must seek in a disciplined way to employ reason and the information he or she has gained through formal education ... so that understanding may be achieved. A great effort has to be made to pierce the barriers that exist between one situation, the situation of the interpreter, and another, the situation that existed when and where the text was produced. It is precisely this conscious willed effort of overcoming distances and cultural barriers that makes knowledge of other societies and cultures possible – and at the same time limits that knowledge. At that moment, the interpreter understands himself or herself in his or her human situation and the text in relation to *its* situation ... This can occur only as the result of self-awareness animating an awareness of what is distant and alien but human nonetheless. (Said 1997: 164–5)

One might say that the process described here is perfectly *circular*. Its result – the 'self-awareness animating an awareness of what is distant and alien but human nonetheless' – being in fact also its precondition. I believe, one has to admit this hermeneutic circularity, but not necessarily to picture it as a 'vicious circle'. This is linked to the fact that Said is never reluctant to investigate the various *anomalous positions* with respect to the hegemonic distribution of places and discourses which provide conditions for the production of counter-interpretations or the emergence of alternative affiliations: heretical 'communities of interpretation'. There is an affinity with

the Lyotardian allegory of the 'pagan' here, but I am also tempted to recur
to the category of *heterotopia*, which comes from Foucault (1998: 175–85).
One of the possible names for heterotopia is also 'exile'.

Any description of the politics of translation as a conflict between
communities over 'interpretation' inevitably leads to asking a question
about *who* displaces the established pattern, and how it becomes
possible to displace it? This is not – rather, it is not only – a Marxian
and Gramscian question of the *forces* involved in a relationship or an
antagonism, even if we are ready to admit that there are 'communicative
forces' (e.g. *mass media*) as well as 'productive forces' involved in social
conflicts. It is rather – in Said's preferred formulation – a question of
'speaking truth to power' (Said 1994: 85–102) or it is a question of a
discursive agency which requires a 'mode of subjectivation'. But when we
discuss it also as an agency of interpretation and translation, this becomes
the question of the 'subjective' relationship to language and the plurality
of languages which provides at least some of the conditions for a critical
action against dominant modes of interpretation. Said expressed himself
on this question, being careful, however, not to propose his personal case
as a model, but also trying to understand what made it a critical predisposition to the subversion of existing patterns of translation, whereby we
retrieve the subject–object dialectic of 'self-awareness'. We can read here
a passage from the opening pages of his autobiography, *Out of Place*
(1999):

> The travails of bearing such a name were compounded by an equally
> unsettling quandary when it came to language. I have never known
> what language I spoke first, Arabic or English, or which one was
> really mine beyond any doubt. What I do know, however, is that
> the two have always been together in my life, one resonating in the
> other, sometimes ironically, sometimes nostalgically, most often each
> correcting, and commenting on, the other. Each *can* seem like my
> absolutely first language, but neither is. I trace this primal instability
> back to my mother, whom I remember speaking to me in both English
> and Arabic, although she always wrote to me in English ... Certain
> spoken phrases of hers ... were Arabic, and I was never conscious
> of having to translate them or ... knowing exactly what they meant.
> They were a part of her infinitely maternal atmosphere ... promising
> something in the end never given. But woven into her Arabic speech
> were English words like 'naughty boy', and, of course, my name,
> pronounced 'Edwaad'. I am still haunted by the memory of the sound
> ... Her English deployed a rhetoric of statement and norms that has
> never left me ... I hadn't then any idea where my mother's English
> came from or who, in the national sense of the phrase, she was: this
> strange state of ignorance continued until relatively late in my life.
> (Said 1999: 4–5)

This development takes us far away from generalities on 'hybridity' and 'multiculturalism', to a veritable 'differend of phrases' located in the most basic layer of subject-formation, but also reconstructed retrospectively in the form of a narrative, or through a method of 'dramatization'. It is interesting to compare it with a development in Derrida's also largely autobiographic essay, *Monolingualism of the Other or the Prosthesis of Origin* (published in 1996 in French), to discover a quite different relationship to the enigma of the 'first language', which nevertheless also exhibits an internal distanciation:

> My attachment to the French language takes forms that I sometimes consider 'neurotic.' I feel lost outside the French language. The other languages which, more or less clumsily, I read, decode, or sometimes speak, are languages I shall never inhabit. Where 'inhabiting' begins to mean something to me. And dwelling [*demeurer*]. Not only am I lost, fallen, and condemned outside the French language, I have the feeling of honoring or serving all idioms, in a word, of writing the 'most' and the 'best' when I sharpen the resistance of my French, the secret 'purity' of my French, the one I was speaking about earlier on, hence its resistance, its relentless resistance to translation; translation into all languages, including another such French. Not that I am cultivating the untranslatable. Nothing is untranslatable, however little time is given to the expenditure or expansion of a competent discourse that measures itself against the power of the original. But the 'untranslatable' remains ... Word for word, if you like, syllable by syllable. From the moment this economic equivalence – strictly impossible, by the way – is renounced, everything can be translated, but in a loose translation, in the loose sense of the word 'translation.' In a sense, nothing is untranslatable; *but in another sense*, everything is untranslatable; translation is another name for the impossible. ... The language called maternal is never purely natural, nor proper, nor inhabitable. *To inhabit*: this is a value that is quite *disconcerting* and equivocal; one never inhabits what one is in the habit of calling inhabiting. There is no possible habitat without the difference of this exile and this nostalgia. Most certainly. That is all too well known. But it does not follow that all exiles are equivalent. From this shore, yes, *from this* shore or this common drift, all expatriations remain singular. For there is a twist to this truth. This *a priori* universal truth of an essential alienation in language – which is always of the other – and, by the same token, in all culture. (Derrida 1996: 97–114; 2006: 56–8)

A full interpretation of these lines would doubtless situate them in relation to the entire linguistic and philosophical tradition, at the origin of which appears the name of Humboldt and at the end of which lies that of Benveniste. This tradition poses the question of *subjectivity in language* in terms of reciprocal appropriation: the appropriation of the subject by language, at least the one which is for him/her 'maternal' or 'first', and the appropriation of language by the subject, through the first impregnation in infancy relayed through learning, which is also in part a translation process. This linguistic and philosophical tradition always inscribed such moments of appropriation within a 'community' of interlocutors, who trace the 'borders' of membership (of the nation, but also of class, or in a culture), making the *mutual comprehension* of a 'shared language' between these interlocutors the means of passing or re-passing endlessly from I to We, from We to I (see Benveniste 1966/1974). What, then, does Derrida mean when he writes: 'I only speak one language, and yet this (unique) language is not mine', if what he calls 'the language of the other' does not mean 'a foreign language' but rather concerns the foreignness (*étrangèreté*) and strangeness (*étrangeté*) of the *mother tongue* itself?

In the text, the response to this question combines three aspects, each of which is situated at a different level of experience. The first aspect is *biographical*, marked by a dramatic episode in the author's childhood. The Jews of Algeria were deprived of their entitlement to the French citizenship that they had received two generations earlier (with the Crémieux Decree of 1870) in order to distinguish them from the other 'natives' (*indigènes*). The Vichy government took advantage of the defeat to institute anti-Semitic legislation.[8] That loss resulted in exclusion from the public schools, which in France are principally concerned with the internalization of language as the principal institution of national identity.

Here, thus, we encounter the second aspect, which is *cultural*. The French language, with which Derrida tells us he shares a 'neurotic' or ultra-perfectionist 'purist' relation, is an imperial language, protecting itself from contamination by other 'inferior' or 'subaltern' idioms, whether from linguistic minorities in the metropolis, or colonized populations, who are contradictorily compelled both *to assimilate* to the dominants and *to stay in their own place*, i.e. remain dominated, and are thus held in a situation of *internal exclusion*. It therefore rests implicitly on a 'communitarian' hierarchy that is simultaneously the object of a powerful denial, the counterpart of which is the 'haunting' of the dominant language by dominated languages and the more or less vast permeability of its expressions of social class.

We see here also a third *philosophical* aspect that we can call 'transcendental' in the technical sense, since it concerns the *conditions of possibility* for the subject's access to language which conditions his insertion into the world. Instead of instituting equality, putting the speaking individual into a simple relation with a community in which he naturally 'inhabits' language, it forms a relation to language as much 'expropriated' as it is 'appropriated', which is riddled with difficulties and permanent conflict (here Derrida coins the portmanteau term 'exappropriation' to express this contradiction). The subject is 'at war' with language, and fundamentally, through the subjects who utilize it, it is language that is 'at war' with itself, with its 'proper' instituted existence (Derrida 2006: 63–4). But the representation of this internal conflict also opens onto a constructive practice: that of translation. A subject or speaker (*locuteur*) who is not in a natural relation of belonging with his 'mother' tongue is always already inscribed into a process of 'translation' of his own (*propre*) language, a process made all the more difficult precisely because there are no rules or codes for it. This is what Derrida after Benjamin calls 'absolute translation' (Derrida 2006: 61), which operates in relation to all *others* – that is to say to all 'encounters' with foreign languages – both as a predisposition and as an obstacle.

At this point it is interesting to return from Derrida to Said, who draws from personal experience in the opposite direction to give us a proposition that nevertheless converges in part on the relations of politics to translation. As we remember, Said – the son of a Palestinian father who acquired US citizenship but returned to settle in Egypt, and a Lebanese mother from a family of Baptist ministers, with an English first name and an Arabic last name, not to forget the middle name, which was his father's – recounted the impossibility in which he found himself as he tried to determine which of the two languages he learned as a child was 'his language', even though they had never been interchangeable (Said 1999). We have here another form of uncertainty, which seems to be more 'objective', but also locates translation as the condition for access to language in an unconscious zone that precedes the formation of individual consciousness. In his critical and political works, Said gradually worked out the conflictual and cultural dimensions of this uncertainty, which took the form of an *unstable* relation between the dominant and dominated languages of the 'imperial' world.

The transformation in his thought is particularly visible when we compare his formulations related to the *representation of the non-European other* in *Orientalism* with the essays from 1981 to 1987 that I quoted a moment ago on the treatment of Islam by the American media (Said 1997) and the criticism collected in *Culture and Imperialism* (1993). Between these two moments, the Iranian Revolution and the First Gulf War had taken place, as had the Oslo Accords on the 'settlement' of the Palestinian question, to which Said, a member of the Palestinian National Council, was opposed from the outset. Rightly he predicted that they would be used by Israel to intensify its colonization, and tie the Palestinian Authority to its colonial interests. In *Orientalism*, the theory of 'hegemony' and its reproduction beyond the moment of formal decolonization rests on the detection of a *double asymmetry: between those who 'represent' and those who are 'represented', and between those who 'translate' and those who are 'translated'*. Along with idioms of different status come the *narratives* that assign a more or less mythical personality to peoples and cultures, as well as the academic disciplines which allow them to be managed. But in his later works things become complicated because Said is confronted with the fact that the discourse of domination can be *reappropriated* by the 'dominated' themselves, who use it either to express demands for autonomy, or to overturn and expose imperialism to its image of itself. Something more 'dialogic' but always conflictual is added to the apparatus (*dispositif*) of 'power-knowledge', in which the representations of East and West produce effects far more *ambivalent* than can be seen in the simple schema of colonial domination. *Nationalism* and especially the *politico-religious discourse* of Islamic 'fundamentalism' are always susceptible to co-optation, since their own representation of the 'Orient' as a system of values incompatible with those of the 'Occident' regenerates an essential 'untranslatability' between the two halves of the world.

Said's critique, which, as we know, is not universally accepted, operates simultaneously *on two fronts*, which are bound together in a common task of demystifying the stereotypes of cultural difference. The unity of the 'representation of the other' and of 'asymmetrical dialogue' is precisely what Said also calls *interpretation*. Its subjects or agents are not individuals so much as they are historically and institutionally constituted 'communities of interpretation' within the framework of a certain distribution of power between the various parts of the world and of humanity. But this distribution gives way to a dislocation of the relations of forces: in the face of the hegemonic disciplines and established discourses, which reproduce the stereotypes of alterity, we discover the existence of *antithetic interpreters* who produce effects of contestation and nurture resistance by modifying the regime of translation (Said 1997: 135). We thus discover a lesson comparable to that proposed by Lyotard in terms of the 'differend' and by Derrida in terms of 'exappropriation', despite all the divergences that separate these authors from one another. It was on the basis of this comparison, and also this idea of the *singularity* of all expatriations, that I asked what kind of relation Said has to 'exile', not only as a personal experience, but as a *general condition* for the deconstruction of the monopolies of interpretation in the post-colonial world. This is not, it seems to me, a relationship of simple identification, but rather a more oblique, overdetermined relationship, which involves identification and distance. This becomes clear when we read again the essay 'Reflections on Exile' (from which the title of the namesake book is derived). It begins like this:

Exile is strangely compelling to think about but terrible to experience. It is the unhealable rift forced between a human being and a native place, between the self and its true home: its essential sadness can never be surmounted. And while it is true that literature and history contain heroic, romantic, glorious, even triumphant episodes in an exile's life, these are no more than efforts meant to overcome the crippling sorrow of estrangement. The achievements of exile are permanently undermined by the loss of something left behind forever. (Said 2002: 173)

But, following a quotation (taken from Auerbach) of the medieval monk and mystic Hugo of St Victor ('The man who finds his homeland sweet is still a tender beginner; he to whom every soil is as his native one is already strong; but he is perfect to whom the entire world is as a foreign land'), it ends like this:

> For an exile, habits of life, expression, or activity in the new environment inevitably occur against the memory of these things in another environment. Thus both the new and the old environments are vivid, actual, occurring together contrapuntally. There is a unique pleasure in this sort of apprehension, especially if the exile is conscious of other contrapuntal juxtapositions that diminish orthodox judgment and elevate appreciative sympathy. There is also a particular sense of achievement in acting as if one were at home wherever one happens to be. This remains risky, however ... Exile is life led outside habitual order. It is nomadic, decentered, contrapuntal; but no sooner does one get accustomed to it than its unsettling force erupts anew. (ibid.: 186)

My suggestion therefore is not that Said identifies with exile or elevates its experience to the meaning of a symbol of post-national identity, but rather that he struggles to retain with it a relationship of uneasy vicinity, or familiarity, that makes it also possible to picture the correspondences between *different exiles*, which remain 'singular' in Derrida's words, or perhaps are separated by some irreducible 'differend' in the sense of Lyotard, i.e. will never become unified under common names and narratives. They will remain at war, literally or metaphorically, and they will foster translation as much as postpone it indefinitely.

Notes

1   This lecture is based on a paper that I presented three years ago at the International Symposium on Edward W. Said organized by the American University of Beirut, with the title 'Politics as Translation: Lyotard, Derrida, Said', in the presence, in particular, of Mariam Said.

2   Being part in this sense of the great contemporary debate launched by Foucault in his lectures on *Society Must Be Defended* from 1976 (2003), where he puts forward the idea of 'reversing' the well-known Clausewitzian formula on 'war as a continuation of politics by other means'.

3   This is especially the case when I try to think about the historical function of Europe in the process of modernization and globalization: see my essay 'Europe as Borderland' (2009).

4   *Le différend* was published in French in 1983, and translated into English in 1988.

5   Montesquieu's famous expression in *The Spirit of the Laws*: '*le doux commerce*', is often cited in this regard. It refers to a broad and differentiated notion of commerce, 'anthropological' *avant la lettre,* which includes both commodity exchange and relations of 'civility' or 'politeness' – especially as they are established by the initiatives of women within the framework of a civilization based around a court society (see Elias, 1983 and Spector, 2004). The complexity of the semantic spectre of 'commerce' in the classical age can be located in the English *intercourse* and in the German *Verkehr* as well.

6   Note that I do not say 'cultural', precisely because the examination of the question of the differend is one of the means we have to *put into question* the notion of 'culture' itself, hitherto promoted by anthropology, which is in the process of being renounced here.

7   For an extensive discussion of the opposition between *filiation* and *affiliation, s*ee in particular 'Introduction: Secular Criticism', in Said 1983: 23 sv.

8   See Stora 2006. We must recall, as Derrida insists, that the German troops did not occupy Algeria – the government of the French state was not obeying in this case any external coercion, but following its own tendencies.

References

Balibar, E. (2009), 'Europe as Borderland', *Society and Space* 27 (2): 190–215.

Benveniste, E. (1966/1974), 'La subjectivité dans la langue'. In *Problèmes de linguistique générale*. Paris: Gallimard.

Chakrabarty, D. (2000), *Provincializing Europe: Postcolonial Thought and Historical Difference*. Princeton: Princeton University Press.

Derrida, J. (1996), *Le monolinguisme de l'autre ou la prothèse d'origine*. Paris: Galilée.

Derrida, J. (2006), *The Monolingualism of the Other, or, the Prosthesis of Origin*, trans. Patrick Mensah. Stanford, CA: Stanford University Press.

Elias, N. (1983), *The Court Society*. New York: Pantheon.

Fanon, F. (1961 [1968]), *The Wretched of the Earth*, trans. Constance Farrington. New York: Grove.

Foucault, M. (1998), 'Different Spaces'. In J. Faubion (ed.), *Aesthetics, Method, Epistemology*. New York: The New Press.

Foucault, M. (2003), '*Society Must Be Defended*': *Lectures at the Collège de France, 1975 1976*. London: Picador.

Lyotard, J.-F. (1983), *Le Différend*. Paris: Éditions de Minuit.

Lyotard, J.-F. (1988), *The Differend: Phrases in Dispute*, trans. Georges Van Den Abbeele. Minneapolis: University of Minnesota Press.

Said, E. W. (1978), *Orientalism*. New York: Vintage Books.

Said, E. W. (1983), *The World, the Text, and the Critic*. Cambridge, MA: Harvard University Press.

Said, E. W. (1993), *Culture and Imperialism*. New York: Vintage Books.

Said, E. W. (1994), *Representations of the Intellectual, The 1993 Reith Lectures*. New York: Vintage Books.

Said, E. W. (1997), *Covering Islam: How the Media and the Experts Determine How We See the Rest of the World*. New York: Vintage Books.

Said, E. W. (1999), *Out of Place: A Memoir*. New York: Vintage Books.

Said, E. W. (2002), *Reflections on Exile and Other Essays*. Cambridge, MA: Harvard University Press.

Spector, C. (2004), *Montesquieu: Pouvoirs, richesses, et sociétés*. Paris: Presses Universitaires de France.

Stora, B. (2006), *Les trois exils juifs d'Algérie*. Paris: Stock.

CHAPTER TWELVE

We, the Non-Europeans

Engin F. Isin

Is the crisis of Europe *not* more fundamental than the current crisis that engulfs it? Although it is tempting to immerse ourselves in the question of crisis in the present, I want to present a more fundamental crisis implied in the question 'what is called Europe?' This is not equivalent to asking 'what is Europe?' I want to enter this question with Jacques Derrida. When, in May 1990, he delivered a lecture on 'the other heading' during a colloquium in Turin on 'European Cultural Identity' he was in many ways responding to the question of Europe and how to approach it. Yet, I want to argue, Derrida's question of Europe is much older than that. To put it emphatically, Europe had been a 'question' for Derrida from the moment he encountered Edmund Husserl and engaged with a cluster of problems that Husserl had articulated as 'the crisis of Europe', a cluster that inspired various reflections on Europe by Martin Heidegger, Jean-Paul Sartre and Emmanuel Levinas. So there is a danger in beginning with 'the other heading' and forgetting that Derrida's ethical and political problem of Europe had exercised him practically all his public life.

What I wish to address in this chapter is how Derrida's question of Europe can be brought into sharper relief with late Edward Said's (2003) lecture on Freud and the non-European. I want to draw a lesson from the fact that 'late' Said had become exercised by the question of Europe or 'what is called Europe?' from a different angle than his earlier work *Orientalism* (1979). In 2003, his Museum of London lecture on Freud, Said indicated a path after orientalism, a path towards thinking about Europe through non-Europe. I want to argue that Said articulates, through Freud, a problem that was much deeper than orientalism, of which orientalism was a symptom. That is why I want to consider this path as 'after' orientalism. But before I go on I'd better say something about why I want to read Derrida with Said.

It is true that Derrida and Said rarely, if at all, are discussed or read together. This is not quite accidental and there is a good reason for this (see

Karavanta and Morgan 2008). Said was critical of Derrida. He found a 'crippling limitation in those varieties of deconstructive Derridean readings that end (as they began) in undecideability and uncertainty' (Said 2004: 66). For Said, the readings that Derrida provides 'defer too long a declaration that the actuality of reading is, fundamentally, an act of perhaps modest human emancipation and enlightenment that changes and enhances one's knowledge for purposes other than reductiveness, cynicism, or fruitless standing aside' (Said 2004: 66).

Moreover, Said thought that Derrida would not recognize the demand that we as citizens 'enter into the text with responsibility and scrupulous care' (see Spivak 2005). This view can perhaps be traced to an early essay where Said misunderstood Derrida and Michel Foucault as occupying opposed positions on reading (Said 1978). Since Marzec (2008) and Radhakrishnan (2010) discuss Said's vexed relations to Derrida and Foucault respectively I will not deal with that question here. Just as I am not interested in consigning Derrida and Said to their separate posts (post-colonialism and poststructuralism), I am not quite interested in making Derrida and Said speak to each other – a posthumous reconciliation. Rather, my aim is to selectively read, or at least invite you to read, Derrida with late Said on the question of Europe as the question of the non-European. For I am convinced that both Derrida and Said converged on the fundamental crisis of Europe as being the inability to approach the non-European with the openness that it required. I will shortly elaborate on this notion of 'openness' but my view is that Said and Derrida together present a fuller picture of the depth of the question of Europe and non-Europe than does either thinker alone. To put it differently, the question is not even 'what is called Europe?' as I suggested above but 'what is called non-European?' For both Derrida and Said this question is simultaneously an ethical, political, psychoanalytical and philosophical question, each aspect irreducible to the others and yet each complicating the other.

Let me start with Said's reflections on Freud and the non-European, then discuss the question of the non-European in Derrida and draw these readings together with reflections on social and political thought in Europe today to conclude the chapter.

Said begins his London lecture with the observation that Freud's knowledge of other cultures was deeply inflected by his education in Judaeo-Christian tradition, especially European humanism and scientism. Perhaps for this reason Said says that Freud was not bothered much by the other as a general problem but as a problem of the non-European. This may appear as a strange statement since Freud can arguably be considered the classic figure in the invention of the other. Yet the other that preoccupied Freud, Said suggests, is a 'European' other (Said 2003: 14). According to Said 'Freud was deeply gripped by what stands outside the limits of reason, convention, and, of course, consciousness: his whole work in that sense is about the Other, but always about an Other recognisable mainly to readers who are well acquainted with the classics of Greco-Roman and Hebrew Antiquity and European languages' (Said 2003: 14). So Said paints a picture of Freud as a quintessential European intellectual both in disposition and audience and of Freud's concern with the Other as a problem of the non-Europe.

Both in *Totem and Taboo* (Freud 2001a) and in *Moses and Monotheism* (Freud 2001b) Said finds an implicit resistance by Freud to establish an insurmountable difference or gap between the European and the non-European (Said 2003: 19). For Said it is this resistance, albeit implicit, that can be said to constitute Freud's ethics towards the non-European. But Said thinks that Freud goes even deeper and claims that the very fabric of the European is made up of non-European elements. This is, for Said, the kernel of Freud's politics of the non-European. The main impetus for this claim is about the identity of Moses. Said notes that Freud becomes adamant about Moses's identity: 'Moses was an Egyptian, and was therefore different from the people who adopted him as their leader – people, that is, who became the Jews whom Moses seems to have later created as his people' (Said 2003: 35). What Said observes is not so much the historical accuracy of Freud's interpretation – in fact he remains unconvinced and unsatisfied – but its audacity, given how aware Freud was of the dangers of his interpretation and how uncertain he was about it (Said 2003: 39). What Said highlights, and this is of utmost importance to us when we discuss Derrida's articulation of the question of non-Europeans, is that 'in excavating the archaeology of Jewish identity, Freud insisted that it did not begin with itself but, rather, with other identities (Egyptian and Arabian) which his demonstration in *Moses and Monotheism* goes a great distance to discover, and thus restore to scrutiny' (Said 2003: 44). Freud's audacity was to have argued that the founder of Jewish identity was himself a non-Jewish Egyptian. Said concludes from this that 'identity cannot be thought or worked through itself alone; it cannot constitute or even imagine itself without that radical originary break or flaw which will not be repressed, because Moses was Egyptian' (Said 2003: 54). This may be thought, as Judith Butler did, an expression of what philosophers would call ineradicable alterity to indicate that otherness is an absolute condition of identity (Butler 2012: 31). Yet, the ethico-political question that it opens up yields surprising if not counterintuitive responses.

Consider Bonnie Honig's interpretation. In her brilliant reading of Rousseau and Freud on democracy and the foreigner, she puts it starkly that 'Moses is foreign to the people he founds' (Honig 2001: 26). Yet, Honig warns against participating in the myth of the foreigner as the founder by recognizing that there was more to Freud's recognition that Moses is foreign to the people he founds. For Honig it is not because Moses was foreign that the Israelites experienced trauma but because the law imposed by Moses was *so* alien that its founders had to be narrated as foreign (2001: 31).

Honig argues that Freud misses this point by assuming that the foreignness of Moses consisted in his being Egyptian whereas it can be thought that the law he imposed in founding a people was the source of his foreignness. This is an intriguing argument which Honig uses effectively to illustrate the meanings of democracy, but on the question of otherness of Moses, Said provides another, perhaps a more nuanced, possibility. The question is not whether Moses is foreign or not and the sources of foreignness, but that the founding of a people cannot occur without its outside. A people cannot constitute or imagine itself, as Said finds Freud saying, without that radical originary rupture. Reading Said, Butler concludes that 'it is not the Moses who leads the people out of the wilderness who is most important here, but rather the one who wanders, a motif that is affirmed time and again by Jewish philosophers' (Butler 2012: 215). The ethico-political question becomes how does a people respond to this rupture or trauma of being founded by the one who wanders.

It is this ethico-political question that Derrida considers as the problem of the non-European. For both Said and, as I shall now discuss, Derrida, the European is always already the non-European. Non-Europe is Europe's rupture or trauma, if you like. But this is not a thesis of identity. Again, as Butler notes, 'it is clear that what [Said] likes most in Freud's embrace of Moses as the non-European, the Egyptian founder of the Jews, is the challenge the figure of Moses poses to a strictly identitarian politics' (Butler 2012: 31). It is not a claim that European is equivalent to non-European or that there is no difference between the European and the non-European. It is a thesis of impurity. It is the assertion of an impossibility of any social group – a people, a nation or a profession – being able to identify itself with itself without any relation or reference to the other or without having already the other within itself.

Rudolph Gasché (2009) closely examines how Derrida approaches Europe through its trauma. It is helpful to discuss him briefly as he struggles with the very meaning of Europe and how the name Europe already contains the ethico-political question we just named. Gasché illustrates how Derrida inherits a tradition in which Europe never figures as a geographic or political entity but is always something other, which has been called by various names. Gasché (2009: 9) reminds us how Europe is called an idea (Husserl), a figure, an image (Valéry), a category (Badiou), a schema (Guénoun) and 'a little thing' (Derrida); he could also include a 'vanishing mediator' (Balibar).

If Europe is not merely an entity, what are its origins as a name? As Gasché says, although Europe as a name originates in the seventh century BC, it is doubtful that it meant the same thing in subsequent centuries. Arguably, the name was inherited by the Greeks from Asia, where its possible meaning – 'dusk' – designated the 'land of evening'. Intriguingly, Gasché surmises, the Greeks may well have not thought of themselves as Europeans but those who were glancing towards dusk, looking towards the land of evening. Thus, in later centuries, by naming itself as Europe, Europe arguably constituted itself with a name that originated outside itself. In a very strong sense, and following Derrida, Gasché says this is perhaps what Europe evokes: it calls itself by the name of the other (Gasché 2009: 10). Europe comes to name itself, is able to name itself, only through the other, or the name inherited from the other. This is the same motif that we saw earlier Said drawing from Freud. Europe comes to itself from outside of itself.

> What the name Europe refers to is thus not primarily the proper name of a land but a name for a movement of separation and tearing (oneself) away in which everything proper has always already been left behind. It is thus an extension prior to all confinement within oneself, thus constituting an exposure to the foreign, the strange, the indeterminate. (Gasché 2009: 11)

But just why did 'Europe' become the name of the continent? Peter Gommers (2001) considers various possible explanations. He considers, for example, etymological, topographical and mythological explanations (2001: 62–7). Yet these ostensibly true explanations fail in giving a full account why Europe became the name of the continent. Gommers then provides an intriguing fourth account. This involves divine name-givers of non-Greek, if not 'oriental' origin. This is how it goes. In ancient Greece a goddess Europa was worshipped at the Pelasgian oracle of Dodona. This goddess 'became' the partner of Zeus – as the name of a goddess Europe is found as geographical names across Greece. Yet, the Phoenician princess has had the honour through centuries of being the name-giver of Europa due to her relation to Zeus; however, it now appears that the Phoenician princess is an incarnation of the Pelasgian goddess (2001: 67). This is, of course, the well known myth of Europa. But, as Michael Wintle (2009) illustrates, if we oppose myth to truth we will entirely miss the performative force the myth of Europa played in forging an image of Europe. So what was the 'relation' of Europa to Zeus? The myth of Europa, the daughter of the Phoenician king born on the oriental coast of the Mediterranean, and abducted (or fled) to Crete by Zeus disguised as a bull becomes the name-giver of Europe not only in ancient history but, more importantly, in modern history where the myth of Europa becomes iconized in numerous art, science and philosophy depictions (Wintle 2009; Gasché 2009: 10–12). Of course, there are various ways of interpreting the performative force of this myth. If we read it as an abduction of Europa by Zeus we can see it symbolizing the colonization of the orient by 'Europe'. If we read it as an escape of Europa from oppression (as many paintings depict Europa appearing with ecstatic femininity on Zeus with masculine virility) then Europa can appear as a symbol of liberation. So the 'relation' between Europa and Zeus is afflicted with tension and ambiguity. Martin Bernal has illustrated how the figures Homer and Hesiod played on this tension and ambiguity (Bernal 1987: 85).

Europe is not a proper name and the name comes to Europe from outside. The name Europe designates an obscure part of the world where the sun sets. 'The name itself names Europe's origin in a movement of departure from everything native' (Gasché 2009: 13). Europe always glances towards the distance being always ahead of itself with the other (Gasché 2009: 14). How then must Europe respond to this rupture or trauma? This question yields a surprising answer. *Europe is, or rather must stand for, an openness to the world.* 'To elicit the name Europe is not only to evoke the continent and its history – Europe as a geographical and political entity, as well as the history of its many accomplishments and its many failures – but something else as well (even though one does not know exactly what this is)' (Gasché 2009: 16). That something else may well be the demand to remain open to its impurity. This demand to remain open is radical as it is not about toleration, hospitality, accommodation or recognition of an imagined or otherwise 'other' but it is about getting to grips with its own impurity of being already meshed with the other.

For this reason, and perhaps unfairly, Gasché criticizes post-colonial thought for creating a blind spot of Europe by assuming its unity and hegemony and glossing over its ambiguity instead of articulating it as a question. Yet, it was post-colonial thought and literature that struggled against inheriting words and deeds as one finds them but translating them into other vocabularies and languages. This was expressed most forcefully and poignantly by Derek Walcott when he imagined a colonial subject (in this case Caribbean) delivering herself or himself from servitude by creating a language which goes 'beyond mimicry, a dialect which had the force of revelation, as it invented names for things, one that finally settled on its own mode of inflection' (quoted in Burkett 2001: 131). But in articulating Europe as a concept that takes its name from outside, Gasché provides a strong sense of the kind of thing Europe is (Gasché 2009: 17). This sense is clearly indebted to Derrida, as Gasché readily admits, but it also locates Derrida within a project, or rather, as belonging to a project, or better still, as inheriting a task, a task that is Europe.

Derrida himself intimated this with his emphasis on the relationship between inheritance and responsibility, or rather, inheritance as responsibility. For Derrida, being European means taking responsibility for the heritage of thought that reflects upon what Europe is. This is not a responsibility that is chosen. It imposes itself upon us. For Derrida, being what we are is first of all this inheritance and this inheritance is our task (Gasché 2009: 265). Derrida goes as far as to say that 'we are insofar as we inherit' (Derrida 1994: 68). Taking responsibility for this inheritance means keeping the openness of the concept of Europe through its relation to the other, non-Europe. The task consists in a double movement of being faithful to the concept of Europe and remaining committed to its openness

(Gasché 2009: 266). It requires recognizing that Europe is the name of an identity involving conflicting demands and that it produces a mode of being that is infinitely open to what is other than itself. It is in this sense that Europe is a project that is yet to come (2009: 286). It also means a critical openness. The responsibility that this inheritance imposes upon itself as an intellectual responsibility is not about peddling Europe's ostensible values in a list of Enlightenment accomplishments. As Hannah Arendt put it starkly in the preface to the first edition of *The Origins of Totalitarianism* (1951), 'we can no longer afford to take that which was good in the past and simply call it our heritage, to discard the bad and simply think of it as a dead load which by itself time will bury in oblivion' (1951: ix). This was because 'the subterranean stream of Western history has finally come to the surface and usurped the dignity of our tradition. This is the reality in which we live' (ibid.). For her, 'all efforts to escape from the grimness of the present into nostalgia for a still intact past, or into the anticipated oblivion of a better future, are vain' (ibid.). Five decades later Derrida would echo Arendt: 'without Eurocentric illusions and pretensions, without the slightest pro-European nationalism, without even much trust in Europe as it is or in the direction it is taking, we must fight for what this name represents today, with the memory of the Enlightenment, of course, but also with a guilty conscience for and a responsible awareness of the totalitarian, genocidal, and colonialist crimes of the past' (Derrida 2006: 410).

It is in this sense that Europe is an ethico-political question of non-Europeans. We, the non-Europeans, are a problem for Europe, Europa (of Phoenician origin who is abducted or escaped from oppression), Derrida (of Algerian-French and Jewish upbringing) and Said (of Arab-Christian and Palestinian upbringing) seem to announce, only in so far as Europeans are already contaminated by non-Europeans. It is also in this significant sense that 'the question of Europe is not merely one question among others' (Gasché 2009: 287). It is a question that projects itself beyond its boundaries and beyond its limits, especially those of a geographical, political and cultural nature. The question of Europe is always 'at once a chance and a danger' (2009: 287).

The preliminary conclusion I want to draw from this argument is that the starting point of reflecting on Europe cannot be its ostensible unity or value. Perhaps this is an obvious if not a banal conclusion. But if the beginning point, its originary promise, is its openness, or rather, its commitment to openness, defining itself with other than what it is, placing itself and its impurity always under question, then the question of Europe is at once inside and outside, itself and the other. We have just seen that taking the myth of Europe seriously means not to dismiss it but to draw out the performative force of its ambiguity as the source of an ethico-political question about ourselves (European or non-European). If the question is not about Europeans as such but Europeans as non-Europeans then Europe is that name which signifies the commitment to place itself under question regarding what it itself is not. That is why Europe is not a geography, a polity, a culture or even a civilization, but stands for the radical openness of that space which took as its name the name of the other. That is also why we, the non-Europeans, are a historical problem – and not toleration, hospitality, accommodation or recognition – *for* Europeans.

How did Derrida struggle, consciously or unconsciously, with this ethico-political problem? When Derrida insists that it is 'essential to study and take seriously into account ... beginning with the Greece of Plato and Aristotle, of Hellenism and Neoplatonism, what gets passed on, transferred, translated from Europe by pre- and post-Koranic Arabic, as well as by Rome', I would like to think that he is expressing this ethico-political question about ourselves opening the question of the impurity of European philosophy (Derrida 2005: 31). He pleads:

> we feel strongly the seriousness of the question of whether philosophy was born in Greece or not, whether it is European or not, whether one can speak of Chinese philosophy, whether one can speak of African philosophy, or whether the destination of philosophy is marked by a singular source, thus by a singular language or a network of singular languages. (Derrida 1995: 377)

For Derrida, then, the fact that Europe's origin is not identical to itself should lead to a historical understanding of the multiple sources of its identity not ostensibly placed outside but located within. Derrida was convinced that it is wholly inappropriate to regard the identity of Europeans historically as solely Greek, with some additional Jewish, Christian, and Islamic elements. Rather, Europeans are all these things and these things are all open to them at once.

The openness that Said anticipates in his reflections on Freud and the way Derrida approaches Europe as an open project (Derrida 1992b) are radical in the sense that they place ethico-political demands on us, Europeans and non-Europeans alike, to reconfigure our relations with our multiple sources of identity and identifications. For Europeans the urgency of this reconfiguration becomes immediately apparent with regard to the ancient Greeks.

For major European philosophers Europe always comes into existence with the ancient Greeks. As Enrique Dussel argued, the single line of development Greece–Rome–Europe is an invention of the dominant Eurocentric thought in the eighteenth and nineteenth centuries (Dussel 2000: 466–7). For Dussel, 'Today, this is considered to be the standard, traditional sequence. Few consider this to be an ideological invention that first kidnapped Greek culture as exclusively western and European and then posited both the Greek and Roman cultures as the center of world history' (Dussel 2000: 468). To put it differently, the birth certificate of Europe as philosophy is staged as inescapably Greek (Gasché 2009: 291). Derrida complicates this relationship with Greece as Europe's birth certificate. It is not that he disowns that originary moment. It is that he multiplies the sources of Europe as philosophy. Derrida accepts that what we rigorously recognize as philosophy as such does not exist elsewhere than Greece. Philosophy, as thought of as being and existence, was born in Greece. To make this recognition requires neither orientalism (or occidentalism depending on the point of view of evaluation) nor historicism. But it means also to recognize that it will have traces of non-Europeans in it.

A year after his Turin lecture Derrida was invited in 1991 to respond to two contributions by Éric Alliez and Francis Wolff, who had discussed the relations of Derrida, Foucault and Gilles Deleuze to ancient Greeks during a colloquium organized by Barbara Cassin. Derrida's presentation was subsequently published as 'Nous autres Grecs' (Derrida 1992a) and has been recently translated into English as 'We Other Greeks' (Derrida 2010). As the translators note, the phrase Derrida uses in the original title can mean 'we who are Greek', but can also mean 'we too are Greeks' as an affirmation, or, 'we Greeks of another kind', as a claim of difference (2010: 17, n1). As the editors note, this is perhaps the most extensive if not the most explicit of Derrida's reflections on his relationship to ancient Greeks (2010: 17).

This piece clearly illustrates that the question of the inheritance of the ancient Greeks is a troubling question for Derrida. It places us in the presence of

> an intrusion of the other, of the wholly other, who forces the limits of identification and the relationship of language, the corpus, or the system to itself. It is thus a question of locating the traces of this intrusion (traumas, inclusion of the excluded, introjection, incorporation, mourning, and so on) rather than defining some essence or self-identity of the 'Greek', the originary truth of a language, corpus, or system. (2010: 19, n.2)

To be sure, Derrida welcomes the efforts of the organizers to discuss resonances and resemblances amongst contemporary philosophers to identify a generation of approaches to the Greek question. Yet he says this is not enough. 'We and the Greeks' as a question is too fractured and impure to shape a generation. Derrida does not feel comfortable with being associated with a generation. For Derrida it is equally urgent to recognize the limits of these resonances and analogies (2010: 21). By saying that he has his own Greeks, followed by a pun, 'to each according to his Greeks' Derrida, in my view, signals the impossibility of a generation that will delimit all the resonances and analogies (2010: 19–20). He notes, for example, his difficult relationship to the way Nietzsche or Heidegger relates to the 'Greek thing' and for whom the Greek never appeared as a question. Rather, for Nietzsche and Heidegger it was a question of which Greeks. Neither ever considered the question of Greeks as a question of inheritance: what is being inherited, why is it inherited and how it ought to be inherited? Quite rightly Derrida wonders why in the twentieth century many scholars have chosen Greek words to name historical formations such as '*epoche*' (Heidegger), 'paradigm' (Kuhn), 'episteme' (Foucault), and '*themata*' (Holton) (2010: 22, n.11). These acts of naming are not constative acts. They are performative utterances that bring into being a particular relationship of inheritance between the modern and ancient Greeks. For Derrida these acts perform three things at once: '(1) the invention of the new, namely, a concept that is irreducible to those circulating in everyday language; (2) the supposed invention of the new as archaeological rediscovery: restoration, reactivation, or liberation of an occluded or even a forbidden memory; (3) finally, the authority attached to the use of rare words or of ancient languages considered to be learned languages' (ibid.). All three are performatives that, despite their claims to discontinuity, establish continuity with the Greeks as their source of authority. As for his own Greeks, Derrida resolutely and emphatically asserts:

> It is not only the non-Greek that attracted me in/to (*chez*) the Greek (it's a question of knowing in short what *chez* means), not only the other of the Greek (the Egyptian, the Barbarian, or whoever is determined by the Greek as his other, and so is excluded-included, posed as opposable), but the wholly other of the Greek, of his language and his *logos*, this figure of a wholly other that is unfigurable by him. This wholly other haunts every one of the essays I have devoted to 'Greek' things and it often irrupts within them: under different names, for it perhaps has no proper name. (2010: 25)

Derrida insists that we must resist an either/or injunction where we as Europeans are obligated to announce ourselves as Greeks by an automatic inheritance or as having broken with them by a law of liberation. 'If we are still or already Greeks, we ourselves, we others (*nous autres*), we also inherit that which made them already other than themselves, and more or less than they themselves believed' (2010: 27). It follows that,

> if the legacy of the thought (of truth, of being) in which we are inscribed is not only, not fundamentally, not originarily, Greek, it is no doubt because of other convergent and heterogeneous foliations, other languages, other identities that are not simply added on like secondary attributes (the Jew, the Arab, the Christian, the Roman, the German, and so on); it is no doubt because European history has not simply unfolded what was handed down to it by the Greek; it is especially because the Greek himself never gathered himself or identified with himself. (2010: 31)

Approaching it from another angle, Said similarly critiqued identitarianism by identifying its two moves. First, Said says 'if you know in advance that the African or Iranian or Chinese or Jewish or German experience is fundamentally integral, coherent, separate, and therefore comprehensible only to Africans, Iranians, Chinese, Jews, or Germans, you first of all posit as essential something which, I believe, is both historically created and the result of interpretation – namely the existence of Africanness, Jewishness, or Germanness, or for that matter Orientalism and Occidentalism' (Said 1994: 31). This is the first of the two moves of identitarianism. Through the second move 'you are likely as a consequence to defend the essence or experience itself rather than promote full knowledge of it and its entanglements and dependencies on other knowledges. As a result, you will demote the different experience of others to a lesser status' (1994: 31–2).

I mentioned earlier that for both Derrida and Said the fundamental crisis of Europe is the inability to approach the non-Europeans with the openness it demands. This may have sounded like a call for hospitality. Yet, notwithstanding Derrida's work on hospitality, Derrida's call with Said's is in my view more radical than that gesture. Calling attention to the fundamental crisis of Europe is no less than re-evaluating the multiple origins that constitute Europeans and their relationships to non-Europeans. It requires not only revisiting the 'Greek thing' and the inheritance that it implies but also re-evaluating a whole series of ostensible differences that have been put into play especially over the last few decades. It also requires exposing a whole series of differences that have been concealed within Europe as the question of others within Europe.

The infinite task of Europe is infinite not because it is over the horizon beckoning us to orient ourselves towards it. It is infinite because many contemporary problems are rooted in the fundamental crisis of Europe's inability to approach the non-European with the openness it demands. As William Connolly (2006) indicated recently, the task is not a heroic undoing of Europe but one of painstakingly and patiently revealing, rediscovering and remapping its subjugated knowledges and inheritance or, more provokingly, its minority lineages, traces and movements. For Connolly, 'The task is to modify the terms of engagement within Europe writ large by projecting the minor tradition of enlightenment more vibrantly onto the field of politics, and to build upon that entry to inspire a new spiritualization of political engagement inside and outside Europe' (2006: 90–1). Yet, symptoms of confronting this ethico-political question are all around us, to which I now want to turn by way of concluding this chapter.

One such symptom, for example, is the way in which European social and political thought always begins with its distinctiveness as the originary place of democracy, liberty, rights and citizenship. As Euben puts it: 'Those who take the West as shorthand for a series of "values" – for example, democracy, liberalism, constitutionalism, freedom, the separation of church and state – rarely recognize the extent to which such values are defined in contradictory ways and are belied by the very diversity of practices within the West' (Euben 2006: 4). Yet Said and Derrida urge us to go beyond this sentiment and affirm that Europe is not only diverse but its diversity, its minorities, are made up of many elements both European and non-European. European thought has been unable to open itself up to the possibility that such fundamental institutions are not originary but connected with non-European histories, or rather, originate from dialogical relations between European and non-European histories. European social and political thought has not been able to approach non-European forms of thought with the openness they demand because it has created an insular aura about its origins and distinctiveness, and even (and this is something that Said has taught us) superiority. Examples from its history are many but the contemporary difficulty of creating at least a modicum of comparative political thought, for example, attests to its continuing hold on the life of the European intellectual life (Freeden and Vincent 2013).

When this insularity and closeness persist in European social and political thought it is not surprising to find xenophobia, not as prejudice against non-Europeans both within Europe and without but as an endemic condition of politics (Bonjour et al. 2011). Today differences among Europeans generate responses that are just as xenophobic and searing with resentment as responses to non-Europeans (El-Tayeb 2011). From the acrimony surrounding the accession of Turkey into the European Union to utterly dangerous and disingenuous approaches to China and India, and from disparaging statements about Greek, Italian, Spanish or Portuguese political cultures to the treatment of the Roma and Sinti peoples in Germany, France and elsewhere, yet again, the contemporary symptoms of the fundamental crisis of Europe that Derrida and Said invite us to see are clearly visible.

How do we respond to this task in social and political thought? How do we assume responsibility for it despite its immense challenge? An intriguing proposal was made by Étienne Balibar in his *We, the People of Europe?* (2004). Balibar reflects on the idea of Europe as a vanishing mediator – inspired by Frederic Jameson (1973) – to mean a figure that enables an imaginary of the new during the process of transformation of a society, as the old gradually fades away (Balibar 2004: 233). It is an imaginary of the moment between no longer and not yet. This may sound as though Balibar reflects on Europe merely as a historical project; he actually uses 'translation' as a metaphor for the project of Europe. Balibar thinks that this idea of the vanishing mediator is not much different from the process of translation of ideas from one idiom to another. For Europeans – Balibar now speaks as belonging to 'we, the people of Europe' – this might well constitute the exceptional character of Europe, as translator or mediator of cultures. He admits that Europe is not the only space in the world to translate cultures from one language to another, but argues that 'nowhere – not even in India or in China – was it necessary to organise to the same

degree the political and pedagogical conditions of linguistic exchanges'
(2004: 234). Balibar expands this task of Europe as vanishing mediator
in two ways. First, he includes Arabic, Turkic, Urdu and other languages
that are already spoken within Europe. Second, he also stretches the idea
of translation from language to culture. For this utopia or myth – for
Balibar admits its enigmatic character and its impossibilities – Europe can
become an interpreter of the world, translating cultures and languages in all
directions (2004: 235). Although Balibar immediately recognizes that the
practice of translation cannot be enclosed within the borders of Europe since
these languages can never remain within the national cultures of Europe,
burdening Europe with an exceptional project raises all the questions that
Derrida and Said ask of the European project. Why imagine Europe as an
exceptional space (of translation)? Why consider Europe as a unique space
of interpretation (of other cultures)? Why consider non-Europe as if it is
already outside Europe? I am afraid imagining Europe as an exceptional or
unique space with sui generis burdens runs the risk again of placing Europe
outside history when the task is, as both Derrida and Said suggest, to place
it back firmly within (rather than outside) history – *of* world history.

It is tempting to place European history within world history only
since the fifteenth-century colonization and the rise of European empires.
After all, is it not European colonization that rendered continents with
names that Europe invented? Can we imagine Asia outside European
colonization? Can we imagine Africa without European empires? Can we,
after all, imagine the Americas without European colonization? If Europe
created a world that we inherit we need to understand how it diffused itself
through five centuries. We can read such diffusion as European diffusionism
spreading out from a centre and transplanting itself in other continents,
which Blaut (1993) named as a colonizer's view of the world, or it can also
be seen as Europe having incorporated the others within itself. It is in this
sense that the impurity of Europe is the task we inherit. Still, the task we
inherit as Europe has deeper resonance now in world history than in the
last 500 years. I hope I have shown, with Derrida and Said together, that
becoming open to that history symbolized by the myth of Europa or Moses
is also part of that task and that the crisis of Europe is embodied in the
traumas of Europa and Moses.

I argued that Derrida and Said together provide a unique perspective
on thinking about Europe as a political question. That both developed
their insights as non-Europeans makes them especially European in the
sense we have seen in this chapter. Derrida (1992b: 7) called himself an
over-colonized European hybrid, and Said (1999: 295) described his life as
always out of place and dissonant. Throughout this chapter, you will have
noticed, I alternated between their voices as Europeans and non-Europeans.
Balibar calls this multidirectional linguistic and cultural translation a utopia
or a myth to indicate perhaps the impossibility of the task; it also places
urgent and immediate demands on both Europeans and non-Europeans

to place themselves *within* world history. For practitioners of social and political thought especially, the demand is no less than to re-evaluate many of the central concepts with which we perform ourselves as Europeans and others as non-Europeans: democracy, rights, citizenship, law, territory and state. Tracing the impure histories of these concepts, the ways in which they traversed different cultures and spaces, and the ways in which each rationalized and justified pure origins while masking other differences is now an intellectual responsibility for both Europeans and non-Europeans. This should perhaps be the task of social and political thought – merging and joining disparate elements and multiple languages to assemble new concepts while considering the traces of the way in which they have been constituted as distinct. Whether we conceive this task as deconstructing or decolonizing, given how difficult it has been for only one of those institutions named above – citizenship – the task ahead for social and political thought is no mean challenge.

Acknowledgements

The research leading to these results has received funding from the European Research Council under the European Union's Seventh Framework Programme (FP7/2007–2013) / ERC grant agreement no. 249379. I am grateful to Jack Harrington for reading an earlier draft and providing insightful comments. A shorter version was published in *Europe after Derrida: Crisis and Potentiality*, edited by Agnes Czajka and Bora Isyar (Edinburgh University Press). I would like to thank Agnes Czajka and Bora Isyar for their diligent queries and corrections on a later draft. A draft was delivered as a lecture at Edward Said Memorial Conference, 15–17 April 2013, University of Utrecht. I am grateful to Étienne Balibar, Judith Butler and Miriam Said for their insightful questions and comments on the lecture. I am also grateful for comments by the participants of two workshops in which I presented later versions of this chapter: Tara Atluri, Dana Rubin, Lisa Pilgram, Zaki Nahaboo, Alessandra Marino, Andrea Mura, Aya Ikegami, Deena Dajani and Jack Harrington for their comments during an Oecumene workshop on 18 September 2013 and Humeira Iqtidar, Leigh Jenco, Rochana Bajpai, Ammara Maqsood and Faysal Devji for their insightful comments during a workshop of London Comparative Political Theory on 20 September 2013. The comments and suggestions made during an Oecumene symposium on 22 November 2013 by Agnes Czajka, Nacira Guénif and William Outhwaite were most helpful in preparing the final draft of this paper. I am grateful to Rosi Braidotti and Paul Gilroy for providing critical comments on the latest draft.

References

Arendt, H. (1951), *The Origins of Totalitarianism*. New York: Harcourt Brace Jovanovich.

Balibar, É. (2004), *We, the People of Europe?: Reflections on Transnational Citizenship*. Princeton, NJ: Princeton University Press.

Bernal, M. (1987), *Black Athena*. New Brunswick, NJ: Rutgers University Press.

Blaut, J. M. (1993), *The Colonizer's Model of the World: Geographical Diffusionism and Eurocentric History*. New York: Guilford Press.

Bonjour, S., A. Rea and D. Jacobs (eds) (2011), *The Others in Europe*. Brussels: Institut D'Etudes Europeennes (IEE).

Burnett, P. (2001), *Derek Walcott: Politics and Poetics*. Gainesville, FL: University Press of Florida.

Butler, J. (2012), *Parting Ways: Jewishness and the Critique of Zionism*. New York: Columbia University Press.

Connolly, W. E. (2006), 'Europe: A Minor Tradition'. In D. Scott and C. Hirschkind (eds), *Powers of the Secular Modern: Talal Asad and His Interlocutors*. Stanford, CA: Stanford University Press, pp. 75–92.

Derrida, J. (1992a), 'Nous Autres Grecs'. In Barbara Cassin (ed.), *Nos Grecs et Leurs Modernes: Les Stratégies Contemporaines D'appropriation de L'antiquité*. Paris: Éditions du Seuil, 251–76.

Derrida, J. (1992b), *The Other Heading: Reflections on Today's Europe*. Bloomington: Indiana University Press.

Derrida, J. (1994), *Specters of Marx: State of the Debt, the Work of Mourning and the New International*. London: Routledge.

Derrida, J. (1995), *Points ...: Interviews, 1974–1994*, ed. Elisabeth Weber, trans. Peggy Kamuf. Stanford, CA: Stanford University Press.

Derrida, J. (2005), *Rogues: Two Essays on Reason*. Stanford, CA: Stanford University Press.

Derrida, J. (2006), 'A Europe of Hope', *Epoché* 10 (2): 407–12.

Derrida, J. (2010), 'We Other Greeks'. In Miriam Leonard (ed.), *Derrida and Antiquity*. Oxford: Oxford University Press, 17–39.

Dussel, E. (2000), 'Europe, Modernity, and Eurocentrism', *Nepantla* 1: 465–78.

El-Tayeb, F. (2011), *European Others: Queering Ethnicity in Postnational Europe*. Minneapolis: University of Minnesota Press.

Euben, R. L. (2006), *Journeys to the Other Shore: Muslim and Western Travelers in Search of Knowledge*. Princeton, NJ: Princeton University Press.

Freeden, M. and Vincent, A. (2013), *Comparative Political Thought: Theorizing Practices*. London: Routledge.

Freud, S. (2001a), *The Complete Psychological Works of Sigmund Freud: Totem and Taboo and Other Works*, ed. J. Strachey, 13. New York: Vintage.

Freud, S. (2001b), *The Complete Psychological Works of Sigmund Freud: Moses and Monotheism, an Outline of Psychoanalysis and Other Works*, ed. J. Strachey, 23. New York: Vintage.

Gasché, R. (2009), *Europe, or the Infinite Task: A Study of a Philosophical Concept*. Stanford, CA: Stanford University Press.

Gommers, P. H. (2001), *Europe: What's in a Name*. Leuven: Leuven University Press.

Honig, B. (2001), *Democracy and the Foreigner*. Princeton, NJ: Princeton University Press.

Jameson, F. (1973), 'The Vanishing Mediator: Narrative Structure in Max Weber', *New German Critique* 1: 52–89.

Karavanta, M. and Morgan, N. (2008), 'Introduction: Humanism, Hybridity, and Democratic Praxis'. In M. Karavanta and N. Morgan (eds), *Edward Said and Jacques Derrida: Reconstellating Humanism and the Global Hybrid*. Newcastle: Cambridge Scholars Publishing, 1–21.

Marzec, R. P. (2008), 'Said, Derrida and the Undecidable Human: In the Name of Inhabitancy'. In M. Karavanta and N. Morgan (eds), *Edward Said and Jacques Derrida: Reconstellating Humanism and the Global Hybrid*. Newcastle: Cambridge Scholars Publishing, 304–23.

Radhakrishnan, R. (2010), 'Edward Said and the Possibilities of Humanism'. In A. Iskandar (ed.), *Edward Said: A Legacy of Emancipation and Representation*. Berkeley: University of California Press, 431–47.

Said, E. W. (1978), 'The Problem of Textuality: Two Exemplary Positions', *Critical Inquiry* 4 (4): 673–714.

Said, E. W. (1979), *Orientalism*. New York: Vintage.

Said, E. W. (1994), *Culture and Imperialism*. New York: Vintage.

Said, E. W. (1999), *Out of Place: A Memoir*. London: Granta.

Said, E. W. (2003), *Freud and the Non-European*, ed. Jacqueline Rose. London: Verso.

Said, E. W. (2004), *Humanism and Democratic Criticism*. Basingstoke: Palgrave Macmillan.

Spivak, G. (2005), 'Thinking About Edward Said: Pages from a Memoir', *Critical Inquiry* 31 (2): 519–25.

Wintle, M. J. (2009), *The Image of Europe: Visualizing Europe in Cartography and Iconography*. Cambridge: Cambridge University Press.

CHAPTER THIRTEEN

Musical Dis-Possessions

Stathis Gourgouris

My work on the thought of Edward Said over the years has focused primarily on the significance of his notion of secular criticism, as well as his widely misunderstood call for – in his own words – a non-humanist humanism.[1] The overarching impetus has been to highlight Said's commitment to thinking against the grain of any sort of orthodox modes of being – in theory and in practice – which unavoidably implicate themselves in the creation, establishment and sustenance of transcendentalist mentalities. The transcendental element here would be signified, in Said's terms, as anything that occludes and represses the *worldliness* inherent in any and every human action regardless of how such action might be conceived, represented or justified as otherworldly. On this basis, we can perhaps speak, rather generally but none the less pointedly, of the epistemology of Edward Said, which brings together the great variance and heterogeneity of his writing throughout his life into a coherent core.

On this occasion, I extend the constellation of this engagement with Said's writing by turning specifically to his musical thinking. Music was central to Said's being, and one may argue that musical thinking is embedded at the crux of all of his work, not unlike it is for Theodor Adorno – a thinker whose enormous influence Said recognized explicitly, certainly in the domain of exilic intellect but most urgently in terms of the centrality of music to his philosophical outlook. Said's writing on music aspires not to musicology per se, which is an expert mode of analysing musical structures, but to a mode of thinking that begins with the recognition that music enables one to understand the profound significance of listening as a mode of social and political being. In this latter sense, and without necessarily sticking to Said's own determinations of what specific forms of musicality are pertinent to the problem, the thoughts that follow belong to an ongoing concern that circles around the notion of 'transgressive listening' – a notion I have yet to define in a satisfactory way but, as nebulous as it remains, seems most apt to the task of addressing a nexus of problems and questions that arise from the relation of whatever might be deemed musical – and here the general categories of the sonic and the auditory would be granted equal play with non-musical domains, such as the visual, the technological and the political.[2]

Perhaps it will be helpful to be reminded of how Said understood specifically the transgressive element of music. I quote three instances from *Musical Elaborations* (1991), which, in their juxtaposition, can actually come across as a step by step elaboration of a broader argument.[3]

> What I mean by 'transgression' is something completely literal and secular at the same time: the faculty that music has [in order to] to travel, cross over, drift from place to place in a society, even though many institutions and orthodoxies have sought to confine it. (1991: xix)

Here, the transgressive element of music is characterized literally by a condition of mobility, perhaps we might even say a certain translational capacity, taking translation, again, literally, in the way Said is suggesting we do: namely, the process of crossing boundaries against the grain of various institutional and ideological tendencies that confine us in a self-contained, self-referential space. This space constitutes itself in its fundamental correctness – *orthodoxy* – and is therefore dogmatic. Curiously, for Said, this space is as far away from the literal as one can imagine, even though the typical tendency is to identify literalness with dogmatism or fundamentalism. For Said, on the contrary, the dogmatic and fundamentalist (orthodox) is deceitfully presented to reside close to the letter, for it is in fact constitutively abstracted and transcendentalized, therefore placed as far away from the literal as one can imagine and, in this precise way, rendered 'untranslatable': uninterpretable, inflexible, immobile. Music is, instead, the faculty that stands against this space and these tendencies of immobility. It returns us to the literal precisely because of its worldly transgressiveness. Moreover, the fluid mobility of music that enables it to transgress boundaries does not mean that music exists beyond language, as it would be understood through a Romantic sensibility, but as what perhaps enables the translation of language – or of languages, in the plural – at the same time that it is itself *literally* a language of translation.

The different operation of the 'trans' in translation and transgression as opposed to transcendence is of crucial significance, but expounding on it here would take us far afield. Suffice it to say, the 'trans' in transcendence implies an arrest of movement, a way out that relies on a state of arrival in some permanent monolingual elsewhere, even if that resists being precisely bounded or determined. Transgression remains kinetic and, if it is to remain worthy of its name, it cannot be ultimately instrumentalized. This is why transgression is implicated in the work of the secular. The language that Said goes on to use is quite indicative:

A secular attitude warns us to beware of transforming the complexities of a many-stranded history into one large figure, or of elevating
particular moments or monuments into universals ... In its most literal
sense, transgression means to cross over ... Secular transgression chiefly
involves moving from one domain to another, the testing and challenging
of limits, the mixing and intermingling of heterogeneities, cutting
across expectations, providing unforeseen pleasures, discoveries, experiences. (1991: 55)

Here, we have an elaboration of how the two key terms standing right next
to each other in the previous quotation (the secular and the literal) work
to qualify transgression. In so far as the secular is linked directly to transgression, it is also understood to be linked conceptually to movement. Yet,
it isn't just a matter of movement simply, but more of a certain crossing
against the current, which for Said is a key significance of the secular. What
is more directly significant here in terms of our discussion is that Said's
otherwise ubiquitous thinking about the secular takes place in – and on the
basis of – the language of music. Said speaks of music enacting 'a whole
series of transgressions': indeed 'an invasion by music into non-musical
realms' or 'consistent transgressions by music into adjoining domains – the
family, school, class and sexual relations, and even large public issues'
(1991: 56). The attention is placed on what Said, borrowing explicitly from
Gramsci (and, it must be noted, thinking specifically within the terms of
'Western' culture), understands to be music's elaboration of civil society.
Whatever may be the possible charges of musical formalism (behind which
resides in particular the enormous weight of Romantic thinking), Said
endows music with a constitutively transgressive nature:

The transgressive element in music is its nomadic ability to attach itself
to, and become a part of, social formations, to vary its articulations
and rhetoric depending on the occasion as well as the audience, plus the
power and the gender situations in which it takes place. (1991: 70)

In other words, as opposed to transcendence, transgression never aspires
to an arresting point, no matter how it may be instrumentalized retrospectively in various acts of assessment and interpretation that presume to lock
down its meaning. Constitutively, transgression belies movement, a kind of
itinerant – Said explicitly calls it 'nomadic' – drive across bounded constituencies of meaning. Having said that, however, the transgressive nomadic
element of music does not just bear a negative capacity as a gesture against
the grain, but is, in addition, also affirmative in procuring an irreverent
attachment (or affiliation, if we want to use Saidian language) that in
fact alters the situation. The transgression that Said claims to be literally
constitutive of music – simply speaking, the basic fact that music crosses
the historical-geographical terrains of language – turns out to be essential

to social formation. It isn't merely a matter of aesthetics, even when we speak of music as such, of music's hardcore elemental constituents. Music is radically unique as an art form, especially as it defies the constraints of verbal signification, but it is also, *always at the same time*, implicated in the elaborations of the worldliness of sociality, the constituencies of the social imagination.

Musical elaboration – which, let's be clear, involves the full range of all pertinent realms, from composition to improvisation and from performance to interpretation – is thus unavoidably secular. No doubt, there is a great deal more one can say here about how Said signifies the secular but this would lead us into another conversation. In passing – and to round out this preliminary framework that serves as an introduction to the musical instances I discuss below – let me reiterate what I have been arguing consistently about the ways to understand the secular. Namely, unlike much of the fashionable discourse nowadays, the bottom line of what Said signals as secular is what subverts established patterns and what enables connections between otherwise heterogeneous elements. The secular, in this respect, involves not only the dislocation and alteration of authorities and orthodoxies, but also a certain kind of movement or endemic displacement against forces of confinement which reconfigures the meanings of the itinerant and the mutable.

To mine further the musical metaphors that the above quotations demand, the secular is a mode of orchestrating disparate elements against the grain of established, expected, or confining associations or arrangements, thereby undoing or altering situations and creating new and unforeseen possibilities of (social) composition. In this respect, Said argues, there is something intrinsically transgressive in the secular and music bears this out. I don't know of any other occasion where Said associates this intrinsically trans-gressive element specifically with music, or with any other art form for that matter, an exclusivity that certainly bears a long discussion, but for the sake of argument here I shall take it up axiomatically. I do need, however, to reiterate that, in thinking of music in this fashion, neither Said's terms nor mine would concede to an essentially Romantic investment in music as superior to language or any other such notion of 'language beyond language' (which would easily register as a designation of the sacred), nor, moreover, to the equally typical tendency that takes music to signal the alleviation of social antagonism as a designated space of social or spiritual harmony.

I will trace these Saidian contours in relation to two scenes that illustrate his understanding of the transgressiveness of music, albeit away from his acknowledged preference for Western classical music and indeed drawn from the inventory of his Arab mode of worldliness, which curiously – apart from a few pages here and there about the great Egyptian singer Um Kalthoum – never quite found an analogous elaboration in his musical thinking. My more extensive focus will be on Lebanese avant-garde musician and artist Mazen Kerbaj, but I will first turn to something directly pertinent to the multiple intersection between the musical, the visual and the popular, which will, additionally, help link Said's understanding of musical transgression with his broader investment in Palestinian politics and culture. In both cases, music becomes the primarily significant mode of dealing with inexorable conditions of dispossession in both the social and the psychical sphere.

Palestinian filmmaker Elia Suleiman is celebrated for creating a unique cinematic universe whose chief mobilizing force is not narrative or even speech as such, but a gestural amalgam of image, sound and bodily space, where the kinetic (cinematic) components are most often perceived from the standpoint of arrest, of stillness. In Suleiman's characteristically static or slow-moving image-universe, sound (which, in obvious ways, includes silence) often takes the lead in the configuration of meaning. On certain occasions, a song might intervene in the action not, let us say theatrically, in order to act as choral interpretation or commentary, but rather as the force that animates filmic action at a primary level. In Suleiman's film *Divine Intervention* (2002), a key scene near the end is animated by the insertion into the action – literally, as the protagonist inserts a cassette in his car stereo – of the song 'I Put A Spell On You' as it is performed by the Egyptian singer Natacha Atlas.

The scene involves an encounter of two people in adjacent cars coming to a stop at a red traffic light: the film's protagonist (Suleiman himself) and an Israeli nationalist, perhaps a settler, in a station-wagon covered with all kinds of nationalist insignia, most of them in English. Inaugurated by the insertion of the cassette which floods the screen with Atlas's spellbinding voice, the scene consists of the protagonist staring at the man in the car

FIGURE 13.1 *Possessed object of gaze. Still from Elia Suleiman's film* Divine Intervention, *2002, produced by Elia Suleiman and Humbert Balsan*

FIGURE 13.2 *Spell-binding gaze of dis-possession. Still from Elia Suleiman's film* Divine Intervention, 2002, *produced by Elia Suleiman and Humbert Balsan*

next to him behind his dark glasses – and, of course, at the spectator who is trained on the screen. There is no movement, no other gesture, just a shot/counter-shot frame in which the person stared at, interpellated by the song, looks back increasingly paralysed by the intensity of the gaze (see Figures 13.1 and 13.2 above). The stillness of the spellbinding stare/counter-stare animated and kept suspended by the plentiforous sound of the music is disrupted by the outraged honking of the drivers behind the two men as the light turns green, in the classic sort of gag characterizing Suleiman's films in the manner of Jacques Tati or Buster Keaton.

   This scene comes third in what may be deemed to be a triptych of spellbinding actions. In an earlier scene at the Al-Ram checkpoint (where whatever passes as action takes place throughout the film) the protagonist releases from the sunroof of his car a red balloon on which he has drawn a recognizable caricature of Arafat's face. As the balloon, propelled by the wind, begins to drift across the checkpoint the Israeli guards are overtaken by a spellbound paralysis staring at the high-flying Arafat crossing into Israel unchecked, so that the protagonist and his girlfriend can drive through unnoticed.[4] This follows the very first such instance at the earliest point in the film when the protagonist's girlfriend hypnotizes the guards by sheer female walking bravado. Indeed, the song serves to retrospectively underline this consistent motif: the politics of spellbinding as a mode of resistance against surveillance.

   The choice of song and its specific rendition is clearly deliberate and thought out at length. 'I Put A Spell On You' is a classic R&B tune, written in 1956 by Screamin' Jay Hawkins and famously performed by him with inimitable voodoo extravagance. The song has been covered in various ways by a dozen artists, the most memorable being the one by Nina Simone

(1965), which bears not only a musical innovation (an added motif of strings and horns) but a radical shift in affect and meaning that makes it the undeniable precursor to this version. Suleiman uses an equally innovative rendition by Natacha Atlas, originally recorded in Cairo with Egyptian musicians and Atlas's old band Transglobal Underground in 2001, a year before *Divine Intervention*. In this respect, the song is also featured in the film as a cultural imprint of contemporaneity – indeed, as an insertion of popular culture (Arab but also cosmopolitan) into a mythographic terrain of Palestinian cinema.

Palestinian cinema is not a national cinema, as the categorization usually goes, but a cinema of occupation and dispossession. In this context Suleiman's specific mode of filmmaking is distinct, in the sense that it deliberately undermines the primacy of spoken language and straightforward dramatic narrative, opting instead for what, borrowing from Bertolt Brecht, we can call a gestic idiom. The characters in Suleiman's films, starting from the filmmaker who casts himself as the protagonist, hardly ever utter a word. Rather, communication between characters mostly happens through muted signals, silent eye contact, inscrutable gestures.[5] Hence the hyper-extension of an almost documentary visuality even in parts that extend to pure fantasy. Because Suleiman's films also lack any sort of action in the typical cinematic sense, we are treated to a hyper-visuality of the banal. Indeed, what Suleiman calls *the choreography of the banality of life*[6] produces a curious cinematic design, alternately wondrous and frustrating, evocative and confusing, alarming and hypnotizing, at times hilarious and other times unnerving – hence the puzzled responses of many viewers, whether in the film community or the public at large.

In this muted and inactive cinematic design, one can see how important music can become – as Brecht himself, after all, understood music to reside at the core of the gestic universe.[7] On this occasion, Suleiman additionally draws from the gestus of the music-video genre. By the time the song is staged we come to realize retrospectively that, in the entire time of its unfolding, the film has been literally illustrating the song before it actually appears by depicting acts of spellbinding. Suleiman uses music to dramatize those instances where the forbidden is openly transgressed, whether literally by crossing through the border checkpoint or allegorically by enacting a series of passages from dispossession to possession.

A spell, after all, belongs to the discursive order of possession. 'I put a spell on you, cause you're mine': the lyric gives cause and account for what is already announced in the word 'spell' and instantly corroborated by the image of the spellbinding stare. The spell that possesses is an act that reiterates what is already possessed: 'you're mine'. The spellbound Israeli turns his head exactly at the interpellation of 'you' in the song. It is the language of the song that actually casts the spell, not the stare behind dark sunglasses; this is what Brecht's gestic music is about. In this sense, the visual choreography of stares in the shot/counter-shot sequence subjectifies what the song proposes, so that facial images actually perform the work of the pronouns (I/you). The lyric resonates transgressively – as Said understands transgression – in its translation to a whole other situation, enabling a whole other situation by moving against the confinements of specific genre and context.

The song is based on a rather typical blues lyric about a problematic relationship:

> I put a spell on you,
> cause you're mine.
> You better stop the things you do,
> I ain't lyin'
> I can't stand it
> when you're running around,
> I can't stand it
> when you put me down.
> I put a spell on you,
> cause you're mine.

As I mentioned, the precursive transgression against the expectations of this basic blues lyric already took place when Nina Simone radically altered the conventional gendering of a bluesman's complaint by additionally tampering both with the song's melody and with its arrangement. Simone's musical contribution is more than a rendition, a version or an interpretation. She created an original, which not only secured a memorable place in music history (and specifically within the music history of Black song) in its own right, but spawned a whole other range of possibilities, especially for other women singers. Natacha Atlas, in this respect, draws more from Nina Simone than from the Screamin' Jay Hawkins original.

Atlas transgresses this nexus further, of course, by a kind of unabashed orientalization that takes shape through the contemporary music elements (ethno-trance and trip-hop) that constitute her recognizable musical style. Suleiman's casting of the song's gestus is yet another step further in this trail of transgression. The film throws a love lyric that is initially woven around a play of possession – in more ways than one – into a terrain of social and political dispossession: a Palestinian confronts an Israeli settler or a host of checkpoint guards. Thus, the phrases 'You better stop the things you do' or 'I can't stand it when you put me down' take up a whole other meaning as indexes of dispossession, as do the affirmations of 'I ain't lyin'' or the core lyric itself 'I put a spell on you, cause you're mine'. It should be obvious how this staging radicalizes the claim 'you're mine' as a kind of dialectical reversal, a dis-possession of dispossession, if you allow me the Hegelianism. This is dramatized further in the checkpoint scene, where this dis-possession of dispossession enables the unchecked passage of two Palestinians into Jerusalem, where a whole other framework of possession (and of enormous symbolic gravity) is indeed played out. Nothing spells out more precisely the grammar of dis-possession than a spell-casting song in a spellbinding cinematic performance of an otherwise perfectly real political scene.[8]

Sometimes, one can apprehend history through the coordination, inter-section or coexistence (symphony) of anonymous sounds. We suppose that all sounds begin and end in some name, but we rarely really know it. In all cases, however, the time, place and name of sound bear a relentless precision. On the night of 15 July 2006, Mazen Kerbaj came out on the terrace of his home in Beirut to play his trumpet. He had no audience, no public. He did have, however, a fellow player. On the hill across the way he could even see this player; he could see and feel the catastrophic reverberations of Israeli bombers. Kerbaj came out on his terrace to play a duet with the bombs.

No musician, even the most solitary and ascetic, can remain in the position of utter singularity. Even when self-enclosed in your own sound – and there have been a great many such musicians in all sorts of epochs who continue to magnetize us – you must at some point emerge from your abode. Music itself makes this exit certain. Even if you have dedicated yourself to the most hermetically enclosed solo, you are riveted by an unsurpassable otherness. You wrestle with some instrument, you try to master it or submit to it, but whichever way, the music emerging out of you emerges through it – even if this instrument is your own body, your vocal chords. Even when you sing on your own, unaccompanied and unattended, you are speaking out into the night or day. Mediation coexists even with the most uncompro-mising immediacy which is your own body. Like all other art forms, music can emerge out of solitude, but automatically, materially, it dissolves this solitude. This is because sound itself is a musician's closest companion, even when it is confronted as an enemy in one's most desperate nights – say, for instance, the last nights of Charlie Parker in March 1954, in some wretched downtown LA hotel when he would set fire to the bed and play saxophone next to the trash bins with intoxicated insanity.

Practically of the same age as was then the hapless legendary saxophonist, Mazen Kerbaj perhaps had the advantage that history knocked on his door with greater clarity and condensed sharpness than the dark and murky fate of a 'free' black man in America. The comparison ultimately is not the issue. Kerbaj felt that the Israeli planes bombarding his city for several nights already could no longer keep him locked up indoors. He came out on his terrace to greet them, to confront them on his own battlefield, sound to sound. Not sound against sound – here is the key difference. Kerbaj came out on his terrace one sweet summer night in Beirut to confront those who were ruining it. Not going against them, but playing with them, accompa-nying their sound and thereby altering their exclusive mark.

Kerbaj doesn't play trumpet as one would expect. Certainly, in this specific musical interaction with the bombs, he strips his instrument from recognizable references to the musical traditions that inform it. He evades

FIGURE 13.3 *Photos of performances of Mazen Kerbaj, courtesy of Mazen Kerbaj*

traditionally coded notes, as if he is trying to find, through a musical instrument, the sonic grammar of breath itself. He often uses just the mouthpiece, which he connects directly to the amplifier or various gadgets of distortion effects. In the variety of photographs where he might be sitting cross-legged on the floor, surrounded by various musical toys, or on a chair (Figure 13.3), his playing is akin to smoking a hookah.

The recording begins with the almost inaudible sound of crickets interrupted occasionally by the distant barking of a dog – sounds of a city deserted by humans, when even at a distance nature can be heard. The trumpet follows exactly this ineffable motif, a hard-pressed exhalation, as if a weakened mouth is wrestling to breathe against the world. Then, a momentary silence. When the first bomb explodes (and then soon after, the second and the third), the trumpet sound happens to be at a point where you almost think that it too is about to explode – not in a high frequency, but rather as something rumbling and turgid, like a wound straining to open. Along with the bombs, the sounds of the city return – sirens, ambulances, car alarms. And then the long baritone sound of aeroplanes, echoing the bombs they leave behind – the unwaning sound of destruction. Kerbaj does not lower the scale of his exhalation. It now seems that the trumpet seeks to get to know the bombs up close; it falls into bizarre bass depths that don't actually exist in the trumpet range, but they exist in the musician who, through a trumpet, expresses what keeps him living. Indeed, if there is something immediately emerging from this *syn-ode* it is that a man is straining to inscribe the traces of his life intact, his very own breath, on the traces of a history that is destroying him.

We can only wonder at the brave irony that brings the musician to call the piece he records on the terrace *Starry Night*.[9] The history in which he consciously intervenes – the history which at this moment, through his crazy idea to bring it into music, he transgresses – is here rendered as nature. Nature by distortion, of course. Music here manifests the hidden nature of history. It reinscribes history on the motifs of nature, not in order to freeze it, to immortalize it as art – *nature morte* – but to highlight the fact that its consequences touch upon the depths of human earthly nature. Here, history does not merely destroy history, does not annihilate the creations of a society. It kills and irreparably alters nature itself. It destroys lives, pollutes the seas, threatens the planet.[10]

The sort of music that does not make its way beyond reality has little to say. Surely, such music does not even make its way out from within reality. It remains ignorant of what produces it, of what allows it even to exist, and so this music is mute, it says nothing. On the contrary, whatever makes its way out from within reality has the power to make its way beyond it, even if this does not happen often. Kerbaj achieved something unique. He chose to play straight up against reality and simultaneously to reach beyond it – to create through it (and from within it) a sort of music that is perfectly unreal. In *Starry Night* shines precisely what outshines the stars (the bombs), but also what the bombs cannot quite efface, something that shines beyond the light because it's something that resounds – along with the bombs, in an outrageous duet, and yet beyond the bombs.

No doubt, it matters a great deal that this iterative moment was consciously recorded, thus effacing at once its ephemeral singularity. To carry out the gesture of a music that makes its way outside of reality Kerbaj conceived and took up the responsibility, not only to record this moment, but to release it on the Internet. That is, he didn't merely immortalize the moment – he didn't extinguish the unrepeatable nature of the moment like a snapshot – but he surrendered it to the most relentless regime of repetition that exists in our time.

I doubt there is another document of the 2006 Israeli bombing of Beirut registered with such immediacy. Surely, there must exist archived reportage of all kinds and all purposes. And there may even be private footage – the probability nowadays is high. But it's certain that no other such double document exists: double because it records the reality of history and yet also the history of another reality, not parallel but intersecting, a reality that is other precisely because, although it emerges from the hard imposition of a conjuncture, it none the less dares play with this conjuncture on its own terms, transforming it in the very instance of recording it indelibly as history. In this sense, Kerbaj's gesture resists the categorization of sonic journalism. *Starry Night* is not a field recording. Whatever is indisputably documentary about it is riveted by the expressionist intervention of the musician. This hardly abolishes the documentary element, of course, but it certainly exceeds it by the artistic elaboration that renders it musical, that manifests its musicality. Becoming artwork, reality thus emerges even sharper from the underside of its mere documentation.

The case of Mazen Kerbaj is no accident. For more than a decade he has resided at the centre of a powerful, even if not widely known, experimental movement in the art and music sphere of Beirut, which demonstrates directly how a city that has suffered multiple destructions manages yet to retain the unmasterable creative tradition that characterizes it throughout the twentieth century as the most cosmopolitan and experimental art space in the Arab world.[11] I would argue that one of the ways to account for the vehemence with which the Israeli army has repeatedly demolished the infrastructure of this city (beyond the purposes of strategic interest) has to do with its unwillingness to accept the capacity of Arabs to blossom as a modern secular society. Israel would always prefer the image of Arab societies as a fanatic and uncivilized mob, incapable of creating and managing any conditions of autonomy. Hence the immediate demolition of any element that might suggest an autonomous life, from the regularized sabotage of the operations of The Freedom Theater in Jenin to the relentless brutality of bulldozing Palestinian homes and olive groves. And although, regarding the latter, the context is rural and the act is perceived as the destruction of tradition, it is none the less perfectly analogous to the destruction of the cosmopolitan space of Beirut. To perceive Beirut's devastation as de facto demolition of secular life is accurate, yet there is nothing more secular (and essential to one's social autonomy) than a centuries-old tradition of olive cultivation.

Kerbaj stands at the forefront of a circle of musicians and artists that deserves to be called avant-garde. As a musician he belongs to a space deriving from the aesthetics of 1960s jazz, and specifically the chief expressions of free improvisation we find in America at the time: Sun Ra Arkestra, Ornette Coleman, Cecil Taylor, Anthony Braxton, Albert Ayler, etc. Along with them exists a subsequent but broad European experimental jazz tradition, mainly in Britain, Germany and Scandinavia, but also more eccentrically (and in fact clandestinely) in the Czechoslovakia of the Soviet period. Even the gesture of using the mouthpiece connected to a tube can be seen in various other European avant-gardists – Alvin Curran and Alfred Harth come quickly to mind. Yet, the Lebanese musicians experimenting in this genre are impressively learned and skilled, not at all plagiarists of a certain mannerism. In fact, their inventiveness breathes new life to another domain that characterizes the European tradition: electro-acoustic music and *musique concrète*.

At the same time, Kerbaj has distinguished himself equally as a painter and graphic artist. His sketches don't actually show a refined technique. Rather, his approach testifies to an explosive improvisational expression analogous to his music. During the 2006 bombings, Kerbaj produced

FIGURE 13.4 How can I show sound in a drawing? *Artwork by Mazen Kerbaj, courtesy of Mazen Kerbaj*

FIGURE 13.5 *Artwork by Mazen Kerbaj, courtesy of Mazen Kerbaj*

FIGURE 13.6 In each poet two eyes in each eye, *by Mazen Kerbaj, courtesy of Mazen Kerbaj*

FIGURE 13.7 Day after day I am smoking myself, *by Mazen Kerbaj, courtesy of Mazen Kerbaj*

more than a dozen sketches a day, in an effort to document – much like he did with *Starry Night* (which he also renders in a sketch – see Figures 13.4 and 13.5) – not only the history of a city under bombardment, but how this history is undercut by an everyday reality that does not subside under duress, a mode of living that resists any prospect of subjugation and annihilation.

From this standpoint, the sketches – like the musical duet with the bombs out on the terrace – become documents not of an occasion in which history becomes present, but of an occasion where history is created, even when one is acting defensively and on the run under the threat of mass death and without any sort of military prospect of resistance. Creating history by mere living entails, in the last instance, a transformative encounter with the historical archive – not so much in deliberately tampering with the archive as established historical documentation, but as archive-making in itself, which in that very respect, in its creative emergence out of the space of mere living, produces waves of inadvertent interference that reconfigure the established archival parameters of historical documentation.

Kerbaj's gesture of putting out on the Internet a fragment from the terrace recording is itself a gesture of this mode of living. It is the same mode that prompted many Lebanese (but also Israelis) to begin blog journals from the outset of the war. In his own blog, Kerbaj hardly ever speaks – and in this sense too he is innovative, if we consider that blogging is the quintessential chattering genre. He mainly posts bunches of sketches, occasionally accompanying them with laconic quips, sometimes in verse mode. These tiny poems – if we can call them that – are not performed exclusively in a literary domain. What may be called, literally, a poem is the aggregate: sketch + verse. The visuality of this artistic pair remains foundational; the verses work to make the image denser (see Figures 13.6 and 13.7).

No doubt, the Internet has radically changed the conditions of production and reception of art. Any artist automatically, with a mere click, can send out whatever fragments of inner fantasy to a receptive space which, in essence, has no limits of reproducibility. Thinking against the grain, we can say that this new horizon of possibility returns to the artist a big part of the ownership of the means of production that is otherwise revoked by the market. At the same time, however, it forces the artist to abandon any requisition from the mechanisms of the market (publication, advertising, distribution or sales) to protect and promote the artwork. Generally speaking, the dissemination of the artwork on the Internet presupposes a substantial distancing of the artist from the work, or even more, the reconciliation of the artist with the fact that the artwork will be disseminated as a simulacrum. The art object as such – the specific sculpture, painting or book – can only hope to continue to exist in a parallel life of much narrower purview and without exclusivity.

It is no longer useful, it seems to me – perhaps it's even pointless – to believe that we need to choose between these two lives. Those who have nostalgia for the original artefact should not forget that we are all, without exception, subjected to the fetishism of commodities. Paradoxically, the unknown public that comes into contact with the sketches or the music of Kerbaj on the Internet – an out-of-place and out-of-time public in relation to the work's conditions of production – evades this logic of commodity fetishism. Of course, it's but a momentary evasion, as ephemeral as is one's passage from one website to another. This is not the most interesting aspect of the problem. What matters most are the basic questions that emerge from these conditions, which concern specifically this notion of public. How do we understand the notion of Internet public? How can we speak of public when the encounter with the artwork (or any document of reality) takes place so exclusively in private in front of one's own digital screen? What is the space of the *commons* between all these solitary figures across the multilateral spaces around the globe, when out of place and out of time they encounter the simulacrum of the same artwork on a website? Whatever the veneration of social media technologies as a new development in the negotiation of public/private, or even in the explicitly political space of social struggle (evidenced, for example, in the extensive discussion about their role in the events of the Arab Spring), there is no way to outmanoeuvre the staunch presence of social and political practices that still depend on the proximate existence of real bodies – of real subjects and objects – in the real time–space continuum of the street, the anonymous, but so very personal, public space.

In the Kerbaj case, at least concerning the musical duet with the bombs, the media reaction (mainstream and Internet) was voluminous and immediate, even if not immediately positive. While bombardments were continuing, a substantial part of this public not only refused to entertain this act as an artwork, but rather deemed it to be blasphemous against both art and reality. And while Kerbaj was accused of aestheticizing war and destruction, he was also constructed as an Internet and television news item. Kerbaj refused invitations to take part in a discussion on camera, therefore retaining control over the means of (re)production of the specific gesture and thereby clearly distinguishing between the Internet and the satellite televisual image as media of translation of both the artwork and the creative thought behind it.

Kerbaj insists that his blog does not engage in politics, that it simply invests reality with art. But his art is interwoven with reality. It doesn't merely interpret reality, nor merely document it. It also interrupts it and alters it. Kerbaj's reality – contrary to the reality of most of us who live in conditions of settled somnambulance – obviously has a different relation to art. In our reality art counts when it unsettles our condition, so much in fact that after a shattering performance we may yearn to return to the safety of our somnambulance, even if we can't. The very realization of this debilitated desire – if in fact it actually registers – may make possible an awakening that will then lead us productively elsewhere. But in Kerbaj's war-torn world, reality is what everyone is trying to get away from, and here art does the exact opposite. It remains in the place of dispossession, even while it retains an investment in reality's possession.

I close by returning for a moment to Said. Near the end of *Musical Elaborations*, Said confronts exactly this problem of the public/private negotiation of music and reality. Reflecting on Brahms's Sextet Variations, he finds himself 'coming to a sort of unstatable, or inexpressible, aspect of [Brahms's] music, the music of his music, which I think anyone who listens to, plays, or thinks about music carries within oneself' (1991: 93). While no doubt this kind of deeply personal, almost ineffable, characterization can be read as a subjectivist investment in a sort of musical formalism, I would argue that it's not. Kerbaj's case illustrates dramatically the significance of 'the music of his music' in the very gesture of showing how the sound of this music encompasses the alien magnitude of Israeli bombers. In the context of the same argument, Said goes on to elucidate precisely this worldly encompassing: 'Musical elaboration itself – the composition and performance of music – is an activity in civil society and is in overlapping, interdependent relationship with other activities ... In fact, music has always taken place, so to speak, in mixed public and private circumstances ... [and] serious musical thought occurs in conjunction with, not in separation from, other serious thought, both musical *and* non-musical' (1991: 97).

These two statements are thus not contradictory at all, even though each retains a hardcore position within the clear-cut boundaries of what is private and what is public. Nothing indeed can be more private – more *idiomatic* – than the music of one's music, the music that is self-possessed, to use here a term that very much resounds in the context of our discussion yet resounds also, on its own, in a number of contestable significations in social theory. I certainly don't mean to interpret Said to be privileging something that, by virtue of the language of self-possession, belongs to the realm of the liberal individual. But I do want to underline his insistence that we cannot compromise on how profoundly the power of music resides in its singularity. For Said, of course, what makes singularity matter is its worldliness. All idioms, even the most hermetic and unreadable, exist in a social-historical sphere and in the midst of multiple languages, not necessarily addressing each other or communicating, but often intersecting, sometimes conflicting, and surely coexisting.

In a brilliant reading of these particular passages in Said's *Musical Elaborations*, which very much evokes Said's spirit and language, Michael Wood (2004) has stressed this entanglement between the deeply personal 'music of one's music' and the constitutively social 'music of non-music' with an eye to how we come, not merely to convey or carry out a politics, but to *form* a politics, to create future constituencies and to alter situations that are taken to be unassailable.[12] On the one hand, Wood says, we have the situation where music 'creates a space of its own, a form of solitude that doesn't remove us from the world but makes a sort of hole in the world, a secret zone where there really is nothing but music' (2004: 143). And, on the other hand, the 'music that explores the music of its own music may offer us the image of a future politics, a world where solitude turns into freedom and undiluted respect, a world that is full but not crowded because no invasions – of individuals or of groups – are taking place. We are not alone and we are not silent; but we have given up none of the privileges of solitude and silence. We hear the music, and we hear the music of the music. The music of a possible politics, we might say' (2004: 144). This musical possibility of a future politics may indeed be utopian, Wood adds, but the meaning of utopian would have to be configured in the terms that only Said, very much against the grain of all that is conventionally recognized as utopian, would dare define in the closing sentence of *Musical Elaborations* by the most transgressive (that is to say, musical) conditionality: 'if by utopian, we mean worldly, possible, attainable, knowable' (Said 1991: 105).

Notes

1   See indicatively: 'Transformation, Not Transcendence', *boundary 2* 31: 2 (Summer 2004): 55–80; '*Orientalism* and the Open Horizon of Secular

Criticism', *Social Text* 87 (Summer 2006): 11–20; 'The Late Style of Edward Said', in Ferial Ghazoul (ed.), *Edward Said and Critical Decolonization* (Cairo: American University of Cairo Press, 2007).

2   The literature on the problem of listening is vast and vastly increasing by the day. It is difficult to disengage it from the broad nexus of problems that has destabilized the once unassailable epistemological integrity of the categories of music, sound, noise or silence. Key recent works on the problem of listening would be: Peter Szendy, *Listen: A History of Our Ears* (Fordham University Press, 2008); Salomé Voegelin, *Listening to Noise and Silence* (Continuum, 2010); Brian Kane, *Sound Unseen* (Oxford University Press, 2014). An essential conversation on this intersection of problems takes place in Georgina Born's edited volume *Music, Sound, and Space: Transformations of Public and Private Experience* (Cambridge University Press, 2013).

3   See Edward Said, *Musical Elaborations* (Columbia University Press, 1991). Henceforth cited in the text.

4   The two scenes from *Divine Intervention*, as a sort of music video for the song, can be found here: http://www.youtube.com/watch?v=nJvD6weya3k. A stunning video of Natacha Atlas performing the song with Transglobal Underground can be found here: http://www.youtube.com/watch?v=FamqM4rI6DE

5   I can only think here of Edward Said's haunting description of Palestinian sensibility – it is especially pertinent to Suleiman's cinematic universe: 'We are a people of messages and signals, of allusions and indirect expression. We seek each other out, but because our interior is always to some extent occupied and interrupted by others – Israelis and Arabs – we have developed a technique of speaking **through** the given, expressing things obliquely and, to my mind, so mysteriously as to puzzle even ourselves.' See Edward Said, *After the Last Sky* (Columbia University Press, 1999), 53.

6   'A Quick Chat with Elia Suleiman'. Interview with Jason Wood, 13 December 2002. Quoted from www.kamera.com.uk, no longer available.

7   Bertolt Brecht, 'On Gestic Music' [1932] in *Brecht on Theatre*, John Willett ed. and trans. (New York: Hill and Wang, 1974), 104–6. Note that, for Brecht, the use of *Gestus* (and *gestisch*) emerges from a specific understanding of the situation of music in theatrical performance; the terminology was likely borrowed from Kurt Weill's 1929 essay 'Über den gestischen Charakter der Musik'.

8   My thinking here has had much to gain from the dialogue between Judith Butler and Athena Athanasiou on the intrinsically aporetic notion of dispossession, the elusive difference between being and becoming dispossessed (which may also be a valuable way to understand the notoriously difficult to determine difference between metaphysics and politics), as well as the inevitable gendering (and, surely, sexualization) of the notion, which is also evident in my example, and finally its political performativity which goes hand in hand with its epistemological precariousness. A dialectical undoing of dispossession – which, if we are strict about dialectics, happens from within and also preserves dispossession at the same time that it alters its condition

– seems to me an interesting way to address (though surely not resolve) this aporia. See Judith Butler and Athena Athanasiou, *Dispossession: The Performative in the Political* (Polity Press, 2013).

9 A fragment of the piece (6:31 minutes) can be found at: http://www.muniak. com/mazenkerbaj.html (accessed 13 November 2015). It bears the following information: 'A minimalistic improvisation by Mazen Kerbaj / trumpet and the Israeli Air Force / bombs. Recorded by Mazen Kerbaj on the balcony of his flat in Beirut, on the night of 15th to 16th of July 2006.'

10 I cannot help but recall here Walter Benjamin's last entry in his *One Way Street* (1928), where, working very much against the background of the 'starry night' being one of Kant's figures for the sublime, he points out precisely how the technology of human history produces 'nature' on a planetary scale. See Walter Benjamin, *Selected Writings*, vol. 1, (Harvard University Press, 1997), pp. 486–7.

11 For an overview of this specific experimental art and music scene in Beirut, see Sharif Sehnaoui's 'Global Ear: Beirut' in *Wire* 271 (September 2006): 16. For a general perspective, see Thomas Burkhalter, Kay Dickinson and Benjamin J. Harbert (eds), *The Arab Avant-Garde: Music, Politics, Modernity* (Wesleyan University Press, 2013).

12 Michael Wood, 'The Music of His Music: Edward Said 1936–2003', *October* 109 (Summer 2004): 143–9.

CHAPTER FOURTEEN

In the Time of Not Yet: On the Imaginary of Edward Said[1]

Marina Warner

Edward Said first met Daniel Barenboim by chance, at the reception desk of the Hyde Park Hotel, London, in June 1993; Said mentioned he had tickets for a concert Barenboim was playing that week. They began to talk. Six years later, in Weimar, they dreamed up the idea of a summer school in which young musicians from the Arab world and from Israel could play together. They hoped, Said remembered in *Parallels and Paradoxes* (2004), that it 'might be an alternative way of making peace'. It was in Weimar, he noted, that Goethe had composed 'a fantastic collection of poems based on his enthusiasm for Islam … He started to learn Arabic, although he didn't get very far. Then he discovered Persian poetry and produced this extraordinary set of poems about the "other", *West-östlicher Divan*, which is, I think, unique in the history of European culture' (2004: 7). The West-Eastern Divan: the orchestra had a name; it was never discussed again.

It seems odd that Said, the fierce critic of European orientalism, chose to use the title of a work that, on the face of it, belongs in the orientalist tradition. Goethe's poems are filled with roses and nightingales, boys beautiful as the full moon, wine, women and song. Yet as Said saw it, Goethe's lyric cycle is animated by a spirit of open enquiry towards the East, grounded in a sense of the past in art and culture, not in dogma or military and state apparatuses. He read it as calling for an understanding of individuality as a process of becoming and therefore fluid. He also believed that poetry can have the metaphorical power to proclaim a visionary politics. The cycle represented for him an alternative history and epistemology, concerned with the cross-pollination between East and West. It seemed to confirm the orchestra's principle that 'ignorance of the other is not a strategy for survival' (Barenboim 2012).

Said's approach was always historical; his work as a critic and intellectual was rooted in an examination of context, both cultural and political, and the orchestra, which in summer 2015 toured South America, embodies his commitment to the work of art as an actor in its time. The word *theoria*, he liked to remind us, means 'the action of observing'; for him, theory was a dynamic, engaged activity, not a matter of passive reception. The theorist-critic should be a committed participant in the works he observes, and the works themselves aren't self-created or autonomous but precipitated in the crucible of society and history. 'My position is that texts are worldly', he writes in *The World, the Text, and the Critic*. 'To some degree they are events, and, even when they appear to deny it, they are nevertheless a part of the social world, human life, and of course the historical moments in which they are located and interpreted' (Said 1983: 4). The making of music is an event in this sense too.

Said had long been interested in the historic entanglements of East with West. He always felt himself to be 'out of place' (this was the title of his autobiography), and was strongly attracted by displacements that brought one culture in contact with another. He evolved from that sense of dislocation his theory of 'contrapuntal' reading, put forward in his essay 'Reflections on Exile':

> Most people are principally aware of one culture, one setting, one home; exiles are aware of at least two, and this plurality of vision gives rise to an awareness of simultaneous dimensions, an awareness that – to borrow a phrase from music – is contrapuntal. For an exile, habits of life, expression or activity in the new environment inevitably occur against the memory of these things in another environment. (Said 2000: 186)

As a Palestinian who grew up in Egypt and was educated in Cairo and later in the United States, Said was well used to such antiphonal switches of viewpoint. He was a translated man, between East and West, and in between and back again.

The *West-Eastern Divan* is an example of this contrapuntal consciousness, and its publication in 1819 marks an apogee in the oriental renaissance, the era retrospectively named by the French literary scholar Raymond Schwab in a magnificent book, published in 1950, which explored how the culture and civilization of the West was shaped by the encounter with Arabic, Middle Eastern and Asian cultures in ways not sufficiently recognized. In a wonderful phrase, picked up by Said, Schwab wrote that enthusiasm for the East 'multiplied the world'; he went on to describe the change in the West's image of the Orient, from 'incredulous bedazzlement' to 'condescending veneration'. 'There is', Said wrote in a 1976 essay, 'a saddening impoverishment obviously, from one image to the other.' Schwab's approach to the Orient was one that the critic of orientalism could recognize and support, and Said found a similar approach in Goethe's passage between East and West, across languages, period and genre. The *West-Eastern Divan* must also have appealed to Said because of his theory of 'contrapuntal criticism':

in Goethe's oriental masquerade, his impersonation of an exotic alter ego, accompanied by a creative throwing of the voice, acts as a literary analogue to musical counterpoint. No exile in fact, he transmuted Weimar into medieval Shiraz out of a desire to be reborn, renewed.

Oriental masquerade had been the height of fashion throughout the eighteenth century, on the stage, in fiction and fable, as well as in philosophy and politics. Montesquieu, in *Lettres Persanes*, adopted the viewpoint of a foreign visitor, and Voltaire's acerbic oriental tales, his *Contes philosophiques*, are an obvious instance of the West putting on Eastern dress in order to examine itself more clearly and skewer iniquities at home, or point the way to social and medical reforms. Said loved *Così fan tutte*, the last collaboration between Mozart and Lorenzo Da Ponte, which was first performed in Vienna in January 1790. The opera stages very knowingly and farcically an oriental masquerade, when Don Alfonso devises a trick for the two young men to play on their fiancées, Dorabella and Fiordiligi. They will disguise themselves as Orientals and test the young women's steadfastness. When they reappear in their masquerade (the word is used often in the opera), the maid Despina immediately draws attention to the new visitors' appearance, expressing horror at their outlandish moustaches (lots of opportunity here for stage designers to indulge in pantomime excess – gigantic turbans, glittering damasks, swaggering seductiveness). She supposes they must be from the Ottoman Empire, the Balkans or Turkey – later they settle on Albania.

One might have expected Said to find all this demeaning and the worst sort of orientalism. Instead, he points up the doubts the libretto casts on stable identities and notes the perplexing shifts in the characters' emotions. His keen interest in the fluidity of the self, something explored by several of his favourite writers, returns again and again in his thoughts on late style, which are attentive to surprise changes of direction, to inconsistency, experiment, 'anachronism and anomaly'. Don Alfonso, he writes, devises a game 'in which human identity is shown to be as protean, unstable and undifferentiated as anything in the actual world' (Said 2002).

In a splendid comic aria, stuffed with innuendo, Guglielmo asks the two women to admire him:

> Look at us,
> Touch us,
> Take stock of us:
> We're crazy but we're charming,
> We're strong and well made,
> And as anyone can see,
> Whether by merit or by chance,
> We've good feet,
> Good eyes, good noses.
> Look, good feet; note, good eyes;

Touch, good noses; take stock of us;
And these moustaches
Could be called
Manly triumphs,
The plumage of love.

The mock serenade reverses the usual direction of a singer's praise: Guglielmo and Ferrando vaunt their own charms, not the beauty of their love objects. And beneath the froth and wit, the scene stages a double demand: the young women are being asked to look at the Orientals without being prejudiced against them on account of their unfamiliar features (those moustaches); and to see through the men's disguises to discern their true lovers beneath. The women fail, but in doing so, come to realize their ignorance.

Such recognitions underlie the movement of fairy tales towards their happy endings: Cinderella is seen for who she is, not a slattern after all. In some ways, *Così fan tutte* also uses oriental masquerade to warn that one should never trust appearances, not because they are deceptive but because everyone is burdened with prejudicial baggage. The Albanian disguises of the fiancés trigger uncharacteristic behaviour in the two young women: they fall for oriental seductiveness, even when play-acted. (It's piquant that fashion later adopted the oriental moustache so wholeheartedly that every good Victorian paterfamilias cultivated luxuriant whiskers.)

Said was the *Nation*'s music critic for many years, and paid close attention to Peter Sellars's productions of Mozart – he always found them compelling, if not entirely successful. Sellars is notorious for his extreme updates: his Don Giovanni is a heroin addict, and he recently set *Zaide*, an early sketch of *The Abduction from the Seraglio*, in an Asian sweatshop. Said found much to praise in Sellars's *Così fan tutte*, singling out the way his production illuminated the opera's portrait of human personality as almost infinitely capable of mutation: 'What Sellars has picked up with great brilliance is the void at the centre … a void that allows an infinite series of substitutions, so long as each is internally consistent in its patterns and conceits' (Said 1989). 'La donna è mobile' indeed. But not only in the sense of 'fickle': Said, in his thoughts on contrapuntal harmonies, points out that 'flightiness', in the strongest and best sense, could refer to flights of the mind. He discerns a presentiment in *Così fan tutte* of the more ambiguous, serious meaning that Goethe gave to masquerade, and productions today often refuse to provide a sense of serene closure at the end. What the characters have discovered has unsettled their complacent sense of virtue. They have experienced contrapuntal consciousness and are changed.

Goethe's oriental impersonation, which culminates in the poems of the *West-Eastern Divan*, published twenty-nine years after the first performance of *Così fan tutte*, invites us to imagine a similar projection of the self into another. He first read *The Arabian Nights* in Antoine Galland's French translation of 1704–17; it was one of the spurs to his lifelong curiosity about Eastern literatures and languages, which began with the Bible and soon took him to Islam's sacred scriptures. The *West-Eastern Divan*, which he began between 1814 and 1815, is a long, elaborate lyric cycle which draws on Persian and Arabic verse forms, themes and imagery, and sings fervent praises to oriental attitudes towards love, pleasure and ethics.

Goethe knew the language well enough to write some poems in Arabic script; he read the Koran with care, and acknowledged it as a profound inspiration: Islam seemed to him a liberating alternative to the Christian morality of Germany. 'The poet considers himself a traveller', he wrote of himself in the 'announcement' for these poems. 'He has already reached the Orient. He enjoys its ways, its customs, objects, religious beliefs and views' (Goethe 1816). Though he recoiled from the puritanism of Islam (he was a keen tippler), he felt able to declare that he 'does nothing which would rebut any suspicion that he himself could be a Muslim' (ibid.).

The result of this immersion is a dramatic spiritual – and carnal – odyssey told in exclamatory lyrics, by turns ecstatic and tender, comic and ferocious; the verses are highly wrought, lapidary, difficult to render into English without producing something that sounds like patter or nursery rhymes. Occasionally, the poems step to the rough music of the vernacular forms developed by Schiller and Heine as well as Goethe himself, inspired by the European oral tradition: ballads, curses, spells, tales, dirges, lullabies, serenades and other kinds of love song. But Goethe chiefly adapts Persian and Arabic lyric forms. As the Arabist Jaroslav Stetkevych has observed, 'Arabic poetry was admitted in an unmitigated way into European literary sensibility' through Goethe's enthusiastic *imitation*.[2] Stetkevych is careful to distinguish this development from the study of Arabic culture as a form of scientific ethnography designed to contain and control it, which came later and developed along a different path.

Goethe was captivated above all by the medieval poet Hafiz, who had recently been translated by the orientalist Joseph von Hammer-Purgstall. Hafiz, who lived in Shiraz, survived the turmoil that resulted from Tamburlane's invasion, and wrote passionate poetry about drinking and loving well into his later years; he died aged around 70 in c. 1389. Hailed as a Sufi mystic as well as the hedonist's patron saint, Hafiz is celebrated as a virtuoso of rhyme and metre, a poète maudit and a great man. He is still a much loved and much quoted poet in Iran. In the souk in Shiraz, there's said to be a fortune-teller with a pet pigeon: once you pay your rials, the bird pecks a screwed-up bit of paper from a tray on which, as in a fortune cookie, you'll find a line or two of verse to guide you on your way. They are all from Hafiz. Goethe rhapsodizes: 'And though the whole world sink to ruin, I will emulate you, Hafiz, you alone! Let us, who are twin spirits, share pleasure and sorrow! To love like you, and drink like you, shall be my pride and my life-long occupation.'

The Napoleonic Wars brought Goethe into further contact with Islamic culture, and in unexpected ways. He was a believer in omens, and took it for a sign when a soldier, just returned to Weimar from the Spanish campaign, handed him a manuscript page from a Koran he had taken as booty, which contained Muhammad's order: 'Say, "I take refuge with the Lord of men ... from the evil."' This spoke luminously to Goethe: he must take refuge from the gods and values of his own milieu. His oriental studies were, he wrote, 'a kind of Hegira, one flees from the present into distant times and regions where one expects something of paradisal quality' (Goethe, op.cit., p. xi). (He called an opening poem in the *West-Eastern Divan* 'Hegira'.)

The word *divan*, a novelty in German at that date, originally meant 'cushion' in Arabic, and then came to designate the seat of the ruler as he presides over his council of advisers. Its meaning widened so that it could be used to describe an assembly or collection, and in turn a collection of writings, or a book. An analogy in English might be using the word *cathedra* – 'throne' – for a volume of poetry. The use of the word *divan* also underlines a significant aspect of oriental attitudes towards literature and its role, to which Goethe in Germany and the Romantics in England (in their early days as radical idealists) also subscribed: poets, Shelley's 'unacknowledged legislators of the world', must not dissociate themselves from politics.

The titles of the twelve books that make up the *West-Eastern Divan* – 'The Book of the Singer', 'The Book of Love', 'The Book of Proverbs' and so on – are given in German and Farsi, and lend the sequence a scriptural feel, echoing both the Bible and the Koran. The sequence opens with a quatrain which invokes the Barmecides, a clan famed for their wealth and munificence, who lived in the time of the caliph Haroun al-Rashid and feature in many of *The Arabian Nights*; this is the Golden Age in the Islamic imaginary, an era of civilized luxury and benevolent rule, when Baghdad was the richest and most populous city in the world. The mood is one of retrospective nostalgia (the translation is John Whaley's of 1998):

> Twenty years I let time run
> And enjoyed the lot I drew;
> Unmarred lovely years, each one,
> Like the Barmecides once knew.

Goethe also borrows motifs and tropes from Firdusi and Rumi: their verse is erotic, languishing, potent, full of deep stirrings of desire and passion, the desire of the moth for the flame, but it's also humorous and lively, as they extol the pleasures of nights of love and drinking. He adopts their verse forms: paeans, epigrams, revenge songs and, above all, the *ghazal*, the most important form in Persian poetry, a complex antiphonal song in which each verse stands alone, moving in a different direction with a new theme, to jagged and colloquial effect.

Goethe seems to want his readers to imagine that he's channelling the poems rather than originating them himself. In the oriental tradition, lyric poetry – with or without music – dominates. This mode seeks to create verbal music with a tempo that readers and listeners experience physically, as in dancing; poetry here attempts to free itself from the constraints of reference, meaning, even sense, and to reach a wordless state of transport (even of self-annihilation – hence the accompaniment of excessive drinking). In this way, lyric institutes an ordering of thought that might contribute to a realigning of values and a remoulding of alliances and allegiances, both personal and social.

The *West-Eastern Divan* cycle is known today for the rhapsodic suite of love poems in 'The Book of Suleika'. 'Suleika' is an oriental mask for the young actress, musician and writer Marianne von Willemer, thirty-five years younger than Goethe, one of a long sequence of women with whom he fell rapturously in love. These erotic invitations encapsulate oriental lyricism in the Romantic era and have been much anthologized, giving a distorted sense of the whole cycle. Marianne was the youngest performer in a troupe of travelling players when at the age of sixteen she was taken into the household of the Frankfurt banker Johann Jakob von Willemer to be educated with his daughters. She became his third wife in 1814 when she was twenty-nine, and he seems to have been the most complaisant of husbands, even offering Goethe a ménage à trois (an arrangement to the poet's taste – this wasn't the first time).

The two began their love story in Eastern costume: the lovesick Goethe called himself Hatem, after Hatem Thai, a poet to whom Hafiz often refers, who was celebrated for his 'unsurpassed generosity'. Marianne cast herself as Suleika, the Islamic name for the woman known in the Western tradition as 'Potiphar's wife'. As in the Bible, she's smitten by the young Joseph and makes amorous advances to him; when he flees, leaving his torn shirt behind in his eagerness to escape, she tells her husband he assaulted her. In the West, the story takes the form of a cautionary tale of entrapment and has a distinguished career in the annals of misogyny; in Christian moral exempla, in pictures and in stories, Potiphar's wife embodies women's lust and treachery. By contrast, Sura XII ('Yusuf') in the Koran relates that Suleika calls her attendants together to witness the power of Joseph's beauty for themselves, and they are so overcome that they cut themselves with fruit knives – an odd but convincing insight into the perverse effects of desire and the springs of some forms of self-harm. Later, Suleika agrees to put the love of God above her lust for Joseph and her self-restraint earns her a place in the highest rank of Muslim saints.

Goethe deals with the ecstatic erotic strains in this story, rather than the later sanctity: the poems are filled with caresses exchanged, kisses given and taken on her face, her breasts. The poems have become famous in Schubert's settings, in which the piano wafts and swells, and the voice, closely following the freight of metaphor in the verses, transforms the lifting and freshening of the summer wind into kisses, fondling and pent-up breath:

> What means this stirring?
> Does the east wind bring me good news?
> The fresh moving of his wings
> cools my heart's deep wound …
>
> Ah, the true heart's message,
> breath of love, life renewed,
> can be granted me only from his mouth,
> from his breath.

This poem, along with several others, has since been attributed to Marianne von Willemer herself, and has become an emblem of German Romantic women's poetry. If Marianne wrote the lyrics, and Goethe appropriated them, she seems to have taken this as part of the masquerade – at least at first (she claimed authorship in old age). If Goethe wrote them, Marianne was providing him with yet another oriental mask, a female one.

Although the *West-Eastern Divan* is chiefly known today for its blazing love poetry, to focus on this would be to ignore the truculent rebelliousness of several other books, in which Goethe emulated another aspect of Hafiz's work. 'The Book of Displeasure', above all, with its dyspeptic epigrams and savage cynicism, is reminiscent of Ovid at his most worldly. In the wake of Napoleon's defeat, Goethe found himself at odds with most of his contemporaries in his resistance to nationalism and sympathy for the French. His opposition to the power politics of European nations refracts Hafiz's ferocious disgust with his times. In spite of all the roses, moonlight and nightingales, Hafiz also makes rough music, not so much in the sound of his poetry as in its effects: shaking up received ideas, breaking through borders. In keeping with his spirit, Goethe's songs change their mood and bristle with anti-worldly scorn.

Passionate lyric is usually considered a game for the young. When he wrote the *Divan*, Goethe was in his sixties. That was old in 1814 (though we don't think so now: on Saidian principles, the experience of age is itself being changed by history). In the same decade of his life, Said was terminally ill with leukaemia, and his thoughts turned to the effects of lateness. For him, late style is not merely a matter of chronological or biographical facts, but is rather a way of thinking and making, composing and writing; it can bring a newly discovered freedom of speech, a renewed courage in risk-taking and experiment, and open the mind to the potential for productive change. Goethe's break with the past, on the one hand, and his contrapuntal projections, contradictions and harmonies, on the other, made him in his old age a perfect presiding spirit for the new orchestra.

The arts play a crucial part, Said maintained, in creating and fostering the historical memory vital in the foundation of a nation state. His argument grows in force when considered along with Paul Gilroy's analysis in *Darker than Blue: On the Moral Economies of Black Atlantic Culture* (2010). In eloquent indignation, Gilroy sets out how 'the wholesale privatisation of culture' transforms the 'mechanisms of social memory' (2010: 129), damaging people's sense of social groups, their history and consequently their identities. Gilroy sees music, and especially live music performed to live audiences, as a powerful mode of cultural expression, with the potential to supersede individual interests and political antagonisms. The performers in the West-Eastern Divan Orchestra are, in Gilroy's phrase, working as 'responsible troubadours' (2010: 122). The time in which they play and perform is the time of the 'not yet', of one day soon – the time of the Blues. 'The pursuit of an alternative future', he writes, 'necessitates the cultivation of counter-memory. Even time … "loses its power when remembrance redeems the past"' (2010: 125). Barenboim and Said's orchestra is drafting an alternative future by living a different present, engaged in the making of these counter-memories.

Said in his own late style argues an oblique, difficult way back to politics, specifically to a politics of culture capable of admitting contradiction and in which the difficulties of reconciliation and harmony are confronted. It is a late style of furious advocacy as well as invective. He never lost this fine fury, but his many antagonists are blind to the humanism he embraced in this late period, and his belief in the possibility that culture might be able to cross borders and even move them. The name of the orchestra he founded sets up a counterpoint of voices across time: Goethe speaks to and through Persian poetry; the orchestra plays under the aegis of Said and Barenboim, independent-minded and interculturally tolerant.

To do something 'in concert' means to combine together towards an enterprise. There is an overtone of difficulty – concerted effort – and an echo (which has no etymological rationale) of concentration. Concord, concordance and the chord itself also sound in the word. A concert is a performance in unanimity but not in unison: different voices, different sounds are necessary to its full expression. A concert can also be a historic occasion, a landmark in human experience, as when the West-Eastern Divan Orchestra played in Ramallah in 2005. The orchestra has not played a concert in Israel, in Jerusalem. Not yet. We are still in the time of 'not yet'.

Notes

1   This article first appeared in the London Review of Books: www.lrb.co.uk

2   Jaroslav Stetkeyych, 'Arabic Poetry and Assorted Poetics', in Malcolm Kerr, ed., *Islamic Studies: A Tradition and its Problems* (Malibu: Undena, 1980, 113).

References

Gilroy, P. (2010), *Darker than Blue: On the Moral Economies of Black Atlantic Culture*. Cambridge, MA: Belknap Press of Harvard University Press.

Goethe, J. W. (1816), *Morgenblatt für gebildete Stände*. [*Morning Herald for Cultured Audiences*], 24 February.

Goethe, J. W. (1998), *Poems of the East and West: West-Eastern Divan-West-osticher Divan, Bi-lingual edition of the Complete Poems* (Germanic Studies in America 68). Verse translation by John Whaley, ed. Katharine Mommsen. New York, Paris et al.: Peter Lang, pp. 14–15.

Goethe, J. W. and J. Whaley (trans.) (1998), *Poems of the West and East: West-Eastern Divan*. New York: Peter Lang.

Knowledge Is The Beginning (Documentary Including The Ramallah Concert) (West-Eastern Divan Orchestra/Daniel Barenboim) (Euroarts: 2054338) [DVD] (2012), sleeve notes.

Said, E. W. (1976), 'Raymond Schwab and the Romance of Ideas', *Daedalus* 105 (l): 151, 167.

Said, E. W. (1983), *The World, the Text, and the Critic*. Cambridge, MA: Harvard University Press.

Said, E. W. (1989), 'Peter Sellars's Mozart', *The Nation*, 18 September.

Said, E. W. (2000), *Reflections on Exile and Other Essays*. Cambridge, MA: Harvard University Press.

Said, E. W., (2006) 'On Late Style', p. 66.

Schwab, R. (1950), *La Renaissance orientale*. Paris: Payot.

Stetkevych, J. (1979), 'Arabic Poetry and Assorted Poetics'. In M. H. Kerr (ed.), *Islamic Studies: A Tradition and Its Problems*. Malibu, CA: Undena Publications.

Warner, M. (2012), *Stranger Magic: Charmed States and the Arabian Nights*. London: Chatto & Windus.

INDEX

The letter *f* after an entry denotes a figure